Principles of External Auditing

Principles of External Auditing

Brenda Porter
Jon Simon
David Hatherly

JOHN WILEY & SONS
Chichester · New York · Brisbane · Toronto · Singapore

Other Wiley Editorial Offices

John Wiley & Sons, Inc., 605 Third Avenue,
New York, NY 10158-0012, USA

Jacaranda Wiley Ltd, 33 Park Road, Milton,
Queensland 4064, Australia

John Wiley & Sons (Canada) Ltd, 22 Worcester Road,
Rexdale, Ontario M9W 1L1, Canada

John Wiley & Sons (Asia) Pte Ltd, 2 Clementi Loop #02-01,
Jin Xing Distripark, Singapore 129809

Library of Congress Cataloging-in-Publication Data

Porter, Brenda.
 Principles of external auditing / Brenda Porter, Jon Simon, David
Hatherly.
  p. cm.
 Includes bibliographical references and index.
 ISBN 0-471-96212-0
 1. Auditing. 2. Auditing—Law and legislation. 3. Auditors'
reports. 4. Auditing—Automation. I. Simon, Jon. II. Hatherly,
David J. III. Title.
HF5667.P633 1996
657'.45—dc20   96–23713
                CIP

British Library Cataloguing in Publication Data

A catalogue record for this book is available from the British Library

ISBN 0-471-96212-0

Typeset in 10/12pt Times from the author's disks by Dorwyn Ltd, Rowlands Castle, Hants
Printed and bound in Great Britain by Redwood Books Ltd, Trowbridge, Wilts
This book is printed on acid-free paper responsibly manufactured from sustainable forestation, for which
at least two trees are planted for each one used for paper production.

Contents

Preface

This book provides an introduction to the principles of external auditing in both the private and the public sector in the United Kingdom (UK) and Republic of Ireland. It describes and explains, in readily comprehensible, non-technical language, the nature of the audit function and the principles of the audit process.

The book is designed for *anyone* interested in understanding the principles which underlie external auditing in the UK and Ireland. It provides an ideal foundation for *all* those studying auditing and is particularly suitable as a text for introductory courses in external auditing in universities and for professional examinations such as the ACCA's *The Audit Framework* Certificate Level Paper 6. For more advanced courses, the book may be supplemented by specialist articles and other reading material drawn from professional and academic journals. Some suitable articles are indicated in the 'Additional Reading' which is provided at the end of most chapters.

The book commences with four chapters which form the 'back-drop' for an understanding of the audit process. These chapters explain the nature and development of auditing, outline auditors' statutory, common law and professional duties, and discuss two concepts which are central to auditing, namely, 'independence' and 'true and fair view'.

In Chapter 5, the meaning of 'audit evidence' is explained and an overview is provided of the process by which the evidence is gathered. In Chapter 6, some administrative aspects of conducting an audit are considered – staffing, documenting and controlling the quality of an audit.

By the end of Chapter 6, the scene has been set for an examination of the audit process. In the next seven chapters (Chapters 7 to 13), the reader is taken step by step through the audit process – from gaining an initial understanding of the audit client, to issuing audit reports to parties both external and internal to the reporting entity. Auditors' statutory audit reports, their reports on listed companies' statements on corporate governance matters, and management letters, are all discussed.

In Chapter 14, the impact of information technology (IT) on auditing is considered from two perspectives, namely:

- the changes which result from entities adopting increasingly sophisticated IT systems to capture and process accounting data; and
- the changes which result from auditors increasing their reliance on the computer as an audit tool.

In Chapter 15 the issue of auditors' liability is examined – in particular, how liability arises under both contract and common law and how auditors' duty of care to third parties has evolved. The *Caparo* case, and its effect on the development of auditors' duty of care, is discussed in some detail, and some relevant cases decided subsequent to *Caparo* in the UK, Australia and New Zealand are also reviewed. Chapter 16 follows on from the examination of auditors' liability in Chapter 15. It describes measures audit firms and the auditing profession have taken (and are taking) to help auditors avoid exposure to liability by conducting high quality audits. The chapter also outlines proposals which have been advanced as means of limiting auditors' liability, namely, incorporation of audit firms, the imposition of a statutory cap on auditors' liability, and the introduction of proportionate (or contributory) liability.

In February 1996, the Auditing Practices Board published *The Auditors' Code*. This Code, which is reproduced inside the front cover of this book, sets out 'the nine fundamental principles of independent [or external] auditing'. These principles constitute the foundation on which the external audit function rests and are all pervasive. As a consequence, we have not devoted a chapter to the Code. However, for each fundamental principle, we have identified the chapter where the principle seems to have greatest application and have presented the principle at the beginning of that chapter.

It should be noted that, as this book explains the principles of external auditing as they relate to entities in both the private and the public sector, unless a contrary intention is clear from the context in which the words are used, in each of the following cases the terms should be understood to have similar meanings:

• *'True and fair view'* (as used in companies legislation and some public sector legislation) and *'fairly presents'* (as used in some public sector legislation).
• *Board of Directors* (the governing body of companies) and *management* (the nearest equivalent in most public sector entities). In this regard it should be remembered that the Companies Act 1985 requires directors to be elected by shareholders to *manage* the affairs of the company. Although the directors frequently delegate responsibility for the day-to-day management of the company to executives, they nevertheless remain part of the company's management structure. In this book, the term 'management' and 'managers', when used in relation to companies, embraces non-director executives, and both non-executive and executive directors.

This book owes many things to many people and to record all those who have provided help, and all the help we have received, would result in a very long list. However, we would like to thank the numerous students and our auditing colleagues whose insightful feedback has been invaluable. Thanks are also due to family, friends and colleagues for their patience, understanding, encouragement and support throughout the period the book has absorbed our time, energy and attention. Particular and special thanks go to Sheila Hart and Fiona Lloyd, whose talents as expert typists in preparing drafts of this book have been truly magnificent.

Brenda Porter
Jon Simon
David Hatherly

Chapter 1

What is Auditing?

LEARNING OBJECTIVES

After studying the material in this chapter you should be able to:
- explain the general nature of the audit function;
- distinguish between financial statement audits, compliance audits and operational audits;
- distinguish between external and internal audits;
- describe how auditing differs from accounting;
- explain why financial statement audits are necessary;
- discuss the benefits which arise from the external audit function for:
  - users of financial statements
  - the auditee (i.e. the entity whose financial statements are audited)
  - society as a whole.

The following publication and fundamental principle of external auditing are particularly relevant to this chapter:

Publication:
- Statement of Auditing Standards (SAS) 100: *Objectives and General Principles Governing an Audit of Financial Statements* (APB, 1995).

Fundamental principle of external auditing: *Providing Value*

Auditors add to the reliability and quality of financial reporting; they provide to directors and officers constructive observations arising from the audit process; and thereby contribute to the effective operation of business, capital markets and the public sector.

1.1 INTRODUCTION

Under United Kingdom (UK) legislation, all companies with a turnover of £350,000 or more, and all public sector entities, are required to produce annually, audited financial statements. The audits of these financial statements are big business. As shown in Figure 1.1, in 1995 the audit fees of just 10 of the largest companies listed on the London Stock Exchange amounted to some £55.4 million. From this it is evident that the statutory audits of UK corporate entities as a whole involve a substantial amount of resources. But the question arises, What is an audit? Further, why are audits necessary? Do they provide benefits which are commensurate with their cost?

We address these questions in this chapter. More specifically, we examine the nature of the audit function and distinguish between financial statement audits, compliance audits and operational audits and also between external and internal audits. We consider the factors which make financial statement audits necessary and discuss the value of these audits for users of financial statements, for auditees (that is, the entities whose financial statements are audited), and for society as a whole.

Figure 1.1   1995 Audit Fees of 10 of the Largest Companies Listed on the London Stock Exchange

Company	Audit fee £million	Auditor
HSBC Holdings plc	9.4	KPMG Peat Marwick
Unilever plc	7.0	Coopers & Lybrand
Hanson plc	6.0	Ernst & Young
British Petroleum plc	5.5	Ernst & Young
Lloyds TSB plc	5.2	Price Waterhouse
BTR plc	5.0	Ernst & Young
Barclays Bank plc	4.6	Price Waterhouse
Grand Metropolitan plc	4.4	KPMG Peat Marwick
The Peninsular and Oriental Steam Navigation Company (P & O)	4.2	KPMG Peat Marwick
National Westminster Bank plc	4.1	KPMG Peat Marwick
Total:	£55.4	

Source: *Accountancy Age*, 6 June 1996, p.7

1.2   WHAT IS AN AUDIT?

Anderson (1977) conveys the essence of auditing and puts the audit function in perspective when he states:

> The practice of auditing commenced on the day that one individual assumed stewardship over another's property. In reporting on his stewardship, the accuracy and reliability of that information would have been subjected to some sort of critical review [i.e. an audit]. (p.6)

Audit is a Latin word meaning 'he hears'. Auditing originated over 2,000 years ago when, firstly, in Egypt, and subsequently in Greece, Rome and elsewhere, citizens entrusted with public funds were required to present themselves publicly, before a responsible official (an auditor), to give an oral account of their handling of those funds.

In order to understand what an audit is and how it is conducted in the modern context, a definition is needed. A comprehensive definition of auditing with general application is as follows:

> Auditing is a systematic process of objectively gathering and evaluating evidence relating to assertions about economic actions and events in which the individual or organisation making the assertions has been engaged, to ascertain the degree of correspondence between those assertions and established criteria, and communicating the results to users of the reports in which the assertions are made.[1]

This definition conveys that:

- auditing proceeds by means of a logical, structured and organised series of steps;
- auditing primarily involves gathering and evaluating evidence. In pursuing this activity the auditor maintains an objective unbiased attitude of mind;
- the auditor critically examines assertions made by an individual or organisation about economic activities in which they have been engaged;
- the auditor assesses how closely these assertions conform to the 'set of rules' which govern how the individual or organisation is to act and/or report to others about the economic events which have occurred. This 'set of rules' comprises the established criteria which enable the auditor to evaluate whether the assertions represent the underlying facts;
- the auditor communicates the results of this evaluation in a written report. The report is available to all users of the document(s) in which the assertions are made.

The major features of an audit are presented diagrammatically in Figure 1.2 overleaf.

1.3 TYPES OF AUDIT

Audits may be classified in various ways. They may, for instance, be categorised according to:

- the primary objective of the audit; or
- the primary beneficiaries of the audit.

1.3.1 Classification by Primary Audit Objective

Based on primary audit objective, three main categories of audits may be recognised, namely:

(i)   Financial statement audits,
(ii) Compliance audits,
(iii) Operational audits.

---

[1] Adapted from the definition provided by the American Accounting Association's (AAA) Committee on Basic Auditing Concepts (1973, p.8).

Figure 1.2   Major Features of an Audit

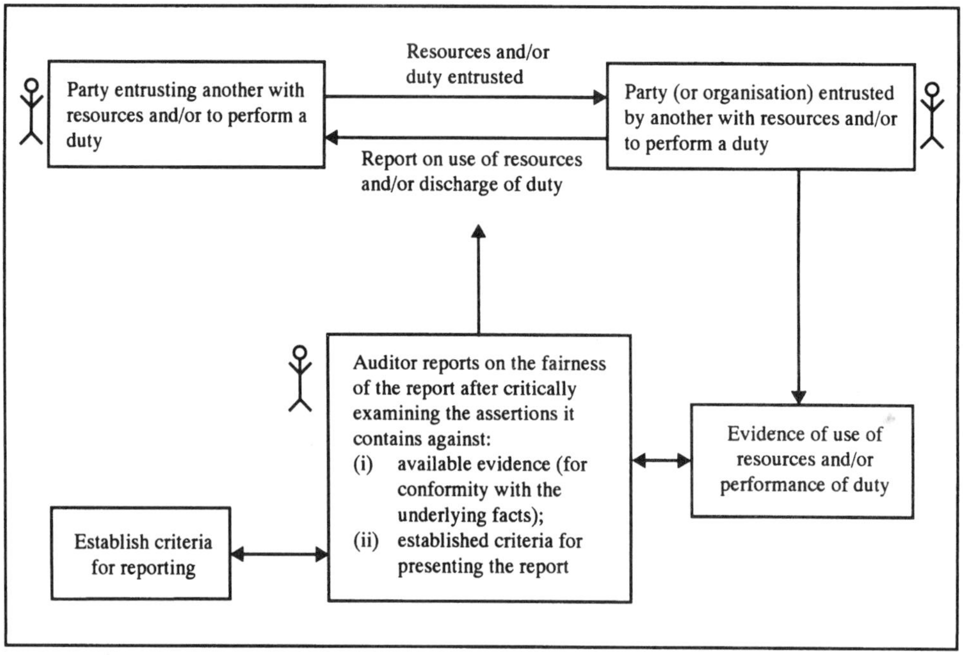

(i)   *Financial Statement Audits*

A financial statement audit is an examination of an entity's financial statements, which have been prepared for shareholders and other interested parties outside the entity, and of the evidence supporting the information contained in those financial statements. It is conducted by an expert, who is independent of the entity, for the purpose of expressing an opinion as to whether or not the financial statements provide a true and fair view of the entity's financial position and performance, and comply with relevant statutory and/or other regulatory requirements.

The major features of a financial statement audit are presented in Figure 1.3.

Under the provisions of the Companies Act 1985 (as amended by the Companies Act 1989) and relevant public sector legislation, the directors (or their equivalent) of all companies and all public sector entities are required:

i)   to prepare annually, financial statements which include:
   - a balance sheet, showing the entity's financial position as at the last day of the financial year;
   - a profit and loss (or income and expenditure) account, showing the results of the entity's operations for the financial year; and
   - if required by an applicable financial reporting standard, a statement of cash flows, showing the entity's cash flows over the financial year;
ii)   to attach an auditor's report to these financial statements.

Thus, *prima facie*, all companies and all public sector entities must, by law, subject their financial statements to an external audit. However, companies with a turnover of

Figure 1.3   Major Features of a Financial Statement Audit

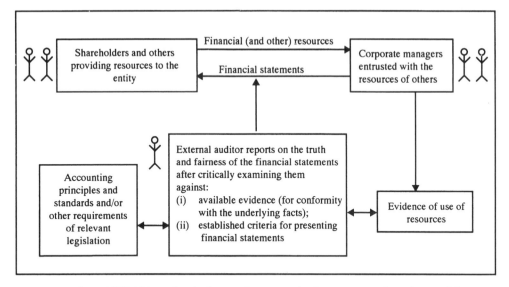

not more than £350,000 and a balance sheet total of not more than £1.4 million are exempt from a statutory audit,[2] but those with a turnover of between £90,000 and £350,000 are required to have an exemption report in place of an audit report.[3]

Companies taking advantage of the audit exemption, and also partnerships and sole traders (which do not need to appoint an auditor), may still require financial statement audits for specific purposes. For example, if one of these entities approaches a bank for a loan, the bank may require audited financial statements as a basis for deciding whether or not to grant the loan. Further, it is usual for clubs and societies to include in their constitution a requirement to have their annual financial statements audited.

(ii)   *Compliance Audits*

The purpose of a compliance audit is to determine whether an individual or entity (the auditee) has acted (or is acting) in accordance with procedures or regulations established by an authority, such as the entity's management or a regulatory body. The audits are conducted by experts (internal or external to the auditee) who are appointed by, and report to, the authority which set the procedures or regulations in place.

Examples of compliance audits include those conducted by the Customs and Excise Department which are designed to ascertain whether individuals or organisations have complied with legislation governing imports and exports. They also include audits conducted within companies to ascertain whether company personnel are complying with the system of internal controls established by management.

---

[2] The audit exemption is not available to a company if, at any time during the financial year, it was a public company, a banking or insurance company, an authorised person under the Financial Services Act 1986, or a parent or subsidiary company, or if members holding an aggregate of 10% or more of the nominal value of the company's issued shares request an audit (Companies Act 1985, s.249B).

[3] The exemption report (and attendant requirements) is discussed in Chapter 3 (section 3.2.2).

(iii) *Operational Audits*

An operational audit involves a systematic examination and evaluation of an entity's operations which is conducted with a view to improving the efficiency and/or effectiveness of the entity. In private sector entities such audits are usually initiated by the entity's management and are conducted by experts (internal or external to the organisation) who report their findings to management. An operational audit may apply to the organisation as a whole or to an identified segment, such as a subsidiary, division or department. The objectives of the audit may be broad, for example, to improve the overall efficiency of the entity, or may be narrow and designed, for example, to solve a specific problem such as excessive staff turnover.[4]

1.3.2 Classification by Primary Audit Beneficiaries

Based on primary audit beneficiaries (that is, those for whom the audit is conducted), audits may be classified as:

  (i) external audits, or
 (ii) internal audits.

(i) *External Audits*

An external audit is an audit performed for parties external to the auditee. Experts, independent of the auditee and its personnel, conduct these audits in accordance with requirements which are defined by or on behalf of the parties for whose benefit the audit is conducted. Probably the best known and most frequently performed external audits are the statutory audits of companies' and public sector entities' financial statements (that is, financial statement audits). However, compliance audits conducted, for instance, by the Customs and Excise Department and the Inland Revenue, are also examples of external audits.

(ii) *Internal Audits*

In contrast to external audits, internal audits are performed for parties (usually management) internal to the entity. They may be performed by employees of the entity itself or by personnel contracted in from an outside source (such as an accounting firm). However, in either case, the audit is conducted in accordance with management's requirements. These may be wide-ranging or narrowly-focused, and continuous (on-going) or one-off in nature. They may, for example, be as broad as investigating the appropriateness of, and level of compliance with, the organisation's systems of internal control,[5] or as narrow as examining the entity's policies and procedures for ensuring compliance with health and safety regulations.

---

[4] As explained in Chapter 3 (section 3.3), in public sector entities, broadly-based operational audits (or value for money audits) are generally required as part of the statutory audit function. However, additional more specific operational audits may also be initiated by the entity's management and conducted along the lines of those undertaken in private sector entities.

[5] Internal controls are discussed in Chapter 9.

1.3.3 Commonality of Audits

It should be noted that, although different categories and types of audit may be recognised, all audits possess the same general characteristics. Whether they are financial statement, compliance or operational audits, and whether they are conducted for parties external or internal to the entity, they all involve:

- the systematic examination and evaluation of evidence which is undertaken to ascertain whether statements or actions by individuals or organisations comply with established criteria; and
- communication of the results of the examination, usually in a written report, to the party by whom, or on whose behalf, the auditor was appointed.

1.4 AUDITING VS ACCOUNTING

This book is concerned with external financial statement audits. However, before focusing attention on these audits we need to distinguish between auditing and accounting.

Accounting data, and the accounting systems which capture and process this data, provide the raw materials with which auditors work. In order to understand these systems, and the data they process, an auditor must first be an accountant. However, the processes involved in auditing and accounting are significantly different. Accounting is essentially an *imaging* process which involves identifying, organising and communicating information to reflect economic events. Auditing, on the other hand, is essentially a *critical* process. It involves gathering and evaluating audit evidence, and communicating conclusions based on this evidence about the fairness with which the communication resulting from the accounting process (that is, the financial statements) reflects the underlying economic events.

1.5 WHY ARE EXTERNAL FINANCIAL STATEMENT AUDITS NEEDED?

1.5.1 The Need to Communicate Financial Information

Over the last 150 years or so, business organisations have grown from owner-operated entities which employed a handful of family members, to vast multi-national corporations staffed by thousands of employees. Such growth has been made possible by channelling financial resources from many thousands of small investors, through the financial markets and credit-granting institutions, to the growing corporations.

As corporate entities have grown in size, their management has passed from shareholder-owners to small groups of professional managers. Thus, corporate growth has been accompanied by the increasing separation of ownership interests and management functions. As a consequence, a need has arisen for corporate managers to report to the organisation's owners and other providers of funds, such as banks and other lenders, on the financial aspects of their activities. Those receiving these reports need assurance that they are reliable. They therefore wish to have the information in the reports 'checked out' or audited.

However, this gives rise to three questions:

1. Why might the information in the reports not be reliable?
2. Why is it so important to the receivers of the reports that the information is reliable?
3. Why do the receivers of the reports not audit the information for themselves?

The answers to these questions can be found in four main factors, namely, a conflict of interests, consequences of error, remoteness, and complexity.

1.5.2 The Need to Have the Communication Examined

(i) *Conflict of Interests*

An entity's financial statements are prepared by its managers[6] and these managers essentially report on their own performance. Users of the financial statements want the statements to portray the entity's financial performance, position and cash flows as accurately as possible. However, they perceive that the managers may bias their report so that it reflects favourably on their management of the entity's affairs.

Thus, it can be seen that there is a potential conflict of interest between the preparers and users of the financial statements. The audit plays a vital role in helping to ensure that managers provide, and users are confident in receiving, information which is a fair reflection of the organisation's financial affairs.

(ii) *Consequences of Error*

If users of an entity's external financial statements base their decisions on unreliable information, they may suffer serious financial loss as a result. Therefore, before basing decisions on financial statement information, they wish to have the information confirmed as reliable and, thus, as 'safe' to act upon.

(iii) *Remoteness*

In general, as a consequence of legal, physical and economic factors, users of a corporate entity's external financial statements are not able to verify for themselves the reliability of the information contained in the financial statements. Even if, for example, they are major shareholders in a company, they have no legal right of access to the company's books and records. Further, they may be many miles distant from the company which prevents easy access to it, and/or they may not be able to afford the

---

[6] In the Preface to this book it is noted that the term 'managers' is defined to mean executive directors, non-executive directors, and non-director executives in companies and their equivalent in public sector entities. Under the Companies Act 1985 (s.226) it is the responsibility of a company's directors to prepare the company's annual financial statements.

time and cost which would be involved if they were to check the information personally, should they have the legal right to do so.[7]

As a result of legal, physical and economic factors preventing users of external financial statements from examining personally the information provided by an entity's management, an independent party is needed to assess the reliability of the information on their behalf.

(iv) *Complexity*

As organisations have grown in size, the volume of their transactions has increased. Further, especially in recent years, economic transactions, and the accounting systems which capture and process them, have become very complex. As a result, there is greater likelihood of errors occurring in the accounting data and the resulting financial statements. Additionally, with the increasing complexity of transactions, accounting systems and financial statements, users of external financial statements are less able to evaluate the quality of the information for themselves. Therefore, there is a growing need for the financial statements to be examined by an independent qualified auditor, who has the necessary competence and expertise to understand the entity's business, its transactions and its accounting system.

1.6 BENEFITS DERIVED FROM EXTERNAL FINANCIAL STATEMENT AUDITS

In section 1.5 above, we noted that external financial statement audits are necessary because the ownership and management functions of corporate entities have become increasingly separated, and because of factors such as a potential conflict of interest between preparers and users of financial statements and the inability of financial statement users to verify the information for themselves.

In this section we consider the benefits derived from external financial statement audits by financial statement users, auditees, and society as a whole. These benefits are reflected in the fundamental principle of external auditing – *providing value*:

> Auditors add to the reliability and quality of financial reporting; they provide to directors and officers constructive observations arising from the audit process; and thereby contribute to the effective operation of business, capital markets and the public sector.

1.6.1 Financial Statement Users

The value of an external audit for financial statement users is the credibility it gives to the financial information provided by the management of corporate entities. This credibility arises from three forms of control which an audit provides:

---

[7] However, it should be noted that many influential financial institutions, including pension funds, insurance companies and unit and investment trusts, which are significant shareholders of large UK companies, visit companies and question their managements. These institutions have considerable influence, especially if the companies are not performing adequately.

(i)   *Preventive control:* Employees involved in the capture and processing of account-
      ing data and/or the preparation of the entity's financial statements, who know
      that their work will be subject to the scrutiny of an auditor, are likely to work
      more carefully than they would in the absence of an audit. It is probable that the
      extra care taken by employees prevents at least some errors from occurring.
(ii) *Detective control:* Even if employees in the auditee entity process the accounting data
      and prepare the financial statements with great care, errors may still occur. The audi-
      tor may detect these errors during the audit and draw them to management's atten-
      tion. They may then be corrected prior to publication of the financial statements.
(iii) *Reporting control:* If the auditor detects material errors in the financial state-
      ments and refers them to management, but management refuses to correct them,
      the auditor draws attention to the errors by qualifying the audit report (that is,
      the auditor states that all is not well, giving reasons for this conclusion). In this
      way, users of the financial statements are made aware that, in the auditor's
      opinion, the information provided is not reliable.

It is interesting to note that, while UK legislation is silent on the qualifications of
those who may prepare company financial statements, the Companies Act 1989 specifies that the auditor of these statements must hold an 'appropriate qualification' and
be 'registered'.[8] This implies that, although the preparer of the financial statements
need not be a qualified accountant, the auditor must be a well qualified, competent
and experienced professional. It therefore seems that Parliament looks to auditors to
protect the interests of financial statement users by giving assurance that the financial
statements are reliable, or providing a warning that they are not.

1.6.2 Auditees

During the course of an external financial statement audit, the auditor becomes very
familiar with the organisation, its business, its accounting system and all aspects of its
financial affairs. Added to this, the auditor is a highly qualified and experienced
individual, who comes to the auditee as an independent objective outsider, divorced
from the day-to-day running of the entity.

These factors place the auditor in an ideal position to observe where improvements
can be made. (S)he is able to advise the auditee on matters such as strengthening
internal controls; the development of accounting or other management information
systems; tax, investment and financial planning; and general management of the organisation. In addition, should it be necessary, the auditor is able to provide advice on
such things as share floats or liquidation proceedings. The provision of these services is
a very valuable by-product of the audit for the auditee entity. Indeed, as Anderson
(1977) has pointed out:

> In many cases, it is the presence of these collateral services which makes the audit an
> economical package from management's point of view. The professional auditor must
> always be alert for opportunities to be of service to his or her client while at the same time
> discharging conscientiously his or her responsibilities to the users of the audited financial
> statements. (p.6)

─────────────────────────────

[8] The required qualifications and registration of auditors is discussed in Chapter 3.

Notwithstanding the value of these services for the auditee, there is a potential danger which auditors need to bear in mind. In recent years, the fees paid by audit clients to their auditors for non-audit services have grown to such an extent that in some instances they match, or even exceed, the audit fees. This has led to concerns that auditors may not be sufficiently critical in their auditing duties for fear of upsetting the entity's management and consequently losing lucrative non-audit contracts. (The dangers to auditors' independence of providing non-audit services to audit clients is discussed in Chapter 4).

1.6.3 Society as a Whole

Over the last 150 or so years, as financial, human and other nonfinancial resources have been channelled by individuals and groups in society to corporate entities, so these entities have grown in size. As they have become larger, these entities have gained significant social, economic and political power. Today, large national and multinational corporations dominate the lives, and control the well-being, of whole communities and have a major impact on society in general. However, in a democratic society, power is not absolute. Mindful of Lord Acton's dictum that 'power corrupts and absolute power corrupts absolutely', society has set in place checks and balances designed to prevent possible abuse of power. Accountability is demanded of corporate managements as a means of ensuring they do not abuse the power bestowed upon them through the provision of resources: they are held accountable for the responsible use of the resources entrusted to them. This accountability is secured primarily by requiring corporate managers:

- to provide publicly available annual financial statements which report on their use of resources;
- to submit these financial statements to a critical examination by an independent expert (that is, an audit).

Thus, auditors may be seen as an integral part of the process of securing the accountability of corporate managements who control and use the resources of various groups in society such as shareholders, debtholders, creditors, employees, suppliers, customers and the general public. Legally, a company auditor is appointed by, and reports to, shareholders. In reality, however, all stakeholders who provide resources to corporate managements (or who are otherwise affected by corporate managements' decisions) have an interest in the accountability process of which auditing is a part.

Therefore, in addition to protecting the interests of financial statement users by giving credibility to the financial statements, and providing ancillary services to auditee entities, the external audit, functioning as an element of social control within the corporate accountability process, is also of value to society as a whole.

1.7 SUMMARY

In this chapter we have considered the nature of the audit function and distinguished between financial statement audits, compliance audits and operational audits and between external and internal audits. We have also noted the difference between accounting and auditing and discussed why external financial statement audits are needed. In the final section of the chapter we have examined some of the benefits derived from these audits by financial statement users, auditees, and society as a whole.

In the next chapter we trace the development of auditing, noting in particular how auditing has responded over time to changes in its socio-economic environment.

SELF-REVIEW QUESTIONS

1.1 Give a comprehensive definition of auditing.

1.2 Explain briefly the following words and phrases included in the definition of auditing given in this chapter:
  (i)   systematic process
  (ii) objectively gathering and evaluating evidence
  (iii) assertions
  (iv) degree of correspondence between assertions and established criteria
  (v)   communicating the results.

1.3 List the major elements which are present in all audits.

1.4 Explain briefly the major differences between the following types of audit:
  (i)   Financial statement audits
  (ii) Compliance audits
  (iii) Operational audits.

1.5 Under the provisions of the Companies Act 1985 an auditor's report must be attached to a company's financial statements. Is this true for all companies? Explain.

1.6 Distinguish between auditing and accounting.

1.7 Explain briefly why external financial statement audits are necessary.

1.8 It is said that the value of an audit for financial statement users lies in the credibility it provides for the financial statements which are prepared by management.

  Explain briefly the three types of control which help an audit to give credibility to audited financial statements.

1.9 Explain briefly the benefits which an external financial statement audit provides for an auditee.

1.10 Explain briefly the value of external financial statement audits for society as a whole.

REFERENCES

Anderson, R.J. (1977). *The External Audit I: Concepts and Techniques*. Toronto: Cropp Clark Pitman.

ADDITIONAL READING

Benston, G. (1985). The market for public accounting services: Demand, supply and regulation. *Journal of Accounting and Public Policy*, **4**, 33–79.

Commission on Auditors' Responsibilities. (1978). *Report, Conclusions and Recommendations* (The Cohen Commission). (pp. 3–12). New York: AICPA.

Hatherly, D. (1992a). Company auditing: a vision of the future. *Accountancy*, **110**(1187), 75.

Hatherly, D. (1992b). Can auditing work without a break with tradition? *Accountancy*, **110**(1189), 85.

Humphrey, C. & Moizer, P. (1990). From techniques to ideologies: An alternative perspective on the audit function. *Critical Perspectives on Accounting*, **1**, 217–38.

Chapter 2

The Development of Auditing and Audit Objectives

LEARNING OBJECTIVES

After studying the material in this chapter you should be able to:
- describe and explain the changes which have taken place in audit objectives in the English-speaking world over the last 150 years;
- explain the relationship between changes in the external audit function and changes in the socio-economic environment of the English-speaking world over the last 150 years.

The following fundamental principle of external auditing is particularly relevant to this chapter:

Fundamental principle of external auditing: *Accountability*

Auditors act in the interests of primary stakeholders, whilst having regard to the wider public interest.

The identity of primary stakeholders is determined by reference to the statute or agreement requiring an audit: in the case of companies, the primary stakeholder is the general body of shareholders.

2.1   INTRODUCTION

In this chapter we discuss the evolution of audit objectives in the English-speaking world over the last 150 or so years, and examine the ways in which the external audit function has responded to changes in its socio-economic environment.

2.2   DEVELOPMENT OF AUDITING

2.2.1   An Overview

Auditing, like all professions, exists to satisfy a need in society. It is therefore to be expected that auditing changes as the needs and demands of society change. Figure 2.1 shows the close link between auditing and the socio-economic environment it serves in the English-speaking world. In particular it shows:

- how audit objectives have changed in response to changes in the socio-economic environment;
- how the main centre of auditing development shifted from the United Kingdom (UK) to the United States of America (US) as the centre of economic development moved across the Atlantic;
- how the procedures adopted by auditors correspond to the objectives auditing is trying to meet.

Figure 2.1 also shows that the development of auditing can be considered conveniently in four phases:

- The period up to 1844
- 1844–1920s
- 1920s–1960s
- 1960s to the present.

2.2.2   The Period up to 1844

During this earliest and longest phase in its development, auditing was primarily concerned with public accounts. Evidence, mainly in the form of markings on tablets and buildings, shows that over 2000 years ago the Egyptians, Greeks and Romans all used systems to check the accounting of officials entrusted with public funds. In the old Greek and Roman Empires, those responsible for public funds were required to appear periodically before a government official to give an oral presentation of their accounts. As noted in Chapter 1, the word *audit* (Latin for 'he hears') dates from these times.

Similarly, in feudal times in England, government officials visited the various manors and estates to check the accounts (now in written form) to ensure that the funds collected and disbursed on behalf of the Crown were properly accounted for.

Prior to the industrial revolution (which began in the late eighteenth century) auditing had little commercial application. Industry was primarily based in cottages and small mills, located where water power was available. These small businesses were owned and managed by the same individuals and therefore there was no need for the business managers to report to the owners on their management of resources – and no need for such reports to be audited.

However, especially during the eighteenth century, overseas trading ventures became important. The captains of the ships engaged in these commercial ventures were required to account for the funds and cargoes entrusted to their care, to those who had financed the undertaking. These accounts were subject to audit. Indeed, private commercial venture audits date from the audits of the accounts of trading ships returning to Britain from the East and the New World.

During this pre-1844 period, concern centred on the honest authorised use of funds by those to whom the funds had been entrusted. Correspondingly, the main audit objective was the detection of fraud. In order to meet this objective, the accounts under audit were subjected to a detailed and thorough examination, with special emphasis on:

- arithmetical accuracy; and
- compliance with the authority given to the custodian of the funds.

2.2.3   1844–1920s

(i)   *Socio-economic Developments*

As in the latter stages of the pre-1844 period, economic and auditing development during the period from 1844 to the 1920s was centred in the UK. This period, which followed the industrial revolution, saw far-reaching changes in the socio-economic environment. In particular, it witnessed the emergence of large scale industrial and commercial enterprises and the displacement of individual (one-off) joint ventures by continuing corporations. Accompanying these changes, the period also witnessed a significant advancement in auditing.

In the late eighteenth century, the industrial revolution, with its associated large factories and machine-based production, led to a demand for vast amounts of capital. At the same time, a new 'middle class' emerged, with small amounts of surplus funds available for investment. As a result, small amounts of capital were contributed by many people, and these were channelled by financial entrepreneurs into the large industrial and commercial undertakings. However, in the eighteenth and early nineteenth centuries, the share market was unregulated and highly speculative, and the rate of financial failure was high. At this time, liability was not limited and the treatment of debtors, including innocent investors who became debtors when 'their' business venture failed, was very harsh. Given this environment, it was clear that the growing number of small investors needed some protection.

(ii)   *Statutory Developments*

As a result of these socio-economic developments in the UK, the Joint Stock Companies Act was passed in 1844. This Act enabled companies to be formed and officially recognised merely by registration. Previously, companies could only become

Figure 2.1 The Inter-relationships of External Auditing

Period	Main Centre of Audit Development	Major Characteristics of Business Enterprises and the Audit Environment	Accountability of Business Enterprises — To Whom?	Accountability of Business Enterprises — For What?	Audit Objectives	Major Characteristics of Auditing Techniques

Pre-1844	United Kingdom	• Cottage industries
		• Individual trading ventures
		• Emergence of industrial organisations (with the Industrial Revolution)
			• Owners (Shareholders)	Honest authorised use of funds	Detection of fraud
					
					(Only Balance Sheet audited)
						• Detailed checking of transactions and account entries
						• Concern for
						  – arithmetical accuracy
						  – agreement between accounts and Balance Sheet amounts

1844–1920s	United Kingdom	• Growth in number and size of companies
		• Separation of ownership and management
		
		(Emergence and increase in number of professional accountants and auditors)
			• Shareholders
			• Creditors
					• Detection of fraud
					• Detection of errors
					• Determination of solvency/insolvency
					
					(Only Balance Sheet of importance)
						• Detailed checking of transactions and account entries
						• Little physical observation of assets or use of external evidence
						• Concern for
						  – arithmetical accuracy
						  – agreement between accounts and Balance Sheet amounts

1920s–1960s	Shift from United Kingdom to United States in the early 1920s	• Increasing concentration of capital in the growth of large corporations • Increasing separation of ownership and salaried	• Shareholders • Creditors • Investors in general	• Honest authorised use of funds • Efficient and effective use	• Lending credibility to financial statements prepared by management • Fraud and error	• Gradual change to reliance on internal controls combined with test checking of selected samples

Period	Country					
		managers • Wall Street Crash and the Depression • Two World Wars • Emergence of institutional investors		of resources	detection lost their significance as audit objectives and became of minor importance (Emphasis gradually shifted to Profit and Loss Statement but Balance Sheet remained important)	• Physical observation of external and other evidence outside the 'books of account' • Concern for the truth and fairness of financial information provided by management
1960s–Present	United States	• Continued growth of large corporations • Corporations increasingly multi-national in character • Dominance of professional management divorced from ownership interests • Increasing importance of taxation • Dominance of institutional investors • Deregulation in the business environment • Increasing competition between business (and audit) firms	• Shareholders • Creditors • Investors • Society in general	• Honest, authorised use of funds • Efficient and effective use of resources • Wider social responsibilities (e.g. pollution)	• Provision of ancillary services to management • Increased responsibility for detecting fraud and reporting doubts about 'going concern' Emerging trends: • Acceptance of responsibility to report to regulatory authorities – fraud detected during an audit – doubts about a company's solvency • Lending credibility to all information provided by management in their annual reports • Systems audits	• Audit based on – a thorough understanding of the client, its business and its industry; – identification of audit risk through analytical review; – assessment of reliance which can be placed on internal controls • Emergence and increasing significance of auditing of and by computers • Examination of evidence from a wide variety of sources – both internal and external to the entity

recognised as such by means of a Royal Charter or a Special Act of Parliament. The first option was very expensive and the latter very slow.

In return for gaining recognition through registration, companies had to comply with certain regulations. These included the following:

- each company's directors had to provide an annual balance sheet to their shareholders, which set out the state of affairs of the company;
- an auditor had to be appointed by the company's shareholders. The auditor was empowered to examine the company's records at reasonable intervals throughout the year and was required to report to the company's shareholders whether, in his opinion, the balance sheet gave a 'full and fair' view of the company's state of affairs. Unlike today, the auditor was not required to be independent of the company's management, nor a qualified accountant. In practice, a shareholder was usually appointed as auditor by his fellow members.

In 1856, the statutory provisions requiring compulsory audits were repealed. Subsequent events proved this move to be ill-advised: of 88,000 companies registered between 1862 and 1904, over 50,000 had come to an end by 1904 (Brown, 1905, p.325). Not surprisingly, compulsory audits were re-introduced in the Companies Act of 1900. Under the auditing provisions of this Act, an auditor was still not required to be a qualified accountant but the need for auditors to be independent of management was recognised. The Act provided that neither a director nor an officer of the company (that is, any of the company's management) could be appointed as auditor.

The new Act also included the following provisions:

- auditors were to be given access to all of a company's books and records which they required in order to perform their duties as auditors. This included access to documents such as contracts and minutes of directors' meetings;
- auditors were to append a certificate to the foot of the audited balance sheet stating that all of their requirements as auditors had been met;
- in addition to the above certificate, auditors were to report to shareholders on the balance sheet stating whether, in their opinion, it conveyed a 'true and correct' view of the state of affairs of the company.

The Institute of Chartered Accountants in England and Wales (ICAEW) sought legal advice on the form the required certificate and report should take. This resulted in the adoption of a standard form of certificate and audit report. These were as follows:

Auditor's Certificate

In accordance with the provisions of the Companies Act 1900, I certify that all my requirements as auditor have been complied with.[1]

---

[1] Reported in an Editorial, *The Accountant's Magazine*, January 1901, p.47.

> **Auditor's Report**
>
> I have audited the above balance sheet and, in my opinion, such a balance sheet is properly drawn up, so as to exhibit a true and correct view of the state of affairs of the company, as shown by the books of the company.[2]

The Companies Act 1900 was a prominent milestone in the history of company auditing. It established compulsory audits, the independence of auditors from company managements, and a standard form of audit report.

(iii) *Corporate Accountability and Audit Objectives*

During the period from 1844 to the 1920s, companies remained relatively small and company managers were generally regarded as accountable only for the safe custody and honest, authorised use of funds entrusted to them. In accordance with society's needs and expectations of the time, audit objectives were designed to protect principally shareholders, but secondarily lenders/bankers, from unscrupulous acts by company managers who had custody of their funds. Hence the main audit objectives were:

- the detection of fraud and error; and
- the proper portrayal of the company's solvency (or insolvency) in the balance sheet.

In general, during this period company managers were considered to be accountable only to the company's shareholders. This is reflected in the fact that the balance sheet was considered to be a private communication between the company's management and its shareholders. Indeed, there was much debate in accounting circles about the auditor's report on the balance sheet. The Act only required that the report be read at the shareholders' annual general meeting and many professional accountants apparently thought it was wrong also to attach it to the published balance sheet. They feared that the auditor might have something to say in the report which, should it become public knowledge, might be injurious to the company. For example, comments which might cause creditors to panic and to demand that their claims be met immediately, causing the company to collapse. Others considered that, logically, the report should be combined and published with the auditor's certificate. In the event, the Companies Act 1908 settled the debate by supporting the latter view and requiring the auditor to provide just one (combined) report (Lee, 1970, p.366).

(iv) *Development of Auditors' Duties*

The decisions of the courts during the period from 1844 to 1920 served to clarify auditors' duties. The two most notable cases were those of *London and General Bank* (1895) and *Kingston Cotton Mill* (1896).

---

[2] Ibid.

- In the renowned case of *In re London and General Bank (No. 2)* [1895] 2 Ch. 673, the auditor had discovered errors in the balance sheet. He had reported the facts to the directors but failed to report the matter to the shareholders.

In his summing up, Lindley L J stated that it was not the duty of the auditor to see that the company and its directors acted prudently or imprudently, profitably or unprofitably, in performing their business activities, but it was the auditor's duty to report to shareholders any dishonest acts which had occurred and which affected the propriety of the information contained in the balance sheet. However, he also said that the auditor could not be expected to find every fraud and error committed within the company. That would be asking too much; the auditor was not an insurer or guarantor. What was expected of him was reasonable skill and care in the circumstances.

- In *In re Kingston Cotton Mill Co Ltd (No. 2)* [1896] 2 Ch. 279, Lopes L J elaborated on the remarks of Lindley L J (above). He stated:

> It is the duty of an auditor to bring to bear on the work he has to perform that skill, care and caution which a reasonably competent, careful and cautious auditor would use. What is reasonable skill, care and caution must depend on the particular circumstances of each case. An auditor is not bound to be a detective or . . . to approach his work with suspicion or with a foregone conclusion that there is something wrong. He is a watchdog not a bloodhound. If there is anything to excite suspicion he should probe it to the bottom; but in the absence of anything of that kind he is only bound to be reasonably cautious and careful.

These two cases reinforced the audit objectives of detecting fraud and error and established the general standard of work expected of auditors. They established that auditors are not expected to ferret out every fraud but are required to use reasonable skill and care in examining the relevant books and records.

Corresponding with the primary audit objective of detecting fraud and error, auditing procedures from 1844 to the 1920s involved detailed checking of the arithmetical accuracy of the accounting records and close examination of the related internal documentary evidence. However, towards the end of the period, judgments by the courts made it clear that auditors were required to do more than merely check the company's books and records. In the case of *London Oil Storage Co Ltd v Seear, Hasluck & Co.* [1904] 31 Acct. LR 1, it was held that the auditor was liable for damage sustained by a company which resulted from his omission to verify the existence of assets stated in the balance sheet. It was established that the auditor, in ensuring that the information given in the audited balance sheet corresponded with the company's books and records, was not merely required to check the arithmetical accuracy of the entries. He was also required to ensure that the data in the books represented fact rather than fiction. This case made it clear, for the first time, that the auditor was required to go beyond the internal books and records of the company for evidence to support his audit opinion.

This position was confirmed and extended in *Arthur E. Green & Co. v The Central Advance and Discount Corporation Ltd* [1920] 63 Acct LR 1. In this case the court held that the auditor was negligent in accepting a schedule of bad debts provided by a responsible officer of the company when it was apparent that other debts not included in the schedule were also irrecoverable. The case established that, not only was the auditor required to go beyond the company's internal documentary evidence, he was also required to relate evidence obtained from different sources.

These cases indicate that, by the 1920s, auditing was rapidly developing into a technical process, requiring the skills of qualified accountants. However, many auditors were still laymen: frequently, they were merely shareholders chosen to be auditors by their fellow members. This reflects the key to this early period in the development of company audits. Company managers were regarded as accountable for the safe custody and honest authorised use of funds entrusted to them, primarily by shareholders. Audits were required to protect the interests of, and secure managers' accountability to, the company's shareholders.

2.2.4 1920s–1960s

(i) Socio-economic Developments

During this period the centre of economic and auditing development shifted from the UK to the US. The period was marked by the continued growth of modern corporations and the development of sophisticated securities markets and credit-granting institutions, designed to serve the financial needs of the growing economic entities.

In the years of recovery following the 1929 Wall Street Crash and ensuing depression, investment in business entities grew rapidly and became widespread. Company ownership became highly diffused and a new class of small investors emerged. Unlike the shareholders of earlier years, who were few in number but closely bound to the companies they partially owned, the new breed of investors were little interested in the management or fortunes of 'their' companies *per se*. They were primarily concerned with the return they could earn on their investment and, if they perceived that better returns could be earned elsewhere, they readily switched their allegiance from one company to another. With these developments, ownership interests and management functions of companies became increasingly separated. The management and control of companies gradually passed to small groups of qualified, professional, salaried managers who, more often than not, owned no shares in the companies they managed.

In this new economic environment, the accountability of company managers was extended from the honest, authorised use of shareholders' funds, to include the efficient and effective use of those funds; business managers became accountable for attempting to generate a reasonable return on the financial resources entrusted to them.

At the same time – as shareholders became increasingly divorced from their companies, and companies grew in size and extended their influence in society – it came to be recognised that the survival and growth of companies rested, not only on the financial resources provided by shareholders, but on the joint contribution of all stakeholders, that is, all those who have a particular 'stake' or interest in the company: its shareholders, debtholders, employees, suppliers, customers and the government. As a consequence, many in society came to regard company managers as accountable to all of their company's stakeholders, and as having an obligation to ensure that each stakeholder group is sufficiently rewarded for its contribution so as to ensure it maintained its 'stake' in the company.

The trend towards society expecting increased accountability from business managers was re-inforced by events such as the 1929 Wall Street Crash and the questionable or downright dishonest acts of company directors which resulted in cases such as the *Royal Mail* case (1932) in the UK and the *McKesson & Robbins* case (1938) in the US.

(ii)   *Developments in Auditing*

During the period from the 1920s to the 1960s, in response to changes in the socio-economic environment, auditing changed in four main ways. These are as follows.

1. *Development of sampling techniques:* As companies grew in size, the volume of transactions in which they engaged made it progressively less feasible for auditors to check in detail all of the entries in the accounting records.

   As companies grew in size, their managers found it necessary to delegate accounting duties to employees. With the growth in the volume of transactions and the delegation of accounting responsibilities, error and fraud became more likely. In order to prevent and/or detect error and fraud, managements introduced systems of internal control.

   As a result of these changes, auditing procedures changed from meticulous checking of accounting records to testing techniques based on samples, combined with a review and evaluation of the company's system of internal control.

2. *Increased emphasis on external audit evidence:* Particularly as a result of decisions in cases such as *London Oil Storage Co. Ltd* v *Seear, Hasluck and Co.* (see above) and the *McKesson & Robbins* case (1938, US) (see Chapter 3, section 3.4), new emphasis was given to the physical observation of assets such as cash and stock, and to the use of external evidence (for example, confirmation of debtors). These duties came to be recognised as being of equal importance to the auditor's traditional task of examining the company's internal books, records and documents.

3. *Auditing the profit and loss statement:* As return on investment became the factor of prime importance for investors, and as companies' stakeholders focused their attention on receiving adequate compensation for their contribution to joint performance, so the emphasis of financial statement users shifted away from the balance sheet and ideas of solvency, towards the profit and loss statement and ideas of earning power.

   This shift in emphasis was led from the US but was dramatically reinforced in the UK by the *Royal Mail* case (*R* v *Kyslant* [1932] 1 KB 442; [1931] All ER 179) which, in the words of De Paula 'fell like an atom bomb and changed the face of the world of accounting' (as reported, Johnston, Edgar and Hays, 1982). This case, more than any other, highlighted the need for the profit and loss statement to be subject to audit. Not surprisingly, the legislators introduced mandatory auditing of the profit and loss statement: in the US in 1934, under the Securities and Exchange Commission Act, and in the UK in the Companies Act 1948.

4. *Change in audit objectives:* Although the other changes which occurred in auditing between the 1920s and 1960s were significant, the greatest single change which took

place was the change in audit objectives. The focus of auditing shifted away from preventing and detecting fraud and error towards assessing the truth and fairness of the information presented in companies' financial statements.

As noted above, as companies grew in size, their ownership and management functions became increasingly separated. In order to ensure that funds continued to flow from investors to companies and to make financial markets function smoothly, it was essential that participants in the financial markets were confident that company financial statements were reliable and presented a true and fair picture of the relevant company's financial position and performance. Responding to these needs, auditors accepted as their primary audit objective, providing credibility to the financial statements prepared by company managers, which essentially reported on their own (that is, the managers') performance.

As providing credibility to financial information emerged as the chief audit objective, the auditor's responsibility for detecting fraud and error declined in importance. This corresponded with the fact that, as companies grew in size:

- their managements established systems of internal control designed to prevent and detect fraud and error; and
- auditing procedures changed from detailed checking of the company's books and records to testing samples of entries, combined with a review and evaluation of the company's system of internal control.

These changes also provided new opportunities for auditors. Through their review of their audit client's accounting system and related internal controls, and from the thorough knowledge of the client entity and its business which auditors gained during the course of their audit, they were well placed to offer ancillary services to the entity's managers. They were, for example, in an ideal position to suggest ways in which the efficiency and effectiveness of the accounting system and/ or internal controls might be improved, and to offer assistance in areas such as financial and tax planning.

By the mid-1960s, companies had become an influential element in society and their managers were regarded as accountable to a wide range of interested parties, not only for the honest, authorised use of resources entrusted to their care, but also for the efficient and effective use of the resources. Auditing had become well established as a profession and auditors' rights and duties, which still pertain today, were embodied in statute and case law. Nevertheless, over the past three decades further notable changes have occurred in both the audit environment and auditing techniques.

2.2.5   1960s to the Present

(i)   *Socio-economic Developments*

Since the 1960s, companies have continued to grow in size and, particularly in the case of national and multinational companies, have become extremely powerful and influential forces in society. The extent of the power held by companies is reflected in the enormous share of the nation's resources which is invested in the corporate sector.

The social and economic influence of companies is also evident in the effect they have on their local communities. This is not restricted to providing employment and generating a flow of funds in their neighbourhoods; they also have an impact through the presence and appearance of their grounds and buildings. Many provide sporting and cultural facilities. They use the local transport network and affect traffic volumes and flows. They produce goods and services desired by consumers. They may help to beautify, or to exploit and pollute, the local environment. When these and other factors are taken into consideration it is clear that even a moderately-sized company can have a significant influence on the economic and social life of the community of which it is a part. Taken as a whole, the corporate sector has an enormous impact on the well-being of society in general.

Given this level of power and influence in society, it is often argued that company managers should be held accountable for behaving in a socially responsible manner. Many believe that corporate managers have an obligation to consider the impact of their decisions on those who will be affected by them, at the same time as they seek to accomplish their traditional economic goals, such as profit-making and long-term survival. To an extent this wider obligation to society is already well established. Company managers are, for example, considered to have an obligation to prevent environmental pollution, to enhance industrial and product safety, to adopt equal employment opportunities and to protect consumers. The state has introduced a considerable volume of statutory regulation covering these issues and company managers must comply. The necessary compliance auditing, however, is not currently the responsibility of the company's financial statement auditors, but it may be carried out by inspectors from a state agency.

Notwithstanding the extension of the accountability expected of company managers in recent years, legislation relating to external reporting by companies in the UK (as elsewhere) has continued to focus on company managers' accountability to shareholders for financial performance. Nevertheless, the legislators have recognised that corporate managers are also accountable to their company's debenture-holders as, under the Companies Act 1985, s.238, companies are required to provide not only shareholders but also debenture-holders with a copy of their annual financial statements, directors' report and auditor's report.[3] However they are not (as yet) required to report to a wider range of stakeholders and/or on their social activities,[4] but these are possible developments for the future and some companies already undertake such reporting voluntarily.

The essence of the present position is reflected in the fundamental principle of external auditing – *Accountability:*

> Auditors act in the interests of primary stakeholders, whilst having regard to the wider public interest.

> The identity of primary stakeholders is determined by reference to the statute or agreement requiring an audit: in the case of companies, the primary stakeholder is the general body of shareholders.

---

[3] The statutory duties of companies with respect to external financial reporting are discussed in Chapter 3, section 3.2.

[4] As shown in Chapter 3, section 3.3, the financial reporting and auditing provisions of public sector legislation are significantly more demanding of public sector entities than are the requirements faced by companies under the Companies Acts 1985 and 1989.

(ii) *Auditing Developments*

The current state of the auditing art is the subject matter of this book. However, it is pertinent to refer here to the major changes in auditing techniques and auditors' duties which have occurred in recent years, or which are presently underway.

As shown in Figure 2.1, three major developments in auditing techniques have taken place in the post-1960s period. These are:

- increased emphasis on examining audit evidence derived from a wide variety of sources, both internal and external to the entity concerned; (this is a continuation of the trend noted in the earlier phases of auditing's development);
- the emergence and increasing significance of computers, both as an audit tool and as an element in auditee entities to be embraced by the audit examination;[5]
- the development of risk-based auditing.[6]

As regards changes in auditors' duties, there has been a discernible increase in emphasis on those duties which reflect the auditor's role as an element in the process of securing corporate accountability. Thus, the auditing profession has recently acknowledged increased responsibility for detecting and reporting corporate fraud and for reporting more explicitly doubts about a company's continued existence. From trends evident overseas, and the level of accountability now expected of corporate managers, it seems likely that in the not too distant future auditors' duties might develop along the following lines:

- giving more general emphasis to reporting fraud or other forms of corporate crime detected during an audit, to regulatory authorities;
- reporting doubts about a company's solvency to regulatory authorities; (steps in this direction have already been taken in the banking and financial sector under the provisions of the Financial Services Act 1986);
- examining, and expressing an opinion about, all of the information (both financial and non-financial) provided by managements in their company's annual reports; the amount and type of information which companies disclose in their annual reports (including their financial statements) may be expected to continue to increase;
- performing management efficiency and effectiveness (or value for money) audits; these are already required as part of the statutory audits of most public sector entities and it may be argued that, in order for audits to reach their potential as elements in the corporate accountability process, efficiency and effectiveness audits should also be required as part of the statutory audits of companies and other private sector entities;
- reporting on the effectiveness of the reporting entity's system of internal control. This has recently been encouraged by The Committee on the Financial Aspects of Corporate Governance (CFACG, the Cadbury Committee, 1992).

---

[5] This topic is discussed in Chapter 14.
[6] This topic is discussed in Chapter 8.

2.3 SUMMARY

In this chapter we have reviewed the development of auditing over the past 150 or so years. In tracing this development, we have emphasised the close link between changes in the socio-economic environment of the English-speaking world and changes in audit objectives and procedures. In particular, we have stressed the relationship between auditing and the accountability expected of corporate managers.

We have also noted that private sector legislation, which governs the preparation and audit of companies' financial statements, may not be attuned, in some respects, to the current level of accountability expected of company managers. It is likely that in the future large national and multinational companies, at least, will be required to produce, and external auditors will be required to audit, more comprehensive accountability reports. However, care will be needed to ensure that the costs associated with securing greater corporate accountability in this way do not outstrip the benefits derived therefrom.

SELF-REVIEW QUESTIONS

2.1 Briefly describe the audit environment in each of the following periods:
   (i)   pre-1844
   (ii) 1844–1920s
   (iii) 1920s–1960s
   (iv) post-1960s.

2.2 Outline the major audit objectives in each of the following periods:
   (i)   pre-1844
   (ii) 1844–1920s
   (iii) 1920s–1960s
   (iv) post-1960s.

2.3 State the major changes which have occurred in auditing techniques during the last 150 years.

2.4 Outline briefly the development of corporate accountability over the past 150 years.

2.5 Explain briefly the significance of the Joint Stock Companies Act 1844 to the development of auditing.

2.6 The Companies Act 1900 has been referred to as 'a prominent milestone in the history of company auditing'. List reasons which help to explain why this Act has been given this title.

2.7 Explain briefly the importance of the following cases to the development of auditors' duties:
   (i)   *In re London and General Bank (No.2)* [1895];
   (ii) *In re Kingston Cotton Mill Co. Ltd (No.2)* [1896].

2.8 List reasons which help to explain why the detection of fraud and error lost its prominence as the primary audit objective during the 1920–1960s period.

2.9 'Changes in auditing reflect, and represent a response to, changes in the socio-economic environment'.

Using an example to illustrate your answer, explain briefly the link between changes in auditing and changes in the socio-economic environment.

2.10 List three ways in which auditors' duties are likely to change in the not too distant future.

REFERENCES

Brown, R. (1905). *History of Accounting and Accountants.* London: Jack.

Committee on the Financial Aspects of Corporate Governance (CFACG). (1992). *Report of the Committee on the Financial Aspects of Corporate Governance* (Cadbury Committee). London: Gee.

Johnston, T.R., Edgar, G.C. & Hays, P.L. (1982). *The Law and Practice of Company Accounting,* 6th ed. Wellington: Butterworths.

Lee, T.A. (1970). A brief history of company audits: 1840–1940. *The Accountant's Magazine,* **74**(782), 363–68.

ADDITIONAL READING

Anderson, R.J. (1977). *The External Audit 1: Concepts and Techniques* (pp. 6–11). Toronto: Cropp Clark Pitman.

Auditing Practices Board (APB). (1992). *The Future Development of Auditing.* London: APB.

Auditing Practices Board (APB). (1994). *The Audit Agenda.* London: APB.

Auditing Practices Board (APB). (1996). *The Audit Agenda – Next Steps.* London: APB.

Cadbury, A. (1992). Keeping the State from the corporate door. *Accountancy,* **110**(1187), 71.

Chandler, R.A., Edwards, J.R. & Anderson, M. (1993). Changing perceptions of the role of the company auditor, 1840–1940. *Accounting and Business Research,* **23**(92), 443–59.

Elliott, R.K. (1994). Confronting the future: choices for the attest function. *Accounting Horizons,* **8**(3), 106–24.

Elliott, R.K. (1995) The future of assurance services: implications for academia. *Accounting Horizons,* **9**(4), 118–27.

Flint, D. (1971). The role of the auditor in modern society: An exploratory essay. *Accounting and Business Research,* **1**(4), 287–93.

Flint, D. (1988). *Philosophy and Principles of Auditing.* Basingstoke: Macmillan Education Ltd.

Hoskins, M. (1993). The future of auditing: a Big Six view. *Accountancy,* **111**(1198), 88.

Humphrey, C., Moizer, P. & Turley, S. (1993). The audit expectations gap in Britain: an empirical investigation. *Accounting and Business Research,* **23**(91A), 395–411.

Institute of Chartered Accountants of Scotland (ICAS). (1993). *Auditing into the Twenty-first Century.* Edinburgh: ICAS.

Morison, A.M.C. (1970). The role of the reporting accountant today. *The Accountant's Magazine,* **74**(783), 409–15, and **74**(784), 467–72.

Porter, W.T., & Burton, J.C. (1970). Auditing in the US: Past, present and future. *The Accountant's Magazine,* **74**(786), 610–15.

Power, M. (1994). *The Audit Explosion.* London: Demos.

Chapter 3

Legal and Professional Duties of Auditors

LEARNING OBJECTIVES

After studying the material in this chapter you should be able to:
- **state which entities must have an audit;**
- **list the rights, responsibilities and duties of external auditors under:**
  (a) legislation
  (b) decisions of the courts
  (c) professional standards;
- **describe the relationship between the auditor and the client;**
- **explain the auditor's responsibility, compared with directors'/management's responsibility, for the financial statements;**
- **discuss the auditor's responsibility for detecting and reporting fraud.**

The following statutes and professional publications are particularly relevant to this chapter:

- Companies Acts 1985 and 1989
- Local Government, England and Wales: The Accounts and Audit Regulations 1996 (Statutory Instruments 1996 No. 590)
- Statement of Auditing Standards (SAS) 110: *Fraud and Error* (APB, 1995)
- Statement of Auditing Standards (SAS) 120: *Consideration of Law and Regulations* (APB, 1995)
- Statement of Auditing Standards (SAS) 620: *The Auditors' Right and Duty to Report to Regulators in the Financial Sector* (APB, 1994)
- *Code of Audit Practice for Local Authorities and the National Health Service in England and Wales* (The Audit Commission, July 1995).

3.1 INTRODUCTION

The rights, responsibilities and duties of auditors are defined by three separate institutions:

- Parliament – in statute law;
- The Courts – in case (or common) law;
- The profession – represented by The Auditing Practices Board (APB)[1] – in Auditing Standards and Guidelines.

The impact of these three institutions on auditors' duties is cumulative in the sense that:

- statute law requires company and public sector entity audits to be conducted and sets out the administrative details of the auditor's appointment, removal and remuneration. It also specifies who may be an auditor and the duties the auditor is to perform;
- case law expands on statute law by explaining the standard of work expected of auditors in the performance of their statutory duties;
- professional Standards and Guidelines provide more specific guidance to auditors on what is required of them when conducting an audit.

The relationship between these three institutions and auditors' legal and professional duties is presented diagrammatically in Figure 3.1.

In this chapter, we discuss the statutory requirements for audits, and the rights and duties of auditors in relation to both the private and the public sector. We also consider the auditor's relationship with the client, and examine the auditor's (*vis-à-vis* management's) responsibility for the audited financial statements and for detecting and reporting corporate fraud.

3.2 AUDITS AND AUDITORS' DUTIES UNDER STATUTE LAW: PRIVATE SECTOR ENTITIES[2]

3.2.1 Overview

The main statutory provisions governing the audits of companies are contained in the Companies Act 1985 as amended by the Companies Act 1989. These Acts require

---

[1] The Auditing Practices Board, which was established in 1991 by the Consultancy Committee of Accountancy Bodies, issues auditing standards in its own right. The composition and functions of the Board are discussed in section 3.5.

[2] We will restrict our discussion to all companies subject to audit. Other private sector organisations, such as building societies, trade unions and employer associations, housing associations, certain charities and unincorporated investment businesses are subject to specific audit regulations. These entitites are generally subject to separate legislation.

Figure 3.1 Defining the Legal and Professional Duties of Auditors

```
                                    AUDITOR
                  ┌────────────────────┼────────────────────┐
                  │                    │                    │
           ┌─────────────┐      ┌─────────────┐     ┌──────────────┐
           │ Statute Law │      │ Common Law  │     │ Professional │
           └─────────────┘      │ (Case Law)  │     │  Standards   │
                                └─────────────┘     └──────────────┘
```

COMPANIES ACT 1985 AND 1989
- Who may be auditor (CA 1989 s.25-27)
- Appointment and remuneration (CA 1985, s.384-388, 390A)
- Resignation and removal (CA 1985, s.391-392A)
- Duties and rights (CA 1985, s.235, 237, 389A, 390)

DUTIES: WHAT auditors must do
A) Form an opinion and report to shareholders as to whether the financial statements
   - give a true and fair view of the company's state of affairs and profit or loss
   - are properly prepared in accordance with the Companies Acts
B) Form an opinion as to whether
   - information and explanations have been received
   - proper accounting records have been kept
   - the financial statements agree with the accounting records
   - proper returns adequate for the audit have been received from branches not visited
   - directors' report is consistent with the financial statements
   AND report to shareholders in cases where the above criteria are not met

PUBLIC SECTOR LEGISLATION
eg Local Government Finance Act 1982
National Audit Act 1983.
Different public sector entities are governed by different legislation. Administration and duties of auditors differ for different types of public sector entity.

DUTIES for local authority auditors include:
A) Form an opinion and report to the local authority as to whether the financial statements
   - present fairly the authority's financial position and income and expenditure
   - comply with relevant legislation
B) Form an opinion as to whether
   - there are adequate accounting systems and internal controls
   - there are adequate arrangements
     • to secure economy, efficiency and effectiveness of use of resources
     • to prevent and detect fraud and corruption
     • to ensure the legality of transactions
     • for collecting and publishing performance indicators

Guidance on HOW duties are to be performed: standard of work required

OVERRIDING STANDARD
Reasonable skill, care and caution in the circumstances *(In re Kingston Cotton Mill [1896])*

This standard changes as business conditions and society's attitudes and expectations change over time

INDIVIDUAL CASES define the standards required in specific areas of the audit, in specific circumstances, and at a specific time.
Examples:
- *London Oil Storage Co. Ltd* v *Seear Hasluck & Co.* (1904)
- *Arthur E Green & Co* v *The Central Advance and Discount Co* (1920)
- *McKesson & Robbins* case (1938) U.S.

LANDMARK CASES draw together and restate the principles enunciated in individual cases over preceeding years.
Example:
Pacific Acceptance Corp. Ltd v *Forsyth and others* (1970) (Australia)

AUDITING STANDARDS
Principles and procedures indicating what is required to meet the standard of 'reasonable skill and care'

GUIDE TO PROFESSIONAL ETHICS
Guidance on ethical conduct expected.
Examples:
- Independence, Integrity Objectivity
- Competence

ACCOUNTING STANDARDS (SSAPs/FRSs)
Compliance with accounting standards is, in general, required for true and fair view to be given

companies to provide audited financial statements annually to their shareholders and debenture holders. They also set out:

- who may be an auditor;
- who is responsible for appointing and remunerating auditors;
- how auditors may resign or be removed;
- the basic duties and rights of auditors.

Each of these factors is considered below.

3.2.2 Requirement for Audited Financial Statements

Under the provisions of the Companies Act 1985 (CA 1985), two types of company are recognised, namely:

(i) Public Companies – companies with a memorandum stating that it is a public company and a name which must end with 'public limited company' (plc).
(ii) Private Companies – companies which are not public. In most cases, the name of these companies must end with the word 'limited'.

Only a public company may issue shares or loan stock to the general public.

The directors of all companies (whether public or private) must prepare and provide to all of the company's shareholders and debenture holders, and to the Registrar of Companies, a balance sheet and profit and loss statement for each financial year[3] (CA 1985, s.226, 241, 242). These financial statements must present a true and fair view of the state of affairs and profit or loss of the company for the financial year and comply with the disclosure requirements of the Fourth Schedule to the Act (CA 1985, s.226).

The Companies Act does not define the meaning of 'true and fair view' but it is generally accepted that in order for financial statements to give a true and fair view they must comply with the Financial Reporting Standards (FRSs) and Statements of Standard Accounting Practice (SSAPs) issued by the Accounting Standards Board (ASB). Support for this stance seems to be provided by clause 36A of the Fourth Schedule to the CA 1985. This requires financial statements to state whether they have been prepared in accordance with applicable accounting standards[4] and to provide details of any material departure from the standards together with reasons therefor. Nevertheless, the CA 1985 also provides that, if compliance with its provisions is insufficient for a true and fair view of the company's state of affairs and profit or loss to be presented, additional information is to be provided so that the required true and fair view is given [CA 1985, s.226(4)]. Further, if in special circumstances compliance with any of the Act's provisions would result in a true and fair view not being given, then that provision should be departed from to the extent necessary for a true and fair view to be presented [CA 1985, s.226(5)].[5]

---

[3] Companies with subsidiaries are also required to prepare and submit group financial statements (that is, financial statements which treat the parent company and its subsidiaries as a single entity) (CA 1985, s.227).

[4] 'Applicable accounting standards' refers to the standards issued by the ASB.

[5] The concept of 'true and fair view' is discussed in detail in Chapter 4.

In addition to requiring all companies to prepare annual financial statements, the CA 1985 requires that these statements be audited.[6] However, in 1994, the CA 1985 was amended to relax the audit requirement for small companies.[7] More specifically:

- companies with a turnover of not more than £90,000 and a balance sheet total of not more than £1.4 million are exempt from an audit requirement [CA 1985, s.249A(3)];
- companies with a turnover of more than £90,000 but not more than £350,000 and a balance sheet total of not more than £1.4 million are exempt from an audit but are required to have an 'exemption report', prepared by a reporting accountant,[8] in place of an audit report.

An exemption report is required to state whether, in the reporting accountant's opinion:

- the financial statements are in agreement with the underlying accounting records;
- the financial statements have been drawn up in accordance with the Companies Act;
- the company has met the criteria enabling it to qualify for an exemption report in place of an audit throughout the year (CA 1985, s.249C).

3.2.3 Who May be an Auditor of a Company?

The Companies Act 1989 (CA 1989) introduced a regime for regulating auditors which is in line with the Eighth EU Company Law Directive. This regime is designed 'to ensure that only people who are properly supervised and appropriately qualified are appointed as company auditors, and that audits are carried out properly, with integrity and with the proper degree of independence' (Beattie, 1989, p.5). Since 1991 (1993 in Northern Ireland), only 'registered auditors' have been eligible for appointment as company auditors. In order to become registered, an individual must first qualify with one of the six Recognised Qualifying Bodies (RQB)[9] and then register with one of the five Recognised Supervisory Bodies (RSB).[10] In order to become an RSB, a professional body must have rules relating to, *inter alia*, auditors being fit and proper persons, technical standards applying to audit work, procedures for maintaining competence, monitoring and enforcement of the RSB's rules, investigation of

---

[6] With the exception of the financial statements of a dormant company, that is, a company which has not undertaken any significant accounting transactions during the financial year.

[7] The audit exemption is not available to a company if, at any time during the financial year, it was a public company, a banking or insurance company, an authorised person under the Financial Services Act 1986, or a parent or subsidiary company, or if members holding an aggregate of 10% or more of the nominal value of the company's issued shares request an audit (CA 1985, s.349B).

[8] To qualify as a 'reporting accountant', a person must be either: a member, holding a practising certificate, of one of the five supervisory bodies (see footnote 10); or a registered auditor (see section 3.2.3).

[9] The six RQBs are The Institute of Chartered Accountants in England and Wales (ICAEW), The Institute of Chartered Accountants of Scotland (ICAS), the Institute of Chartered Accountants in Ireland (ICAI), the Chartered Association of Certified Accountants (ACCA), the Association of Authorised Public Accountants (AAPA), and the Association of International Accountants (AIA).

[10] The five RSBs are ICAEW, ICAS, ICAI, ACCA and AAPA. Although most individuals qualify and register with the same professional body, this is not a requirement. They may, if they wish, qualify with one body and register as an auditor with another.

complaints, and meeting claims arising out of audit work (professional indemnity insurance). (Details of the requirements for recognition as an RSB are set out in the CA 1989, Schedule 11, Part II).

The CA 1989 [s.25(2)] provides that either a firm or an individual may be appointed as a company's auditor. Under the Act, firms may be registered auditors if a majority of their principals are qualified individuals (that is, qualified with an RQB), however, under the rules of the professional bodies, 75% of the principals (rather than just a simple majority) must be qualified individuals before the firm may be registered as an auditor.

In addition to being a registered auditor, in order to be appointed as a company's auditor, the individual or firm must *not* be:

a) an officer or employee of the company;
b) a partner or employee of an officer or employee of the company;
c) a partnership in which a person included in (a) or (b) above is a partner [CA 1989, s.27(1)].

The purpose of the Companies Act specifying who may and may not be appointed as a company's auditor is to ensure that the auditor is:

• competent and experienced, and also bound by the rules and standards of the accountancy profession;
• independent of the entity to be audited.

3.2.4 Who is Responsible for Appointing and Remunerating an Auditor?

The CA 1985 [s.385(2)] provides for a company's shareholders to appoint the auditor at each general meeting at which the financial statements are presented and also to determine how the auditor's fees and expenses are to be fixed (s.390A). However, in practice, the company's directors usually decide who is to be appointed as auditor and their decision is merely ratified by the shareholders at the general meeting. Normally, the shareholders also delegate to the directors responsibility for fixing the auditor's fees and expenses. However, in order to secure 'transparency' with respect to the fees paid to the auditor, the CA 1985 (s.390A) requires the company to disclose the audit fee in the notes to its financial statements. Additionally, under regulations issued by the Secretary of State (in accordance with CA 1985, s.390B), companies are required to disclose (separately from the audit fee) fees paid to the auditor (or audit firm) for non-audit work.

As noted above, auditors are appointed at each general meeting of the company where the annual financial statements are presented. They hold office from the conclusion of that meeting until the conclusion of the next such meeting and, in general, there is no automatic reappointment. However, under the CA 1985 (s.386), a private company may dispense with the obligation to appoint an auditor annually and, in this case, the auditor is automatically reappointed.

Although shareholders are given responsibility for appointing the company's auditor annually, if an auditor ceases to act as such during the year (for whatever reason), the directors are permitted to appoint a replacement auditor. This auditor holds office until the conclusion of the following general meeting. The directors are also permitted to appoint the first auditor of the company – to hold office until the first general meeting of the company. If an initial auditor is not appointed by the directors, the shareholders are required to appoint the first auditor at a general meeting of the company. In any case where no auditor is appointed, the Secretary of State may appoint an auditor (CA 1985, s.385, 387, 388).

3.2.5 How May an Auditor Resign or be Replaced?

Auditors may resign by simply giving notice to that effect to the company in writing (CA 1985, s.392). However, where an auditor ceases to hold office (for whatever reason, including resignation or failure to seek re-appointment), (s)he is required to deposit at the company's registered office a statement of any circumstances (s)he considers should be brought to the attention of the company's shareholders or creditors, or a statement that there are no such circumstances. If there are such circumstances, unless the company applies to the court for a judgment on whether the auditor is seeking needless publicity for defamatory matter, the company must send a copy of the auditor's statement to all those entitled to receive copies of the company's financial statements. If application is made to the court, the auditor must be notified accordingly. In the absence of such notice, the auditor must send a copy of his or her statement to the Registrar of Companies (CA 1985, s.394).

Just as an auditor may resign from office at any time, so a company may remove its auditor at any time by passing an ordinary resolution to this effect at a general meeting. Similarly, if a company wishes to appoint another auditor in place of the retiring auditor, it must pass a resolution to appoint another auditor at a general meeting. Resolutions to remove or replace an auditor may not be passed at a general meeting unless at least 28 days' notice of the resolution has been given to the existing auditor and (s)he has been given the opportunity to make representations to the shareholders on the appointment of another auditor (CA 1985, s.391A).

The provisions enabling auditors to inform shareholders of their reasons for not seeking reappointment, or the perceived reasons for their replacement, are particularly important where company directors wish to remove auditors for the wrong reasons – for example, because they have uncovered questionable acts by directors or senior managers of which the shareholders are not aware and of which they would not approve. Directors lacking integrity may wish the company to engage less diligent auditors.

3.2.6 Auditors' Statutory Duties

The auditor's primary duties are set out in the CA 1985, sections 235 and 237. Under these provisions, auditors are required to report to the company's shareholders stating whether, in their opinion, the company's financial statements:

- give a true and fair view of the company's state of affairs and its profit or loss for the financial year; and
- have been properly prepared in accordance with the Companies Act 1985.[11]

---

[11] In applicable cases, auditors are also required to report whether group financial statements give a true and fair view of the state of affairs and profit or loss of the group of companies included in the consolidated financial statements, and have been properly prepared in accordance with the Act.

Auditors are also required to form an opinion as to whether:

- proper accounting records have been kept by the company, and proper returns adequate for their audit have been received from branches not visited by them;
- the financial statements are in agreement with the underlying accounting records;
- the information given in the directors' report is consistent with the financial statements;
- they have received all the information and explanations they required for the purpose of their audit.

In any case where auditors consider that one or more of the above requirements has not been met, they are required to state that fact in their audit report.

As noted in section 3.2.2 above, the CA 1985 requires the directors of companies to prepare financial statements which give a true and fair view of the company's financial position and performance; and that it is generally accepted that, in most circumstances, providing such a view requires the financial statements to be prepared in accordance with applicable accounting standards. It was also noted that, if it is necessary in order for financial statements to present a true and fair view, information additional to that required by the Companies Act provisions should be provided and/ or a provision of the Act should be departed from. It follows from this that auditors, in forming their opinion on the company's financial statements, need to assess:

- whether the financial statements comply with applicable accounting standards and relevant provisions of the CA 1985;
- if they do not so comply, whether the departure was necessary in order for the financial statements to give a true and fair view;
- if they do comply whether compliance results in either:
  - financial statements which are insufficient to provide a true and fair view and, if so, whether additional information and explanations which have been given result in financial statements which give the required true and fair view; or
  - financial statements which do not give a true and fair view. (In this case, which would arise only in extremely rare circumstances, departure from the Act should have occurred in order for a true and fair view to be presented.)

Under the provisions of the CA 1985, section 233, the company's financial statements must be approved by the board of directors and the balance sheet must be signed on behalf of the board by one of the directors. This approval and signing signifies acceptance by the board of its responsibility for the financial statements. The board of directors must also send a copy of the financial statements, together with the auditor's report thereon and a copy of the directors' report, to all of the company's shareholders, and debenture holders, and also to the Registrar of Companies (s.238, 242).

3.2.7 Auditors' Statutory Rights

The CA 1985 provides auditors with rights which facilitate the performance of their duties. They are, for example, given a right of access, at all times, to all of a company's accounting records and other documents, and the right to require directors and employees of the company to provide any information and explanations they consider necessary for the performance of their duties as auditors (s.389A).

Auditors are also entitled to attend any general meeting of the company, to receive notices and other communications relating to any general meeting which a shareholder is entitled to receive, and to speak at any general meeting on matters that concern them as auditors (s.390).

3.3 AUDITS AND AUDITORS' DUTIES UNDER STATUTE LAW: PUBLIC SECTOR ENTITIES

3.3.1 Requirement for Audited Financial Statements, Accounting Records and Control Systems

The accounting and audit requirements of public sector entities vary according to the type of entity and the legislation to which it is subject. However, the requirements faced by local authorities under the Accounts and Audit Regulations 1996 may be cited as fairly representative of those pertaining to public sector entities in general.

Under the Accounts and Audit Regulations 1996, each local authority must have a 'responsible financial officer' who, amongst other things, is required to maintain:

- an accounting system and ensure it is observed; and
- accounting records which comply with proper practices and are kept up to date [Reg. 4(2)].

The accounting control system is to include:

- measures to ensure that financial transactions are recorded as soon as reasonably practical and as accurately as reasonably possible, measures to enable the prevention and detection of inaccuracies and fraud, and the ability to reconstitute any lost records;
- identification (and division of duties) of officers dealing with financial transactions;
- procedures for uncollectable amounts such that bad debts are not written off without proper approval and that approval is shown in the accounting records [Reg. 4(4)].

The accounting records are to contain:

- entries recording all monies received and expended by the local authority and the matters to which the income and expenditure account relate;
- a record of the local authority's assets and liabilities; and
- a record of income and expenditure of the local authority in relation to claims made (or to be made) for any contribution, grant or subsidy from any Government Department or agency, or a Community institution [Reg. 4(3)].

Each local authority is also required:

- to ensure that an adequate and effective system of internal audit of its accounting records and control systems is maintained (Reg. 5);
- to prepare a statement of accounts for each accounting period. This is to include, *inter alia*:
  - an explanatory introduction;
  - summarised statements of the income and expenditure of each fund for which a separate account is required by statute;
  - a summarised statement of capital expenditure showing the sources of finance of the total capital expenditure in the period;
  - a statement of accounting policies adopted and any changes of policy which have a significant effect on the results shown by the statement of accounts;
  - a consolidated revenue account;
  - a consolidated balance sheet;
  - a consolidated cash flow statement (Reg. 6).

The statement of accounts is to be approved by a resolution of the local authority's Council, meeting as a whole, or by a committee there of, within six months of the end of the relevant accounting period. However, prior to this approval being given, the responsible financial officer is to sign and date the statement of accounts, and certify that it presents fairly the financial position of the local authority at the end of the period to which it relates and its income and expenditure for that period (Reg. 8).

From the above, it is evident that the accounting requirements faced by public sector entities are more specific and demanding than those faced by companies under the Companies Act 1985. This applies, in particular, to the requirement for public sector entities to maintain an accounting control system and an effective system of internal audit, and for the responsible financial officer to certify that the financial statements present fairly the entity's financial position and income and expenditure.

3.3.2   Overview of External Audit Requirements

Like the accounting requirements, the audit requirements of public sector entities vary with the type of entity being audited and the legislation to which it is subject. Nevertheless, in all cases, as for the external audits of companies, the external audits of public sector entities involve examining the entity's financial statements and supporting evidence and preparing an audit report. However, like the accounting requirements, the audit requirements faced by public sector entities go beyond those faced by companies.

In general, the components of public sector audits may be compared to those of private sector audits on three levels:

1. On the first level are the basic requirements which apply similarly to the audits of entities in both sectors, that is:
   - forming and expressing an opinion as to whether the entity's financial statements present a true and fair view of (or present fairly) the entity's financial position and performance (or income and expenditure) and are prepared in accordance with relevant legislation;

- forming an opinion as to whether proper accounting records have been kept, all required information and explanations have been received, and whether the financial statements agree with the underlying accounting records. In cases where the auditor concludes that any of these requirements have not been met, (s)he is required to state this fact in the audit report.
2. On the second level are components which are explicit requirements of public sector audits but which are also, to a lesser extent, features of private sector audits. These include:
   - assessing the adequacy of the entity's accounting systems and related internal controls;
   - evaluating the entity's policies and procedures for preventing and detecting fraud.
3. On the third level are requirements which apply in public sector audits but which do not, in general, feature in private sector audits. Examples include:
   - ascertaining whether the entity has acted outside its powers (that is, acted *ultra vires*), for example, purchasing unauthorised assets;
   - evaluating the economy, effectiveness and efficiency with which the entity has used the resources under its control;
   - expressing an opinion on the value for money outcomes of significant decisions.

Although it is possible to make some general statements about public sector audits, as indicated above, significant differences exist in the audits of specific types of public sector entity. These differences are highlighted in sections 3.3.3 to 3.3.8 below.

3.3.3   English and Welsh Local Authorities

Local authorities are responsible to local electors and central government, both of whom provide the authority with finance. A local authority must assess and prioritise local needs and then ensure money is spent accordingly. However, a tension sometimes develops when central government is not sympathetic to the authority's assessment of local needs and wishes to restrict the available finance either by withdrawal of central funding or by 'capping' the authority's ability to raise funds locally through the council tax. In general, the local authority auditor operates in, and must be mindful of, a sensitive political environment.

Local authority auditors are appointed by the Audit Commission. Both the District Audit Service and private sector accounting firms with the necessary expertise are eligible for appointment. The District Audit Service is part of the Audit Commission but operates as an arm's-length agency, quite separate from that part of the Commission which makes audit appointments.

Although the District Audit Service has been in existence since 1846, the Audit Commission was established more recently, as an outcome of the Local Government Finance Act 1982. The Commission, in addition to appointing local authority auditors, undertakes projects designed to improve the economy, effectiveness and efficiency with which local authorities use their resources. It does this by encouraging the authorities to learn from examples of 'good practice'. It also investigates the impact of government legislation on local authorities, and performs quality control procedures on the District Audit Service and private sector auditors conducting local authority audits. Additionally, the Audit Commission draws up a Code of Local Government Audit Practice which is approved by Parliament. This Code is updated every five years and outlines how local authority audits should be conducted. It is generally kept in line with the APB's Auditing Standards and Guidelines. In fact, the APB includes four public sector members who represent the Audit Commission, the National Audit Office (NAO), the Department of Trade and Industry (DTI), and its Irish equivalent. In 1995, the Audit Commission issued draft guidance notes on the application of the APB's Auditing Standards to the audits of local authorities and National Health Service bodies. The Code of Audit Practice is a concise and readable summary of local authority audits and the following paragraphs draw heavily upon it.

The primary objective of local authority auditors is to make an independent assessment of the following matters:

a) whether the financial statements present fairly the financial position and income and expenditure of the audited body and have been properly prepared in accordance with relevant legislation;
b) the adequacy of authority's accounting systems;
c) the adequacy of the arrangements:
    – to secure economy, efficiency and effectiveness (value for money or VFM) in the use of resources,
    – for preventing and detecting fraud and corruption;
    – for ensuring the legality of transactions with a possible financial consequence;
    – for collecting and publishing performance information;
d) the general financial standing of the audited body.

The scope of the VFM audit work may include, for example, a review of the local authority's:

• strategic direction;
• systems for planning and financial management;
• asset management;
• human resource issues;
• service delivery and performance, evaluated against good practice.

In order to assist VFM auditing, the Commission publishes the findings of national studies of specific service providers such as the fire service. These studies are conducted by special teams with a range of expertise, backed up by local auditors. In addition to the national studies, auditors of each local authority devote a proportion of their audit time to a local study or review of selected services not covered by the national studies. The Audit Commission supports these efforts by publishing statistical profiles of each Council. These serve as an attention directing device. One of the difficulties encountered in VFM audits is drawing a distinction between policy and the arrangements for securing efficient and effective implementation of that policy. As noted earlier, public sector auditors operate in a politically sensitive environment and it is not part of the VFM auditor's role to evaluate or criticise policy as such.

Local authority auditors pay special attention to activities which are particularly vulnerable to fraud and corruption which, if present, could be material to the authority's finances or financial statements. Areas where corrupt practices may be found include:

- tendering and the award of contracts;
- settlement of contractors' claims;
- related party interests of Council members and officers;
- secondary employment of staff which may affect the objectivity of their work for the local authority;
- canvassing for appointments;
- hospitality and pressure selling;
- the award of planning consents and licences;
- the disposal of assets.

At the conclusion of the audit, the local authority auditor issues a report on the financial statements,[12] a report to officers and, where appropriate, to Council members on the results of the VFM and regulatory audits, and a management letter addressed to Council members which gives a summary of the audit and significant matters arising therefrom.

The auditor's report on the financial statements is sent to the local authority and made available to the public who have a right to question the auditor and make objections to the financial statements. In addition, if it is in the public interest to do so, the auditor can issue an immediate report on any serious matter coming to his or her attention. Such reports must be made public by the local authority. It is for the auditor to judge when a report in the public interest is justified, although the Code of Audit Practice provides guidance. Public interest reports are used sparingly, but reports on local authorities with particularly difficult problems or poor financial management have been effective in promoting change. Legal consequences do not flow automatically from the issue of a public interest report but, in some instances, such reports have been the prelude to formal action being taken in relation to misconduct by local authority officers or Council members.

Another distinctive feature of local authority auditing is that audit firms working for the Audit Commission are precluded from providing non-audit services (consulting) for their local authority auditees, unless they can demonstrate that there is no conflict of interest between the audit and non-audit work and that their firm is the most economical or best suited for the contract. All such contracts exceeding £10,000 must be submitted to the Commission for approval.

The Local Government Finance Act 1982 gives auditors both powers and responsibilities. This Act also places a responsibility on the local authority's responsible financial officer to report unlawful expenditure and situations where expenditure is likely to exceed the available revenues and/or borrowings. This report must be sent to the auditors and councillors and a meeting must be arranged to consider the report. The financial officer is prohibited from committing any further resources to similar expenditures until the matter is resolved. The auditors are also able to issue such a prohibition order. If necessary, the matter may go to the High Court to be resolved.

---

[12] An example of an auditor's report on the financial statements of a local authority is presented as Figure 13.9 in Chapter 13.

3.3.4   Scottish Local Authorities

In Scotland, auditors of local authorities are appointed by the Accounts Commission which fulfils much the same role as the Audit Commission in England and Wales. In fact, the Accounts Commission predates the Audit Commission by almost ten years, being established by the Local Government (Scotland) Act 1973.

3.3.5   Central Government

The National Audit Office (NAO), established by the National Audit Act 1983, is responsible for auditing all central government departments, the National Health Service, executive (government) agencies and many non-departmental public bodies.[13] It is headed by the Comptroller and Auditor General who reports the audit results to Parliament. The NAO is concerned to see that the monies allocated to government departments etc. are properly accounted for, appropriately spent, and value for money obtained. The potential field for NAO value for money audits is huge, covering annual cash flows of over £450 billion. The NAO has published reports covering such wide ranging matters as school buildings, the operation of the Royal Dockyards under commercial management, the management of computer systems for Training and Enterprise Councils, and the quality of consular services (CIPFA, 1994, p.10).

   In recent years, the tendency has been to emphasise VFM audits but the prevention and detection of fraud and corruption are also important audit objectives. Indeed, these latter objectives may be increasing in importance as a result of widespread public concern about integrity within the government. Another area receiving greater NAO attention is working with government departments and agencies to develop performance measures. The audit of performance measures, which are published along with the financial information, is undertaken as part of the annual financial statement audit. Like local authority auditors, the NAO applies the APB's Auditing Standards in its audits of financial statements. Indeed, in 1996, the APB issued a Practice Note (No. 10) which provides guidance on the application of its Auditing Standards in the audit of financial statements in the central government sector.[14]

   The NAO's reports are laid before Parliament and published. The VFM reports are normally also issued to the media. In addition, the Public Accounts Committee (a senior select committee of the House of Commons, chaired by a member of the Opposition), holds regular public sessions in which the Committee interviews the accounting officers of organisations audited by the NAO. These sessions result in recommendations to which the Government responds, usually accepting the Committee's recommendations.

---

[13] The NAO also audits the Audit Commission and occasionally carries out joint projects with the Audit Commission on value for money issues.

[14] An example of an audit report issued by the NAO on a government agency's (Serious Fraud Office: Administration) financial statements is presented as Figure 13.7 in Chapter 13.

3.3.6 The National Health Service (NHS)

The NAO audits the financial statements of the NHS as a whole, but the health authority audits are the responsibility of the Audit Commission.[15] The Audit Commission also appoints auditors for NHS Trusts. As for local authority audits, the Audit Commission can appoint either District Auditors or private sector audit firms to perform these audits. In the case of health authorities, the auditors have a duty to report whether or not the financial statements of the authority present fairly the financial position and income and expenditure of the authority. The audit opinion on the financial statements of the NHS Trusts is stated in terms of their being 'true and fair', rather than 'presenting fairly'.

3.3.7 Nationalised Industries/Regulated Businesses

Nationalised industries are held accountable under specific Acts of Parliament which require auditors to be appointed. As they are commercial organisations, they tend to be audited by private sector firms in similar ways to companies. This includes providing an opinion as to whether or not the financial statements give a true and fair view of the reporting entity's financial position and performance, and comply with relevant legislation. Most of the traditional nationalised industries, such as telephone and gas, have been privatised, often with the appointment of a regulator to protect customer interests. This has raised the question of whether the auditor should have any reporting duties to the regulator. Whilst auditors have, in general, no formal duty to report to the regulators of former nationalised industries, they do have statutory reporting duties in respect of regulated businesses such as banks and building societies. The auditor of these businesses must report to the regulator any matters relevant to the regulator's work, of which the auditor becomes aware during the course of the audit.

3.3.8 Universities

Universities are required by their Royal Charter or Act of Parliament to appoint auditors. These auditors are usually private sector firms.[16] Additionally, the universities' use of public funds can be investigated by the NAO: for example, as a result of a VFM study on university purchasing, the NAO projected savings of £30 million annually through more effective purchasing by the universities (reported in CIPFA, 1994, p.10).

3.3.9 Conclusion Regarding Statutory Audits of Public Sector Entities

The audits of the financial statements of public sector entities are conducted along similar lines – and comply with the same Auditing Standards – as those conducted for private sector companies. However, a distinctive feature of the external audits of

---

[15] This responsibility was given to the Audit Commission by the National Health and Community Care Act 1990. Indeed, in 1990, the Audit Commission was renamed 'the Audit Commission for Local Authorities and the National Health Service in England and Wales'.

[16] An example of an audit report issued by Ernst & Young on Edinburgh University's financial statements is presented as Figure 13.8 in Chapter 13.

public sector entities is that they help to ensure that the entities are held properly accountable for their use of public funds. It is for this reason that public sector auditors usually have explicit responsibilities to consider, as part of their audits, value for money matters, the propriety of transactions, and possible fraud and corruption.

3.4 AUDITORS' DUTIES UNDER COMMON LAW

Although statute law requires the financial statements of both private and public sector entities to be audited, and specifies the duties auditors are to perform, it has been left to the courts to determine what is expected of auditors in the performance of their statutory duties. To date, all of the major cases relevant to the performance of auditors' duties have involved auditors engaged in private sector audits. However, it seems likely that, should it be put to the test, the courts would impose similar standards of performance on auditors irrespective of whether they are engaged in private or public sector audits. If this is so, then the findings of the courts, as outlined below, are as applicable to auditors of public sector entities as they are to those engaged in private sector audits.

The general standard of performance required of auditors was laid down by Lopes L J in *In re Kingston Cotton Mill Co. (No.2)* [1896] 2 Ch. 279, when he said:

> It is the duty of an auditor to bring to bear on the work he has to perform that skill, care and caution which a reasonably competent, careful and cautious auditor would use. What is reasonable skill, care and caution must depend on the particular circumstances of each case.

Clearly, what is regarded as 'reasonable skill, care and caution in the circumstances' will change over time, as changes occur in society, in society's attitudes and values, and in the 'technology' of auditing.

As noted in Chapter 2, until the 1920s, auditors were primarily concerned with detecting fraud and error and ensuring that the solvency position of the reporting entity was fairly portrayed in the balance sheet. In accordance with this, auditors carefully checked the detailed entries in, and arithmetical accuracy of, the entity's books, and made sure that the amounts shown in the balance sheet corresponded with the ledger account balances. If this was all that auditors did today, they would be regarded as grossly negligent. They are now expected to examine sufficient appropriate evidence, drawn from a variety of sources (from both inside and outside the entity), on which to base an opinion about the truth and fairness of the entity's financial statements.

Over the years, various parties who have suffered loss after relying on audited financial statements have taken auditors to court on claims of negligence, that is, on grounds that the auditors did not perform their duties properly and, as a result, failed to detect errors in the financial statements. Many of these cases have helped to clarify specific duties of auditors. The following cases serve as examples.

- In *Leeds Estate Building and Investment Co.* v *Shepherd* (1887) 36 Ch D 787, the auditor was found to be negligent for failing to ensure that the audited balance sheet was drawn up in accordance with the company's Articles of Association.

- In *The London Oil Storage Co. Ltd* v *Seear, Hasluck & Co.* (1904) Acc LR 30, it was established that auditors are required to verify the existence of assets stated in the balance sheet. In this case the cash book balance did not agree with the actual cash balance, a fact that the auditors failed to check or discover. This case is particularly significant, for it was the first time that the court made it clear that auditors are expected to go beyond the books and records of the client company for evidence to support their opinion about the truth and fairness of the financial statements.
- In *Arthur E Green & Co.* v *The Central Advance and Discount Corporation Ltd* (1920) 63 Acc LR 1, an auditor was held to be negligent for accepting a schedule of bad debts provided by a responsible officer of the company when it was apparent that other debts not included in the schedule were also irrecoverable. The case settled that auditors may not blindly accept evidence given to them by officers of the auditee. They must properly relate it to other evidence gathered during the course of the audit.
- In the infamous *McKesson and Robbins* case (US, 1938), the auditor failed to uncover a massive fraud involving fictitious accounts receivable (debtors) and inventory (stocks). The court held that auditors have a duty to verify the existence of these assets. This extended the *London Oil Storage Company* case, making it clear that auditors must verify assets stated in the balance sheet, even when those assets are at a distant location.

Occasionally when a case comes before the court, the judge takes the opportunity to bring together the specific duties of auditors settled in a number of previous cases, and to enunciate general principles. One of the most renowned cases of this type is the Australian case, *Pacific Acceptance Corporation Limited* v *Forsyth and Others* (1970) 92 WN (NSW) 29.

In his long judgment, Moffit J provided comprehensive guidance on auditors' duties and responsibilities. Among the important legal principles he confirmed or established are the following:

1. When auditors accept an engagement to conduct a statutory financial statement audit they can be taken to have promised, not only to make the report required by legislation (for example, by s.235 of the Companies Act 1985), but also to conduct such examination as is necessary to form their opinion, and to exercise due skill and care in so doing.
2. Auditors' duties are not confined to an examination of the company's books and records at balance sheet date, but extend to an audit of the company's financial affairs in general, and for the whole of the relevant financial period.
3. The duty to audit involves a duty to pay due regard to the possibility that fraud may have occurred. The audit programme and audit procedures should be structured so that the auditor has a reasonable expectation of detecting material fraud if it exists.
4. Auditors have a duty to make prompt and frank disclosure, to the appropriate level of management, of material matters discovered during the course of an audit. This includes a duty to report promptly to the company's directors if suspicious circumstances are encountered.
5. The auditor's duty to report includes a duty to report to shareholders at their general meeting any material matters discovered during the audit. This

responsibility cannot be shirked on the grounds that it involves an adverse reflection on the board, a director, or a senior executive, or on the pretext that public disclosure may damage the company.
6. The auditor has a paramount duty to check material matters for him or herself. However, reliance may be placed on enquiries from others where it is reasonable to do so. Nevertheless, reliance on others is to be regarded as an aid to, and not a substitute for, the auditor's own procedures.
7. The use of inexperienced staff or the failure to use an adequate audit programme do not, of themselves, establish negligence. However, if audit failure occurs (that is, a material misstatement in the financial statements is not uncovered by the audit), then the use of such staff and/or the absence of a satisfactory audit programme may be taken as evidence that the failure occurred as a result of negligence.

In his judgment, Moffit J noted that professional standards and practice must change over time, to reflect changes in the economic and business environment. He further observed that the courts, in trying to ascertain what qualifies as 'reasonable skill, care and caution . . .', are guided by professional standards and best auditing practices of the time. However, the courts will not be bound by these standards. If they see fit, they will go beyond them. It is the courts, not the profession, which determine, in the light of society's prevailing norms, what is reasonable skill and care in the particular circumstances of the case.

The relevance of these points is evident when it is realised that the duties which Moffit J attributed to auditors were not generally practised at that time. Indeed, Kenley (1971, pp. 153–61) noted that the case brought to light key matters which required the immediate attention of auditors. These included the following:

1. The need to have an adequate written audit programme, and the need to correlate this with a review of the audit client's system of internal controls, and to modify it as necessary during the course of the audit to ensure that it adequately covers all material aspects of the entity.
2. The need to ensure that audit samples are drawn from throughout the financial period, not just the period around the balance sheet date.
3. The need to ensure that audit staff are properly supervised by both partners and managers, and that proper instructions are given to assistants with limited qualifications and/or experience.
4. The need to carefully assess the level of management from which the auditor seeks information and the need to record in audit working papers appropriate details of responses to enquiry.
5. The need to report promptly and forthrightly to the appropriate level of the audit client's management, deficiencies in transactions or accounting records examined by the auditor.

Today all of these matters have become what is regarded as 'usual practice'. Indeed, the *Pacific Acceptance* case has had a profound impact on auditing, as the principles enunciated by Moffit J underlie the Auditing Standards which have been promulgated by professional accountancy bodies throughout the Western world.

3.5 AUDITORS' DUTIES UNDER PROFESSIONAL AUDITING STANDARDS AND GUIDELINES

Unlike statute and case law, which impose duties on auditors from outside the profession, Auditing Standards and Guidelines are set, monitored and amended (as appropriate) by the auditing profession itself. Rather than each of the professional bodies in the UK and Ireland setting its own Auditing Standards and Guidelines, these bodies have established the Auditing Practices Board (APB) to perform this function. The APB has up to 18 voting and five non-voting members. The Chairperson and up to eight other voting members are required to be practising auditors; the membership also includes 'persons from the business and academic worlds, the public sector and the legal profession' (APB, 1993, para 2, 3).

In its *Scope and Authority of APB Pronouncements* (1993, paras 1 and 18), the APB explains that its pronouncements fall into three principal categories:

- Statements of Auditing Standards (SASs);
- Practice Notes, which 'assist auditors in applying Auditing Standards of general application to particular circumstances and industries'; and
- Bulletins, which 'provide auditors with timely guidance on new or emerging issues'.

The APB also explains that:

> SASs contain basic principles and essential procedures ('Auditing Standards') . . . with which auditors are required to comply, except where otherwise stated in the SAS concerned, in the conduct of any audit of financial statements. (para 4)

> SASs also include explanatory and other material which, rather than being prescriptive [that is, mandatory], is designed to assist auditors in interpreting and applying Auditing Standards. (para 6)

The APB has issued (and is issuing) its SASs in a structured series. This is shown in Figure 3.2.

It should be noted that compliance with the Auditing Standards contained within the SASs is mandatory. If an auditor fails to comply with the Standards, disciplinary action may be taken against him or her by the RSB with which (s)he is registered. Such disciplinary action may result in withdrawal of registration and hence of the auditor's eligibility to perform company audits (APB, 1993, paras 9 and 11).

It thus may be seen that Auditing Standards serve two main purposes: they provide guidance to individual auditors regarding the standard of work required of them in the performance of their duties, and they also help to protect the reputation of the profession as a whole. As the standards of work required of auditors are set out clearly, and as they are binding on all members of the profession in the conduct of all audits, any auditor falling short of the required standards when performing an audit is exposed to disciplinary action. This helps to ensure that all members of the profession perform their duties in accordance with the profession's standards.

It is pertinent to observe that, although the explanatory material included in SASs and the APB's Practice Notes and Bulletins is persuasive rather than mandatory, the APB notes that all of its pronouncements 'are likely to be taken into account when the adequacy of the work of auditors is being considered in a court of law or in other contested situations' (para 13).

Figure 3.2 Structure of the APB's Statements of Auditing Standards

Series numbers	Matters addressed	Date of Issue
Series 001/099 010	**Introductory matters** The scope and authority of APB pronouncements	May 1993
Series 100/199 100 110 120 130 140 150 160	**Responsibility** Objective and general principles governing an audit of financial statements Fraud and error Consideration of law and regulations The going concern basis in financial statements Engagement letters Subsequent events Other information in documents containing audited financial statements	 March 1995 January 1995 January 1995 November 1994 March 1995 March 1995 March 1995
Series 200/299 200 210 220 230 240	**Planning, controlling and recording** Planning Knowledge of the business Materiality and the audit Working papers Quality control for audit work	 March 1995 March 1995 March 1995 March 1995 March 1995
Series 300/399 300 310	**Accounting systems and internal control** Accounting and internal control systems and audit risk assessments Auditing in an information systems environment	 March 1995 Not yet issued
Series 400/499 400 410 420 430 440 450 460 470	**Evidence** Audit evidence Analytical procedures Audit of accounting estimates Audit sampling Management representations Opening balances and comparatives Related parties Overall review of financial statements	 March 1995 March 1995 March 1995 March 1995 March 1995 March 1995 Not yet issued March 1995
Series 500/599 500 510 520	**Using the work of others** Considering the work of internal audit The relationship between principal auditors and other auditors Using the work of an expert	 March 1995 March 1995 March 1995
Series 600/699 600 610 620	**Reporting** Auditors' reports on financial statements Reports to directors or management The auditors' right and duty to report to regulators in the financial sector	 May 1993 March 1995 March 1994
Series 700/799	**Engagements other than audits of financial** **statements**	Not yet issued
Series 800/899	**Particular industries and sectors**	Not yet issued

In addition to the APB's SASs, Practice Notes and Bulletins, the following Auditing Guidelines (which were issued by the APB's predecessor body, the Auditing Practices Committee) provide guidance to auditors with respect to specific aspects of their audits:

3.401 Bank reports for audit purposes
3.405 Attendance at stocktaking
3.412 Prospectuses and the reporting accountant
3.503 Reports by auditors under company legislation in the United Kingdom
3.504 Reports by auditors under company legislation in the Republic of Ireland
3.506 The auditors' statement on the summary financial statement.

The APB plans to revise these Guidelines at some future date.

3.6 AUDITOR-CLIENT RELATIONSHIP IN PRIVATE SECTOR ENTITIES

In the private sector, the legal relationship between the auditor and the client company, and the auditor and the company's shareholders, is somewhat unusual. It was noted in section 3.2 above that under the provisions of the Companies Act 1985 shareholders are responsible for appointing the auditor, and it is implicit in the statutory provisions that the auditor is appointed primarily to protect shareholders' interests. However, after being appointed at the company's general meeting, the auditor has no contact with the shareholders until the brief audit report is sent to them (after the end of the financial period), together with the audited financial statements.

Notwithstanding that auditors are appointed by the company's shareholders (at least, technically), the contractual arrangement for the audit is between the auditor and the client company. As a result, the auditor owes a contractual responsibility to the company *per se*, not to its shareholders. Further, in conducting the audit, a close working relationship necessarily develops between the auditor and the company's management, and it is the company's management (not its shareholders) who receive the auditor's management letter – a detailed report of the auditor's findings.[17] The auditor's relationship with the client company and its shareholders is represented diagrammatically in Figure 3.3.

Given auditors' dual relationship with the company and its shareholders, it is essential that they adhere strictly to the profession's fundamental principle of objectivity and independence: that they remain objective and independent of the entity and directors.[18]

3.7 AUDITORS' *VIS-À-VIS* DIRECTORS'/MANAGEMENT'S RESPONSIBILITY FOR THE FINANCIAL STATEMENTS

In both private and public sector entities, responsibility for the preparation of the entity's financial statements lies squarely with the entity's directors or management.

---

[17] Management letters are discussed in Chapter 13.

[18] The importance of auditors maintaining their independence and objectivity is discussed in Chapter 4.

Figure 3.3 The Auditor's Relationship with the Client Company and its Shareholders

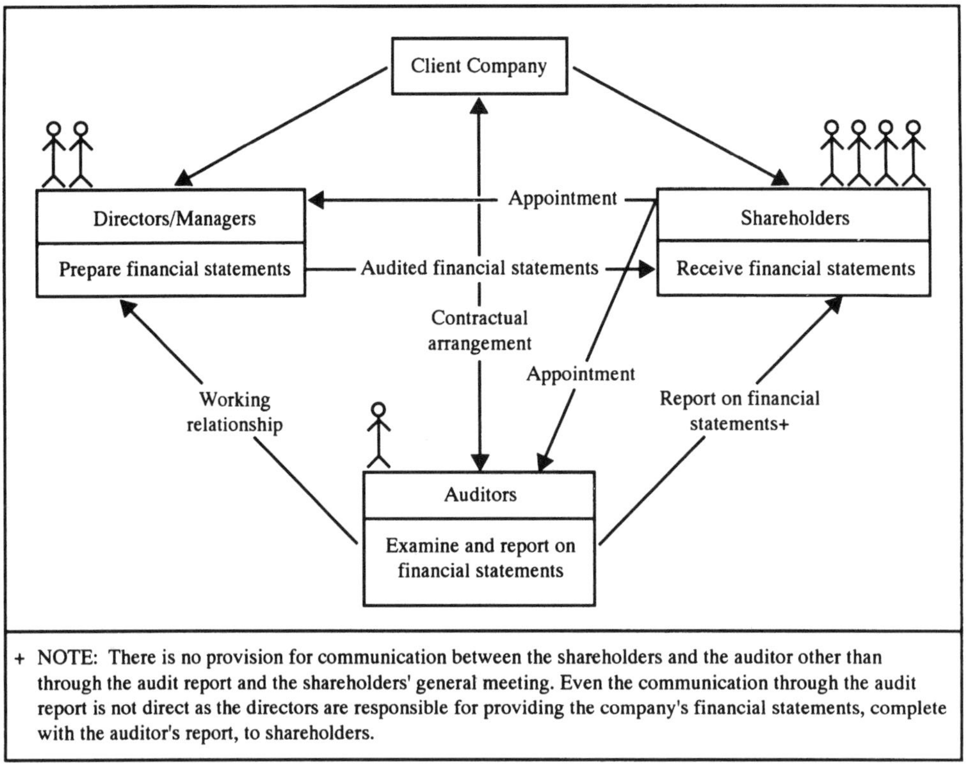

+ NOTE: There is no provision for communication between the shareholders and the auditor other than through the audit report and the shareholders' general meeting. Even the communication through the audit report is not direct as the directors are responsible for providing the company's financial statements, complete with the auditor's report, to shareholders.

As noted in section 3.2 above, the Companies Act 1985 requires the directors of all companies to provide financial statements annually to their shareholders and debenture holders. It also requires all companies to keep proper accounting records. These are records which, among other things, facilitate both the preparation and audit of the company's annual financial statements.

In section 3.3 above, it was noted that public sector legislation generally goes further than this. For example, local authorities are required to prepare financial statements and maintain an adequate and effective system of internal audit. Additionally, the responsible financial officer of a local authority is required to maintain an accounting control system and proper accounting records, and also to certify that the financial statements present fairly the authority's financial position and income and expenditure.

The APB, in SAS 600: *Auditors' Reports on Financial Statements*, requires auditors to distinguish between their responsibilities and those of the auditee's directors for the audited financial statements. It states:

(a) Auditors should distinguish between their responsibilities and those of the directors by including in their report
   (i)   a statement that the financial statements are the responsibility of the reporting entity's directors;
   (ii) a reference to a description of those responsibilities when set out elsewhere in the financial statements or accompanying information; and

      (iii) a statement that the auditors' responsibility is to express an opinion on the financial statements.
  (b) Where the financial statements or accompanying information (for example the directors' report) do not include an adequate description of directors' relevant responsibilities, the auditors' report should include a description of those responsibilities. (para 20)

A typical statement of directors' responsibilities is that provided in the 1995 Annual Report of First Choice Holidays plc:

DIRECTORS' RESPONSIBILITIES
Company law requires the Directors to prepare financial statements for each financial year of the Group which give a true and fair view of the state of affairs of the Company and the Group and of the profit or loss for that period. In preparing those financial statements, the Directors are required to:

- select suitable accounting policies and then apply them consistently;
- make judgements and estimates that are reasonable and prudent;
- state whether applicable accounting standards have been followed, subject to any material departures disclosed and explained in the financial statements; and
- prepare the financial statements on the going concern basis unless it is inappropriate to presume that the Group will continue in business.

The Directors are responsible for keeping proper accounting records which disclose with reasonable accuracy at any time the financial position of the Company and to enable them to ensure that the financial statements comply with the Companies Act 1985. They have general responsibility for taking such steps as are reasonably open to them to safeguard the assets of the Group and to prevent and detect fraud and other irregularities.

The audit report includes the following statement:

RESPECTIVE RESPONSIBILITIES OF DIRECTORS AND AUDITORS
As described above, the Company's Directors are responsible for the preparation of financial statements. It is our responsibility to form an independent opinion, based on our audit, on those statements and to report our opinion to you.

The public sector regulators have endorsed the APB's stance with respect to disclosure of management's responsibility for external financial reporting. This is reflected, for example, in the *Code of Practice on Local Authority Accounting in Great Britain 1995* (the Code), with which local authorities are required to comply. The Preface states that the Code reflects the requirements of the APB's SAS 600, 'by requiring a statement of responsibilities for the [local] authority's statement of accounts'. An example of such a statement is included in Bedford Borough Council's 1995 Annual Report. It includes the following statements:

THE AUTHORITY'S RESPONSIBILITIES
The authority is required:
- To make arrangements for the proper administration of its financial affairs and to secure that one of its officers has the responsibility for the administration of those affairs. In this authority, that officer is the Director of Finance.
- To manage its affairs to secure economic, efficient and effective use of resources and safeguard its assets.

THE DIRECTOR OF FINANCE'S RESPONSIBILITIES
The Director of Finance is responsible for the preparation of the authority's statement of accounts which, in terms of the Code of Practice on Local Authority Accounting in Great

Britain ('the Code'), is required to present fairly the financial position of the authority at the accounting date and its income and expenditure for the year (ended 31 March 1995).

In preparing this statement of accounts, the Director of Finance has:
- selected suitable accounting policies and then applied them consistently;
- made judgments and estimates that were reasonable and prudent;
- complied with the Code.

The Director of Finance has also:
- kept proper accounting records which were up to date;
- taken reasonable steps for the prevention and detection of fraud and other irregularities.

As for First Choice Holidays plc, Bedford Borough Council's audit report includes a statement explaining the respective responsibilities of the Chief Finance Officer and the auditors:

As described on page 14 the Chief Finance Officer is responsible for the preparation of the statement of accounts. It is our responsibility to form an independent opinion, based on our audit, on the statement and to report our opinion thereon.

Statements of this nature, explaining the respective responsibilities of directors/ managements and auditors for the financial statements, are helpful in informing users of the financial statements where responsibility for their preparation lies. Research conducted prior to the issue of SAS 600 indicated that many financial statement users were not aware of this fact.

Surveys conducted by Lee and Tweedie (reported by Chandler, 1983, pp.56–57), for example, provided evidence which suggested that one quarter of institutional investors and more than half of private investors had little or no understanding of who is legally responsible for company financial statements. Similarly, Porter (1993), in a survey conducted in New Zealand, found that just over a quarter of the general public were of the opinion that auditors are responsible for preparing company financial statements.

3.8 AUDITORS' RESPONSIBILITY TO DETECT AND REPORT FRAUD

3.8.1 Fraud Defined

Before considering auditors' duties with respect to fraud, it is necessary to establish what is meant by 'fraud'. There are basically three types of corporate fraud:

1. misappropriation of corporate assets;
2. manipulation of accounting information;
3. deception of a third party.

1. *Misappropriation of corporate assets.* Evidence suggests that this type of fraud is most likely to be committed by employees who are not directors or senior managers. However, when it is carried out by senior management it can be on a massive scale. Misappropriation is usually undertaken for personal gain and is an action against the entity.

2. *Manipulation of accounting information.* This type of fraud is intended to result in financial statements which give a false impression of the entity's financial affairs. It is almost always perpetrated by management but, rather than being committed for direct personal financial gain, it is usually motivated by what the individual concerned sees to be in his or her own best interests in terms of reporting the entity's financial position or (more commonly) its performance.

3. *Deception of a third party.* This generally involves misappropriation of a third party's assets and/or deception through the provision of false information to a third party. The person committing the fraud may believe (s)he is acting in the entity's best interests. An example, is making false representations to the Inland Revenue in order to minimise the company's tax liability.

3.8.2 A Controversial Issue

Auditors' responsibility for detecting fraud is one of the most controversial issues in auditing. There is a discrepancy between what the courts, investors and the general public expect of auditors in this regard and what auditors acknowledge to be their duty. The Cohen Commission (CAR, 1978), for example, reported:

> Court decisions, criticism by the financial press, actions by regulatory bodies, and surveys of users indicate dissatisfaction with the responsibility for fraud detection acknowledged by auditors. Opinion surveys . . . indicate that concerned segments of the public expect independent auditors to assume greater responsibility in this area. Significant percentages of those who use and rely on the auditor's work rank the detection of fraud among the most important objectives of an audit. (p.31)

3.8.3 Changes in the Profession's Attitude to Fraud Detection

The stance of the auditing profession in relation to detecting and reporting fraud has changed markedly over the last 70 or so years. From the time compulsory audits were first introduced in 1844 until about the 1920s, the prevention and detection of fraud and error were regarded as primary audit objectives. Nevertheless, as noted in Chapter 2, it was decided in the *Kingston Cotton Mill* case (1896) that auditors were not required to nose out every fraud (auditors are 'watchdogs not bloodhounds'), but they were expected to exercise reasonable skill, care and caution appropriate to the particular circumstances. Further, if anything came to their attention which aroused their suspicions, they were expected to 'probe the matter to the bottom' and to report it promptly to the appropriate level of management.

Between the 1920s and 1960s the importance of fraud detection as an audit objective was steadily eroded. During this period companies grew in size and complexity and, as a consequence, corporate managements set in place accounting systems to capture and process accounting data. These systems incorporated internal controls designed to prevent or detect errors and irregularities (i.e. fraud) and thus to protect the integrity of the accounting information. At the same time, growth in the volume of company transactions made it impractical, within the limits of reasonable time and cost constraints, for auditors to check every entry in the accounting records. Auditing procedures changed accordingly, from meticulous checking of every transaction, to techniques based on testing samples of transactions, combined with a review and evaluation of the reliability and effectiveness of the accounting system and its internal controls (see Chapter 2, section 2.2.4).

Given this environment, auditors argued that preventing and detecting fraud were the responsibility of management and that they were best achieved through the maintenance of a good system of internal controls. They also argued that auditing procedures were not designed, and could not be relied upon, to detect fraud.

The general attitude of the profession from the 1940s to 1960s is reflected in the AICPA's *Codification of Statements on Auditing Procedure*, published in 1951. It states:

> The ordinary examination incident to the issuance of an opinion respecting financial statements is not designed and cannot be relied upon to disclose defalcations and other similar irregularities, although their discovery frequently results. In a well-organized concern reliance for the detection of such irregularities is placed principally upon the maintenance of an adequate system of accounting records with appropriate internal control. If an auditor were to discover defalcations and similar irregularities he would have to extend his work to a point where its cost would be prohibitive . . .

By the 1960s the profession's position on fraud was subject to criticism from both inside and outside the profession. Since that time, as corporate fraud has grown in both incidence and size, so dissatisfaction with the extent of responsibility for detecting fraud acknowledged by auditors has increased. The level of discontent is evident from the following illustrations.

- Woolf (1978), drew attention to the pertinent question raised by the investment analyst whose solo efforts were responsible for exposing the notorious *Equity Funding* fraud in the US in the early 1970s:

  > If routine auditing procedures cannot detect 64,000 phoney insurance policies [two thirds of the total number], $25 million in counterfeit bonds, and $100 million in missing assets, what is the purpose of audits? (p.62)

- In a similar vein, Carty (1985), a member of the Auditing Practices Committee (the forerunner of the APB), observed:

  > [T]he public do not readily accept the limitations on the scope of an audit that the auditors inevitably build into their approach. Whenever there is a revelation in the press of a fraud, there is public outcry and the usual question, 'Why didn't the auditors pick this up years ago?' (p.30)

3.8.4 Recent Developments

In recent years pressure has mounted, especially in the UK and US, for auditors to assume greater responsibility for detecting fraud. In the mid-1980s, faced by the rising wave of corporate fraud in the UK, Fletcher and Howard, successive Ministers of Corporate and Consumer Affairs, made it clear that they viewed auditors as being in the front line of the public's defences in the fight against corporate fraud, and they called upon auditors to extend their duties in this regard. Their stance was supported by fraud investigators, who stated that they considered it both practical and desirable, within the limits of cost and auditing procedures, for auditors to accept a general responsibility to detect fraud (Smith, 1985, p.10).

In response to these and similar pressures, the auditing profession has changed its stance. In various parts of the English-speaking world the professional bodies now acknowledge greater responsibility for detecting fraud and, additionally for reporting fraud to both shareholders (via the audit report) and to regulatory authorities.

In the US, for example, the AICPA, in SAS no.53, *The Auditor's Responsibility to Detect and Report Errors and Irregularities* (issued in 1988) has adopted a new positive approach in defining auditors' duties with respect to fraud. In place of its former defensive tone and insistence that audits cannot be relied on to disclose irregularities, it now states:

> Because of the characteristics of irregularities, particularly those involving forgery and collusion, a properly designed and executed audit may not detect a material irregularity. [However], the auditor should exercise (a) due care in planning, performing and evaluating the results of audit procedures, and (b) the proper degree of professional skepticism to achieve reasonable assurance that material errors or irregularities will be detected. (paras 7–8)

In the UK, SAS 110: *Fraud and Error* (published in 1995) requires auditors to design audit procedures so as to have a reasonable expectation of detecting material misstatements arising from fraud. It also requires auditors:

- if they suspect or discover fraud, to communicate their findings as soon as practicable to the appropriate level of management, the board of directors or the audit committee; even if the potential effect of a fraud or suspected fraud is immaterial to the financial statements, the auditor should still report it to the appropriate level of management (para 41);
- to qualify their audit report when they form the opinion that, as a result of fraud, the financial statements do not give a true and fair view. Similarly, they should qualify the audit report if they disagree with the accounting treatment, or with the extent or lack of disclosure, of the fraud or its consequences (para 45).

SAS 110 also recognises that there may be circumstances in which auditors should go beyond their duty to report instances of fraud to the entity's management or audit committee and, in appropriate cases, to qualify their audit reports (as outlined above) and to report suspected or actual instances of fraud to an appropriate external authority. The Standard requires auditors becoming aware of suspected or actual fraud to consider whether the matter ought to be reported to a proper authority in the public interest (para 50). In normal circumstances, the auditor's duty of confidentiality to the client is paramount and, in line with this, SAS 110 notes that 'confidentiality is an implied term of the auditor's contract'. However, the Standard goes on to state: 'In certain exceptional circumstances auditors are not bound by their duty of confidentiality and have the right or duty to report matters to a proper authority in the public interest' (para 53). In particular:

> When a suspected or actual instance of fraud casts doubt on the integrity of the directors, auditors should make a report direct to a proper authority in the public interest without delay and without informing the directors in advance. (para 52)

Provided auditors (acting in that capacity) report an actual or suspected fraud in the public interest to an appropriate body and the disclosure is not motivated by malice, they are protected from the risk of liability for breach of confidence or defamation (para 55).

When deciding whether disclosure of a detected or suspected fraud to a proper authority is justified in the public interest, the auditor is required to consider factors such as (para 56):

- the extent to which the fraud is likely to affect members of the public;
- whether the directors are taking corrective action or are likely to do so;
- the extent to which nondisclosure of the fraud is likely to enable it to recur with impunity;
- the gravity of the matter;
- the weight of evidence and degree of suspicion that fraud has occurred.

Acceptance of a duty to report to a proper authority when it is in the public interest to do so, represents a significant extension to the responsibility acknowledged by auditors as regards detecting and reporting company fraud. Prior to SAS 110, professional auditing standards interpreted public interest reporting as a right rather than a duty, and it remains to be seen how this duty is discharged by auditors. As was noted in section 3.3.3 above, public interest reporting in relation to public sector entities – in particular, local authorities – as been a feature of public sector audits for some years.[19]

3.8.5 Conclusion: Auditors' Duties With Respect to Fraud

It is clear that auditors' duties with respect to fraud, as recognised by the auditing profession, have changed markedly over the last 70 or so years. The pendulum has swung from one extreme of recognising fraud detection as the primary audit objective (prior to the 1920s), to the other extreme of grudging acceptance of minimal responsibility, combined with an insistence that audits are not designed, and cannot be relied upon, to detect fraud. This attitude typified the 1950s and 1960s. In recent years, in response to mounting pressure on auditors to accept greater responsibility with respect to fraud, the pendulum seems to have swung back a considerable way.

The changes evident in professional publications and auditing practices over the past 70 or so years provide an example of auditors' duties responding to, and reflecting changes in, the socio-economic environment of which it is a part (as discussed in Chapter 2). Today, professional publications still emphasise the fact that non-managerial employee fraud is best prevented and detected by corporate managers through the maintenance of an adequate system of internal control. However, they also affirm that auditors have a responsibility to remain alert throughout an audit to the possibility that fraud may have occurred, and to plan their audits so as to have a reasonable expectation of discovering material frauds which may impact on the accounting records or the financial statements. Further, in the UK auditors have acknowledged some responsibility to report detected (or suspected) fraud to third parties.

---

[19] SAS 120: *Consideration of Law and Regulations* also imposes a duty on auditors to report to an appropriate authority when they encounter suspected or actual noncompliance with law and regulations relating to the preparation of, or disclosure of items in, the financial statements and it is in the public interest to so report. (This Standard is discussed further in Chapter 6, section 6.5).

3.9 SUMMARY

In this chapter auditors' legal and professional duties have been reviewed. It has been shown that auditors' duties are derived from statute law, case law and professional promulgations.

Statute law (primarily embodied in the Companies Act 1985 as amended by the Companies Act 1989 for private sector entities, and the Local Government Finance Act 1982 and National Audit Act 1983 for public sector entities) provides for audits to be conducted and sets out the administrative framework for the auditor's appointment, remuneration, rights, duties, and resignation or removal. Statute law is silent on the standard expected of auditors in the performance of their statutory duties, but case law has provided guidance on what is required. Auditing Standards and Guidelines, issued by the APB, provide further and more detailed guidance to auditors on what is required of them when conducting an audit.

In this chapter we have also discussed the somewhat unusual three-way relationship between auditors, the client company and the company's shareholders, and emphasised that responsibility for an entity's financial statements lies with its directors (or their equivalent), and not with the auditors. The auditor's responsibility is limited to forming and expressing an opinion on the truth and fairness of the entity's financial statements and their compliance (or otherwise) with relevant legislation.

In the final section of the chapter we have examined the controversial issue of auditors' duties in relation to corporate fraud. In this regard we have noted that auditors today acknowledge responsibility to detect fraud which is material to the financial statements and also to report detected or suspected fraud to an appropriate level of management within the entity. Further, in cases where a material fraud (or suspected fraud) is not appropriately dealt with in the financial statements, auditors are required to report this to shareholders by qualifying the audit report. Additionally, when it is in the public interest to do so, they are required to report detected or suspected fraud to an appropriate public authority.

SELF-REVIEW QUESTIONS

3.1 State the institutions which define the rights, responsibilities and duties of auditors and the particular part played by each.

3.2 State who may and who may not be appointed as an auditor of a company.

3.3 In relation to a company, list those parties who may:
   (i) appoint the auditor,
   (ii) remove the auditor from office,
   and the circumstances in which these parties can exercise their rights.

3.4 List the items which the Companies Act 1985 requires auditors to include in their reports to shareholders.

3.5 List three significant differences in the statutory provisions relating to the audits of public and private sector entities.

3.6   State the fundamental standard required of auditors in the performance of their duties as laid down in the *Kingston Cotton Mill* case (1896).

3.7   Explain briefly:
(i)   the purpose of the profession's Auditing Standards;
(ii) how Auditing Standards differ from Auditing Guidelines.

3.8   Explain the responsibilities of:
(i)   an entity's directors/management; and
(ii) its auditors,
with respect to the entity's financial statements.

3.9   Distinguish briefly between the three types of corporate fraud.

3.10 The importance of detecting fraud as an audit objective has changed markedly over the period from 1844 to the present time. State the significance of fraud detection as an audit objective in each of the following periods:
(i)   1844–1920s
(ii) 1920s–1960s
(iii) 1960s to the present.
List reasons to explain the change in the importance of fraud detection as an audit objective during these periods.

REFERENCES

Auditing Practices Board (APB). (1993). Scope and Authority of APB Pronouncements, *Accountancy*, **114**(1198), 117–18.

Beattie, A. (1989). Regulation of auditors; how will it affect you? *The Accountant's Magazine*, **93**(999), 45.

Carty, J. (1985, September). Fraud and other irregularities. *Certified Accountant*, p.30.

Chartered Institute of Public Finance and Accountancy (CIPFA). (1994). *Auditing the Public Services: A Contribution to the Debate on the Future of Auditing*. London.

Chandler, R. (1983). The annual report: Spelling out the responsibility. *Accountancy*, **94**(1081), 56–7.

Commission on Auditors' Responsibilities (CAR). (1978). *Report, Conclusions and Recommendations*. (The Cohen Commission). New York: AICPA.

Kenley, W.J. (1971). Legal decisions affecting auditors. *The Australian Accountant*, **41**(4), 153–61.

Porter, B.A. (1993). An empirical study of the audit expectation-performance gap. *Accounting and Business Research*, **24**(93), 49–68.

Smith, T. (1985, 22 August). Expectation gap trips up fraud fight's 'front line'. *Accountancy Age*, p.10.

The Audit Commission. (1995). *Code of Audit Practice for Local Authorities and the National Health Service in England and Wales*. London: Audit Commission.

Woolf, E. (1978). Profession in peril – Time running out for auditors. *Accountancy*, **89**(1014), 58–65.

ADDITIONAL READING

Bingham, A., Huntington, I. & Jones, M. (1996). *Taking Fraud Seriously*. London: Audit Faculty of the Institute of Chartered Accountants in England and Wales.

Bowerman, M. (1994). The National Audit Office and the Audit Commission: Co-operation in areas where their VFM responsibilities interface. *Financial Accountability & Management*, **10**(1), 47–64.

Humphrey, C., Turley, S. & Moizer, P. (1993). Protecting against detection: The case of auditors and fraud? *Accounting, Auditing & Accountability Journal*, **6**(1), 39–62.

Knox, J. (1994). Why auditors don't find fraud. *Accountancy*, **113**(1206), 128.

Knox, J. (1996). Prosecution for deception of auditors. *Accountancy*, **117**(1232), 79.

Lee, T.A. (1993). *Corporate Audit Theory*. Chapter 8, The corporate auditor's duty of care, pp.115–36. London: Chapman & Hall.

McAlpine, S. (1995). When fraudster and auditor meet. *Accountancy*, **115**(1219), 100.

Tweedie, D.P. (1991). Fraud – management's and auditors' responsibility for the prevention and detection. In Sherer, M. & Turley, S., *Current Issues in Auditing*. 2nd ed, Chapter 2. London: Paul Chapman Publishing.

Wells, J.T. (1990). Six common myths about fraud. *Journal of Accountancy*, **167**(2), 82–8.

Chapter 4

Two Fundamental Concepts: Independence and True and Fair View[1]

LEARNING OBJECTIVES

After studying the material in this chapter you should be able to:
- explain the concept of independence as it applies to external auditors;
- explain why independence is essential to the audit function;
- describe the circumstances in which the auditor's independence may be, or may appear to be, compromised;
- discuss the steps taken, or proposed to be taken, to strengthen auditors' independence;
- explain the concept of 'true and fair view';
- state the requirements to be met in order for financial statements to provide a true and fair view;
- discuss the problems which the concept of 'true and fair view' presents to auditors.

The following publications and fundamental principle of external auditing are particularly relevant to this chapter:

Publications:
- Guide to Professional Ethics Statement (GPES) 1.201: *Integrity, Objectivity and Independence* (ICAEW, ICAS, ICAI;[2] 1996).
- *Report of the Committee on the Financial Aspects of Corporate Governance* (the Cadbury Report) (1992).

Fundamental principle of external auditing: *Objectivity and Independence*

Auditors are objective. They express opinions independently of the entity and its directors.

---

[1] As noted in the Preface to this book, 'true and fair view', as used primarily in private sector legislation, is similar to 'presents fairly' in public sector legislation.

[2] GPES 1.201 is published separately, but in identical form, by each of the three Institutes: ICAEW, ICAS and ICAI.

4.1 INTRODUCTION

In this chapter we examine two concepts which are fundamental to external auditing, namely, 'independence' and 'true and fair view'. The first relates to a personal attribute required of auditors and the second goes to the heart of the auditor's work. These concepts are discussed primarily in the context of company, rather than public sector entity, audits. However, many of the issues addressed are applicable similarly to private and public sector auditing.

4.2 INDEPENDENCE AND AUDITING

4.2.1 The Cornerstone of Auditing

Independence has been referred to as 'the cornerstone of auditing' (Stewart, 1977). This reflects the fact that if auditors are not independent of parties, and other factors, which might influence the opinion they express in the audit report, the audit function will be virtually worthless.

Let us examine this more closely. Auditors are essentially intermediaries between the management of an entity and external parties interested in the entity. They have a duty to form and express an opinion as to whether or not the entity's financial statements (which are prepared by management for shareholders and other interested parties outside the organisation) present a true and fair view of the entity's financial position and performance. If users of the financial statements are to believe and rely on the auditor's opinion, it is essential that the auditor is, and is seen to be, independent of the entity, its management[3] and any other interested party. This is reflected in the fundamental principle of external auditing – *Objectivity and Independence* which states:

> Auditors are objective. They express opinions independently of the entity and its directors.

If auditors are considered not to be independent of the entity, its management and other interested parties, their opinion will carry little credibility and users of financial statements will gain little, if any, assurance from the audit report regarding the truth and fairness (or otherwise) of the financial statements. As a consequence, the audit function will have little purpose or value.

4.2.2 The Meaning of Independence in the Auditing Context

If independence is so critical to the audit function it is clearly important to examine what the concept means.

It is well accepted that independence, in the sense of being self-reliant and not subordinating one's professional judgment to the opinions of others, is a fundamental

---

[3] As noted in the Preface to this book, in the context of companies, the term 'management' embraces executive and non-executive directors, and non-director executives.

hallmark of all professions. However, in auditing, the term has come to have special meaning. In essence it means maintaining an independent attitude of mind and avoiding situations which would tend to impair objectivity or create personal bias. As the Guide to Professional Ethics Statement (GPES) 1.201: *Integrity, Objectivity and Independence* explains:

> Objectivity is essential for any professional person exercising professional judgment . . . Objectivity is the state of mind which has regard to all considerations relevant to the task at hand but no other. It is sometimes described as 'independence of mind'. (para 2)

With respect to auditing, if interested parties are to rely on the auditor's opinion, it is essential that the auditor is both:

- *independent in fact*, that is, the auditor maintains an unbiased, objective attitude of mind which enables him or her to evaluate a set of financial statements (and supporting evidence) as a disinterested but expert observer, and to form and express an opinion in the audit report uninfluenced by personal bias; and
- *independent in appearance*, that is, avoiding situations which might cause others to conclude that the auditor might not be maintaining an unbiased objective attitude of mind.

4.2.3   Factors that may Compromise Auditors' Independence

Stipulating that auditors must be independent in fact and independent in appearance may seem to be a straightforward and, in view of the critical nature of independence to auditing, an obvious requirement. However, in practice, such independence may be difficult to achieve. GPES 1.201 recognises five broad 'threats' to auditors' independence, namely:

- *the self-interest threat* – the threat to an auditor's independence resulting from a financial or other self-interest conflict (para 2.2);
- *the self-review threat* – the difficulty of maintaining objectivity in situations where a product or judgment of a previous audit, or non-audit, assignment needs to be challenged or re-evaluated in reaching audit conclusions (para 2.3);
- *the advocacy threat* – the threat to an auditor's objectivity resulting from the auditor becoming an advocate for (or against) the client's position in any adversarial proceedings or situations (para 2.4);
- *the familiarity or trust threat* – the threat arising from an auditor becoming over-influenced by the personality and qualities of the client's directors and/or senior managers and consequently too sympathetic to their interest. Alternatively, the auditor may become too trusting of management representations, and thus inadequately rigorous in his or her audit testing (para 2.5);
- *the intimidation threat* – the possibility that an auditor may be intimidated by threat, by a dominating personality, or by other pressures, by a director or manager of the client or by some other party (para 2.6).

In addition to recognising these general situations which may threaten an auditor's independence, GPES 1.201 identifies more specific circumstances in which an auditor may find it difficult (or may be perceived as likely to find it difficult) to maintain an unbiased, objective attitude of mind. These include situations where:

- the auditor has some financial involvement with the audit client as a shareholder, debtholder or creditor;
- the auditor participates (or plans to participate) in the affairs of a client in a capacity other than that of auditor (for example, as a director of, or consultant to, the client);
- the auditor has a mutual business interest with the audit client, or with an officer or senior employee of the client;
- the auditor receives favourable treatment from the client in the form of goods, services or hospitality;
- the auditor (or the auditor's firm) depends on the audit client for a substantial portion of total fee income;
- the auditor is actually or potentially involved in litigation against the client;
- the auditor (or the auditor's firm) provides non-audit services to the audit client.

4.2.4 Steps Taken, or Proposed, to Strengthen Auditor's Independence

From section 4.2.3 above, it is clear that a fairly wide range of circumstances may cause auditors' independence to be impaired. Both the legislators and the accounting profession, conscious of the critical importance of independence to the audit function, have established measures designed to ensure that auditors' independence is not compromised.

As regards the legislative provisions, the Companies Act 1989, s.27, stipulates that the following persons may not be appointed as auditor of a company:

- an officer or employee of the company;
- a partner or employee of an officer or employee of the company.

This provision is clearly designed to ensure that the auditor is not exposed to a conflict of interests as a result of working for the company (directly or indirectly) in a capacity other than that of auditor. Additionally, the Companies Act 1985, s.390A, provides that a company must disclose in its annual report, the amount paid or payable to the auditor (or audit firm) for the year in respect of audit fees and expenses. Also, under regulations issued by the Secretary of State (in accordance with s.390B of the 1985 Act), companies are required to disclose in their annual report, fees (and expenses) paid to their auditors (or an associate thereof) for non-audit services. This requirement ensures that financial statement users are provided with information which enables them to assess the likelihood of any impairment of the auditor's independence as a consequence of too great an involvement with the audit client.

In addition to the legislative provisions, the professional accountancy bodies have promulgated a series of 'rules' designed to prevent auditors' independence from being compromised. These 'rules' are of two types:

1. general environmental safeguards;
2. specific safeguards appropriate for identified situations where independence may be at risk.

1. *General Environmental Safeguards*

GPES 1.201 notes that certain safeguards against auditors' independence being impaired are embodied in the general environment of the auditing profession and audit firms. It notes, for example, that:

- chartered accountants are taught from the outset of their training contracts to behave with integrity in all their professional and business relationships and to strive for objectivity in all professional and business judgments [para 3.3(i)];
- firms should set great store on their reputation for impartiality and objectivity [para 3.3(iv)];
- the profession has a long standing ethical code which imposes specific prohibitions in circumstances where the threat to auditors' objectivity is so significant, or is generally perceived to be so, that no other appropriate safeguards would be effective [para 3.4(i)];
- the profession's policing system investigates complaints made by members of the public or members of the profession and, where necessary, commences disciplinary proceedings against an offending member [para 3.4(iii)];
- firms establish internal procedures which help to provide reassurance that the required audit objectivity has been preserved. These include:
  - arrangements to ensure that staff are adequately trained and empowered to communicate any issue of objectivity that concerns them to a separate principal (or partner) of the firm;
  - the rotation of audit engagement partners and staff;
  - formal consideration of the propriety of accepting all potential and continuing audit engagements;
  - the overall control environment, starting with a professional approach towards matters of quality and ethics, and embracing staff training, development and performance appraisal (para 3.5).

2. *Specific Safeguards for Identified Situations of Risk*

These may be considered conveniently under the following headings:
(a) financial involvement with an audit client;
(b) personal or business relationships with an audit client;
(c) favourable treatment from an audit client;
(d) litigation and other external pressures on the auditor;
(e) undue dependence on an audit client for fee income;
(f) provision of non-audit services to an audit client.

(a) *Financial Involvement with an Audit Client:* Financial involvement with an audit client may arise through a shareholding in or loan to or from the client, or through any other direct or indirect beneficial interest in the client: this includes a beneficial interest arising through a trust (as trustee or beneficiary) and a Personal Equity Plan which has an audit client among its investments.

To safeguard auditors' independence from being compromised as a result of financial involvement with an audit client, GEPS 1.201 provides that:

- except in cases where a client is in the business of borrowing and lending money (for example, a bank), no audit firm or principal of a firm should directly or indirectly make any loan to, or receive any loan from, an audit client, or give or accept any guarantee in relation to a debt of the client, firm or principal (paras 4.10 to 4.12);
- in cases where significant fees are overdue from an audit client, or group of connected clients, a principal not involved in the audit is required to undertake a review to ascertain whether the overdue fees, together with the fees for the current audit assignment, could be regarded as a significant loan (paras 4.13 and 4.14);
- no principal in an audit firm, nor anyone closely connected with a principal (such as a spouse and dependent children), should have any beneficial interest in shares or other direct investment in an audit client. Similarly, no principal in an audit firm should have a Personal Equity Plan which has an audit client among its investments (paras 4.31 and 4.36);
- if an employee in an audit firm, or a person closely connected with an employee, has a beneficial interest in shares or other investments of an audit client, that employee should not take part in the audit of that client (para 4.32);
- if a principal in an audit firm, or person closely connected with a principal, holds a beneficial interest in a trust which has a shareholding in an audit client, and the principal is a trustee of the trust, the audit firm should cease to be the auditor of the client. If the principal is not a trustee of the trust, the firm may retain the client but the principal should not be involved in the audit (paras 4.39 to 4.41);
- in cases where shares or other relevant investment(s) in an audit client are acquired involuntarily by a principal in an audit firm, for example, through inheritance, marriage or a takeover, the investment(s) should be disposed of at the earliest practicable date when the disposition would not be considered to amount to insider trading (para 4.37);
- in cases where the audit client's Articles of Association require the auditor to be a shareholder, the auditor should hold no more than the minimum number of shares necessary to comply with the provision in the Articles (para 4.38). Additionally, the auditor is precluded from voting at any general meeting of the company in relation to the appointment, removal or remuneration of the company's auditor(s) (para 4.49).

(b) *Personal or Business Relationships with an Audit Client:* As for financial involvement, the professional bodies have recognised that personal, family and business relationships with an audit client (or officer or senior employee of an audit client) may impair auditors' independence. GPES 1.201 stipulates, for example, that no member of the profession should personally take part in the audit of a company in which (s)he has been an officer or employee during the current accounting period or the preceding two years (para 4.24). Along similar lines, GPES 1.201 states that where a principal or senior employee of an audit firm joins an audit client, appropriate steps should be taken to sever any significant connections between that former principal or employee and the audit firm. Where such a person plans to join an audit client, (s)he should be removed from the audit team immediately this is known, and any significant audit judgments made by that person with respect to the client should be reviewed (paras 4.26 to 4.29).

(c) *Favourable Treatment from an Audit Client*: The professional bodies have recognised that auditors' independence may be compromised as a result of receiving a benefit by way of goods, services or hospitality from an audit client. As a consequence, audit firms and persons closely connected with the firm (principals and employees) are prohibited from accepting such goods, services and hospitality from a client, except where 'the value of any benefit is modest' (GPES 1.201, para 4.15). What amounts to a 'modest benefit' is left to the auditor's (or audit firm's) judgment.

(d) *Litigation and Other External Pressures on the Auditor*: Where litigation between an auditor and audit client is in progress, or is likely to take place, it seems most unlikely that the auditor will be able to maintain an independent attitude of mind when evaluating the client's financial statements and supporting evidence. Even if the auditor is, in fact, able to maintain his or her objectivity, independence in appearance will be impaired. This applies whether the client has sued the auditor for negligence, for example, or the auditor has brought a case against the client for occurrences such as fraud or deceit (GPES 1.201, paras 4.16 to 4.19).

The professional bodies have also recognised that an auditor's independence may be threatened as a result of pressures being exerted by an associated audit firm or an outside source introducing business, such as bankers or solicitors. In this regard, GPES 1.201 notes:

> The threat to objectivity [in such circumstances] will depend upon . . . the strength of an associate's interest in the [auditor or audit] firm's retaining a client, and the extent to which the introduction of business by an outside source is able to affect the [auditor's or audit] firm's fee income. (para 4.51)

In order to mitigate the likelihood of auditors' independence being compromised as a consequence of pressures being brought to bear by outside sources, GPES 1.201 precludes the audit firm from employing on the audit any person who is subject to such pressures. The Statement also notes that potential dangers to auditors' independence resulting from external pressures 'should be borne in mind and provided for in the [audit] firm's review machinery' (para 4.53) (that is, the measures incorporated in the control environment, such as considering the propriety of accepting or continuing audit engagements prior to their acceptance).

(e) *Undue Dependence on an Audit Client for Fee Income*: GPES 1.201 (para 4.1) recognises that auditors' objectivity may be threatened or appear to be threatened by undue dependence for fees on any one audit client or group of connected clients. While noting that new firms may not be able to meet the criteria, GPES 1.201 recommends that auditors should avoid situations where recurring fees (from audit and non-audit services) from one client, or group of connected clients, exceed 15 per cent of the gross income of the practice. If the client is a listed company (or of particular interest to the public) the fees should not exceed 10 per cent of the practice's gross income (para 4.2). GPES 1.201 emphasises that the 15 per cent and 10 per cent noted above 'indicate only the extremes beyond which the public perception of a member's objectivity is likely to be at risk.' It goes on to state that an audit firm:

should, before accepting an audit appointment and as part of its annual review, carefully consider . . . the propriety of accepting or retaining each audit client or group of connected clients the fees from which for audit and other recurring work . . . represent 10 per cent or more of the gross practice income . . . In the case of a listed company or other public interest company . . . a figure of not more than 5 per cent is the appropriate point to initiate review. (para 4.9)

Although serious, dependence on a particular audit client (or group of connected clients) for a significant proportion of fee income is not the only threat to auditors' independence arising from audit fees. It is a widely held view that auditors are unlikely to be truly independent of their clients all the time audit fees are settled through direct negotiation with the client's management. Auditors are perceived as unlikely to bite the hand that feeds them!

A significant proposal designed to divorce company officials from negotiating the audit fee with their auditors is that of having audit fees determined according to a fixed scale. The main difficulty with this proposal is identifying a suitable base for developing a scale of fees. The most common suggestion has been the size of the audit client, but there is no consensus as to the appropriate indicator of size. Should it be, for example, total assets? total revenue? total profits? and, if so, before or after exceptional items? before or after tax? etc.

Even if agreement could be reached about the 'best' indicator of size, this may not be an appropriate basis for determining audit fees. The time, effort and skills required for an audit frequently depend on factors other than size; for example, whether the audit is an initial or subsequent engagement (an initial audit requires additional time to become familiar with the client, its business, its accounting system, etc.); the complexity (or simplicity) of the client's organisational structure and business operations; the quality of the client's internal controls; the expertise of the client's accountancy staff; the presence (or absence) of circumstances which might motivate client-personnel to manipulate the financial statements (for example, plans to float shares or issue debentures during the ensuing accounting period, or managers' bonuses being tied to reported profits).

Further, even if a satisfactory scale of fees could be developed which accommodated factors recognised as affecting the time and skills needed for audits, there is the danger that auditors would be tempted to tailor individual audits to the set fees rather than to the particular circumstances of the audit. In some cases this could result in over-auditing: that is, auditors conducting audit tests beyond those which are strictly necessary because additional time is 'available' under the set fee. In other cases, under-auditing may result: auditors failing to perform tests which are required because the fee is insufficient to cover the time needed.

Although direct negotiation of audit fees between auditors and audit-client managements is a serious obstacle to securing and maintaining auditors' independence, it is an obstacle which is difficult to overcome. A mechanism which can mitigate the difficulties, by ensuring that executives who are responsible for the day-to-day management of the entity are not involved in negotiating audit fees with the auditors, is that of an audit committee. This is discussed in section 4.2.5 below.

(f) *Provision of Non-audit Services to an Audit Client*: Like placing undue dependence on audit clients for fee income, the provision of non-audit services to audit clients is generally regarded as a serious threat to auditors' independence – both in fact and in appearance. However, there are two sides to this issue. These are as follows.

• During the course of an audit, the auditor becomes familiar with all aspects of the audit client – its business, organisation, accounting system, internal controls, policies, key personnel, etc. This familiarity places the auditor in an ideal position to provide financial and management advice to the audit client. The auditor, unlike other outside consultants, does not have to spend time getting to know the client. This clearly reduces the costs involved. Furthermore, because the auditor is familiar with every aspect of the client's organisation, (s)he is able to anticipate the likely impact on all parts of the organisation of any advice given to management. An outside consultant is likely to become familiar only with the aspect of the entity related to the particular task in hand. This consultant may not, therefore, appreciate the wider ramifications within the organisation of advice given to the entity's management.

• While it is generally agreed that auditors are well placed to provide financial and management advice to their audit clients more efficiently and effectively than other outside consultants, it seems likely that providing these services is at the cost of at least some of the auditor's independence. The threat to auditors' independence comes from three main sources:

i) Self-interest. As GPES 1.201 notes:

> All work that creates a financial relationship between the auditor and the audit client may appear to create a self-interest threat ... [T]he auditor's objectivity might be impaired by a need to remain on good terms with the directors of the audited company in order to preserve a working relationship. The perceived threat grows with the size of the fees and is thus increased by work or services additional to the audit. (para 4.58)

ii) Self-review of non-audit work. If an auditor (or audit firm) advises an audit client on, say, a new accounting system and the client, acting on that advice, installs the new system, in any subsequent audit the auditor (or members of the audit firm) will be reviewing the outcome of their own advice. In this circum-stance, it is difficult to accept that the auditor will evaluate the system with the same level of objectivity as (s)he would apply had the advice on the system come from an outside consultant. Even if the auditor is, in fact, able to maintain an objective and unbiased attitude of mind, it may be difficult for an outside observer to accept that this is the case and so, as a minimum, independence in appearance is impaired.

A similar situation exists when an auditor both prepares and audits a set of financial statements. Even if the auditor manages to maintain an unbiased attitude of mind while performing the audit, it may be difficult for an outside observer to conclude that this is the case. The situation might be helped if some other person or group within the auditor's firm provides the advisory service or compiles the financial statements, as the case might be. However, independence in appearance, if not in fact, is still at a lower level than would apply if the audit firm were not involved in providing any advisory service or accounts prepara-tion to the audit client (GPES 1.201, paras 4.60 to 4.63).

iii) Familiarity threat. If an auditor provides non-audit services to an audit client (s)he may be perceived as too closely involved with the audit client's management to be able to conduct the audit in an unbiased objective manner.

Despite the potential threat to auditors' independence resulting from the provision of non-audit services to audit clients, the profession's ethical guidance is quite permissive in this regard. GPES 1.201 for example, observes:

> It is economic in terms of skill and effort for professional accountants in public practice to be able to provide other services to their clients since they already have a good knowledge of their business. Many companies (particularly smaller ones) would be adversely affected if they were denied the right to obtain other services from their auditors. (para 4.56)

However, auditors are also warned that 'care must be taken to ensure [they do] not perform management functions or make management decisions' (para 4.56). They are also counselled to be mindful of the limits placed on the fee income which may be derived from an audit client (discussed above) and to ensure that safeguards are put in place to prevent the provision of non-audit services from adversely affecting their objectivity [see, for example, GPES 1.201 paras 4.58, 4.60 and 4.64].

The question of whether auditors' independence is or is not impaired by the provision of non-audit services to audit clients has been hotly debated for many years. Commentators such as Cowen (1980) have emphasised that there is little or no empirical evidence to suggest that the provision of non-audit services to audit clients impairs auditors' independence. Similarly, the Commission on Auditors' Responsibilities (1978) concluded that, 'there is no evidence that provision of services other than auditing has actually impaired the independence of auditors' (p.94). However, other commentators, both from inside the auditing profession, such as Briloff (1986), and from outside the profession, such as Congressman Dingell (a vocal critic of auditors in the US) and Austin Mitchell MP (a vocal critic of auditors in the UK), are adamant that the provision of non-audit services to audit clients must, and does, impair auditors' independence.

Analysis of the arguments advanced by proponents of each viewpoint suggests that the answer to the question of whether auditors' independence is compromised by the provision of non-audit services to audit clients depends less on whether such services are provided than on the nature and amount of such services. As noted in section 4.2.4 above, under the Companies Act 1989 (s.27) and regulations issued by the Secretary of State, respectively, companies are required to disclose in their annual reports, the amounts paid or payable to the auditor (or audit firm) for the year for audit fees and (separately) for non-audit services. By requiring companies to disclose this information, interested external parties are able to assess for themselves the extent of non-audit services provided by the auditor, and thus to form a judgment as to whether the auditor's independence is likely to have been impaired as a result. However, at present, no information on the nature of the non-audit services provided to the auditee is disclosed in the auditee's financial statements.

4.2.5 Other Proposals for Strengthening the Independence of Auditors

From sections 4.2.3 and 4.2.4 above, it is evident that there are a number of factors which serve to threaten auditors' independence. Yet, if auditors do not maintain their independence (both in fact and in appearance), the credibility of the opinion they express in the audit report will be undermined and the value of the audit function will be lost.

Many members of the auditing profession, as well as a number of politicians, financial journalists and others, have recognised the critical importance of auditors' independence to the future of the audit function. They have also seen the dangers posed to that independence, particularly as a result of auditors becoming too familiar with their audit clients' managements, and being dependent on those managements for their fees and continued appointment. Commentators have expressed concern about the ineffectiveness of the legislative provisions and professional bodies' pronouncements (such as GPES 1.201) in dealing with the problem. Their concerns have given rise to three further proposals designed to maintain and strengthen auditors' independence, namely:

1. mandatory auditor rotation;
2. the appointment of auditors by the state or a state agency; and
3. audit committees.

1. *Mandatory Auditor Rotation*

Two forms of auditor rotation have been proposed:

- rotating the partners responsible for a particular audit but retaining the audit within the audit firm;
- rotating the firms responsible for a particular audit.

Support for both proposals has been expressed from time to time in most English-speaking countries but the rotation of audit firms has received particularly serious consideration in the US. There, the proposal gained prominence in 1976 when Ralph Nadar, and other members of the Corporate Accountability Research Group, recommended to the US Senate Committee on Commerce that Congressional legislation be passed requiring large publicly held corporations to change their external auditors every five years (Hoyle, 1978, p.69). Since the mid-1970s, a number of other politicians, most notably Senator Metcalfe and Congressman Moss in the 1970s, and Congressman Dingell since the mid-1980s, have continued to call for mandatory auditor rotation. Auditor rotation has also been called for by UK critics of the profession such as Austin Mitchell MP.

Four main arguments are usually advanced in favour of auditor rotation. These are as follows:

i)   The quality and competence of auditors' work tends to decline over time as auditors become 'over-familiar' with particular audit clients and, as a consequence, begin to make unjustified assumptions. An auditor may, for example, make assumptions about such things as the effectiveness of certain internal controls and the reliability of management's representations based on the findings of previous audits, instead of objectively evaluating current evidence.

ii) A long-term relationship with an audit client is likely to result in the development of a close personal relationship between the auditor and the client's management.

This is likely to cause some diminution in the auditor's objectivity and unbiased attitude of mind when conducting the client's audits.

iii) Many auditors provide (non-audit) management advisory services (MAS) to their audit clients and the extent of these services is likely to increase directly in proportion to the time the audit is retained. Proponents of mandatory auditor rotation contend that the auditor is unlikely to evaluate the results of management advice (s)he has given to the client as objectively as (s)he would the results of advice proffered by other, unrelated advisors. As Hoyle (1978) has said, 'It is difficult . . . to understand how a CPA [Certified Public Accountants] firm could remain totally objective in viewing financial statements that reflect on the credibility of the CPA firm's MAS advice' (p.71).

iv) The longer the auditor retains the audit of a particular client, the more significant MAS work is likely to become. As MAS work increases, so does the dependence of the auditor on the client for fee income. It seems likely that such dependence will cause some impairment of the auditor's independence – in appearance, if not in fact.

Reviewing these arguments it should be noted that, while rotation of audits amongst audit firms could be expected to reduce all four of the problems indicated, rotation of audits within firms affects only the first two.

Those who oppose mandatory auditor rotation support their position with contrary arguments. These include the following:

i) The complexity of most modern business organisations renders short-term audit engagements inappropriate. It takes an auditor time to gain a thorough knowledge of a business, its policies, operations, accounting system, internal controls, key personnel, etc. – an essential requirement for an efficient and effective audit in today's environment. As Olson, then President of the American Institute of Certified Public Accountants (AICPA), stated to the US Senate Committee on Commerce in 1976:

> The most effective audits are generally performed by auditors who have acquired a thorough knowledge of the business entity under review. It is generally recognized that such knowledge is best gained through actual audit experience over a considerable period of years. (Cited by Hoyle, 1978, p.74)

If mandatory auditor rotation were introduced, a company might have to appoint new auditors just as the quality of audit work was improving.

ii) Auditor rotation would result in significantly increased audit fees. The initial years of any audit are very costly. During these years the auditor must devote considerable time and effort to becoming familiar with the client and its business. This is not necessary in later years. With mandatory auditor rotation, the costly initial period of any audit would occur more frequently than at present, and the benefits to be gained from subsequent, lower cost years, would not be fully realised.

iii) The overall quality of audits would fall. Opponents of mandatory auditor rotation contend that, because auditors would know that a particular audit engagement is to be terminated after a limited number of years, they would not be motivated to perform audits with maximum efficiency and effectiveness.

When evaluating the desirability (or otherwise) of mandatory auditor rotation, the benefits of such a measure need to be weighed against the costs. According to Hoyle (1978):

> Too many of the arguments for rotation have never been substantiated . . . [Further] to say that, [for example], the overall quality of audit work would improve under a rotation system ignores the problems of initial audit engagements and the complexity of the modern business organisation.

> The idea of mandatory rotation is somewhat like trying to swat a fly with a baseball bat. Although it is possible that the problem [of compromised auditor independence] may be solved, the accompanying damage may be irreparable. Mandatory auditor rotation is simply too drastic a step to take without proof that the benefits are worth the . . . costs . . . (p.75)

However strong the arguments against auditor rotation may appear to be, it seems that the profession has been somewhat swayed by those advanced in favour of rotation of audit partners. In the UK, the profession was encouraged to move in this direction by the Committee on the Financial Aspects of Corporate Governance (CFACG, the Cadbury Committee). This Committee looked specifically at ways of improving corporate governance in listed UK companies and considered, amongst many other things, mandatory auditor rotation. It decided against the compulsory rotation of audit firms but was favourably disposed towards the suggestion of rotating audit partners. (It went so far as to ask the accountancy profession to produce guidelines with a view to implementing an appropriate scheme). Following on from this, in 1994 the ICAEW, ICAS and ICAI introduced a requirement (through GPES 1.201, para 15.1) for audit engagement partners of public listed companies to be rotated every seven years. A similar requirement was introduced in the US for all firms joining the AICPA's Securities and Exchange Commission (SEC) Practice Section.[4] All such firms are required, as a condition of membership of the Section, to rotate the audit engagement partner of an SEC registered audit client every seven years (Wood and Sommer, 1985, p.122).

2.   *The Appointment of Company Auditors by the State or a State Agency*

As noted earlier, it is a widely held view that auditors will not be truly independent of their audit clients' managements all the time those managements are influential in their (the auditors') appointment and payment. This has given rise to the suggestion that auditors' independence could be strengthened if company auditors were appointed by the state or by a state agency.

However, this suggestion is not without significant difficulties. For example, if the state were to control auditors' appointment and fees, then the state would, in effect, also control the audit function. This would introduce the possibility of auditors becoming susceptible to the political agendas of the day and of the audit profession losing its professional independence. Further, if auditors were appointed by a state agency, they would be accountable to the state through that agency. If, at the same time, the directors of companies remained accountable to their shareholders, a conflict of the directors' and auditors' accountabilities could arise, with consequential difficulties for the achievement

---

[4] See Chapter 16, section 16.2.3.

of an effective audit. In the case of public sector audits, where auditors are frequently employed or appointed by a state agency (such as the National Audit Office or Audit Commission), a conflict of accountabilities does not arise as both the entity's management and its auditors are accountable to the state (or a section thereof).

3. Audit Committees

Audit committees afford a further suggested means of strengthening auditors' independence. An audit committee is a committee of the governing body (board of directors or equivalent) of a corporate entity which has delegated responsibility from that body for, *inter alia*, overseeing the external financial reporting process and the internal controls of the entity.

Over the past two decades, the value of audit committees as a means of enhancing external financial reporting and ensuring the independence of external auditors has been recognised and these committees have become widely established in many parts of the world. Their development has varied from country to country but, interestingly, it has been stimulated in each case by unexpected corporate failure and/or reports of misconduct by senior executives or directors. It seems that the public and politicians believe that, if auditors had been properly independent of their audit client's managements, and had performed their duties with due skill and care, then warning bells would have been sounded in at least some of the cases. Following on from this, it is generally reasoned that if audit committees are established, with a majority of non-executive directors,[5] to oversee the appointment of external auditors and the external audit function, then unexpected corporate failure and undetected misconduct by senior officials will be significantly reduced.

Development of Audit Committees in North America and the UK: Audit committees were widely adopted in Canada and the US during the 1970s, largely as a result of 'several well-publicised instances of corporate wrongdoing and questionable conduct that severely tarnished the image of big business in North America' (CICA, 1981, p.1).

Following the collapse of Atlantic Acceptance Corporation Ltd in Canada in 1965, in 1971 audit committees became a legal requirement for public companies incorporated in Ontario. In 1973, a similar requirement became effective for public companies incorporated in British Columbia, and in 1975 for federally incorporated companies. Since then audit committees have become a universally accepted feature of corporate life in Canada.

In the US, audit committees received their first major endorsement, from both the New York Stock Exchange (NYSE) and the SEC, as a result of the infamous *McKesson and Robbins* case in the late 1930s. However, few audit committees were established until the 1970s, when interest in them was revived as a result of several factors. These included a number of legal decisions (including the *BarChris Construction Corporation* case) which emphasised that executive and non-executive directors are equally responsible for the company's affairs and equally liable for misleading financial statements. Other factors included the unexpected collapse of Penn Central Company, the notorious Equity Funding fraud, and the widespread

---

[5] Directors who are not involved in the day-to-day management of the entity.

incidents of corporate misconduct which came to light during the enquiries which led to the passing of the Foreign Corrupt Practices Act 1977 – in particular, the admittance by hundreds of companies that they had made significant unrecorded payments overseas (CICA, 1981, pp.98–99).

Since the mid-1970s, politicians in the US have been vocal in their demands that public companies be required to establish audit committees, and such committees have also been actively promoted by the SEC. In June 1978 they became a listing requirement of the NYSE. The adoption of audit committees was further encouraged in 1987 when the National Commission on Fraudulent Financial Reporting (The Treadway Commission, 1987) recommended that they be established by all public companies, and urged the SEC to make such committees a requirement for all companies under its jurisdiction. To date, the SEC has not exercised its regulatory power in this way. However, a survey conducted by Hardiman, Reinstein and Gabhart (1986, p.38) showed that, in 1986, 90 per cent of all publicly traded companies in the US had audit committees, so it is evident that they are very widely supported.

The establishment of audit committees elsewhere in the world has been less widespread and has occurred later than in North America. However, there are signs that they are being adopted at a rapid and accelerating pace in Australia, New Zealand, South Africa, Malaysia, Singapore and elsewhere.

In the UK, adoption of audit committees did not begin in earnest until the late 1980s. Indeed, until 1987 neither the professional accountancy bodies nor the regulatory agencies (such as the Bank of England and the Department of Trade and Industry) seemed to give these committees serious consideration. However in 1987, stimulated by the serious and growing size and incidence of corporate fraud, the ICAEW recommended that public companies be required to establish audit committees, and the Bank of England and PRO-NED[6] also urged these companies to adopt such committees. These moves were followed in 1988 by the introduction of a Private Member's Bill to Parliament which, if enacted, would have required large listed public companies in the UK to establish audit committees. Similar Bills had been introduced by Sir Brandon Rhys Williams in every parliamentary session since 1970 but, unlike its predecessors, the 1988 Bill passed through the House of Commons unopposed. It was subsequently defeated in the House of Lords. Tim Smith (MP), commenting later on the defeat of the Bill, observed:

> Both the government and regulatory bodies are keen that the trend towards audit committees shall continue. Eventually, new rules on audit committees will become law – hopefully before some great company crashes and investors lose out. (As reported, Sammons, 1990)

The adoption of audit committees in the UK received a further boost in 1992, when the Cadbury Committee included in its 'Code of Best Practice', the establishment of an audit committee of at least three non-executive directors (CFACG, 1992, Code of Best Practice, clause 4.3).[7]

---

6 An organisation established in 1982 by the Stock Exchange, the Confederation of British Industry, the Bank of England and other financial institutions to promote the appointment of non-executive directors to Boards of Directors.

7 Although compliance with the Code of Best Practice has not become a requirement in the UK, in April 1993 the London Stock Exchange made it a listing requirement for companies to include in their annual reports a statement as to whether or not they comply with the Code.

Size, Composition and Duties of Audit Committees: The size, composition and duties of audit committees varies widely from country to country and entity to entity. Only Canada and Singapore have legislative requirements for public companies to establish audit committees. In Canada, audit committees must include at least three directors, the majority of whom must not be officers or employees of the company or an affiliate. The committees are required to review, with the external auditor, the company's financial statements before the statements (and a report thereon from the audit committee) are submitted to the full Board of Directors.

Elsewhere, audit committees generally have about three to five members, at least a majority of whom are non-executive directors. Some committees are composed entirely of non-executive directors and this is encouraged by regulatory bodies such as the NYSE.

During the 1970s, the principal duties of audit committees were generally confined to matters related to external financial reporting and the external audit function. They were, for example, typically expected to:

- select the company's external auditors;
- oversee the external financial reporting process – including the external audit; and
- review the external financial statements prior to their submission to the full Board of Directors for approval.

Over the last 10–15 years, the value of audit committees for a much broader function has been recognised – that of maintaining responsible corporate governance. This broader function is reflected in the duties audit committees are now typically expected to perform. They include, for example:

- helping to establish an environment in which internal controls can operate effectively;
- ensuring that an effective accounting system and related internal controls are maintained;
- reviewing the company's accounting policies and reporting requirements;
- assessing the adequacy of management reporting;
- recommending the appointment and remuneration of the external auditor(s);
- appointing the chief internal auditor;
- discussing with the chief internal auditor and external auditor, respectively, the intended scope of the internal and external audit and satisfying itself that no unjustified restrictions have been imposed by executive management;
- reviewing the findings of the internal and external auditors;
- reviewing the entity's financial statements and annual report prior to their submission to the full Board of Directors (or equivalent body);
- reviewing public announcements relating to financial matters prior to their release;
- reviewing, and monitoring compliance with, the corporate code of conduct;
- reviewing the company's compliance with legal and regulatory requirements.

4.2.6 Conclusion: The Independence of External Auditors

From the above discussion it is evident that maintaining auditors' independence, both in fact and in appearance, is crucial to the credibility of the opinion expressed by auditors in their audit reports and, thus, to the future of the audit function. But, it is equally evident that a number of factors serve to undermine this independence – in particular, financial and personal involvement with the client, undue fee dependence, the provision of non-audit services to audit clients, and the influence of executive directors over the auditor's appointment and fees.

The professional bodies have attempted to prevent impairment of auditors' independence by publishing ethical guidelines. These guidelines identify threats, or perceived threats, to auditors' independence, and require auditors to review their exposure to such threats and to introduce appropriate safeguards. However, safeguards additional to those required by ethical guidelines may also be needed. Important proposals which have been advanced as means of securing the required level of auditors' independence are mandatory auditor rotation, the appointment of auditors by the state (or a state agency), and the establishment of audit committees. The suggestions of mandatory rotation of audit firms and the appointment of company auditors by a state agency have not received widespread support, but the rotation of audit partners responsible for the audits of public listed companies has been endorsed by the profession in both the UK and US. Additionally, audit committees have been established in corporate entities in many parts of the world. These committees are regarded as valuable, not only for overseeing the external financial reporting process, but also as a means of securing responsible corporate governance. In the UK, the establishment of audit committees is seen as a fruitful avenue to explore to ensure that the professional independence of external auditors is secured, and is a move which is supported by both the Cadbury Committee and the APB.

4.3   THE CONCEPT OF 'TRUE AND FAIR VIEW'

In Chapter 3 it was shown that the directors of companies and the managements of public sector entities are required by legislation to prepare financial statements which give a true and fair view of (or present fairly) their entity's financial position and performance. However, the legislation does not explain what is meant by a 'true and fair view', nor have the courts clarified the meaning of the phrase. As a consequence, the concept has been subject to differing interpretations. This has been noted, for example by Johnston, Edgar and Hays (1982) who observe:

> It is clear that the interpretation applied by most accountants is that the words 'true and fair' have a technical meaning. It is also clear that many lawyers (as well as investors) are of the opinion that these words have a popular meaning which should be followed by those responsible for their application. (p.259)

The opposing viewpoints indicated in the passage cited above may be illustrated by the following quotations. First that of the lawyers:

> [I]t is probably not an exaggeration to assert that company accounts remain almost unintelligible to the general public, including shareholders and intending investors, and that practices continue which are difficult to reconcile with the statutory obligations that balance sheets give a true and fair view of the company's affairs and that the auditors certify that the accounts give a true and fair view of the company's affairs . . . Essentially, the question is: are the accounts where there has been an undervaluation of

assets[8] 'true'? . . . 'True and fair' are unambiguous words. Practice needs to conform to the legal obligation. (Northey, 1965, pp.41–42)

Although this view may have intuitive appeal, it does not give guidance as to how it may be operationalised. It does not recognise, for example, that a range of possible 'true values' exist – net realisable value, current replacement cost, going concern value, net present value, etc. Which should be used to give a true and fair view of asset values?

Recognising such difficulties, accountants assert that criteria are needed to provide benchmarks against which the 'true and fair' requirement can be judged. This has resulted in accountants giving the phrase a technical interpretation. The Inflation Accounting (Sandilands) Committee (1975) explained this as follows:

> Accounts drawn up in accordance with generally accepted accounting principles, consistently applied, are in practice regarded as showing a 'true and fair view'. . . . The Acts . . . give only limited guidance to the accountancy profession in interpreting the phrase 'true and fair' and it has been traditionally left to the profession to develop accounting practices which are regarded as leading to a 'true and fair view' being shown. (paras 50 and 52)

From the above quotation, it appears that the Sandilands Committee was of the opinion that financial statements prepared in accordance with accounting standards will provide a true and fair view. This stance was supported by the Counsel whose opinion on the matter was sought by the Accounting Standards Board. Counsel stated:

> [A]ccounts which meet the true and fair requirement will in general follow rather than depart from [accounting] standards and [any] departure is sufficiently abnormal to require to be justified. . . . [It is likely] that the Courts will hold that in general compliance with accounting standards is necessary to meet the true and fair requirement. (Arden, 1993, para 7)

However, Counsel went on to observe:

> [T]rue and fair is a dynamic concept. Thus what is required to show a true and fair view is subject to continuous rebirth. (Arden, 1993, para 14)

As will be seen below, the dynamic nature of the true and fair concept is a characteristic which others have also stressed.

It is interesting to note that some eminent commentators have expressed the view, alluded to by the Sandilands Committee (see above), that the legislature deliberately delegated to the accountancy profession the task of defining what qualifies as 'true and fair' financial statements at any point of time. For example, Ryan (1974) (Commissioner for Corporate Affairs in New South Wales) observed that, if a court were called upon to determine whether a particular set of financial statements presented a true and fair view, the fact that they had or had not been drawn up in accordance with the principles embodied in professional pronouncements would be very persuasive. He continued:

> I have come to the conclusion . . . that in selecting the phrase 'true and fair view' as the standard by which the profit or loss of a company and the state of its affairs are to be judged, the Legislature in effect conferred a legislative function on the accountancy profession. It is a legislative function of an ambulatory nature: what is 'true and fair' at any particular point of time will correspond with what professional accountants as a body conceive to be proper accounting principles. The evolution, development and general

---

[8] As a result of adherence to historical cost principles.

acceptance of those principles will cause the concept of what is 'true and fair' to shift accordingly. (p.14)

Notwithstanding the technical interpretation accorded the phrase 'true and fair' by accountants, they nevertheless acknowledge that financial statements drawn up in strict conformity with accounting standards may not, in all circumstances, provide the required true and fair view. This point was emphasised by Flint (1980) when he observed:

> [P]rescription by legislation and professional standards and guidance statements . . . are necessary in the interests of good order and effective communication. . . . But giving a 'true and fair view' must always be a standard of a higher order. Whatever may be the extent of prescription, an overriding requirement to give a 'true and fair view' is, at the lowest level of its utility, a safety valve protecting users from bias, inadequacy or deficiency in the rules; a fail-safe device for the unavoidable shortcomings of prescription. More positively, its real utility is in establishing an enduring conceptual standard for disclosure in accounting and reporting to ensure that there is always relevant disclosure – where necessary beyond the prescription – based on an independent professional judgment. (p.9)

The Companies Act 1985 also acknowledges that compliance with the legislation and accounting standards may not always result in the presentation of a true and fair view of the entity's financial position and performance. Section 226 of the Act provides that, where compliance with the provisions of the Act results in financial statements that are 'not sufficient to give a true and fair view', additional information is to be provided. It also provides that, where compliance with the legislative provisions would result in financial statements which do not give the required true and fair view, the provisions should be departed from to the extent necessary to give a true and fair view. In this situation, the departure, the reasons therefore, and its effect, are to be disclosed in a note to the financial statements. Along similar lines, the Fourth Schedule (clause 36A) to the Companies Act 1985 requires that any departure from applicable accounting standards, and the reasons therefor, are to be disclosed in a note to the financial statements. Presumably, such departure could be justified only on the grounds of providing a true and fair view.

Given the recognition that compliance with relevant legislation and accounting standards does not always result in the provision of a true and fair view, it is suggested that the most appropriate interpretation of the phrase lies somewhere between the lawyers' literal, and the accountants' technical, viewpoints. This interpretation may be explained by drawing a parallel with a good landscape painting. Such a painting portrays the landscape so 'truly and fairly' that anyone seeing the picture will gain an impression of the scene depicted, similar to the one they would have gained had they been present when the picture was painted. In similar vein, in order to meet the 'true and fair' requirement, financial statements must portray the financial affairs of the reporting entity in such a way that anyone reading the statements can gain an impression of the entity's financial position and performance similar to the one they would have obtained had they personally monitored the recording of all of the entity's transactions. (This corresponds to the lawyers' literal interpretation of 'true and fair view'.)

However, many of the items presented in financial statements are subject to judgment.[9] As a consequence, in order to provide a good reproduction of the entity's

---

[9] For example, what allowance should be made for debts which might prove to be 'bad'? For how many accounting periods are long-term assets likely to generate income?

financial picture (and to avoid the impressionist artist's creativity) some conventions or rules are needed to guide and direct the exercise of that judgment. Such 'rules' are embodied in accounting standards (SSAPs and FRSs) and other generally accepted accounting principles. Thus, in order for financial statements to create the 'correct' (that is, true and fair) impression of the entity's financial affairs, adherence to accounting standards is normally necessary. (This reflects the accountants' technical interpretation of the phrase 'true and fair view') (Porter, 1990).

Similar ideas were expressed by Tweedie (1983) when he provided a test for evaluating whether or not a set of financial statements presents a true and fair view:

> While the detailed requirements necessary to show a true and fair view will continually evolve as social attitudes and technical skills change, the basic question to be posed by both director and auditor will remain. "If", they should ask, "if I were on 'the outside' and did not have the detailed knowledge of the company's trading performance and ultimate financial position that I have as I look at these accounts, would I be able to obtain a *clear and unambiguous* picture of that reality from these accounts?" If the picture is poorly painted, or worse, fails to represent reality, then the directors have failed to meet the paramount principle of financial reporting – to show a true and fair view. (p.449)

In concluding this discussion of the concept of true and fair view it is pertinent to note that, irrespective of the opinions of lawyers, accountants, or anyone else about the meaning of the phrase, in the final analysis it will be up to the courts to decide whether or not a particular set of financial statements presents a true and fair view of the financial position and performance of the reporting entity. To date, no case has been brought to throw light on a court's interpretation of the phrase.

4.4 SUMMARY

In this chapter two concepts which are fundamental to auditing have been examined, namely, 'independence' and 'true and fair view'.

'Independence' refers to a personal quality of auditors – an objective, unbiased attitude of mind. This has two dimensions: independence in fact and independence in appearance. Independence in both of these senses must be maintained if the credibility of the opinion expressed by auditors in their audit reports is not to be undermined and, with it, the future of the audit function.

It has been shown that a number of factors, if allowed to do so, could impair auditors' independence but that steps have been taken by the auditing profession to prevent this from happening. Additionally, mandatory auditor rotation, appointment by a state agency, and audit committees have been proposed as means of strengthening auditors' independence. It has been noted that the Institutes of Chartered Accountants in England and Wales, Scotland and Ireland have introduced a requirement for the rotation of audit partners responsible for the audits of public listed companies. It has also been noted that audit committees have been widely adopted by companies in many parts of the world and, in general, they are proving to be valuable, not only for strengthening external auditors' independence from audit-client managements, but also for overseeing the whole of a company's financial reporting process and for securing responsible corporate governance.

The concept of 'true and fair view' refers to a standard which must be reached by financial statements. Although auditors are required by law to form and express an opinion as to whether or not financial statements examined by them reach this standard, the concept has not been defined in statute or by the courts. Further, it is a concept which is dynamic in nature. As a consequence of these factors, the phrase 'true and fair view' is open to different interpretations. However, it is generally accepted that, in the absence of unusual circumstances, for financial statements to present a true and fair view, they must comply with applicable accounting standards. It has also been suggested that a useful test for judging whether a set of financial statements gives the required true and fair view is to ask: 'Do the financial statements provide a reader with the same impression about the reporting entity's financial position and performance as that reader would obtain if (s)he had full (inside) knowledge of all the facts?'

SELF-REVIEW QUESTIONS

4.1 Define 'independence' as it relates to auditing. (Your definition should refer to both independence in fact and independence in appearance.)

4.2 Explain briefly why independence is of critical importance for external auditors.

4.3 List six factors that may result in an auditor's independence being compromised in fact or in appearance.

4.4 Outline the provisions of the Companies Act 1985 which are designed to ensure auditors are independent from their audit clients.

4.5 List the restrictions placed on auditors by the professional accountancy bodies which are designed to prevent auditors' independence from being impaired through:
(i) financial involvement with an audit client;
(ii) personal involvement with an audit client.

4.6 Outline, and briefly evaluate, the recommendations contained in the Cadbury Committee report which are aimed at enhancing the independence of external auditors. (Note: Comprehensive coverage of these recommendations is not provided in this Chapter).

4.7 List two advantages and two disadvantages of each of the following proposals as means of strengthening auditors' independence:
(i) audit fees being paid according to a scale of fees;
(ii) mandatory auditor rotation;
(iii) auditors being appointed by the state or by a state agency.

4.8 Explain briefly what is meant by an audit committee. (Your answer should define an audit committee and refer to the size, composition and major duties of such committees.)

4.9 The auditor of a company is required to form and express an opinion on the truth and fairness of a company's financial statements. Explain briefly:

(i)   the meaning frequently accorded the phrase 'true and fair view' by lawyers;
(ii) why this interpretation is not useful for preparers and auditors of financial statements;
(iii) what is generally accepted by the accounting profession as being required for financial statements to provide the required true and fair view.

4.10 Strict compliance with applicable accounting standards may not, in all circumstances, generate financial statements which meet the 'true and fair' standard. Outline a useful general test which may be applied in order to judge whether or not a set of financial statements presents a true and fair view.

REFERENCES

Arden QC, M., (1993). *The True and Fair Requirement*. (Counsel's opinion). London: Accounting Standards Board. [Also reprinted in Institute of Chartered Accountants in England and Wales. (1994). *Members' Handbook, volume 2*, Appendix to the Foreword, pp.13–20].
Briloff, A.J. (1986, April). *The Auditors' Responsibilities and Irresponsibility*. Unpublished address delivered at the University of Connecticut, Storrs.
Canadian Institute of Chartered Accountants (CICA). (1981). *Audit Committees: A Research Study*. Canada: CICA.
Commission on Auditors' Responsibilities (CAR). (1978). *Report, Conclusions and Recommendations* (The Cohen Commission). New York: AICPA.
Committee on the Financial Aspects of Corporate Governance (CFACG). (1992). *Report of the Committee on the Financial Aspects of Corporate Governance* (Cadbury Report). London: Gee
Cowen, S.S. (1980). Non-audit services: How much is too much? *Journal of Accountancy*, **150**(6), 51–56.
Flint, D. (1980). *The Significance of the Standard of True and Fair View*. Invitation Research Lecture, New Zealand: NZSA.
Hardiman, P.K., Reinstein, A. & Gabhart, D.R.L. (1986). Audit committees for Governmental units – How to. *CPA Journal*, **56**(6), 38–44.
Hoyle, J. (1978). Mandatory auditor rotation: The arguments and an alternative. *Journal of Accountancy*, **146**(5), 69–78.
Inflation Accounting Committee. (1975). *Report of the Inflation Accounting Committee* (Sandilands Committee). London: HMSO, CMND 6225.
Johnston, T.R., Edgar, G.C. & Hays, P.L. (1982). *The Law and Practice of Company Accounting in New Zealand* (6th ed.). Wellington: Butterworths.
National Commission on Fraudulent Financial Reporting. (1987). *Report of the National Commission on Fraudulent Financial Reporting* (Treadway Commission). New York: AICPA.
Northey, J. (1965). *Recommendations for Company Law Reform*. Business Law Symposium.
Porter, B.A. (1990). True and fair view: an elusive concept. *Accountants' Journal*, **69**(110), Editorial.
Ryan, S.J.O. (1974). A true and fair view revisited. *Australian Accountant*, **44**(1), 8–10, 13–16.
Sammons, J. (1990, June). Audit committees – the way forward. *Internal Auditing*, p.1.
Stewart, R.E. (1977). Independence: The auditor's cornerstone. *Accountants' Journal*, **56**(9), 333–37.
Tweedie, D. (1983). True and fair rules. *The Accountant's Magazine*, **87**(925), 424–28, 449.
Wood, A.M. & Sommer, Jr, A.A. (1985). Statement in quotes. *Journal of Accountancy*, **156**(5), 122–31.

ADDITIONAL READING

Auditing Practices Board (APB). (1994). *The Audit Agenda*, Chapter 3. London: APB.

Barkness, L. & Simnet, R. (1994). The provision of other services by auditors: independence and pricing issues. *Accounting and Business Research*, **24**(94), 99–108.

Bartlett, R.W. (1993). A scale of perceived independence: new evidence on an old concept. *Accounting, Auditing & Accountability Journal*, **6**(2), 52–67.

Chartered Accountants' Joint Ethics Committee (CAJEC). (1994). *The Framework – A New Approach to Professional Independence*. London: ICAEW.

Collier, P. (1993). Factors affecting the voluntary formation of audit committees in major UK listed companies. *Accounting and Business Research*, **23**(91A), 421–30.

Currie, B. (1994). The nature of independence. *Accountancy*, **113**(1209), 93.

Flint, D. (1982). *A True and Fair View in Company Accounts*. London: Gee & Co.

Fowle, M. (1992). True and fair – or only fairly true? *Accountancy*, **109**(1186), 29.

Hatherly, D.J. (1992). Can auditing work without a break with tradition? *Accountancy*, **110**(1189), 85.

Hatherly, D.J. (1995). The case for the shareholder panel in the U.K. *The European Accounting Review*, **4**(3), 535–53.

Hoffman, L. & Arden, M. (1983). Legal opinion on 'True and Fair'. *Accountancy*, **94**(1083), 154–56.

Lee, T.A. (1993). *Corporate Audit Theory*, Chapter 7. London: Chapman & Hall.

Lindsell, D. (1992). Blueprint for an effective audit committee. *Accountancy*, **110**(1192), 104.

Nobes, C. (1993). The true and fair view requirement: Impact on and of the Fourth Directive, *Accounting and Business Research*, **23**(13), 35–48.

Rutherford, B.A. (1985). The true and fair doctrine: A search for explication. *Journal of Business Finance and Accounting*, **12**(4), 483–96.

Sadhu, M.A. and Langfield-Smith, I.A. (1994). *A Qualitative Standard for General Purpose Financial Reports: A Review*. Australian Accounting Research Foundation (AARF). Legislative Policy Discussion Paper No. 2. Melbourne: AARF.

Stewart, I.C. (1988). The explication of the true and fair doctrine: A Comment. *Journal of Business Finance and Accounting*, **15**(1), 115–27.

Walton, P. (1991). *The True and Fair View: A Shifting Concept*. Occasional Research Paper No. 7. London: The Chartered Association of Certified Accountants.

Wolnizer, D.W. (1995). Are audit committees red herrings? *Abacus*, **31**(1), 45–66.

Chapter 5

Overview of the Audit Process and Audit Evidence

LEARNING OBJECTIVES

After studying the material in this chapter you should be able to:
- outline the steps in the audit process from 'Appointment' to 'Reporting';
- explain what is meant by 'sufficient appropriate audit evidence';
- explain the relationship between audit procedures, audit evidence and the auditor's opinion;
- distinguish between audit objectives and audit procedures;
- describe the nature of audit evidence;
- list and describe audit procedures which are used to gather evidence;
- discuss the different sources of audit evidence;
- explain the factors which should be considered when deciding which audit evidence to seek.

The following publication and fundamental principle of external auditing are particularly relevant to this chapter:

Publication:
- Statement of Auditing Standards (SAS) 400: *Audit Evidence* (APB, 1995).

Fundamental principle of external auditing: *Rigour*

Auditors approach their work with thoroughness and with an attitude of professional scepticism.

They assess critically the information and explanations obtained in the course of their work and such additional evidence as they consider necessary for the purposes of their audit.

5.1 INTRODUCTION

It was shown in Chapter 3 that the auditor is required, among other things, to form and express an opinion on whether or not a set of financial statements provides a true and fair view of the financial position and performance of the reporting entity. In order to form this opinion, the auditor must gather and examine relevant evidence. This evidence is collected through the audit process.

5.2 OVERVIEW OF THE AUDIT PROCESS

The audit process comprises a series of logical well-defined steps, each of which has a specific objective or purpose and is performed using appropriate audit procedures. An overview of the audit process is presented in Figure 5.1. Additionally, an outline of each step in the process is provided in the Appendix where it has been placed for easy reference.

In order to illustrate the relationship between the audit steps, their objectives, and the procedures used to achieve those objectives, we will refer to Step three of the audit process – 'Understand the client, its activities and its present circumstances' (see Figure 5.1).

What is the objective of this step? Why is it performed? It is performed to ensure the auditor understands events, transactions and practices which may have a significant impact on the financial statements (see Figure 5.1). The auditor needs this understanding, amongst other reasons:

- to ascertain whether there are circumstances which increase the likelihood of errors being present in the financial statements;
- to provide a background against which evidence gathered during the audit can be evaluated to see if it makes sense and 'looks right'.

How is this objective achieved? Audit procedures used to gain this understanding of the client include the following.

- Observing the client's operations, facilities and plant; i.e. visiting the client, touring the premises and meeting key personnel (for example, the managing director, financial director, marketing manager, sales manager, production manager, and personnel manager).
- Making enquiries of relevant personnel; i.e. discussing with key personnel matters such as the trading and financial position of the entity during the past year, and any significant changes in business, accounting or personnel policies and procedures which occurred during the year.
- Inspecting the entity's manuals and legal documents; i.e. reviewing the organisation's legal documents, policy and procedures manuals, and any significant commercial agreements (for example, franchise agreements).

It should be noted that the summary of the audit process presented in Figure 5.1 is designed to give an overview of the process. It is included in this chapter to provide a contextual setting for the detailed discussion of the individual steps in the process

Figure 5.1   Summary of the Audit Process

Audit Step	Objective	Procedures	Discussed in Chapter
1. For companies appointment of auditor at AGM. For public sector entities, appointment of auditor in accordance with relevant legislation.			3
2. Letter of engagement sent to client.	To document the audit arrangements and to clarify matters that may be misunderstood.		7
3. Understand the client, its activities and its present circumstances.	To understand events, transactions and practices that may have a significant impact on the financial statements.	Observation of the entity's operations, facilities and plant. Inquiry of relevant personnel. Inspection of manuals and legal documents.	7
4. Overall analytical review.	To assess audit risk and set materiality limits.	Overall analytical procedures of financial position and results of operations.	8
5. Understand the accounting system and evaluate its internal controls.	To understand how the accounting system 'works' and to identify strengths and weaknesses of internal controls.	Observation, Inquiry, Completion of: - flow charts - internal control questionnaires - narrative descriptions 'Walk through' test.	9
6. Test internal control strengths through compliance testing.	To ascertain whether controls on which audit reliance is planned are functioning properly.	Compliance testing: Examples: Looking for evidence of authorisation, review, reconciliation, etc.	9
7. Test transactions and account balances for their substance (substantive testing).	To evaluate the completeness, accuracy and validity of data produced by the accounting system.	Substantive testing: (a) specific analytical procedures (b) tests of details Examples: Confirmation with outside parties, recomputation,. tracing.	10
8. Completion and review.	To ensure sufficient appropriate evidence has been collected on which to base an opinion.	Review for contingent liabilities and subsequent events. Review and evaluate audit evidence. Form an opinion on the truth and fairness of the financial statements..	12
9. Reporting to: (a) Shareholders and other parties external to the entity.	To inform shareholders and other interested parties of opinion formed regarding the truth and fairness of the financial statements.	Auditor's report	13
(b) Management	To inform management of weaknesses found in the accounting system and any other matters of concern. To offer advice on how financial and accounting efficiency and effectiveness may be improved, etc.	Management letter	
10. Reappointment at AGM.			

which are the subject Chapters 7 to 13 of this book. The chapter in which each step is considered is indicated in Figure 5.1.

5.3   AUDIT EVIDENCE

5.3.1   Sufficient Appropriate Audit Evidence

As the auditor proceeds through the audit process, (s)he accumulates sufficient appropriate audit evidence to support an opinion as to whether or not the financial statements provide a true and fair view of the entity's financial position and performance. More specifically, Statement of Auditing Standards (SAS) 400: *Audit Evidence* requires the auditor to:

> [O]btain sufficient appropriate audit evidence to be able to draw reasonable conclusions on which to base the audit opinion. (para 2)

The standard goes on to explain that:

> Sufficiency and appropriateness are interrelated and apply to audit evidence obtained from both tests of control and substantive procedures.[1] Sufficiency is the measure of the quantity of audit evidence; appropriateness is the measure of the quality or reliability of audit evidence and its relevance to a particular assertion. (para 4)

The Standard makes it clear that there is a direct relationship between audit tests or procedures, audit evidence and the auditor's opinion; compliance and substantive procedures are used to gather evidence on which the auditor bases an opinion about the financial statements. This relationship is presented diagrammatically in Figure 5.2.

Figure 5.2   Relationship Between Audit Procedures, Evidence and the Auditor's Opinion

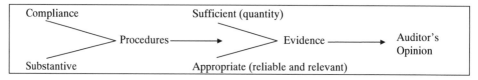

We now need to examine some of these terms to discover what they mean. We will first discuss the meaning and nature of audit evidence and then consider the procedures by which the evidence is gathered.

5.3.2   Definition of Audit Evidence

A particularly useful definition of audit evidence has been provided by Anderson (1977). He defined it as:

> any perceived object, action or condition relevant to the formation of a knowledgeable opinion on the financial statements. Perceived objects may include certain tangible assets

---

[1] As will be shown later in this chapter
- 'tests of control' are usually referred to as 'compliance tests' (see section 5.3.6);
- the terms 'audit tests' and 'audit procedures' are generally used to mean the same thing as each other (see section 5.3.4).

(such as cash funds, inventories and fixed assets), various documents, accounting records and reports, and written representations. Perceived actions generally consist of certain procedures performed by the client's employees. Perceived conditions may include the observed quality of assets, the apparent competence of employees met, the care with which procedures were seen to be performed, or an identified logical relationship with other facts known to the auditor. (p.251)

Thus, in auditing, 'evidence' means all of the facts and impressions the auditor acquires which help him or her to form an opinion about the truth and fairness of the financial statements under review and their compliance (or otherwise) with relevant legislation.

5.3.3 The Nature of Audit Evidence

Unlike legal evidence presented in a court of law, audit evidence does not consist of 'hard facts' which 'prove' or 'disprove' the accuracy of financial statements. Instead, it comprises pieces of information and impressions which are gradually accumulated during the course of an audit and which, taken together, persuade the auditor about the truth and fairness (or otherwise) of the financial statements under consideration. Thus, audit evidence is generally persuasive rather than conclusive in nature.

Also unlike legal evidence, not all of the available evidence is examined by an auditor. The purpose of an audit is not to 'prove' or 'disprove' the accuracy of the financial statements. If it were, auditors would have to collect and evaluate as much evidence as possible. Instead, the objective is to form an opinion as to whether or not the financial statements under review give a true and fair view of the financial position and performance of the reporting entity. To accomplish this, auditors need gather only sufficient appropriate evidence to support their opinion. Thus, rather than examining all of the evidence which is available, auditors usually test only samples of data.

Although audit evidence differs from legal evidence in that it is persuasive rather than conclusive, and only part rather than all of the available evidence is examined, in one regard the two types of evidence are similar. This is in the reinforcing effect of consistent evidence derived from difference sources and, conversely the undermining effect of evidence which is inconsistent. An auditor may wish to reach a conclusion about a particular financial statement item using evidence from different sources and/or of different types. Where such evidence is consistent, (s)he gains cumulative assurance about the item in question. (That is, the assurance the auditor gains regarding the truth and fairness of the item is greater than that obtained from the individual pieces of evidence by themselves.) However, when evidence from different sources or of different types is inconsistent, further evidence may have to be obtained in order to resolve the inconsistency.

5.3.4 Audit Objectives and Audit Procedures

Considerable confusion seems to exist in relation to audit objectives and audit procedures. This has arisen primarily as a result of somewhat careless use of terminology. Three cases in particular have caused misunderstanding, namely:

1. failure to distinguish between audit objectives and audit procedures;
2. use of different terms to mean the same thing;
3. use of the single term 'audit objective' when separate levels of objectives exist.

1. *Failure to Distinguish between Audit Objectives and Audit Procedures*

The term 'compliance tests' or 'compliance procedures' provides an example of this cause of misunderstanding. The term refers to audit procedures which are used to meet the objective of ascertaining whether entity personnel have complied with identified internal controls. The audit procedures adopted (such as enquiry) are not restricted to compliance testing: they are also used to meet other audit objectives. Thus the term 'compliance testing' does not denote a particular set of audit procedures; rather, it indicates the purpose for which the procedures are employed.

2. *Use of Different Terms to Mean the Same Thing*

This cause of confusion may be illustrated by reference to the use, by different authors, of the terms 'audit procedures', 'audit tests', and 'audit techniques', to convey essentially the same meaning, that is, methods used to gather audit evidence. Indeed, the terms are frequently used interchangeably.

Similarly, as illustrated in Figure 5.4, different authors use different terms to refer to the same audit procedure. For example, Anderson (1977) uses the term 'vouching' to refer to the inspection of source documents, but Arens and Loebbecke (1991) and the APB's SAS 400 use the terms 'Documentation' and 'Inspection', respectively, for this audit procedure. (The various audit procedures are outlined in section 5.3.5 below.)

3. *Use of the Single Term 'Audit Objective' when Separate Levels of Objectives Exist*

Notwithstanding use of the term 'audit objective', as shown in Figure 5.3 three distinct levels of audit objectives may be distinguished: the overall audit objective, general audit objectives and specific audit objectives.

An audit objective is the object of the auditor's investigation: it is what the auditor is trying to find out and the purpose for which audit procedures are performed. It is often

Figure 5.3 Hierarchy of Audit Objectives

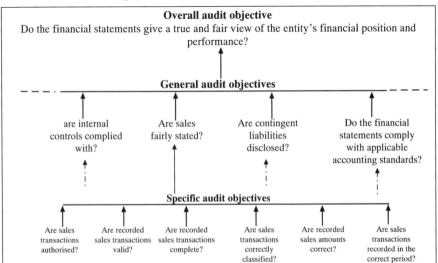

helpful to express an audit objective in the form of a question. From Figure 5.3 it can be seen that the overall audit objective is at the highest level. This is reflected in the question, 'Do the financial statements give a true and fair view of the entity's state of affairs and its profit or loss (or, if a public sector entity, its income and expenditure)?

In order to answer this question, and thus accomplish the overall audit objective, further, more detailed, questions need to be asked. For example, do the financial statements comply with accounting standards? Have the entity's internal controls operated effectively throughout the reporting period? Is the amount shown in the financial statements for, say, sales or trade debtors fairly stated? Questions of this general nature reflect general audit objectives.

To accomplish these general objectives, even more specific questions need to be asked. These are expressions of the specific audit objectives. For example, to accomplish the general objective of ascertaining whether sales are fairly stated in the financial statements, the auditor needs to determine whether:

- sales transactions have been properly authorised;
- recorded sales transactions are valid;
- all valid sales transactions have been recorded;
- sales transactions have been properly classified;
- sales transactions have been recorded at their proper amount;
- sales transactions have been recorded in their proper accounting period.

Each of these factors constitutes a specific audit objective.

5.3.5 Audit Procedures

Audit procedures are the methods used to gather audit evidence. As noted above, the terms 'audit tests' and 'audit techniques' are frequently used in place of, or interchangeably with, 'audit procedures'. Further, different terms are used by different authors for essentially the same procedure. This is illustrated in Figure 5.4 which shows the relationship between the terms used for audit procedures by different authors.

The APB defines the terms used in SAS 400 as follows (paras 20 to 25).

Inspection
20. Inspection consists of examining records, documents or tangible assets. Inspection of records and documents provides audit evidence of varying degrees of reliability depending on their nature and source and the effectiveness of internal controls over their processing. Three major categories of documentary audit evidence, listed in descending degree of reliability as audit evidence, are evidence:
    a) created and provided to auditors by third parties;
    b) created by third parties and held by the entity; and
    c) created and held by the entity.
    Inspection of tangible assets provides reliable audit evidence about their existence but not necessarily as to their ownership or value.

Observation
21. Observation consists of looking at a process or procedure being performed by others, for example the observation by auditors of the counting of stock by the entity's staff

Figure 5.4 Different Terms for the same Audit Procedure

Anderson (1977)	Arens and Loebbecke (1991)	Statement of Auditing Standards 400 (APB, 1995)
Enquiry	Enquiry	Enquiry
Confirmation	Confirmation	Confirmation
Re-performance (of accounting routines)	Mechanical accuracy	Computation
Vouching (of source documents)	Documentation	Inspection
Physical examination (of assets)	Physical examination	
Inspection (of other documents)	Observation	Observation
Observation (of activities)		
Scrutiny of accounting records	Analytical procedures	Analytical procedures
Analysis (into components)		

or the performance of internal control procedures, in particular those that leave no audit trail.

Enquiry and confirmation

22. Enquiry consists of seeking information of knowledgeable persons inside or outside the entity. Enquiries may range from formal written enquiries addressed to third parties to informal oral enquiries addressed to persons inside the entity. Responses to enquiries may provide auditors with information not previously possessed or with corroborative audit evidence.

23. Confirmation consists of the response to an enquiry to corroborate information contained in the accounting records. For example, auditors may seek direct confirmation of debts by communication with debtors.

Computation

24. Computation consists of checking the arithmetical accuracy of source documents and accounting records or performing independent calculations.

Analytical Procedures

25. Analytical procedures consist of the analysis of relationships between items of financial data, or between items of financial and non-financial data, deriving from the same period, or between comparable financial information deriving from different periods or different entities, to identify consistencies and predicted patterns or significant fluctuations and unexpected relationships, and the results of investigations thereof.

5.3.6 Further Clarification of the Jargon

Those first encountering auditing jargon frequently find the distinction and relationship between certain terms far from clear; in particular, the distinction between compliance and substantive procedures, and between tests of details, tests of transactions and tests of balances. The relationship between these terms, and the link between them and some specific audit procedures, is depicted in Figure 5.5.

Figure 5.5   Relationship Between Compliance and Substantive Procedures, Tests of Detail, Tests of Transactions and Tests of Balances

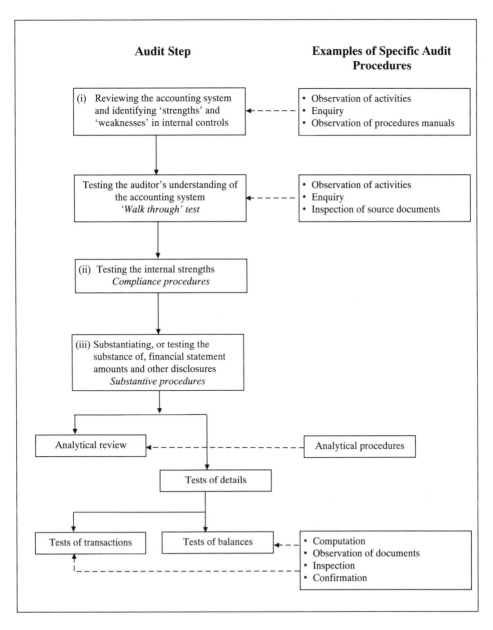

Compliance vs Substantive Procedures

As noted above, the overall objective of an audit is to form an opinion as to whether or not the financial statements under examination give a true and fair view of the financial position and performance of the reporting entity. In order to form this opinion, auditors need, *inter alia,* to ascertain whether each item (or 'statement' or 'assertion') in the financial statements is fairly stated.

Auditors can reduce their work in determining whether each financial statement item is fairly stated if they can assure themselves that the accounting system incorporates effective internal controls (or checks) which can be relied on to prevent and/or detect errors and irregularities in the accounting data. If such internal controls are in place and working effectively, the auditor can feel reasonably assured that the accounting data passing through the system and presented in the financial statements is reliable and accurate.

Thus, an audit includes the following three distinct steps.

(i)   *A review of the accounting system* [see Figure 5.5(i)]:   This review is undertaken for two main purposes, namely:

a) to enable the auditor to understand how the accounting system captures and processes the accounting data, and how it converts the data into the information which is presented in the entity's financial statements;
b) to identify the system's 'strengths' and 'weaknesses', that is internal controls which if operating properly can be relied upon to prevent and/or detect errors and irregularities (strengths), and internal controls which are needed but which are absent or ineffective (weaknesses).

In order to ensure the auditor has a proper understanding of the accounting system and its internal controls, a 'walk through' test is conducted. This test consists of following one or two transactions through the entire accounting system – from their initial recording on source documents to their final inclusion in the financial statements.

(ii)   *Testing internal control 'strengths'* [see Figure 5.5(ii)]:   During the initial review of the accounting system, the auditor identifies internal controls which (s)he considers may be relied upon to prevent and/or detect errors in the accounting data. These are the internal control 'strengths' which, if operating properly, will help to ensure that the accounting data processed by the system is complete, valid, and accurate as to amount, account classification and reporting period. However, before the auditor can rely on these controls to protect the integrity of the accounting data, they must be tested to establish that they are, in fact, operating effectively and that they have been so operating throughout the reporting period. Such tests are referred to as compliance procedures: they are tests or procedures which are performed in order to ascertain whether the internal controls on which the auditor plans to rely have been complied with by personnel within the reporting entity.

(iii) *Testing the financial statement amounts and other disclosures for their substance* [see Figure 5.5(iii)]:   The auditor is required to form and express an opinion on the truth and fairness of the financial statements rather than on the internal controls. Therefore, irrespective of how effective an entity's internal controls may appear to be, tests must always be performed to substantiate, or to test the substance of, the information presented in the financial statements. Such tests are referred to as substantive procedures.

Tests of Detail, Tests of Transactions and Tests of Balances

Substantive procedures fall into two broad categories:

1. analytical procedures;
2. tests of details.

1. *Analytical procedures*:   These analyse meaningful relationships between accounting data in order to establish the 'reasonableness' of financial statement amounts. For example, the relationship between average debt and average interest rates can be used to provide an estimate of an entity's interest expense. If, based on this estimate, the interest expense looks 'reasonable', this may be the extent of the audit tests conducted to substantiate this balance. If, however, there is a marked discrepancy between the estimated amount and the financial statement amount, this discrepancy will need to be investigated.

2. *Tests of details*:   Two subsets of tests of details may be distinguished, namely, tests of transactions and tests of balances.

a) *Tests of transactions* are audit tests or procedures which are applied to transactions, or rather, to the source documents which provide evidence of the transactions. Transaction testing is normally used to substantiate revenue and expense account balances in the profit and loss statement, however it may also be used to substantiate (indirectly) balance sheet account balances. This is because, if the opening balance of a particular balance sheet account is accurate (substantiated by the previous year's audit) and all of the transactions affecting that account during the reporting period are complete, accurate and valid, then the balance shown in the closing balance sheet must also be correct.
b) *Tests of balances* are audit tests or procedures which, rather than substantiating the transactions which generate particular financial statement balances, directly test the completeness, accuracy and validity of the balances themselves. An example is debtors' confirmation, where the auditor writes to an entity's debtors for confirmation of their outstanding account balance.

In relation to tests of transactions, it is important to note that source documents used to substantiate transactions (their completeness, accuracy and validity) may also be used for compliance tests. For example, a customer order and a despatch note may be used to substantiate the validity of a sale (a substantive test). The same source documents might also be examined for evidence indicating that an internal control, designed to ensure that despatches are only made against customer orders, has been complied with (that is, for compliance testing).

5.3.7 Different Sources and Types of Audit Evidence

It was noted in section 5.3.3 that auditors generally examine only part of the evidence available to them. They may select evidence from different sources and of different types. Which evidence they decide to collect depends on a number of factors, in particular its relevance, reliability, availability, timeliness and cost.

- *Relevance* of evidence refers to how closely the evidence relates to the particular objective the auditor is trying to accomplish. For example, observation is a useful procedure for verifying the existence, but not the ownership, of stock. To establish ownership, relevant purchase (or similar) documents need to be scrutinised.
- *Reliability* of evidence refers to how confident the auditor is that the evidence reflects the facts of the matter being investigated. For example, the auditor can have greater confidence in bank reconciliations (s)he has performed personally, than in assurances from client personnel that the entity's bank statements and bank balances have been reconciled.
- *Availability* of evidence refers to how readily the auditor can acquire the evidence. For example, the auditor has ready access to the client's accounting records – including the balances of individual trade debtors. Evidence of these balances, obtained by confirming them with the individuals concerned, is less readily available.
- *Timeliness* of evidence refers to how quickly the evidence can be obtained. For example, the auditor may be aware that the amount of a contingent liability arising from disputed tax will be clarified when the case is heard by the relevant taxation authority. However, if the case is to be deferred for some months, the auditor may decide to forgo that evidence. If audited financial statements are to be useful to external parties interested in the reporting entity, they must be made available – and hence the audit must be completed – on a timely basis.
- *Cost* of evidence. The auditor generally has a choice of evidence which may be used to establish, for example, whether internal controls have been complied with or financial statement amounts are fairly stated. Therefore, the cost of obtaining particular evidence should be weighed against its benefits, that is, the contribution the evidence may make towards the auditor forming an opinion about the degree of compliance with the internal controls, or the truth and fairness of the financial statement amounts, under investigation.

Reviewing the above factors it may be seen that, with the exception of relevance, they are all affected by the source from which the evidence is derived. As is shown in Figure 5.6, audit evidence may be obtained from three sources:

1. direct personal knowledge;
2. sources external to the client;
3. sources internal to the client.

Evidence obtained by direct personal knowledge is the most reliable evidence, it is generally readily available on a timely basis, but it is very costly to acquire. At the other extreme, evidence obtained from sources internal to the client is the least

Figure 5.6   Sources of Evidence and Accompanying Characteristics

	Sources of evidence		
	Direct personal knowledge	**External to the client**	**Internal to the client**
Examples	• Observation • Computation	• Confirmation from third parties • Documents (eg invoices) from third parties	• Accounting records • Client personnel responses to enquiries
Characteristics of evidence			
Reliability	High level of reliability	High to medium level of reliability	Low level of reliability
Availability	Readily available	Less readily available	Readily available
Timeliness	Available on a timely basis	May not be available on a timely basis	Available on a timely basis
Cost	High cost	High to medium cost	Low cost

reliable, but it is generally readily available on a timely basis and is the least costly evidence to obtain. Evidence derived from sources external to the client has an intermediate placing in terms of reliability and cost, but is frequently less readily available and is less timely to acquire than evidence obtained from the other two sources (see Figure 5.6).

SAS 400 requires auditors to obtain sufficient appropriate evidence on which to base an opinion about the truth and fairness of the information presented in the financial statements. The standard goes on to explain that what amounts to sufficient appropriate evidence in any particular case is influenced by a number of factors. These include the following:

- the assessment of the nature and degree of risk of misstatement at both the financial statement level and the account balance or class of transactions level;
- the nature of the accounting and internal control systems, including the control environment;
- the materiality of the item being examined;
- the experience gained during previous audits and the auditors' knowledge of the business and industry;
- the findings from audit procedures, and from any audit work carried out in the course of preparing the financial statements, including indications of fraud or error; and
- the source and reliability of information available. (SAS 400, para 6)

It should also be noted that what amounts to sufficient appropriate audit evidence in any particular case needs to be considered in the light of the fundamental principle of external auditing – *Rigour*.

Auditors approach their work with thoroughness and with an attitude of professional scepticism. They assess critically the information and explanations obtained in the course of their work and such additional evidence as they consider necessary for the purposes of their audit.

Notwithstanding that the factors indicated above (and other similar factors) affect what amounts to 'sufficient appropriate evidence' in particular cases, for any given set of circumstances there is a trade off between the amount of evidence that is required (its sufficiency) and its relevance and reliability (its appropriateness). The greater the relevance and reliability of evidence, the smaller the quantity that is needed to enable the auditor to form his or her opinion about the financial statements. This trade off is depicted in Figure 5.7. All points on the curve represent combinations of quantity and quality of evidence which meet the 'sufficient appropriate' requirement of SAS 400. The particular combination the auditor selects will be affected by considering such factors as availability, timeliness, and cost of the evidence. The auditor will seek the combination which will provide a sufficient amount of reliable evidence, relevant to the information being evaluated, within a reasonable time – at the lowest possible total cost.

Figure 5.7   Sufficient Appropriate Evidence Trade Off

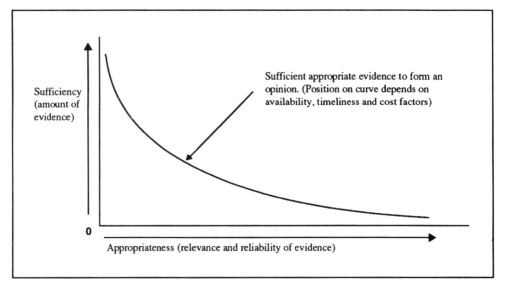

5.4 SUMMARY

In this chapter we have reviewed the audit process. It has been shown that this process consists of a series of well-defined steps through which the auditor proceeds, gradually gathering evidence to enable him or her to form an opinion on the truth and fairness with which the financial statements under examination reflect the entity's financial position and performance, and their compliance (or otherwise) with relevant legislation.

The meaning and nature of audit evidence has been discussed and a distinction has been drawn between audit objectives – the purpose for which audit evidence is obtained – and audit procedures: the methods by which the evidence is gathered. Additionally, three levels of objectives have been identified (overall, general and specific objectives), some common audit procedures have been outlined, and terms such as compliance and substantive procedures, and tests of transactions and tests of balances, have been explained.

In the concluding section of this chapter, factors affecting auditors' choice of evidence have been discussed, namely reliability, relevance, availability, timeliness and cost, and it has been shown that there is a trade off between the quantity of evidence an auditor needs to gather (sufficiency) and the relevance and reliability (appropriateness) of the evidence.

SELF-REVIEW QUESTIONS

5.1 Identify the major steps in the audit process.

5.2 Explain briefly why audit evidence is regarded as being persuasive rather than conclusive.

5.3 Briefly explain the objective of:
(i) compliance procedures; and
(ii) substantive procedures.
For each of these objectives give one example of an audit procedure which is designed to meet that objective.

5.4 List the three levels of audit objectives and provide one example to illustrate each level. (The example may be expressed in the form of a question.)

5.5 List five common audit procedures (or tests) and give one specific example of each procedure.

5.6 Indicate the audit procedure(s) you would use to verify each of the following items. Briefly explain each procedure, indicating how it would be applied in the particular situation.
(i) Value of office supplies on hand at year end.
(ii) Value of a trade debtor's balance outstanding at year end.
(iii) Fire insurance expenses for the year under audit, assuming that the existence of insurance protection has already been tested.
(iv) Value of raw materials purchased for the year under audit.
(v) The liability arising from long service leave available to employees at year end.

5.7 State whether you agree or disagree with the following statement. Briefly explain your answer.

> Gathering evidence in accordance with Auditing Standards requires the auditor to obtain the strongest possible evidence for each item in the financial statements regardless of cost or difficulties that may be encountered.

5.8 For each of the following groups of items of evidence indicate which item you consider to be of superior reliability. Briefly explain why:

(i) In support of the recorded cost of purchased raw materials:
   (a) standard costs used by the company,
   (b) a supplier's quotation list held on file in the purchasing department,
   (c) the actual invoices representing materials purchased.
   How would your answer to (i) differ if you were attempting to support the ending stock of raw materials rather than purchases?
(ii) In support of the valuation of a marketable security held by the company:
   (a) the cancelled cheques used to pay for the security,
   (b) the *Financial Times* dated the last day of the company's financial year,
   (c) both (a) and (b).
   How would your answer to (ii) differ if you were attempting to support a long-term investment rather than a marketable security?

5.9 Indicate the type of error that each of the following audit procedures is designed, or is likely, to disclose.
(i)   Reconciliation of interest expense with loans payable.
(ii) Review of the repairs and maintenance account.
(iii) Confirmation of a sample of trade debtors.

5.10 Explain how an auditor might acquire evidence about each of the following transactions:

(i) Equipment	£3,000	
Cash		£3,000
(ii) Equipment	£4,000	
Creditors		£4,000
(iii) Depreciation expense	£2,000	
Accumulated depreciation – equipment		£2,000
(iv) Insurance expense	£1,000	
Prepaid insurance		£1,000

REFERENCES

Anderson, R.J. (1977). *The External Audit I: Concepts and Techniques*. Toronto: Cropp Clark Pitman.
Arens, A.A. and Loebbecke, J.K. (1991). *Auditing: An Integrated Approach* (5th ed.). New Jersey: Prentice-Hall Inc.

ADDITIONAL READING

Hatherly, D. (1980). *The Audit Evidence Process*. London: Anderson Keenan Publishing, Chs.2 and 3.
Gray, R. (1991). Evidence and judgement. In Sherer, M. & Turley, S., *Current Issues in Auditing*. 2nd Ed, Chapter 9. London: Paul Chapman Publishing.
Pound, G. (1983). Standard audit procedures. *The Australian Accountant*, **53**(4), 281–82.
Tuckey, D. (1996). Proof beyond reasonable doubt. *Accountancy*, **117**(1232), 88–90.

Chapter 6

Staffing, Documenting and Controlling the Quality of an Audit

LEARNING OBJECTIVES

After studying the material in this chapter you should be able to:
- **discuss the requirements with respect to auditors' skills and competence;**
- **explain auditors' responsibilities when part of an audit is performed by other auditors and/or experts;**
- **describe the structure of a 'typical' audit team;**
- **explain the importance of auditors directing, supervising and reviewing the work of assistants;**
- **discuss the purpose and importance of audit working papers;**
- **describe the form, content, and preparation of audit working papers;**
- **explain the importance of working paper review;**
- **outline quality control procedures which auditors should adopt with respect to audit staff, and assignment and supervision of audit work;**
- **discuss auditors' duty of confidentiality to clients.**

The following publications and fundamental principles of external auditing are particularly relevant to this chapter:

Publications:
- Statement of Auditing Standards (SAS) 120: *Consideration of Law and Regulations* (APB, 1995).
- Statement of Auditing Standards (SAS) 230: *Working Papers* (APB, 1995)
- Statement of Auditing Standards (SAS) 240: *Quality Control for Audit Work* (APB, 1995)
- Statement of Auditing Standards (SAS) 510: *The Relationship Between Principal Auditors and Other Auditors* (APB, 1995)
- Statement of Auditing Standards (SAS) 520: *Using the Work of an Expert* (APB, 1995)
- Guide to Professional Ethics Statement 1.205: *Confidentiality* (ICAEW, ICAS, ICAI; 1994)

Fundamental principles of external auditing:

Competence: Auditors act with professional skill, derived from their qualification, training and practical experience. This [principle] demands an understanding of financial reporting and business issues, together with expertise in accumulating and assessing the evidence necessary to form an opinion.

Integrity: Auditors act with integrity, fulfilling their responsibilities with honesty, fairness and truthfulness. Confidential information obtained in the course of the audit is disclosed only when required in the public interest, or by operation of law.

6.1   INTRODUCTION

An audit is usually a major undertaking which must be carefully planned and controlled. This involves, *inter alia*, ensuring that the audit is properly staffed and documented and appropriate quality control procedures are in place. In this chapter we discuss these important administrative aspects of an audit. More particularly, we examine the requirements with respect to the skills and competence an auditor must possess, the auditor's responsibilities in cases where part of an audit is performed by other auditors or experts, and the composition of a 'typical' audit team. We also discuss the importance of the auditor directing, supervising and reviewing work delegated to assistants.

With respect to audit working papers, we consider their purpose, content and preparation and examine the process of working papers review. Before concluding the chapter some quality control procedures relating to audit staff, and the assignment and supervision of audit work, are examined, and the important, but sometimes rather controversial, issue of auditors' duty of confidentiality to their clients is addressed.

6.2   STAFFING AN AUDIT

6.2.1   Audit Personnel

When discussing the staffing of an audit, it is important to distinguish between three categories of audit personnel, namely:

- *the auditor* – the person who is responsible for the audit (usually a partner in an auditing firm); this person is frequently referred to as 'the audit engagement partner';
- *assistants* – professional staff members employed by the auditor's firm, ranging from new entrants to the firm (non-graduates and graduates) to highly experienced audit managers;
- *other auditors and experts* – auditors and experts from outside the auditor's firm who, for a variety of reasons, may be employed by the auditor to perform some part(s) of the audit.

In order for an audit to be performed effectively and efficiently, it is essential that it is adequately staffed by personnel who possess the skills and competence required for the tasks to be performed and that any work delegated to assistants is properly directed and supervised.

6.2.2   Requirements with respect to Skills and Competence

In order to perform an audit to the standard expected of a member of the auditing profession, an auditor requires specialised skills and competence. As noted in the fundamental principle of external auditing – *Competence*:

> Auditors act with professional skill, derived from their qualification, training and practical experience. This [principle] demands an understanding of financial reporting and business

issues, together with expertise in accumulating and assessing the evidence necessary to form an opinion.

The skills and competence required by auditors are acquired through a combination of general education and technical knowledge. These, in turn, are obtained primarily through formal courses of study and practical experience under proper supervision. However, in addition to general education and technical knowledge, in order to be competent to conduct any particular audit, an in-depth knowledge of the industry to which the audit client belongs, is also generally required.

If the auditor does not possess the necessary skills and/or competence to perform or complete a particular audit to the required standard, the audit engagement should be declined or discontinued (as applicable). An exception to this is where the auditor can acquire the skills and competence required to complete the audit satisfactorily through advice or assistance from inside or outside the audit firm. For example, if the auditor lacks the competence needed to perform part of an audit, technical advice may be sought from experts such as lawyers, actuaries, engineers and valuers. This would probably apply, for example, in an audit of an entity specialising in jewellery. If the auditor lacks the competence to evaluate the entity's valuation of, say, its stocks of diamonds, the auditor may (indeed, should!) seek assistance from a jewellery valuation expert.

However, it should be noted that under SAS 520: *Using the Work of an Expert* (para 1), when an auditor seeks advice or assistance from an expert, the auditor remains responsible for all aspects of the audit. It is incumbent upon the auditor to be satisfied that the expert possesses the required degree of skill and competence to perform the task in question, and to obtain reasonable assurance that the work is performed to the appropriate standard. More specifically, the Standard requires the auditor:

- to be satisfied that the expert is properly qualified. Evidence of this may be obtained, for example, through professional certification, licensing by, or membership of, an appropriate professional body, and/or through the expert's experience and reputation in the field (para 11);
- to be satisfied that no relationship exists between the expert and the client such that the objectivity of the expert is likely to be impaired (para 12);
- to be reasonably assured that the expert's work constitutes appropriate audit evidence. Such assurance should be gained by considering:
  - the source data used by the expert;
  - the assumptions and methods used by the expert;
  - when the expert carried out the work;
  - the reasons for any changes in assumptions and methods compared with those used in the prior period;
  - the results of the expert's work in the light of the auditor's overall knowledge of the business and the results of other audit procedures (para 17).

Similar conditions apply when an auditor relies upon the work of another auditor. This may arise, for example, when a branch, division or subsidiary of the audit client is located at a distant geographical location and the auditor relies on another auditor to gather evidence in relation to that branch, division or subsidiary (SAS 510: *The Relationship Between Principal Auditors and Other Auditors* deals with this issue).

Where an auditor relies on assistants (employees of the auditor's firm) to perform audit work, as is the case in most audits of any size, SAS 240: *Quality Control for Audit Work* requires the auditor to ensure that the assistants have the skills and competence necessary to complete satisfactorily work delegated to them (para 6).

6.2.3 A 'Typical' Audit Team

The precise composition of an audit team varies according to the circumstances of the audit, for example, its size and complexity, and whether it is an initial or continuing audit engagement. Additionally, different auditing firms use different terms for the levels of staff constituting their audit teams. However, in general, audit teams comprise a number of levels of staff which we describe as follows:

- *Audit engagement partner:* The audit engagement partner usually has at least seven years' auditing experience. (S)he has overall responsibility for the audit and, as a result, signs the audit report on behalf of the audit firm. The partner visits the audit client occasionally but generally monitors the progress of the audit through regular reports received from the audit manager. Nonetheless, (s)he is almost always present at the final meeting with the audit client's management (or directors) prior to completion of the audit, when the audit and, in particular, any difficult or unresolved issues are discussed.

- *Audit manager:* The audit manager usually has at least five years' auditing experience. In practice, it is the manager, rather than the engagement partner, who supervises the conduct of the audit. (S)he visits the audit client fairly frequently during the course of the audit but, in any event, maintains close contact with the audit supervisor. Difficulties which arise during the audit are generally reported as a matter of course to the audit manager, even if they are resolved by the audit supervisor or some other member of the audit team. This enables the audit manager to obtain an overview of the audit and issues relating to it. Any difficulties which cannot be resolved at a more junior level are addressed by the manager.

  The audit manager usually works with the audit supervisor to develop the overall plan for the audit and (s)he also reviews the audit programme (the detailed procedures to be performed during the audit) which is prepared by the audit supervisor in consultation with the audit senior(s).

- *Audit supervisor:* The audit supervisor generally has about three years' auditing experience. (S)he is usually responsible for the day-to-day performance of the audit and the supervision of audit staff. The audit supervisor visits the audit client daily (or almost so) while the audit is in progress and, if the audit is particularly large or complex, or the audit seniors have limited experience, (s)he may remain at the client's premises for much of the audit.

  As noted above, the audit supervisor generally works with the audit manager to develop the audit's overall plan and (s)he is usually responsible for preparing the audit programme in consultation with the audit senior(s).

- *Audit senior(s):* The audit team may include one or more audit seniors. These seniors generally have about two years' auditing experience and are responsible for directing, supervising and reviewing the work of the audit juniors. They are responsible, for example, for ensuring that the audit procedures set out in the audit programme are properly performed and documented. The audit seniors, like the audit juniors, remain at the client's premises throughout the audit.

- *Audit juniors:* The term 'audit juniors' refers to both 'new recruits' who are in their first year of auditing and 'intermediates' who have completed their first year and are in their second or third year of auditing. These members of the audit team are responsible for performing the audit procedures set out in the audit programme and for documenting the audit work they do, their findings and their conclusions.

It is important that the work delegated to these junior members of the audit team is commensurate with their knowledge and experience and that it is properly directed, supervised and reviewed.

6.2.4 Directing, Supervising and Reviewing the Work of Assistants

As noted in section 6.2.1 above, we use the term 'assistants' to describe all professional staff employed by the auditor's firm (or public sector auditing bodies such as the District Audit Service and National Audit Office) and they range from new entrants to the firm through to audit managers.[1]

SAS 240: *Quality Control for Audit Work* sets out what is required of auditors when they delegate work to assistants. The Standard states that any work delegated to assistants must be assigned to personnel who possess the technical training and proficiency required for the circumstances (para 6). It further states that any work performed by assistants must be carefully directed, supervised and reviewed so as to provide reasonable assurance that the work is performed competently. When deciding on the appropriate extent of direction, supervision and review, the auditor should give due consideration to the skills and competence of the assistants involved (paras 8 and 9).

SAS 240 explains that 'direction' means more than merely giving instructions to assistants on the tasks to be performed. It also involves providing them with background information about the client and the audit so they can understand the importance and context of the auditing procedures they are asked to perform. Assistants should, for example, be provided with information about the nature of the entity's business and possible accounting or auditing problems that may affect the nature, timing and extent of audit procedures with which they are (or will be) involved (para 10).

With respect to supervision, the Standard requires those responsible for supervising assistants' work to monitor the work so as to ensure that the assistants have the skills and competence needed to complete their assigned tasks, that they understand the audit directions, and that they carry out their work in accordance with the overall audit plan and the audit programme. Those with supervisory responsibilities are also required to become informed of and address significant accounting and auditing

---

[1] It should be noted that SAS 240 defines the term 'assistants' to have a wider meaning: it embraces all personnel involved in an audit including experts employed by the auditor [para 3(d)].

questions which arise during the audit, and to modify the overall audit plan and audit programme when it is appropriate to do so (para 12).

As regards reviewing assistants' work, SAS 240 makes it clear that reviews are required in order to ensure that work performed, results obtained, and conclusions reached are all adequately documented. The reviews should also ensure that the objectives of audit procedures have been achieved, that conclusions expressed are consistent with the results of work performed and support the auditor's opinion on the financial statements, and that all significant audit issues have been resolved or are reflected in audit conclusions (para 13).

The provisions of SAS 240 are clearly very important. If an audit is to be conducted effectively, efficiently and with due professional care but, at the same time, much or most of the work is to be performed by assistants, it is essential that care is taken to ensure that work delegated to assistants:

- is within their skills and competence to perform; and
- is carefully directed, supervised and reviewed.

If these responsibilities are not discharged properly, the audit is in danger of being performed inadequately and the door may be opened to allegations of negligence.

Quality control procedures relating to skills and competence of audit staff, and the assignment, direction and supervision of audit work, are discussed in section 6.4 below.

6.3 DOCUMENTING AN AUDIT

6.3.1 Definition, Purpose and Importance of Audit Working Papers

It was noted in section 6.2.4 above that one of the objectives of reviewing assistants' work is to ensure that work performed, results obtained and conclusions reached are all adequately documented. It is essential that all audit work is fully and properly documented in audit working papers. As SAS 230: *Working Papers* indicates, such documentation provides evidence that the audit has been conducted in accordance with Auditing Standards (para 3).

Audit working papers are records, in written or electronic form, which are prepared or obtained by the auditor in order to record the evidence accumulated during the audit and to support the opinion expressed in the audit report. The working papers should include all of the information the auditor considers relevant to the audit. However, as SAS 230 observes:

> The extent of working papers is a matter of professional judgment since it is neither necessary nor practical to document every matter auditors consider. Auditors base their judgment as to the extent of working papers upon what would be necessary to provide an experienced auditor, with no previous connection with the audit, with an understanding of the work performed and the basis of the decisions taken. (para 7)

The Standard also notes that:

> Auditors should record in their working papers their reasoning on all significant matters which require the exercise of judgment, and their conclusions thereon. (para 6)

The overall purpose of audit working papers is to provide evidence that work performed during the audit, the results obtained, and the conclusions reached all accord with Auditing Standards. However, they also serve other more specific purposes. For example, they provide:

(i) *a basis for planning the audit:* Records of preliminary discussions with the client, notes relating to the assessment of audit risk and the setting of materiality limits, and other similar documentation, provide a basis for planning the nature, timing and extent of audit procedures to be performed;

(ii) *a basis for performing the audit:* The audit programme (an important working paper) provides directions on the audit procedures to be performed. Other documents provide evidence of procedures already completed and conclusions reached based on the results of those procedures. Additionally, the audit working papers include notes on any particular matters assistants need to consider or accommodate when performing certain procedures listed in the audit programme;

(iii) *a basis for reviewing work done and evidence gathered:* The audit working papers provide a record of work done by assistants in relation to particular audit objectives. They therefore provide a means of assessing the adequacy of work performed, the quality of results obtained and the validity of conclusions reached;

(iv) *a means of supervising more junior members of the audit team:* This purpose of audit working papers is closely related to that outlined in (iii) above. Because audit working papers record audit procedures to be performed and audit work completed, they enable personnel responsible for supervising the work of more junior members of the audit team to monitor and assess the work performed by their subordinates;

(v) *an aid to planning subsequent audits:* The findings of previous audits, as recorded in the audit working papers, provide a good basis from which to begin the initial planning of a subsequent audit.

6.3.2 Form and Content of Audit Working Papers

The form and content of audit working papers vary from audit to audit and they reflect such things as the size, nature and complexity of the client's activities, the nature and quality of the client's record keeping, accounting system and internal controls, and the needs of audit team members for direction, supervision and review of audit work (SAS 230, para 10). However, certain documents are present in virtually every audit and these are arranged logically in either the permanent file or the current file.

(i) The Permanent Audit File

As Figure 6.1 indicates, the permanent audit file contains documents of a 'permanent' nature which are required in every audit of the client. Typical permanent audit file documents include the following:

(a) *Legal documents:* extracts or copies of legal documents such as the entity's Memorandum and Articles of Association, contracts (including, for example, pension plans and leases) and debenture deeds. A copy of the audit engagement letter is frequently kept in this section of the audit file.

(b) *General information about the client's operations:* information relating to the historical development of the entity, its industry, its economic and legislative

Figure 6.1   Form and Content of Audit Working Papers

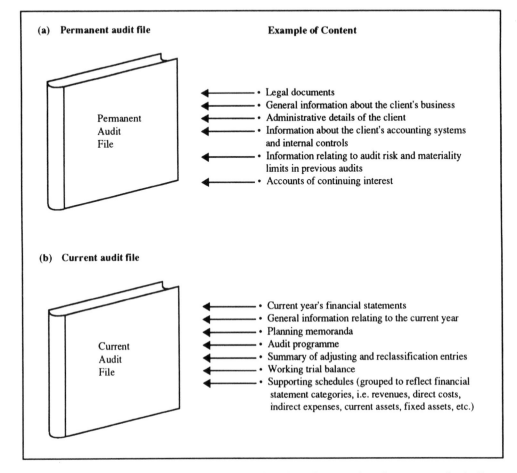

(a) Permanent audit file

Example of Content

Permanent
Audit
File

- Legal documents
- General information about the client's business
- Administrative details of the client
- Information about the client's accounting systems and internal controls
- Information relating to audit risk and materiality limits in previous audits
- Accounts of continuing interest

(b) Current audit file

Current
Audit
File

- Current year's financial statements
- General information relating to the current year
- Planning memoranda
- Audit programme
- Summary of adjusting and reclassification entries
- Working trial balance
- Supporting schedules (grouped to reflect financial statement categories, i.e. revenues, direct costs, indirect expenses, current assets, fixed assets, etc.)

environment, and its present organisational and operational structure including details of any subsidiaries, divisions or departments of the entity (their geographical location, size, principal products, etc.).

(c) *Administrative details of the client:* documents reflecting the client's administrative structure, for example, its organisation chart, chart of accounts, policies and procedures manuals.

(d) *Accounting systems and internal controls:* information relating to the client's accounting systems and internal controls, including flowcharts, internal control questionnaires and evaluations, and narrative descriptions, completed during previous audits. Also, notes made in previous audits on strengths and weaknesses identified in the internal controls, and copies of management letters sent to the client's directors/management.[2] [For large audits, details of the client's accounting

---

[2] Internal controls, and audit documents relating thereto, are discussed in Chapter 9. Management letters are discussed in Chapter 13.

systems (and related internal controls) may be kept in a separate 'systems' file rather than in the permanent audit file].

(e) *Information on audit risk and materiality limits:* the results of analytical review and other information relating to assessment of audit risk and setting of materiality limits in previous audits.

(f) *Accounts of continuing interest:* analyses from previous audits of accounts that are of continuing importance to the auditor; these include shareholders' equity accounts, long-term liabilities, tangible and intangible assets.

(ii)   *The Current Audit File*

As may be seen from Figure 6.1, the current audit file contains information pertaining to the current year's audit. It includes documents such as:

(a) *The financial statements under examination.*

(b) *General information:* information of a general nature relating to the current year's audit; examples include notes on discussions with the client about business, financial, and other matters which have occurred during the reporting period, abstracts or copies of directors' (and similar) meetings, abstracts or copies of contracts or agreements not included in the permanent file, comments on the current year's evaluation of internal controls, and comments arising from working papers review and conclusions reached in relation to various segments of the audit. This section of the file frequently also includes notes relating to difficult issues which have arisen during the audit and how they have been resolved.

(c) *Planning memoranda relating to the current audit.*

(d) *The audit programme:* a list of the audit procedures to be performed. As the audit progresses, each staff member performing a procedure initials and dates the audit programme to indicate that the procedure has been completed.

(e) *Summary of adjusting and reclassification entries:* as the audit proceeds, audit team members almost invariably encounter accounting entries which require correction as to amount or classification. For example, a direct payment into the client's bank account by a credit customer on balance sheet date may not have been recorded as a cash receipt in the current period or office equipment purchased during the year may have been recorded as 'repairs and maintenance' instead of 'office equipment'.

All errors discovered during the audit which require adjusting or reclassification entries are recorded on a summary schedule which is usually located near the front of the current audit file. Such a summary enables the auditor to assess at a glance the significance of individual errors, and the cumulative effect of errors, in relation to the financial statements as a whole and the affected components thereof, such as net or gross profit, current assets, long-term liabilities, etc.

Although the audit team will find and note errors as the audit progresses, no adjustments to ledger accounts or to the financial statements can be made without the consent of the client's management. As noted in Chapter 3, maintaining the accounting records and preparing the financial statements are the responsibility of management. The auditor will request management to adjust entries to correct material errors discovered during the audit. In most cases no difficulty is encountered and management approves the changes. If management refuses to correct what the auditor considers to be material errors, the auditor will have little choice but to issue a qualified audit report. (This report is discussed in Chapter 13.)

(f) *Working trial balance:* Usually, as soon as possible after balance sheet date, the auditor obtains or prepares a list of general ledger accounts and their year-end balances. This is known as a working trial balance.

Frequently, the working trial balance is in the form of a list of balances which appear in the financial statements. Each line of the trial balance is supported by a lead schedule. This lists the general ledger accounts (and their balances) which constitute the relevant financial statement balance.

Each account shown in the lead schedule is, in turn, supported by detailed working papers. These show the audit work performed in relation to the account, the results obtained and the conclusion reached as regards the accuracy or otherwise of the account balance.

The relationship between the financial statements, the working trial balance, the lead schedule and supporting schedules is illustrated in Figure 6.2. This shows that the cash balance presented in the financial statements for 19x7 and recorded in the working trial balance is £54,370. The composition of this balance is detailed in the 'Lead Schedule: Cash'. Audit work has revealed that a receipt from a customer of £120 has not been recorded in the correct period and, as a consequence, an adjusting entry is required.

(g) *Supporting schedules:* The supporting schedules which provide details of audit work performed in relation to individual financial statement balances constitute the major part of the current audit file. Frequently they are grouped in the file in sections which reflect financial statement categories. There may, for example, be sections for revenues, direct costs, indirect expenses, current assets, tangible fixed assets, investments, intangible fixed assets, current liabilities, long-term liabilities and shareholders' funds. Each of these sections may be subdivided into groups of related accounts. The amount of subdivision will largely depend on the size and complexity of the particular audit.

Each group of accounts is fronted by a lead schedule which is cross-referenced to both the working trial balance and the relevant supporting schedules (see Figure 6.2). Each supporting schedule presents, in relation to an individual account balance, details of:

• the objective(s) of audit procedures performed
• the procedures performed
• the results of the procedures
• relevant comments
• the conclusion reached with respect to the account balance investigated.

These features are reflected in Figure 6.3.

Figure 6.2   Relationship Between the Financial Statements and Audit Working Papers

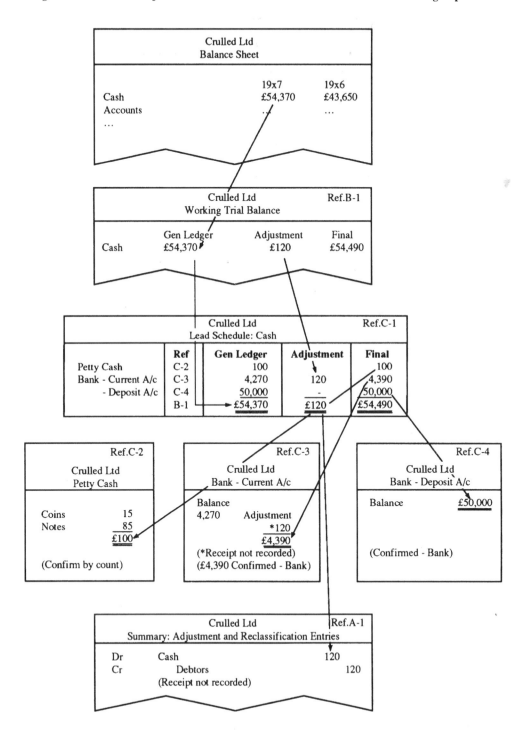

Figure 6.3: Common Features of Audit Working Papers

		Working paper reference
Name of client	→ CRULLED LIMITED	REF: K-2
Audit area	→ Stock Purchases and Cash Payments	Prepared by: RB
Accounting period	→ Year to 31 March 19x7	Date: 10.4.x7
		Reviewed by: MC
		Date: 15.4.x7

Preparer and Preparation date

Reviewer and Review date

Audit Objectives :
• To verify that all merchandise is properly ordered and received and is for legitimate business purposes.
• To verify that expenses (purchases) and assets (stock) are properly valued and classified.
• To verify that cash payments are for legitimate liabilities and properly valued.

Audit Procedures:
\# Traced payment to purchase invoice. Agreed invoice with amount of cheque and payment date. Each payment is 5% less than invoice amount as cash discount received. Recalculated all discounts. (A-6)
< Compared invoice prices with master price list. All agreed except those marked*. (A-7)
Ø Examined purchase invoices for evidence that company employee verified prices, extensions and footings. Markings or initials present in all cases. (A-8)
> Verified arithmetical accuracy of extensions and footings of invoices. (A-9)
v Examined cancelled cheques for amounts, dates, signatures, and payee. (A-10)
t Examined receiving report for agreement with purchase invoice as to description and quantity. All reports were properly signed by Backhouse (Receiving Officer). (A-11)
@ Examined purchase order with receiving report and invoice. Verified account code. All orders agreed with receiving report and were properly approved except those marked + and . (A-12) ← *Audit programme reference*

Sample selection:†
Population: All purchases from Yumslip Products.
Sample: Judgmental. Selected 12 payments for merchandise from Yumslip Products beginning with cheque 1690 from Cash Payments Journal.

Results of Procedures:

Date	Payee	Cheque No.	Amount	1	2	3	4	5	6	7
						Audit Procedure				
10-4-x6	Yumslip Products	1690	£1,432.67	#	<	Ø	>	v	t	@
9-5-x6	Yumslip Products	1725	£2,568.91	#	<*	Ø	>	v	t	@+
15-6-x6	Yumslip Products	1744	£1,021.05	#	<	Ø	>	v	t	@
6-7-x6	Yumslip Products	1769	£456.26	#	<	Ø	>	v	t	@
10-8-x6	Yumslip Products	1780	£461.34	#	<	Ø	>	v	t	@
8-9-x6	Yumslip Products	1795	£1,263.76	#	<*	Ø	>	v	t	@
14-10-x6	Yumslip Products	1841	£1,245.34	#	<	Ø	>	v	t	@
17-11-x6	Yumslip Products	1860	£319.38	#	<	Ø	>	v	t	@
9-12-x6	Yumslip Products	1887	£248.21	#	<	Ø	>	v	t	@
15-1-x7	Yumslip Products	1898	£1,219.47	#	<	Ø	>	v	t	@
13-2-x7	Yumslip Products	1924	£2,639.31	#	<	Ø	>	v	t	@
15-3-x7	Yumslip Products	1953	£1,632.19	#	<	Ø	>	v	t	@

NOTE: Symbols used are shown alongside relevant audit procedure.

Comments:
* Prices on purchases of 9-5-x6 and 8-9-x6 do not agree with master price list by £56.00 and £124.34 respectively. According to Smithson (Purchasing Officer) the differences represent special prices available in May and September which differed from price list. (Confirmed with Yumslip).
+ Purchase order does not agree with receiving report for one item. Smithson indicated that replacement (similar) item was supplied as a result of a stock-out. (Confirmed replacement item ordered).
  Four orders were approved by Thomas (Financial Controller) instead of Mates (Managing Director). According to Smithson only orders in excess of £1,000 need be approved by Mates. (Confirmed with Mates).
  NOTE: Need to alter flow chart to reflect this. (MC 15-4-x7) ← *Follow-up by audit senior*

Audit Conclusion:
(1) The purchases are properly ordered and received and are for legitimate purposes.
(2) Purchases are properly valued and classified.
(3) Payments are properly valued and are for legitimate liabilities.
(4) Purchases and payments transactions are fairly stated in the accounts. (K-1) ← *Lead schedule reference*

† Sample sizes and selection are discussed in Chapter 11.

6.3.3 Preparation of Audit Working Papers

It was noted in section 6.3.1 above that the overall objective of audit working papers is to provide evidence that the audit has been conducted in accordance with Auditing Standards. In order for such evidence to be provided, it is essential that audit working papers are properly prepared.

Although the details of working papers vary according to the nature of the schedule concerned and the specific audit objectives being met, audit working papers should always contain certain features. These are discussed below and illustrated in Figure 6.3.

1. Each working paper should be clearly headed to indicate:
   * the name of the client;
   * the audit area (or account) to which the working paper (schedule) relates;
   * the relevant accounting period.
2. Each working paper should have a unique reference number and be cross-referenced to the relevant lead schedule, working trial balance and/or other related working papers.
3. Completed working papers must show:
   * the initials (or name) of the preparer;
   * the date of preparation;
   * the initials (or name) of the reviewer;
   * the date of the review.
4. Audit working papers also need to show:
   * the audit objectives of the procedures performed;
   * the audit procedures performed (these should be cross-referenced to the audit programme);
   * the results of the audit procedures (these frequently involve the use of tick marks or symbols and all such notation must be clearly explained);
   * the conclusion(s) reached in terms of the objectives, based on the results of the audit procedures performed.
5. Where sampling is used, the relevant working paper should indicate the population from which the sample was drawn, the size of the sample and the means by which the sample was selected.
6. Where any deviation from the expected result of an audit procedure is encountered, such deviation, and an explanation thereof, should be clearly recorded in the relevant working paper. In cases where some follow-up by a more senior member of the audit team is required, the 'senior' must initial the relevant working paper entry to indicate that the follow-up has been performed.

6.3.4 Working Paper Review

It was noted in section 6.2.4 above that SAS 240: *Quality Control for Audit Work* requires the work of assistants to be reviewed. Such review should ensure, *inter alia*, that audit objectives have been met, that audit procedures performed and results obtained have been properly documented, and that conclusions reached are consistent with the results obtained and support the opinion expressed in the audit report.

As observed in section 6.2.2, conducting an audit requires specialised skills and competence. It also requires the frequent exercise of professional judgment – a fact that will become increasingly evident as we study the steps in the audit process in more detail. These characteristics of an audit, combined with the fact that members of the audit team are human and therefore prone to make mistakes and faulty judgments, mean that reliance cannot be placed on audit staff correctly identifying audit objectives, performing appropriate audit procedures, and drawing correct conclusions, on *every* occasion. Clearly, if an effective audit is to be conducted, it is important that the work of each audit team member is reviewed by a superior. This is usually effected in the following manner.

1. As each section of the audit is completed, the working papers of the relevant audit junior are reviewed by his or her immediate superior (the audit senior). The audit procedures performed are compared with those set down in the audit programme, and the results obtained and conclusions reached (based on those results) are evaluated. The working papers are also reviewed for completeness, orderly presentation and cross-referencing to other relevant working papers.
2. *The audit senior* prepares summary notes on each segment of the audit for which (s)he is responsible, regarding:
   • the evidence gathered and conclusions reached;
   • any problems encountered and how they were dealt with;
   • matters requiring the attention of superiors (the audit supervisor or manager);
   • matters to be included in the management letter.
3. *The audit supervisor* reviews the summary notes prepared by the audit senior. (S)he also reviews the detailed working papers prepared by the audit juniors to ensure they contain evidence which indicates they have been reviewed by the audit senior, and also to evaluate the senior's findings. The supervisor discusses with the audit senior any matters which require clarification and any issues which remain unresolved.
4. The audit supervisor prepares summary notes on each major segment of the audit and on the audit as a whole. (S)he comments on:
   • the sufficiency and appropriateness of the audit evidence gathered;
   • the conclusions reached, based on that evidence;
   • problems encountered and how they were resolved;
   • any outstanding unresolved difficulties;
   • matters to be included in the management letter. (The audit supervisor frequently prepares a draft of the management letter.)
5. *The audit manager* carefully reviews the notes and comments of the audit supervisor and discusses with him or her any matters which require elucidation. (S)he also reviews (but in less detail than the audit senior(s) and supervisor) the working papers prepared by the audit juniors.

The audit manager will be particularly concerned to see that:
• all audit problems have been adequately dealt with;
• any unresolved difficulties are either resolved or passed on, by way of audit working paper note, to the audit engagement partner;
• sufficient appropriate evidence has been obtained in each audit segment and for the audit as a whole;

- the conclusions reached are supported by the evidence gathered.
6. The manager prepares summary notes relating to the audit as a whole, making particular reference to:
   - the evidence gathered;
   - the conclusions reached;
   - problems encountered and how they were dealt with;
   - any remaining unresolved issues.

   The audit manager also prepares the management letter. This frequently amounts to approving or amending the draft letter prepared by the audit supervisor.
7. *The audit engagement partner* considers, in detail, the final draft of the financial statements and the summary notes and management letter prepared by the audit manager. (S)he also reviews the audit working papers for completeness, orderliness, adequacy, cross-referencing and evidence of review.

   The audit partner's main concerns are to ensure that:
   (a) (s)he can form an appropriate opinion on the financial statements under examination based on the evidence recorded in the audit working papers, assessed against a background of his or her knowledge of the client, its operations and its financial affairs;
   (b) if the adequacy of the audit is challenged in a court of law, the working papers will:
      - stand up to the scrutiny of the court;
      - clearly show that the opinion expressed in the audit report is supported by audit evidence that is both sufficient and appropriate.

In some audit firms, to ensure that objectives (a) and (b) above are met, the audit working papers are reviewed by a second audit partner who has not had any involvement in the audit in question. A second partner, and/or possibly a relevant committee of the audit firm, may also be consulted if the audit requires particularly difficult judgments to be made, especially where there is also disagreement with the auditee's management.

6.3.5 Ownership of Audit Working Papers

Working papers prepared in relation to an audit engagement, including those prepared by the client at the request of the auditor, are the property of the auditor. The only time anyone else has a legal right to examine the working papers is when they are subpoenaed by a court of law. However SAS 230 *Working Papers* makes it clear that auditors may, if they wish, make parts of, or extracts from, their audit working papers available to the audit client, 'provided such disclosure does not undermine the independence or the validity of the audit process' (para 19). The Standard also requires auditors to 'adopt appropriate procedures for maintaining the confidentiality and safe custody of their working papers' (para 16).

As regards the retention of audit working papers, SAS 230 notes:

> There are no specific statutory requirements regarding the period of retention of audit working papers. Auditors exercise judgment to determine the appropriate period of retention bearing in mind possible needs of their client, for example that audited information may need to be included in a prospectus at some future date, and their own needs,

including any regulatory requirements. Prior to their destruction, auditors consider whether there is likely to be a need to refer to them again. (para 17)

6.4   CONTROLLING THE QUALITY OF AN AUDIT

In order for an audit to be performed in accordance with Auditing Standards, steps must be taken to ensure that its quality is controlled. SAS 240: *Quality Control for Audit Work* provides guidance to auditors on policies and procedures which help to ensure that high quality audits are performed. The Standard requires audit firms to establish appropriate policies and procedures (at both the firm and individual audit level) and to communicate them to their personnel 'in a manner designed to provide reasonable assurance that the policies and procedures are understood and implemented' (para 4).

As noted in SAS 240, important audit quality control policies include the following:[3]

(i)   Evaluating the suitability or otherwise of accepting a new or continuing audit engagement. This includes assessing whether the auditor is independent of the client, whether the client can be properly serviced, and whether the client's management possesses integrity. The pre-engagement investigation which auditors should conduct is discussed in Chapter 7.
(ii) Staffing the audit with personnel who:
    • adhere to the principles of independence, integrity, objectivity, confidentiality and professional behaviour;
    • possess the skills and competence required to fulfil their responsibilities with due care.
(iii) Providing sufficient direction, supervision and review of audit work at all levels.
(iv) Consulting experts from inside or outside the audit firm, wherever necessary.
(v)   Ensuring the audit is properly documented; that is, ensuring the audit working papers:
    • contain all of the relevant information pertaining to the audit;
    • set out clearly the audit procedures performed;
    • record the results obtained from the audit procedures and the conclusions reached.

As indicated above, one of the key features of ensuring that high quality audits are performed is staffing the audit with personnel who possess integrity. This is reflected in the first part of the fundamental principle of external auditing – *Integrity*:

Auditors act with integrity, fulfilling their responsibilities with honesty, fairness and truthfulness.

6.5   AUDITORS' DUTY OF CONFIDENTIALITY TO CLIENTS

During the course of an audit, members of the audit team become very knowledgeable about the client's business, its operations, and its financial affairs. It is imperative that audit staff respect the confidential nature of this knowledge.

---

[3] These and other quality control features are noted in SAS 240. Paras 5 and 6 refer to control policies at audit firm level; paras 7–15 describe control policies (primarily direction, supervision and review of audit work) relating to individual audits. Many of these policies have been discussed earlier in this chapter.

Without reducing the importance of the principle of confidentiality, disclosure of information is generally permitted (according to the Chartered Institutes' Guide to Professional Ethics Statement 1.205: *Confidentiality*) in the following situations:

- when the client gives the auditor authority to disclose information; if this occurs, before making any disclosure, the auditor should consider the interests of all parties concerned, including third parties whose interests might be affected;
- if the auditor is required by law to disclose information, for example, to enable documents to be located or to give evidence in legal proceedings;
- when an auditor has a professional duty to disclose otherwise confidential information, for example, in order to comply with ethical requirements or to protect his or her professional interests in legal proceedings.

As noted, apart from very limited circumstances, such as those referred to above, auditors are required to respect the confidentiality of information which comes to their notice as a result of their audits. However, in recent years this duty of confidentiality to audit clients has been increasingly questioned. This has occurred, in particular, when cases of corporate fraud and other illegal acts by corporate officials have come to light and politicians, the courts, financial journalists and the public have asked why the entity's auditors did not discover such acts and report them to an appropriate authority. The auditors, in response, have traditionally emphasised that, in the absence of a legal requirement to do so, their duty of confidentiality to their clients is paramount and precludes them from reporting matters of concern discovered during an audit to third parties – including regulatory authorities.

It was largely in response to public and political pressure that the APB issued the predecessor of SAS 110: *Fraud and Error* [that is, Auditing Guideline: *The auditor's responsibility in relation to fraud, other irregularities and errors* (APB, 1990)] and SAS 120: *Consideration of Law and Regulations*. As noted in Chapter 3, SAS 110[4] imposes a duty on auditors to report suspected or actual fraud discovered during an audit to a 'proper authority', whenever it is in the public interest to do so. SAS 120 similarly requires auditors to step outside their duty of confidentiality to their audit clients in certain circumstances. The Standard deals with two situations, namely:

(i) where auditors have a statutory duty to report to an appropriate authority (for example, under the Financial Services Act 1986); and
(ii) where auditors have no statutory duty to report to any party outside the client.

The Standard states that when auditors encounter actual or suspected instances of non-compliance with the law or regulations which give rise to a statutory duty to report to an appropriate authority, they should so report without undue delay (para 56). In this case, the need for auditors to override their duty of confidentiality to their client is clear-cut. However, the Standard also requires auditors who become aware of non-compliance with the law and/or regulations which does not give rise to a statutory duty to report, to consider whether the matter ought to be reported to a proper

---

[4] SAS 110 essentially carries forward the relevant provisions from its predecessor Auditing Guideline.

authority in the public interest (para 59). In general, the matter should first be discussed with the audit client's board of directors (including any audit committee). If, after considering any views expressed on behalf of the entity, the auditors conclude that the matter ought to be reported to an appropriate authority in the public interest and the entity does not itself so report, then the auditors should report it to such an authority themselves (paras 59 and 60). If the matter is such that the auditors no longer have confidence in the integrity of the directors, then, according to the Standard, they should report the matter directly to a proper authority, without discussing it with the entity (para 61).

From the above it is clear that, normally, auditors adhere to their duty of confidentiality to their client. However, when a statutory duty exists, or it is in the public interest to do so, auditors should subordinate this duty of confidentiality and disclose matters of concern to an appropriate regulatory authority. The position is reflected in the second portion of the fundamental principle of external auditing – *Integrity*:

> Confidential information obtained in the course of an audit is disclosed only when required in the public interest, or by operation of law.

6.6 SUMMARY

In this chapter we have examined some important administrative aspects of auditing, namely, staffing and documenting an audit, controlling the quality of audits, and auditors' duty of confidentiality to clients. More specifically, we have considered the skills and competence required of auditors, auditors' responsibilities in cases where they rely on other auditors or experts to perform part of an audit, the composition of a typical audit team, and the need for auditors to carefully direct, supervise and review work delegated to assistants. With respect to documenting an audit, we have discussed the purpose and importance of audit working papers, their form, content and preparation, and also working paper review and ownership.

From our examination of these topics it is evident that, in order for an audit to be conducted effectively, efficiently and with due professional care, it must be adequately staffed by personnel who possess the personal qualities of integrity, objectivity and independence, and who also have the skills and competence required to perform the tasks assigned to them. Additionally, work assigned to assistants must be carefully directed and supervised, and all audit work must be fully and properly documented and carefully reviewed. Proper documentation is also required to show that sufficient appropriate audit evidence was gathered during the audit and that the conclusions reached accord with that evidence and support the opinion expressed in the audit report.

In the concluding section of the chapter, the confidential nature of knowledge gained by audit team members was noted and the importance of audit staff respecting their duty of confidentiality to the client was emphasised. However, it was also observed that auditors may have an overriding duty to report to third parties (such as regulatory authorities) when there is a statutory duty to so report or when it is in the public interest to do so.

SELF-REVIEW QUESTIONS

6.1 Distinguish between the following categories of audit personnel:
   (i)   the auditor,
   (ii) audit assistants,
   (iii) other auditors.

6.2 Briefly explain the auditor's responsibilities when (s)he relies on the work of experts to perform part of an audit.

6.3 Outline the requirements of SAS 240: *Quality Control for Audit Work* with respect to:
   (i)   directing,
   (ii) supervising, and
   (iii) reviewing the work of assistants.

6.4 Define 'audit working papers'.

6.5 List five specific purposes of audit working papers.

6.6 (a) Distinguish between the information contained in:
       (i) the permanent audit file
       (ii) the current audit file.
   (b) Give two examples of information contained in each of:
       (i) the permanent audit file
       (ii) the current audit file.

6.7 List 10 features you would expect to see on detailed schedules in the current audit file.

6.8 Explain briefly the task of the audit manager in the process of working paper review.

6.9 Outline the requirements of SAS 230: *Working Papers* with respect to ownership and custody of audit working papers.

6.10 Describe briefly the circumstances in which an auditor may have a duty to override his or her duty of confidentiality to the audit client and report to an appropriate authority matters of concern encountered during the audit. (In your answer you should refer, specifically, to relevant provisions in SAS 110 and SAS 120).

ADDITIONAL READING

Institute of Chartered Accountants in England and Wales (ICAEW). (1993). *Towards Better Auditing*. London: ICAEW.
Whitaker, A. & Western, P. (1985). Quality control of the audit. In Kent, D., Sherer, M. & Turley, S., *Current Issues in Accounting*, Chapter 8. London: Harper & Row.
Woolfe, E. (1994a). Auditing standards: Can small firms comply? *Accountancy*, **113**(1209), 84–5.
Woolfe, E. (1994b). Where's the evidence? *Accountancy*, **113**(1210), 93–4.

Chapter 7

Commencing an Audit
• Engagement Procedures
• Gaining an Understanding of the Client

LEARNING OBJECTIVES

After studying the material in this chapter you should be able to:
- outline the reasons for, and the process of, pre-engagement investigations;
- discuss the purpose and content of audit engagement letters;
- explain the importance of gaining a thorough understanding of the client, its business and its industry;
- identify and discuss external and internal environmental factors which impact on an entity and its external audit;
- outline the audit procedures used to gain an understanding of the client and its business.

The following publications are particularly relevant to this chapter:

- Statement of Auditing Standards (SAS) 140: *Engagement letters* (APB, 1995)
- Statement of Auditing Standards (SAS) 210: *Knowledge of the Business* (APB, 1995)
- Statement of Auditing Standards (SAS) 240: *Quality Control for Audit Work* (APB, 1995)
- Statement of Auditing Standards (SAS) 450: *Opening Balances and Comparatives* (APB, 1995)
- Guide to Professional Ethics Statement (GPES), 1.206: *Changes in a Professional Appointment* (ICAEW, ICAS, ICAI, 1995).

7.1 INTRODUCTION

In this chapter we begin our journey through the audit process. We assume that an auditor (an individual or an audit firm) has been approached by an entity to accept appointment as the entity's auditor. We discuss the steps the auditor should take before accepting the engagement, the audit engagement letter (s)he should prepare, and the all-important audit step of gaining a thorough understanding of the client, its business and its industry.

7.2 PRE-ENGAGEMENT INVESTIGATION

7.2.1 The Need for a Pre-engagement Investigation

In a competitive environment it is not always easy to obtain and retain audit clients. Nevertheless, when an auditor has the opportunity to accept a new or continuing audit engagement, (s)he should consider carefully whether it is prudent to accept the engagement. It is, for example, generally unwise to accept (or continue with) an audit client whose management lacks integrity or constantly argues about the proper conduct of the audit and/or audit fees. Equally, it is important that an audit is not accepted if it cannot be adequately staffed with personnel possessing the necessary levels of independence, skills and competence. As noted in SAS 240: *Quality Control for Audit Work*:

> [P]rospective clients are evaluated and existing clients are reviewed on an ongoing basis. In making a decision to accept or retain a client, the auditors' independence and ability to serve the client properly and the integrity of the client's management are considered. (para 6)

The elements of a pre-engagement investigation may be discussed conveniently under the following headings:

- communicating with the predecessor auditor;
- evaluating the integrity of the client's management;
- assessing the auditor's competence to perform the audit.

7.2.2 Communicating with a Predecessor Auditor

When an auditor is invited to accept nomination for appointment as auditor for a potential client, (s)he should enquire about the entity's existing audit arrangements. If the entity has been audited previously, the auditor should follow his or her professional body's guidance in respect of the matter. For example, the Institutes' Guide to Professional Ethics Statement (GPES) 1.206:[1] *Changes in a Professional Appointment* states that, before accepting nomination to replace an existing auditor, a prospective auditor should communicate with the existing auditor to ascertain whether there are

---

[1] The Guide to Professional Ethics 1.206: *Changes in a Professional Appointment* is published in identical form by the ICAEW, ICAS and ICAI.

any circumstances which might affect his or her decision to accept (or not accept) appointment (para 1.0).

The Institutes' Ethical Guide explains:

> The purpose of finding out the background to the proposed change is to enable the [prospective] auditor to determine whether, in all the circumstances, it would be proper for him or her to accept the assignment. In particular, [prospective] auditors will wish to ensure that they do not unwittingly become the means by which any unsatisfactory practices of the company or any impropriety in the conduct of its affairs may be enabled to continue or may be concealed from shareholders or other legitimately interested persons. Communication is meant to ensure that all relevant facts are known to the [prospective] auditor who, having considered them, is then entitled to accept the nomination if he wishes so to do. (para 1.3)

GPES 1.206 requires prospective auditors, when approached by a client to accept nomination to act as auditor, to explain that they have a professional duty to communicate with the existing auditor. They are also required to request the prospective client to inform the existing auditor of the proposed change and to give the existing auditor written authority to discuss the client's affairs with the proposed auditor. Should the client refuse to grant the existing auditor permission to discuss its affairs, the proposed auditor should not accept nomination (para 1.7).

Once the existing auditor receives permission from the client to disclose information to the proposed auditor, the Ethical Guide requires the existing auditor to advise the proposed auditor 'without delay' of the 'factors within his knowledge of which, in his opinion, the latter should be aware' (para 1.8). If there are no such factors, this should be conveyed to the proposed auditor.

Normally the communication between the existing and proposed auditor is a matter of routine and nothing of significance need be reported by the former to the latter. However, as GPES 1.206, para 1.15, indicates, occasionally circumstances arise which are likely to affect the proposed auditor's decision to accept or reject the nomination. These are the matters the incumbent auditor should communicate to the proposed auditor. They include the following:

a) reasons for the change advanced by the client of which the existing auditor is aware are not in accordance with the facts (as understood by the latter);

b) the proposal to displace the existing auditor arises in his opinion because he has carried out his duties in the face of opposition or evasion/s in which important differences of principle or practice had arisen with the client;

c) the client, its directors, or employees may have been guilty of some unlawful act or default, or [some] aspect of their conduct which is relevant to the carrying out of an audit . . . ought, in the opinion of the existing auditor, to be investigated further by the appropriate authority . . .;

d) the existing auditor has unconfirmed suspicions that the client or its directors or employees have defrauded the Inland Revenue, Customs or Excise or others . . .;

e) the existing auditor has serious doubts regarding the integrity of the directors and/or senior managers of the client company;

f) the client, its directors, or employees have deliberately withheld information required by the existing auditor for the performance of his duties or have limited or attempted to limit the scope of his work. (para 1.15)

From the above, it is evident that the communication between the proposed and existing auditor serves two main purposes:

(i) it reduces the likelihood of the prospective auditor accepting an audit nomination in circumstances where all of the pertinent factors are not known; and

(ii) it protects the interests of the existing auditor when the proposed change arises from, or is an attempt to interfere with, the conscientious exercise of the existing auditor's duty to act as an independent professional.

It is frequently contended that a new auditor should not succeed another if the prospective client owes fees to the existing auditor. However, in relation to this issue, GPES 1.206 states:

> The existence of unpaid fees is not of itself a reason why a prospective auditor should not accept nomination/appointment. If he does accept, it may be appropriate for him to assist in any way open to him towards achieving a settlement of outstanding fees; whether or not he does so is entirely a matter for his own judgement in the light of all the circumstances. (para 1.17)

A further matter relating to a change of auditors concerns the incoming auditor substantiating the balances presented in the financial statements of the period preceding that in which (s)he is appointed. In this regard, SAS 450: *Opening Balances and Comparatives* (para 8) requires auditors to:

> obtain sufficient appropriate evidence that:
> (a) opening balances have been appropriately brought forward;
> (b) opening balances do not contain errors or misstatements which materially affect the current period's financial statements; and
> (c) appropriate accounting policies are consistently applied or changes in accounting policies have been properly accounted for and adequately disclosed.

SAS 450 provides details of procedures designed to achieve the above objectives. The Standard goes on to note:

> [These] procedures normally enable incoming auditors to obtain sufficient appropriate audit evidence about the opening balances, and consultations with predecessor auditors are not normally necessary. Except in the case of certain public sector appointments, predecessor auditors have no legal or ethical obligation to provide information and do not normally allow access to their working papers. However, they are expected to co-operate with incoming auditors to provide clarification of, or information on, specific accounting matters where this is necessary to resolve any particular difficulties. (para 14)

7.2.3 Evaluating the Integrity of the Client's Management

It has been explained in earlier chapters that an auditor is required, *inter alia*, to examine financial statements prepared by an entity's management for parties external to the entity, and to form and express an opinion on whether or not these financial statements present a true and fair view of the entity's financial position and performance and comply with relevant legislation.

Over the past 20 to 30 years, deliberate manipulation of financial statement information has become a problem in many parts of the English-speaking world. Indeed, the problem was so serious in the United States in the mid-1980s that, in 1986, the National Commission on Fraudulent Financial Reporting (the Treadway Commission, 1987) was established to investigate it. In some cases, entity managements have manipulated financial statement information in order to cover up a fraud (as, for example, in the infamous

Equity Funding case); in other cases, management has been motivated by a desire to portray the entity's financial position and performance in a more favourable light than they deserve. This has arisen from management's wish to avoid certain events, such as a decline in the value of the company's shares or liquidation, or its desire to secure certain outcomes, such as a bonus which is linked to reported profits, or raising new debt or equity capital in financial markets on favourable terms.

In the United Kingdom, deliberate but legal manipulation of financial statements has received considerable attention since the mid-1980s and is given the flattering title of 'creative accounting'. The Accounting Standards Board is attempting to reduce these so-called 'creative practices' by issuing more rigorous accounting standards than its predecessor organisation, the Accounting Standards Committee.

If an entity's management lacks integrity, the probability that some manipulation of financial statement information will occur is fairly high. Additionally, such a management is likely to be at pains to deceive the auditor to the extent necessary to ensure that (s)he does not discover the facts of the situation. In this regard it is pertinent to observe that in many of the court cases where auditors have faced charges of negligence as a result of failing to uncover management fraud, it has been revealed that the senior executives and/or directors who were responsible for the fraud had a past history of such deeds. Arens and Loebbecke (1980), amongst others, have drawn attention to this phenomenon. They state:

> An analysis of recent court cases involving management fraud shows that in most instances the individuals responsible for the fraud had also been previously involved in illegal or unethical business practices. (p.176)

A specific example of such a case is afforded by de Angelis, instigator of the massive salad oil fraud in the 1960s at the Allied Crude Vegetable Oil Refining Corporation of New Jersey. During the court hearing it was revealed that de Angelis had a string of previous convictions for fraud and other illegal acts committed whilst acting as a company director.

The importance of auditors evaluating the integrity of a potential client's management is emphasised by Pratt and Dilton-Hill (1982). They suggest that management integrity is probably the single most important factor in the potential for material misstatements in financial statements. They also draw attention to the extent to which an auditor relies on the information and responses from a client's management. The nature of the audit function is such that an auditor makes many decisions based on discussions with management. If the client's management lacks integrity, the information and responses given to the auditor may be untrustworthy and, as a result, erroneous audit decisions may be made. Examples of cases in the UK where auditors have found themselves in court for alleged negligence, in which the integrity of the directors is highly questionable, include Maxwell Communications, Polly Peck and the Bank of Credit and Commerce International (BCCI).

For a continuing audit engagement, the auditor should evaluate the integrity of the client's management by reviewing his or her past experience with that management. However, if significant changes have occurred amongst the client's senior executives and/or directors, further investigation may be necessary, similar to that undertaken for a new audit engagement.

In the case of a new engagement, if the potential client has been audited previously, information pertaining to the integrity of its management can usually be obtained from the predecessor auditor. As noted in section 7.2.2 above, before a proposed auditor accepts an audit engagement nomination, (s)he is required to communicate with the auditor being replaced. It was also noted that one of the matters to be communicated by an incumbent auditor to a proposed auditor is doubts the existing auditor has regarding the integrity of the client's directors and/or senior managers. It was further noted in section 7.2.1 that, under SAS 240: *Quality Control for Audit Work* (para 6), one of the matters to be considered, when deciding whether or not to accept or retain an audit client, is the integrity of the client's management. It therefore seems prudent for nominated auditors to include in their communication with the existing auditor specific enquiries regarding the integrity of the potential client's management.

When a potential client has not been audited previously, relevant enquiries need to be made of appropriate third parties. Such enquiries may be directed to the prospective client's bankers, legal advisors, and others in the financial or business community who may have such knowledge.

In the United States, some auditors and audit firms consider the integrity of a potential client's management to be so important that they hire professional investigators to obtain information about the reputation and background of key members of its management. In the UK, at least until recent years, audit firms have tended to play down the need for a formal pre-engagement investigation of potential clients. It seems that traditionally they have relied on a belief that corporate managements in the UK possess integrity, and also on the likelihood that, as the UK is a country with a relatively well-developed grapevine amongst the auditing and corporate fraternity, any factors which would make it unwise for them to accept a particular audit client would come to their notice. With the spate of unexpected company failures and allegations of corporate fraud which have occurred in recent years, audit firms in the UK have become more diligent about investigating the integrity of senior executives and directors of potential audit clients and more willing to refuse to accept nomination to act as auditors for companies where that integrity is in doubt.

7.2.4 Assessing the Auditor's Competence to Perform the Audit

It has been explained in Chapters 4 and 6 respectively, that auditors are precluded from accepting or continuing audit engagements where they are not independent of their clients and/or they do not possess (or have available) the skills and competence necessary to complete the audit satisfactorily. Thus, before accepting an audit engagement, an auditor must carefully consider whether (s)he:

- possesses the required degree of independence from the (potential) audit client, in both fact and appearance;
- possesses the required levels of training, experience and competence to perform the audit satisfactorily. This includes possessing both:
  - technical skills and experience in auditing; and
  - adequate knowledge of the (potential) client's industry;
- has available, at the appropriate time, adequate assistants who possess the skills and competence necessary to perform the work to be assigned to them;

- is able to direct, supervise and review the work of assistants as required by SAS 240: *Quality Control for Audit Work*;
- has available, at the appropriate time, assistance from other auditors and/or experts, if they are to perform part of the audit.

Additionally, before accepting a new audit client, an auditor must consider the impact of the engagement on his or her audit portfolio. In particular, the auditor should consider whether acceptance of the client would give rise to any conflict of interest with existing clients and whether it would adversely affect his or her ability to service existing clients properly.

7.3 AUDIT ENGAGEMENT LETTERS

Once the pre-engagement investigation is complete and the auditor has decided to accept the engagement, an engagement letter should be prepared. As SAS 140: *Engagement Letters* explains, the purpose of this letter is to confirm the auditor's acceptance of the appointment and to ensure there is no misunderstanding between the auditor and the client as regards the auditor's and directors' responsibilities, the objective and scope of the audit, and the reports the auditor is to provide at the conclusion of the audit (para 14).

Although the details of engagement letters vary according to the circumstances of the particular audit, certain items are almost invariably included. These are as follows:

- A statement outlining the scope (extent) of the audit. Reference is made to any work the auditor is to do in addition to that required for a statutory audit.
- A statement emphasising that the entity's financial statements are the responsibility of the directors (or their equivalent) and that the statements are required to give a true and fair view of the state of affairs and profit or loss of the reporting entity and comply with relevant legislation.
- A statement drawing attention to the directors' responsibility to ensure that all of the company's records and documents, and any other information requested in connection with the audit, are made available to the auditors.
- A statement outlining the auditor's statutory and professional responsibilities, in- cluding his or her responsibility to form and express an opinion on the financial statements and to report if the financial statements do not comply in any material respects with applicable accounting standards, unless the auditor considers that non- compliance is justified in the circumstances.
- An indication of how the auditor will approach the audit and the work to be done; also, in appropriate cases, reference is usually made to the involvement of other auditors or experts in certain aspects of the audit.
- A warning that the audit is not designed to detect significant weaknesses in the company's systems; however, it is noted that any such weaknesses which come to light during the audit will be reported to the directors.
- A statement informing the directors (or their equivalent) that the auditor may request written confirmation of certain oral representations expressed by them to the auditor during the course of the audit. Attention is also drawn, in appropriate

cases, to the legislative provision under which it is an offence for an officer of the entity to mislead the auditors (for example, Companies Act 1985, s.389A).

- A statement to the effect that responsibility for safeguarding the entity's assets and preventing and detecting fraud, error and non-compliance with the law or regulations rests with management; however, it is also pointed out that the audit will be planned so as to have a reasonable expectation of detecting material misstatements in the financial statements or accounting records – including those resulting from fraud, error, or non-compliance with legal requirements.
- Confirmation of any work to be performed by the client's staff – for example, the preparation of schedules such as stock-on-hand (prior to stocktaking) and aged debtors' reports – and any involvement in the audit by the client's internal auditors.
- A statement outlining the form of any reports or other communications which are to be provided by the auditor in relation to the findings and conclusions of the audit.
- A statement confirming any verbal agreements with the client, including the basis on which fees are to be charged.

An example of an audit engagement letter is provided by Figure 7.1. The auditor prepares two copies of the letter: they are both sent to the client for signing; one is retained by the client, the other is returned to the auditor for inclusion in the permanent audit file.

In the case of a continuing audit engagement, the auditor may decide that an engagement letter is not needed. However, as SAS 140 points out, certain factors may cause the auditor to decide that a new letter should be sent. The factors include the following:

- any indication that the client misunderstands the objective and scope of the audit;
- a recent change of management, board of directors or audit committee;
- a significant change in ownership, such as a new holding company;
- a significant change in the nature or size of the client's business; and
- any relevant change in legal or professional requirements. (para 8)

The Standard also notes:

It may be appropriate to remind the client of the original letter when the auditors decide a new engagement letter is unnecessary for any period. (para 8)

Before leaving the subject of audit engagement letters, it should be noted that these letters do not absolve the auditor from any duties in relation to the audit. Their principal purpose is to clarify the objective and scope of the audit and to ensure that the client's directors/management are aware of the nature of the audit engagement and their own responsibilities with respect to the financial statements.

7.4 UNDERSTANDING THE CLIENT, ITS BUSINESS AND ITS INDUSTRY

7.4.1 Importance of Gaining an Understanding of the Client and its Business

In order to perform an effective and efficient audit it is essential that the auditor gains a thorough understanding of the client (its organisation, strategy, key personnel, etc.), its business and its industry. SAS 210: *Knowledge of the Business* states:

Figure 7.1 Example of an Audit Engagement Letter

(This specimen letter is modified to meet the needs of specific circumstances)

To the directors of Foolproof plc

The purpose of this letter is to set out the basis on which we are to act as auditors of the company and its subsidiary undertakings and the respective areas of responsibility of the directors and of ourselves.

Responsibilities of directors and auditors
1.1. As directors of Foolproof plc, you are responsible for ensuring that the company maintains proper accounting records and for preparing financial statements which give a true and fair view and have been prepared in accordance with the Companies Act 1985. You are also responsible for making available to us, as and when required, all the company's accounting records and all other relevant records and related information, including minutes of all management and shareholders' meetings.

1.2. We have a statutory responsibility to report to the members whether, in our opinion, the financial statements give a true and fair view and whether they have been properly prepared in accordance with the Companies Act 1985. In arriving at our opinion, we are required to consider the following matters, and to report on any in respect of which we are not satisfied:
  a) whether proper accounting records have been kept by the company and proper returns adequate for our audit have been received from branches not visited by us;
  b) whether the company's balance sheet and profit and loss account are in agreement with the accounting records and returns;
  c) whether we have obtained all the information and explanations which we consider necessary for the purposes of our audit; and
  d) whether the information given in the directors' report is consistent with the financial statements.
In addition, there are certain other matters which, according to the circumstances, may need to be dealt with in our report. For example, where the financial statements do not give details of directors' remuneration or of their transactions with the company, the Companies Act 1985 requires us to disclose such matters in our report.

1.3. We have a professional responsibility to report if the financial statements do not comply in any material respect with applicable accounting standards, unless in our opinion the non-compliance is justified in the circumstances. In determining whether or not the departure is justified we consider:
  a) whether the departure is required in order for the financial statements to give a true and fair view; and
  b) whether adequate disclosure has been made concerning the departure.

1.4. Our professional responsibilities also include:
  • including in our report a description of the directors' responsibilities for the financial statements where the financial statements or accompanying information do not include such a description; and
  • considering whether other information in documents containing audited financial statements is consistent with those financial statements.

Scope of audit
2.1. Our audit will be conducted in accordance with the Auditing Standards issued by the Auditing Practices Board, and will include such tests of transactions and of the existence, ownership and valuation of assets and liabilities as we consider necessary. We shall obtain an understanding of the accounting and internal control systems in order to assess their adequacy as a basis for the preparation of the financial statements and to establish whether proper accounting records have been maintained by the company. We shall expect to obtain such appropriate evidence as we consider sufficient to enable us to draw reasonable conclusions therefrom.

2.2. The nature and extent of our procedures will vary according to our assessment of the company's accounting system and, where we wish to place reliance on it, the internal control system, and may cover any aspect of the business's operations that we consider appropriate. Our audit is not designed to identify all significant weaknesses in the company's systems but, if such weaknesses come to our notice during the course of our audit which we think should be brought to your attention, we shall report them to you. Any such report may not be provided to third parties without our prior written consent. Such consent will be granted only on the basis that such reports are not prepared with the interests of anyone other than the company in mind and that we accept no duty or responsibility to any other party as concerns the reports.

2.3. As part of our normal audit procedures, we may request you to provide written confirmation of certain oral representations which we have received from you during the course of the audit on matters having a material effect on the financial statements. In connection with representations and the supply of information to us generally, we draw your attention to section 389A of the Companies Act 1985 under which it is an offence for an officer of the company to mislead the auditors.

2.4. In order to assist us with the examination of your financial statements, we shall request sight of all documents or statements, including the chairman's statement, operating and financial review and the directors' report, which are due to be issued with the financial statements. We are also entitled to attend all general meetings of the company and to receive notice of all such meetings.

2.5. The responsibility for safeguarding the assets of the company and for the prevention and detection of fraud, error and non-compliance with law or regulations rests with yourselves. However, we shall endeavour to plan our audit so that we have a reasonable expectation of detecting material misstatements in the financial statements or accounting records (including those resulting from fraud, error or non-compliance with law or regulations), but our examination should not be relied upon to disclose all such material misstatements or frauds, errors or instances of non-compliance as may exist.

2.6. Once we have issued our report we have no further direct responsibility in relation to the financial statements for that financial year. However, we expect that you will inform us of any material event occurring between the date of our report and that of the Annual General Meeting which may affect the financial statements.

Other services
3. You have requested that we provide other services in respect of taxation advice. The terms under which we provide these other services are dealt with in a separate letter.

Fees
4. Our fees are computed on the basis of the time spent on your affairs by the partners and our staff and on the levels of skill and responsibility involved. Unless otherwise agreed, our fees will be billed at appropriate intervals during the course of the year and will be due on presentation.

Applicable law
5. This engagement letter shall be governed by, and construed in accordance with, English law. The Courts of England shall have exclusive jurisdiction in relation to any claim, dispute or difference concerning the engagement letter and any matter arising from it. Each party irrevocably waives any right it may have to object to an action being brought in those Courts, to claim that the action has been brought in an inconvenient forum, or to claim that those Courts do not have jurisdiction.

Agreement of terms
6. Once it has been agreed, this letter will remain effective, from one audit appointment to another, until it is replaced. We shall be grateful if you could confirm in writing your agreement to these terms by signing and returning the enclosed copy of this letter, or let us know if they are not in accordance with your understanding of our terms of engagement.

Yours faithfully

We agree to the terms of this letter

. . . .
Signed for and on behalf of (company)

Source: Adapted from SAS 140: *Engagement letters*, Appendix.

Auditors should have or obtain a knowledge of the business of the entity to be audited which is sufficient to enable them to identify and understand the events, transactions and practices that may have a significant effect on the financial statements or the audit thereof. (para 2)

Knowledge of the business is used by auditors in, for example, assessing risks of error, in determining the nature, timing and extent of audit procedures and in considering the consistency and reliability of the financial statements as a whole when completing the audit. (para 3)

Although the auditor needs to understand the client and its business in order to identify factors that may have a significant effect on the financial statements – that is, for the reason stated in SAS 210, para 2 (above) – this does not reflect the fundamental, all-pervasive importance of auditors possessing this understanding. The explanation provided in para 3 is closer to it, but still does not seem to get to the heart of the matter. By becoming thoroughly familiar with all aspects of the client, and the internal and external factors which affect it, the auditor can understand 'how the client ticks' and (s)he is provided with a background against which evidence gathered during the audit can be evaluated to see if it 'makes sense' and 'rings true'.

As indicated in SAS 210, para 3, the auditor's understanding of the client also provides a basis for:

- assessing whether circumstances exist which increase the likelihood of errors being present in the financial statements; and
- determining the nature, timing and extent of audit procedures for the audit as a whole and for each audit segment.

7.4.2   Obtaining Knowledge of the Client and its Business

In order to understand the client, its business and its industry, the auditor must obtain knowledge of the environmental factors – both external and internal – which affect it.

(i)   *External Environmental Factors*

These include:

- the general economic and competitive conditions of the industry within which the client operates, and the industry's vulnerability to changing economic and political factors;
- major policies and practices of the industry and industry specific accounting policies (if any);
- governmental or other regulatory requirements which affect the client and its industry;
- the client's reporting obligations to external parties such as shareholders, debenture holders, Parliament (in the case of some public sector entities), the Inland Revenue, Department of Trade and Industry, and the Companies Registrar.

(ii) *Internal Environmental Factors*

These include:

* the ownership interests of the client entity;
* its organisational structure and management characteristics;
* its financial characteristics;
* its operating characteristics.

A variety of procedures are available to assist the auditor to obtain knowledge about the client and the environmental factors which affect it. These include the following:

(i)   visiting the client and touring the premises;
(ii)   having discussions with key personnel;
(iii) reviewing the client's documentation;
(iv)   reviewing previous years' audit working papers;
(v)   reviewing industry and business data.

(i) *Visiting the Client and Touring the Premises*

By visiting the client, touring the premises and meeting key personnel (such as the chief executive officer, financial controller and marketing, production and personnel department managers), the auditor can become familiar with the client's layout, organisation and operations.

A tour of the premises enables the auditor to obtain knowledge about the client's production or service provision process, its storage facilities and its dispatching procedures. It also enables him or her to gain insight into the security (or otherwise) of stock on hand and supplies, and the quantity and quality of stock on hand and fixed assets. Additionally, it enables the auditor to obtain information about the client's accounting records, information technology, and the expertise and work habits of its accounting personnel.

(ii) *Having Discussions with Key Personnel*

By having discussions with key personnel (for example, the chief executive officer, the financial controller and the sales and production managers), the auditor is able to learn about the entity's policies and procedures, and any changes thereof which have occurred during the reporting period or are expected to occur in the current or future periods. Such discussions also enable the auditor to ascertain the views of key personnel about the entity's financial position and performance during the past year, and any changes in its operations, organisation, financial structure or personnel which are planned or expected in the near to medium-term future.

Discussions with key personnel should embrace topics such as likely changes in premises or plant facilities, divisions or departments; expected developments in technology, products or services, or production and distribution methods; and any planned changes to the client's accounting system and internal controls.

(iii) *Reviewing the Client's Documentation*

The auditor may gain considerable knowledge about internal aspects of the client by reviewing its documentation. Such documentation includes its legal documents (for example, its Memorandum and Articles of Association and any debenture trust deeds), significant commercial agreements, its organisation chart, its policies and procedures manuals, job descriptions, minutes of directors' and other meetings, reports to shareholders and to regulatory agencies (such as the Inland Revenue), internal financial management reports and internal audit reports.

(iv) *Reviewing Previous Years' Audit Working Papers*

Reviewing previous years' audit working papers may highlight problems encountered during previous audits which need to be followed-up, or watched for, during the current audit. It may also reveal planned or expected developments which are of significance to the present year's audit. For example, plans disclosed during the previous year to expand or change production and sales, or to amend distribution policies, or to alter the accounting system, are likely to have an impact on this year's audit.

(v) *Reviewing Industry and Business Data*

A review of industry and business data, trade journals and magazines, and similar publications relating to the client or its industry, provides the auditor with information which is helpful in understanding the general economic, political and competitive processes likely to affect the client's financial position and performance.

It should be noted that acquiring knowledge and understanding of a client, its business and its industry is not a one-off event which is completed at the commencement of an audit. Rather, it is a continuous and cumulative process which proceeds as the audit progresses. Although information is gathered and assessed as a basis for planning the audit, it is usually refined and added to as the auditor and audit staff learn more about the client and its business.

Clearly, for a new audit engagement, the auditor will need to expend considerable time and effort in establishing a sound understanding of the client and its business. For continuing engagements, less time and effort may be devoted to this audit step but it should not be skipped altogether. The auditor needs to update and re-evaluate information gathered in previous audits to determine whether it is still valid and relevant. Additionally, the auditor should perform audit procedures which are designed to identify any significant changes that have affected the client, its business or its industry since the last audit.

7.5 SUMMARY

In this chapter we have discussed the first steps in the audit process. We have considered why an auditor should conduct an investigation before accepting an audit engagement and pointed out that this investigation involves communicating with the predecessor auditor, evaluating the integrity of the (potential) client's management, and assessing the auditor's competence to perform the audit. We have also discussed the purpose and content of audit engagement letters, and examined the importance of the auditor gaining a thorough understanding of the client, its business and its industry and how this understanding may be obtained. It has been emphasised that gaining an understanding of the client and its business is essential for the performance of an efficient and effective audit. More specifically, it has been noted that this understanding provides a sound basis for planning the audit and a background against which audit evidence may be evaluated.

SELF-REVIEW QUESTIONS

7.1 List three elements of the auditor's pre-engagement investigation.

7.2 Explain briefly the purpose of a proposed auditor communicating with the existing or predecessor auditor, and list three pieces of information the proposed auditor should seek.

7.3 Explain briefly why it is advisable for an auditor to investigate the integrity of a (prospective) client's management before accepting an audit engagement.

7.4 List five factors the auditor should consider before concluding that (s)he is competent to accept a particular audit engagement.

7.5 Explain briefly the purpose of audit engagement letters.

7.6 List five topics which are usually referred to in audit engagement letters.

7.7 Explain briefly the importance of an auditor gaining a thorough understanding of the client, its business and its industry.

7.8 List four external environmental factors and four internal environmental factors which are likely to affect an entity and its external audit.

7.9 List five audit procedures which may be used to gain an understanding of the client and its business.

7.10 Explain briefly the importance of each of the following procedures for gaining an understanding of the client and its business:
(i) touring the client's premises;
(ii) reading trade journals and magazines.

REFERENCES

Arens, A.A. & Loebbecke, J.K. (1980). *Auditing: An Integrated Approach* (2nd ed.). New Jersey: Prentice-Hall Inc.

National Commission on Fraudulent Financial Reporting. (1987). *Report of the National Commission on Fraudulent Financial Reporting* (Treadway Commission). New York: AICPA.

Pratt, M.J. & Dilton-Hill, K. (1982). The elements of audit risk. *The South African Chartered Accountant*, **18**(4), 137–41.

ADDITIONAL READING

Grant Thornton (1990). *Audit Manual*. Chapter 9, Knowledge of the business and environmental assessment. London: Longman, 115–32.

Miller, K. (1996). ISO 9000 and the external auditor. *Accountancy*, **117**(1233), 136.

Woolf, E. (1982). In the ordinary course of business – cautionary tales. *Accountancy*, **93**(1068), 131–2.

Chapter 8

Planning the Audit and Assessing Audit Risk

LEARNING OBJECTIVES

After studying the material in this chapter you should be able to:
- differentiate between the two phases of planning an audit;
- explain what is meant by the auditor's desired level of assurance and factors which affect this;
- discuss the concept of materiality as it relates to auditing;
- define audit risk;
- discuss the four components of audit risk;
- explain the relevance of the concepts of materiality and audit risk to planning the audit;
- discuss the importance of overall analytical review for assessing audit risk and identifying high-risk audit areas;
- describe procedures commonly used for overall analytical review.

The following publications and fundamental principle of external auditing are particularly relevant to this chapter:

Publications:
- Statement of Auditing Standards (SAS) 100: *Objective and General Principles Governing an Audit of Financial Statements* (APB, 1995)
- Statement of Auditing Standards (SAS) 200: *Planning* (APB, 1995)
- Statement of Auditing Standards (SAS) 220: *Materiality and the Audit* (APB, 1995)
- Statement of Auditing Standards (SAS) 300: *Accounting and Internal Control Systems and Audit Risk Assessments* (APB, 1995)
- Statement of Auditing Standards (SAS) 410: *Analytical Procedures* (APB, 1995).

Fundamental principle of external auditing – *Judgment*

Auditors apply judgment taking account of materiality in the context of the matters on which they are reporting.

8.1   INTRODUCTION

If a task is to be accomplished effectively and efficiently it must be carefully planned. This is no less true for an audit than it is for a social event such as a party. The auditor needs to plan what evidence to collect in order to be able to express an opinion on whether the financial statements give a true and fair view of the state of affairs and profit or loss of the reporting entity, and how and when to collect this evidence.

Planning an audit has two phases – audit strategy development and audit programme design. Each of these phases is outlined in this chapter but, as audit programme design is discussed in Chapter 9, it is not considered in detail here. This chapter focuses on developing the audit strategy. More specifically, it examines three concepts which are fundamental to, and an integral part of, developing the audit strategy, namely, desired level of assurance, materiality and audit risk. The chapter discusses factors which affect the auditor's desired level of assurance, the distinction between planning materiality and tolerable error, and the components of audit risk. It also explores the relationship between materiality, audit risk and audit planning, examines the meaning and importance of analytical review and considers the assessment of audit risk through overall analytical review.

8.2   PHASES OF PLANNING AN AUDIT

8.2.1   Benefits and Characteristics of Audit Planning

Statement of Auditing Standards (SAS) 200: *Planning* states:

> Auditors should plan the audit work so as to perform the audit in an effective manner. The audit work planned should be reviewed and, if necessary, revised during the course of the audit. (paras 2 and 16)

The Standard explains that planning is necessary to ensure that appropriate attention is devoted to the different areas of the audit, potential problems are identified, and the work is completed expeditiously (para 5). It also notes that obtaining knowledge of the entity's business is an important part of planning the audit and that the extent of audit planning will vary according to the size of the auditee and the complexity of the audit (paras 7 and 8).

SAS 200, para 3, observes that planning an audit entails two distinct phases, namely:

- developing a general strategy (an overall audit plan); and
- developing a detailed approach for the expected nature, timing and extent of audit procedures (an audit programme).

It explains:

> Auditors formulate the general audit strategy in an overall audit plan, which sets the direction for the audit and provides guidance for the development of the audit programme. The audit programme sets out the detailed procedures required to implement the strategy. (para 4)

The Standard also emphasises that planning is not a 'one-off' affair at the start of the audit but should continue throughout an audit. If changed conditions are encountered and/or audit procedures generate unexpected results, the audit strategy and/or the audit programme may need to be revised (para 17).

8.2.2 The Audit Strategy (Overall Audit Plan)

Once the auditor has gained a thorough understanding of the client and its business (as outlined in Chapter 7), the audit strategy can be developed. That is, the scope and conduct of the audit can be determined or, more specifically, plans can be made regarding:

- how much and what evidence to gather;
- how and when this should be done.

In essence, developing the audit strategy depends on factors such as the following:[1]

- the general economic factors and industry conditions affecting the entity's business and important characteristics of the entity, its business, its financial performance and its reporting requirements;
- the level of assurance (or degree of confidence) the auditor wishes to achieve about the appropriateness of the opinion expressed in the audit report (or, alternatively, the level of risk (s)he is prepared to accept that the opinion expressed in the audit report may be inappropriate);
- the limits beyond which errors in the financial statements as a whole, and in individual financial statement amounts, are to be regarded as 'material'; such errors must be corrected before an unqualified (or 'clean') audit report can be issued;
- the likelihood of material errors being present in the (unaudited) financial statements as a whole, and in certain sections thereof (that is, the level of inherent risk and internal control risk);
- the appropriate segments into which the audit should be divided to facilitate the conduct of audit work;
- the availability of audit evidence from different sources and of different types;
- the likely impact of the use of information technology by the entity or by the auditor;
- the availability of suitable audit staff and, where applicable, other (outside) auditors and experts.

(Establishing the auditor's desired level of assurance, setting materiality limits, and assessing inherent risk and internal control risk are discussed in sections 8.3, 8.4 and 8.5, respectively.)

Once factors such as those outlined above have been determined, the overall audit plan can be developed. This sets out in broad terms:

(i)   the nature of audit procedures to be performed – in particular, the expected emphasis to be placed on, respectively, compliance testing of internal controls and substantive testing of transactions and account balances;

---

[1] SAS 200, para 12, provides a comprehensive list of items the auditor should consider when developing the audit strategy.

(ii)   the timing of audit procedures – the proportion of procedures expected to be performed during the interim audit (part of the audit generally performed some months before the client's year-end) and the final audit (performed after the client's year end);[2]

(iii) the extent of audit procedures – the amount of audit evidence expected to be collected in relation to each audit segment.

8.2.3   The Audit Programme

The audit programme, in effect, operationalises the audit strategy. It sets out in detail the audit procedures to be performed in each segment of the audit, indicating those to be performed during the interim audit and those to be performed during the final audit. It frequently also includes details of such things as the size of samples to be tested and how the samples are to be selected.

As noted in Chapter 6 (section 6.3), the audit programme often lists audit procedures in the form of instructions audit staff can follow. Spaces are provided for staff members to initial and date when each procedure has been completed and for cross-referencing to relevant audit working papers. (Developing the audit programme is discussed in Chapter 9.)

8.3   DESIRED LEVEL OF ASSURANCE (CONFIDENCE LEVELS)

8.3.1   Meaning of Desired Level of Assurance

The Companies Act 1985 requires auditors to state in their audit reports, amongst other things:

- whether, *in their opinion*, the financial statements give a true and fair view of the state of affairs of the company (and, in relevant cases, the group) and its profit or loss;
- whether, *in their opinion*, the financial statements have been properly prepared in accordance with the Companies Act. (emphasis added)

Similarly, public sector legislation requires auditors to express an *audit opinion* on the financial statements of the entity concerned.

It should be noted that, in each case, auditors are required to express an opinion, not to certify that the relevant statutory requirement has been met. Thus, it seems that in passing the legislation, Parliament did not expect auditors to reach a state of certainty with respect to the matters in question. This conclusion is reflected in SAS 100: *Objective and General Principles Governing an Audit of Financial Statements*, which states:

> The auditors' opinion enhances the credibility of the financial statements by providing *reasonable assurance* from an independent source that they present a true and fair view. (para 5, emphasis added)

But, what is reasonable assurance?

---

[2] In general, the interim audit focuses on understanding the entity's accounting system and compliance testing of internal controls; the final audit focuses more particularly on substantive testing.

Although auditors are apparently not expected to be *certain* that financial statements, which they report as giving a true and fair view of the entity's financial position and performance and as complying with the Companies Act or other relevant legislation, are not materially misstated in some respect, they clearly want to be reasonably confident that this is the case. The degree or level of confidence they wish to attain is known as their desired level of assurance. Arens and Loebbecke (1980) define this concept as follows:

> The *desired level of assurance* is the subjectively determined level of confidence that the auditor wants to have about the fair presentation of the financial statements after the audit is completed. The higher the level of assurance attained, the more confident the auditor is that the financial statements contain no material misstatements or omissions.

They continue:

> Complete assurance of the accuracy of the financial statements is not possible. . . . the auditor cannot guarantee the complete absence of material errors and irregularities. (p.142)

This latter theme is echoed by Anderson (1977) who states:

> Absolute certainty in the presentation of audited financial statements is neither possible nor its pursuit economically desirable. The auditor's report adds credibility to the statements to which it is appended, but it cannot add complete certainty. . . . [Audit procedures could be extended, but] the cost of such an extension [beyond some point] would be out of all proportion to the minuscule increment in credibility thereby achieved. (pp.129–30)

It should be noted that the auditor's desired level of assurance is the complement of his or her desired level of audit risk. If, for example, the auditor wishes to be 95% confident that the financial statements on which (s)he issues a 'clean' audit report are free of material misstatements, this means that (s)he is prepared to accept a 5% risk that the financial statements, in fact, contain such errors. (The concept of audit risk is discussed in section 8.5 below.)

8.3.2 Factors Affecting the Auditor's Desired Level of Assurance

An auditor's desired level of assurance will always be high. It is frequently expressed in quantitative terms (a figure of 95% is often quoted as a rule of thumb) but it is clearly difficult to pinpoint when a particular numeric level of assurance has been reached. As a result, in practice, auditors often adopt a qualitative approach and think in terms of a 'high' or 'medium' level of assurance rather than in precise percentage terms.

In certain circumstances, auditors wish to attain a particularly high level of assurance. This applies, for example, in cases where a large number of users are likely to rely on the financial statements, and/or where heavy reliance is placed upon the statements by one or more users (such as when a takeover is contemplated), and/or where there is doubt about the client's ability to continue as a going concern. In each of these cases, if the auditor signifies that the financial statements give a true and fair view of the entity's state of affairs and profit or loss when they contain material error or inadequate disclosure, serious consequences may ensue for both the financial statement users and for the auditor.

Generally speaking, the larger the entity in terms of total revenues or total assets, and the more widely disbursed its ownership and its debts, the greater the number of users of its audited financial statements. A large listed public company, such as Marks and Spencer, Grand Metropolitan or British Telecom, which has extensive economic resources and numerous shareholders, debtholders and creditors, is likely to have its audited financial statements used far more widely than are companies with few shareholders and/or few debtholders and other creditors. Private companies, wholly owned subsidiaries, and companies whose directors hold a large proportion of the company's equity and debt (as applies in some smaller companies) are likely to have relatively few financial statements users who are remote from the company.

As Arens and Loebbecke (1991) point out:

> When the [financial] statements are heavily relied on, a great social harm could result if a significant error were to remain undetected. . . . The cost of additional evidence [that is, raising the auditor's level of assurance] can be more easily justified when the loss to users from material errors is [likely to be] substantial. (p.258)

Furthermore, where audited financial statements have a large number of users, each of whom may suffer loss if the auditor fails to detect material error or inadequate disclosure therein, the auditor may have a wide exposure to potential liability for negligence. Thus, where a large number of users rely on financial statements, it may be in the auditor's own interest to seek a particularly high level of assurance. The same is true where one or more users place heavy reliance on the audited financial statements when making a major investment decision (such as in a takeover situation). If the potential investors decide to make the investment and the audited financial statements on which they rely subsequently prove to be materially misstated, they are likely to suffer serious financial loss. As a result, they are likely to seek redress from the auditors for the loss they sustain.

Another situation in which the auditor may desire a particularly high level of assurance is where there is doubt about the entity's status as a going concern. This is because, if a client is forced into liquidation shortly after receiving a 'clean' audit report and the financial statements are found to contain material errors or inadequate disclosures, the auditor may be exposed to litigation, brought by those who suffer loss as a result of the entity's collapse. If, in such circumstances, the auditor raises his or her desired level of assurance, (s)he will gather more evidence than would otherwise be the case and be particularly concerned to see that the nature of the going concern problem is adequately disclosed in the notes to the financial statements.

As a result of these actions, the auditor will be more likely to detect material errors and/or omissions in the financial statements and, failing this, will be better placed to defend the quality of the audit should a challenge arise.

In order to assess the likelihood of a company collapsing in the near future, the auditor evaluates factors such as:

- the client's liquidity position and, where this is weak, whether it is improving or worsening;
- the client's exposure to financial risk – the ease with which the client can service its debts;

- the client's exposure to business risk – its ability to survive a sudden downturn in business operations, whether this results from reduced demand for its output, an unexpected shortage of raw materials, a depressed economic environment, or other causes;
- the client's profits (or losses) over recent years; if the client has suffered losses over a number of consecutive years and there is little sign of improvement, financial failure is likely;
- the competence of the client's management; a management which is alert to danger signals, and which takes steps to correct perceived deficiencies, is more likely to be able to withstand unexpected difficulties than a management which lacks these attributes.

8.4 MATERIALITY

8.4.1 Definition of Materiality

SAS 100: *Objective and General Principles Governing an Audit of Financial Statements* states:

> In undertaking an audit of financial statements auditors should . . . carry out procedures designed to obtain sufficient appropriate audit evidence . . . [so as] to determine with reasonable confidence whether the financial statements are free of *material* misstatement. (para 2, emphasis added)

The Standard does not explain what is meant by 'material' but guidance on the meaning of this concept is provided in SAS 220: *Materiality and the Audit*:

> 'Materiality' is an expression of the relative significance or importance of a particular matter in the context of financial statements as a whole. A matter is material if its omission . . . or misstatement . . . would reasonably influence the decisions of an addressee of the auditors' report . . . Materiality may also be considered in the context of any individual primary statement within the financial statements or of individual items included in them. Materiality is not capable of general mathematical definition as it has both qualitative and quantitative aspects. (para 3)

The Standard goes on to explain:

> The assessment of what is material is a matter of professional judgment and includes consideration of both the amount (quantity) and nature (quality) of misstatements. (para 4)

> Materiality may be influenced by considerations such as legal and regulatory requirements and considerations relating to individual financial statement account balances and relationships. This process may result in different materiality considerations being applied depending on the aspect of the financial statements being considered. For example, the expected degree of accuracy of certain statutory disclosures, such as directors' emoluments, may make normal materiality considerations irrelevant. (para 7)

This need to consider materiality within a given context is reflected in fundamental principle of external auditing – *Judgment:*

> Auditors apply judgment taking account of materiality in the context of the matters on which they are reporting.

8.4.2 Characteristics of the Concept of Materiality

From an analysis of the extracts from SAS 220 set out above, it is evident that:

- a financial statement item is material if its omission or misstatement is likely to affect the decision or action of a reasonable shareholder (or other legitimate financial statement user) who relies on the information provided in the financial statements;
- materiality in the auditing context has a number of characteristics. These include the following:
  - (i)   deciding what is, and what is not, material in any given circumstance is a matter of professional judgment;
  - (ii) an item may be material by virtue of its quantity or its quality;
  - (iii) materiality needs to be considered at two levels:
    - the overall level: that is, in relation to the financial statements as a whole; and
    - the individual account or disclosure level;
  - (iv) the materiality of an item may be affected by legal and regulatory requirements.

Each of these characteristics is discussed below.

(i)   A Matter of Professional Judgment

SAS 220 does not provide numerical guidelines to assist auditors decide whether an item is or is not materially misstated. Indeed, it points out that 'materiality is not capable of general mathematical definition' (para 3). However, it is generally accepted that a useful starting point is to compare financial statement items with an appropriate base amount. For example:

- profit and loss statement items may be compared with profit before tax and exceptional items for the current year or the average pre-tax profit for the last, say, three years (including the current year), whichever is the more relevant measure of profit having regard to the trend of business over the period;
- balance sheet items may be compared with the lower of:
  - total shareholders' equity; and
  - the appropriate balance sheet class total – for example, current assets, fixed assets, current liabilities, long-term liabilities.

Although SAS 220 does not provide numerical guidelines or endorse their use, in practice the following percentage limit guidelines are widely used.

- A variation of 10% or more of the relevant base amount may be presumed to be material, unless there is evidence to the contrary.
- A variation of 5% or less of the relevant base amount may be presumed to be immaterial, unless there is evidence to the contrary.

• For variations which lie between 5% and 10% of the relevant base amount, determination of materiality (or otherwise) depends on the particular circumstances.

It should be pointed out that these percentage guidelines are not 'magic numbers' and all of the circumstances surrounding the item in question, the reporting entity, and the financial statement users, need to be taken into account.

(ii)   *Quantity vs Quality of an Item*

As noted in SAS 220, para 4 (quoted above), when assessing the materiality of a misstatement, it is not only its amount which is relevant. The nature or quality of the item is also significant. For example, a misstatement of directors' emoluments may be very small relative to the entity's profit and *prima facie* would be considered immaterial. However, the nature of the item may be of such sensitivity that even a small inaccuracy would be material. SAS 220 also notes that material misstatements include 'the inadequate or inaccurate description of an accounting policy when it is likely that a user of the financial statements could be misled by the description' (para 6).

(iii)   *Overall and Account Level Materiality*

(a)   *Overall materiality*:   Overall materiality refers to the amount of error the auditor is prepared to accept in the financial statements as a whole while still concluding that they provide a true and fair view of the state of affairs and profit or loss of the reporting entity. It is the amount of error the auditor considers may be present in the financial statements without affecting the decisions or actions of reasonable users of the statements.

The auditor needs to estimate this level of error, or materiality level, prior to commencing the audit, based on his or her understanding of the client and its business, and his or her assessment of the decision needs of users of the financial statements. It is often referred to as 'planning materiality' or, in terms of SAS 220, as the 'preliminary materiality assessment'. It provides a basis for planning the nature, timing, and more particularly, the extent of procedures to be performed during the audit. The lower the level of planning materiality, the greater the amount of evidence that needs to be collected to ensure that the combined errors in the financial statements do not exceed it.

However, planning materiality must not be viewed as a fixed monetary amount which, if exceeded even by a small margin, will cause the auditor to conclude that the financial statements do not give a true and fair view of the entity's financial position and performance, but which, if not exceeded, will lead to the contrary conclusion. When forming an opinion on a set of financial statements, the auditor considers a myriad of factors, including the size and direction of the difference between the actual error estimated to exist in the financial statements (as estimated at the conclusion of the audit) and the preliminary estimate of error which would be accepted. Planning materiality provides a starting point for the auditor's conclusion.

To emphasise the imprecise nature of planning materiality, auditors frequently express it as a range of monetary amounts, rather than as a single figure. Further, as the audit progresses, the auditor may find that the level of planning materiality needs to be changed. This may occur, for instance, because one of the bases used to establish planning materiality is amended (for example, pre-tax profits: see below) and/or because new information comes to light which causes the auditor to conclude that planning materiality was established at a level which is too high or too low.

When considering planning materiality it is important to remember that during an audit an auditor does not check every transaction and every detail of every account balance. Instead, the accuracy of financial statement amounts is assessed by means of checking samples of data and by procedures such as analytical review. Thus, when ascertaining the amount of error in the financial statements as a whole, in addition to calculating the known (detected) amount of error, allowance must be made for errors which remain undetected because they occur in transactions and/or account balances not examined by the auditor.

Auditing Standards do not require auditors to quantify planning materiality, however, in practice, most auditors do so. Surveys in the United States, New Zealand, and elsewhere, have shown that auditors use a variety of bases for this purpose. A survey conducted in the United States by Read, Mitchell and Akresh (1987), for example, found that the 97 surveyed used nine different bases to establish planning materiality. The most popular base was pre-tax operating income (used by 45% of respondents), followed by total revenue (used by 15%) and after-tax operating income (used by 10%). Other bases used include total assets, current assets, current liabilities and long-term liabilities. Interestingly, 12% of the auditors surveyed did not use a financial statement amount to arrive at a figure (or range of figures) for planning materiality but relied instead on judgment or 'instinct'. The study also showed that even where different auditors adopted the same financial statement base to estimate their planning materiality (such as pre-tax operating income), they applied a variety of percentages to the base. Additionally, the survey indicated that, when establishing planning materiality, some auditors allowed only for known (detected) errors, while others also made provision for undetected errors.[3]

In New Zealand, a survey conducted by Pratt and Cuthbertson in 1988 (reported in Pratt, 1990, p.139) found that the 'Big 7' international accounting firms then represented in New Zealand used guidelines for determining their planning materiality as shown in Figure 8.1.

From Figure 8.1 it may be seen that:

- the seven firms used a fairly wide range of bases for establishing their planning materiality and that, in general, these coincided with the bases used by the auditors in the US study;

---

[3] As noted, planning materiality is the amount of error the auditor is prepared to accept in the financial statements while still concluding that they provide a true and fair view. Therefore, conceptually, planning materiality must always allow for errors which are detected and also those which remain undetected because they occur in transactions or account balances not examined by the auditor. As will be shown in Chapter 11, statistical sampling provides the means to estimate the total error in a population based on errors detected in the samples of evidence examined. As a result, when auditors use statistical sampling, planning materiality is established at a level which allows for both detected and undetected errors. However, when judgmental sampling is used, judgment must be exercised to estimate undetected errors. To avoid this exercise of judgment, some auditors prefer to establish planning materiality, for practical purposes, at a level which allows only for detected errors.

Figure 8.1 Planning Materiality Guidelines used by the 'Big 7' Accounting Firms in New Zealand in 1988[4]

Criteria	Accounting Firms						
	1	2	3	4	5	6	7
Net profit – before tax – after tax	10%*	9–10%	5–10%	5%	5–10%	5–10%	5%
Sales	1–1½%		½–1%	¼–½%		$ #	½%
Gross profit				1–2%			
Total assets	1%		1–2%	½%	1%		½%
Current assets				1%			
Working capital						$ #	
Shareholders' funds			2–5%	1–5%		$ #	

Notes: * The materiality level can be increased to 12½ per cent for subsidiaries within a group.
     # Consideration is given to the dollar amounts involved when determining materiality.

- the percentages applied by different firms to the same financial statement base varied quite widely; for example, the percentages applied to net profit before tax ranged from five per cent, used by Firms 4 and 7, to 10%, adopted by Firm 1. Similarly, the percentages applied to sales ranged from ¼–½ per cent, applied by Firm 4, to 1–1½ per cent, used by Firm 1;
- as found in the US study, the percentage variations seem to indicate that some firms (such as Firm 4) establish planning materiality based on detected errors, while others (such as Firm 1) also make allowance for undetected errors.[5]
- most of the firms arrived at a figure (or range of figures) for planning materiality by reviewing the estimates derived from the various bases and exercising judgment. Only Firm 2 relied on just one base, namely, net profit before tax.

(b) *Account level materiality*: The monetary amount or range established for planning materiality not only defines the amount of error the auditor is prepared to accept in the financial statements as a whole before concluding they are not 'true and fair', it also provides the basis for establishing the maximum amount of error the auditor will

---

[4] Results of a survey conducted by Pratt and Cuthbertson, as reported in Pratt (1990, p.139). Arthur Andersen was not included in the survey as this firm was not represented in New Zealand at the time of the study (1988).

[5] It should be noted that, when evaluating, at the conclusion of the audit, the materiality or otherwise of errors detected in the financial statements, if planning materiality is established at, say 5% of net profit before tax and this estimate allows only for detected errors, then the total of discovered errors should be compared to this materiality estimate. If, however, planning materiality is set at, say, 10% of net profit before tax, and this estimate allows for both detected and undetected errors, the total of errors discovered during the audit is adjusted to allow for undiscovered errors before comparing it with the materiality estimate.

tolerate in an individual account balance before concluding that the balance is materially misstated. Similarly, while the overall level of materiality helps to determine the amount of effort required for the audit as a whole, the account level materiality determines the nature, timing and extent of audit procedures to be performed in relation to each account balance. Use of the term 'tolerable error' for the account level estimate of materiality is a useful means of distinguishing between this level of materiality and overall (or planning) materiality. We therefore adopt this term for use in this book.

At the outset, it must be emphasised that setting the tolerable error for individual accounts is never easy and always involves considerable judgment by the auditor. It should also be noted that different audit firms approach the task in different ways. However, in general, as a starting point, tolerable error for all individual accounts is set at a selected level of planning materiality (for example, it may be set at 75% of planning materiality).[6] The monetary amount thus established may then be adjusted upwards or downwards for individual accounts for factors which are specific to that account. In this way, tolerable error is established for each account balance. Factors the auditor will take into consideration when setting the tolerable error for individual accounts include the following:

- the materiality of the account balance, that is, its likely impact on the decisions of users of the financial statements. The cash balance, for instance, with its implications for corporate liquidity and flexibility may be more material to financial statement users than prepaid expenses. The more important a particular financial statement balance is to users, the more important it is that it is stated accurately; hence, the smaller the tolerable error;
- the size of the account balance; for example, if the debtors balance is £700,000 and the stock balance is £1,500,000, the tolerable error in the debtors account (in monetary terms) is likely to be set at a lower level than for the stock account;
- the auditability of the account. Certain accounts such as cash and loans are capable of more accurate verification than others, such as debtors and depreciation, where provisions need to be estimated; this variation should be reflected in the expectations of financial statement users with respect to the accuracy of account balances; the greater the expected accuracy of an account balance, the smaller the tolerable error;
- the relative significance of understatement and overstatement of an account balance: in general, overstatements of assets and understatements of liabilities are more likely to be material to financial statement users than their counterparts (understatements of assets and overstatements of liabilities), and this can be reflected in the materiality limits; tolerable error may, therefore, be set at different levels for understatements and overstatements in certain accounts.

Some of the ideas presented above in relation to planning materiality and tolerable error may, perhaps, be best understood if illustrated by an example. Let us assume

---

6 If planning materiality is the maximum amount of error the auditor will allow in the financial statements as a whole whilst still concluding that they give a true and fair view of the financial position and performance of the reporting entity, it is clear that the tolerable error (the maximum amount of error the auditor will tolerate in an account balance whilst concluding that the balance is true and fair) cannot exceed the monetary amount of planning materiality.

that, from calculations based on net profit after tax, sales, total assets and share-holders' funds, planning materiality is estimated at £70,000. Let us also assume that, given the particular circumstances of the audit, the auditor considers it appropriate to set tolerable error initially at 75% of planning materiality (£52,500). If the account being considered is, say, stock, the auditor will be aware of, amongst other things, the difficulty of auditing this account as a consequence of, for example, the difficulty of assessing the condition of stock, possible obsolescence, etc. Given such factors, the initial estimate of tolerable error is likely to be adjusted downwards by a relatively small amount to, say, £45,000. On the other hand, if the account being considered is cash, the significance of this account balance for users of the financial statements and their likely expectation that the balance will be stated fairly accurately, is likely to result in the initial estimate of tolerable error being adjusted downwards by a signifi-cant amount – to, say, £10,000. In this case, if the stock or cash balance is found to be misstated by an amount in the region of £45,000 or £10,000, respectively, the auditor will almost certainly require the errant account balance to be adjusted before an unqualified (or 'clean') audit report will be issued.

It should be noticed that we have referred to the stock and cash account balances causing concern for the auditor when they are misstated by an amount *in the region of* £45,000 or £10,000, respectively. This underscores the point that (like planning materiality) the limit set for tolerable error in each account is an estimate, not a 'magic number', which, if exceeded by even a minuscule amount, will cause the auditor to require the account balance to be adjusted but which, if not exceeded, prompts no action. Indeed, *all* errors which are found, even if less than tolerable error, need to be investigated to establish their cause and the likely implications for tolerable error in the account.

Estimating tolerable error for individual accounts is an important step in planning the audit, as the magnitude of the tolerable error has a direct impact on the amount of audit evidence that must be gathered. The smaller the tolerable error, the greater the amount of evidence the auditor must collect in order to be assured that errors in the account in question do not exceed the materiality limit.

(iv) *Legal and Regulatory Requirements*

Many financial statement disclosures are required by statute, government regulation, and/or professional standards (primarily Financial Reporting Standards or Statements of Standard Accounting Practice).[7] For example, disclosure of audit fees is required by the Companies Act 1985, s.390A, and disclosure by lessees of finance lease liabilities, classified into 'amounts payable in the next year, amounts payable in the second to fifth years inclusive from the balance sheet date, and the aggregate amount payable thereafter' is required by SSAP 21, para 52. In most cases, failure to disclose such item(s) will be regarded by the auditor as a material omission.

8.4.3 Amending Materiality Estimates

When considering materiality in the auditing context, it is important to remember that, as noted above, neither planning materiality nor tolerable error in individual

---

[7] Progressively the UK is using the title 'Financial Reporting Standard' (FRS) in place of 'Statement of Standard Accounting Practice' (SSAP).

accounts are 'magic numbers'. They are limits set by the auditor during the planning phase of the audit which reflect his or her considered opinion as to the level of misstatement in the financial statements as a whole, and in individual account balances, at which the decisions or actions of reasonable users of the financial statements are likely to be affected.

The quantitative limits of materiality and tolerable error are determined as objectively as possible. Planning materiality, for example, as explained in section 8.4.2, is frequently established by applying pre-set percentages to pre-selected bases. However, notwithstanding auditors' efforts to arrive at materiality estimates objectively, this does not mean they should be regarded as fixed and unalterable. As noted above, qualitative characteristics of financial statement items are also important and, when the materiality (or otherwise) of a misstatement is evaluated, as much attention should be given to the nature of the misstatement as to its size.

Additionally, during the audit, factors may come to the auditor's attention which suggest that planning materiality, and/or tolerable error in one or more account, is too high or too low. When this occurs, the bases on which the materiality estimates were established need to be re-evaluated. If, upon examining the bases in the light of the new knowledge, the auditor considers that a change in the materiality limits is appropriate, then the change should be made.

In general, auditors find it easier to adjust materiality estimates upwards, but will be less willing to adjust them downwards or to maintain those which are found to have been exceeded. This asymmetry arises because the lower the materiality limit:

• the greater the amount of evidence that needs to be collected to make sure the limit has not been exceeded; and
• the more likely it is that misstatements which are discovered will exceed the limit and thus qualify as 'material'. Such (material) errors, if not corrected by the reporting entity, will give rise to a qualified audit report.

The auditor will not relish having to increase the extent of planned audit procedures, largely because such an extension will have an adverse impact on audit time and cost. Similarly, the auditor will not welcome having to put pressure on the reporting entity's management (if this becomes necessary) to correct misstatements in the financial statements which are judged by the auditor to be material and, in the event of the amendments not being made, issuing a qualified audit report. Such eventualities almost invariably cause a strain in the relations between the auditor and the entity's management.

Thus, when factors are encountered during an audit which raise questions about the propriety of materiality estimates established in the planning phase of the audit, justification for making any amendment must be considered carefully. Upward adjustments should only be made, and downward adjustments should not be resisted, when examination of the bases on which planning materiality and tolerable errors in individual accounts were determined, reveals that the initial materiality estimates were inappropriate. In particular, when the auditor finds that misstatements in individual accounts, or in the financial statements as a whole, exceed the pre-set materiality limits, (s)he must avoid any temptation to adopt spurious arguments to justify adjusting the relevant estimate(s) upwards.

8.5   AUDIT RISK

8.5.1   Definition of Audit Risk

SAS 300: *Accounting and Internal Control Systems and Audit Risk Assessments* defines audit risk as 'the risk that auditors may give an inappropriate audit opinion on financial statements' (para 3). From this definition it is evident that audit risk has two forms:

- α risk: the risk that the auditor may express a *qualified* opinion on financial statements that are *not* materially misstated; and
- β risk: the risk that the auditor may express an *unqualified* opinion on financial statements that *are* materially misstated.

The risk of an auditor expressing a qualified opinion on statements which are not materially misstated is very unlikely. Before qualifying the audit report, the auditor will need good reasons to do so, and such reasons will need to be justified to the relevant entity's directors. If the auditor has drawn invalid conclusions about the financial statements, these are likely to come to light during this 'justification process'. Thus, the term 'audit risk' is commonly used to mean β risk.

As noted in section 8.3 above, audit risk (the risk that a material misstatement is present when an unqualified audit opinion is expressed) is the complement of the auditor's level of assurance (the auditor's level of confidence that a material misstatement is not present). Ultimately, to the auditor, audit risk amounts to exposure to legal liability if, as a result of issuing a 'clean' audit report on financial statements which are materially misstated, a user of the financial statements is misled and suffers a loss as a consequence. However, an auditor expresses an opinion on the financial statements; (s)he does not certify their truth and fairness. As a result, some degree of audit risk is unavoidable. Nevertheless, legal action against an auditor should succeed only if the auditor wittingly or negligently accepts an unreasonably high level of audit risk.

8.5.2   Components of Audit Risk

From the definition and description of audit risk given above, it may be seen that audit risk has two separate components, namely:
(i)   the risk that material error is present in the (unaudited) financial statements; this risk of error occurring results from inherent risk and internal control risk;
(ii) the risk that the auditor will fail to detect material error which is present in the (unaudited) financial statements; this risk component is referred to as detection risk and comprises sampling risk and quality control risk.[8]
These components of audit risk are shown in Figure 8.2 and discussed below.

---

[8] SAS 300 recognises, and discusses as separate audit risk components, inherent risk, control risk and detection risk. Control risk, as defined in SAS 300, equates to what we term internal control risk, and detection risk equates essentially to sampling risk.

Figure 8.2   The Components of Audit Risk

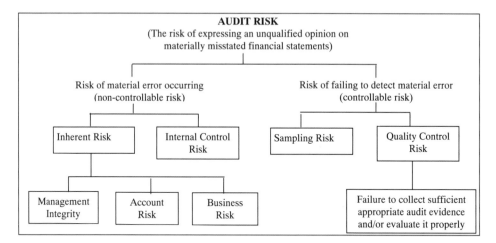

(i)   *The risk that material error is present (Risk of Error Occurrence)*

The likelihood of material error occurring in the unaudited (or draft) financial statements is, for the most part, beyond the auditor's control. This component of audit risk derives from two main sources: inherent risk and internal control risk.

• **Inherent risk:**   Inherent risk is the risk or likelihood of material error being present in the financial statements in the absence of internal controls. As may be seen from Figure 8.2, inherent risk derives from three main sources. These are as follows:

1. ***Management integrity:*** The likelihood of material error being present in the financial statements is strongly influenced by the integrity of the audit-client's management. This integrity has two aspects:
   (a) *inherent integrity*, that is, management's moral and ethical stance; its 'natural' tendency towards being honest or dishonest; and
   (b) *situational integrity*, that is, management's ability to withstand temptation to misrepresent the entity's financial position and/or its profit or loss in situations of pressure; for example, when the entity has failed to meet profit forecasts, or when there are plans to float new shares and the year's profit has been very marginal, management may be tempted to 'artificially improve' the entity's reported profit.
   Where the entity's management lacks integrity, it is likely that the information reported in the (unaudited) financial statements will be manipulated as far as is necessary to portray the entity's state of affairs and profit or loss as desired by management.
2. ***Account risk:*** Material error may also occur in the financial statements as a result of particular account balances (or classes of transactions) being susceptible to misstatement. In the main, these are account balances which involve a high degree of judgment (such as the provision for doubtful debts) or those

where values are uncertain (for example, stands of unsold timber for which market demand is uncertain).[9]

3. **Business risk:** The likelihood of material error occurring in the financial statements is also affected by the nature of the audit–client's business. While some businesses are comparatively risk-free, others are vulnerable to changes in the state of the economy, competition and/or technological advancements. For example, jewellery outlets are affected by changes in consumer wealth; fashion-wear businesses are susceptible to changes in customer 'fads'; and businesses in the electronics industry are particularly prone to changes in technology. In each case, a high risk attaches to the entity's stock valuation (in particular, to stock obsolescence) and possibly also to its ability to sustain sales at the level necessary to meet debt obligations. The latter indicates that business risk also affects the likelihood of situations arising in which management's integrity is put under pressure.

- **Internal control risk:**[10] This is the risk that material misstatement will occur in the audit-client's accounting data (and hence in its financial statements) because it is not prevented or detected by the entity's internal controls. Some internal control risk will always be present because any system of internal control has inherent limitations. However, if an entity has effective internal controls, the likelihood of error occurring in its financial statements can be reduced to a minimum.

In relation to the likelihood of error being present in an entity's unaudited (or draft) financial statements, it is pertinent to note that, although auditors have little or no direct control over inherent risk and internal control risk, they can and should be aware of the circumstances in which these risks are likely to be high. They can perform procedures to ascertain whether these circumstances are present in any given audit and adjust their audit effort and techniques accordingly. (Evaluating the integrity of the client's management and evaluating internal control risk are discussed in Chapters 7 and 9, respectively.)

(ii) *The risk that material error will not be detected (Detection risk)*

Unlike the risk of material error occurring in the unaudited financial statements, the risk of the auditor failing to detect such error is subject to his or her direct control. As Figure 8.2 shows, this component of audit risk derives from sampling risk and quality control risk.[11]

- **Sampling risk:** This is the risk that the auditor may fail to detect material error which is present in the financial statements because not all of the available evidence is examined and a particular transaction or account balance which is materially misstated is not included in the samples of transactions or balances examined during

---

[9] SAS 300 defines inherent risk in terms of account risk (see para 4).

[10] As noted in footnote 8, SAS 300 terms this type of risk 'control risk'.

[11] The definition of detection risk provided in SAS 300, para 6, is broad enough to embrace both of these components of detection risk. However, in para 50 emphasis is given to the sampling risk component.

the audit. Sampling risk also refers to the risk of the sample of evidence selected for examination not being representative of the population from which it is drawn.

When statistical sampling techniques are used, sampling risk is quantifiable and controllable. As explained in Chapter 11, statistical sampling techniques enable sample size to be adjusted so that the desired level of audit (sampling) risk may be achieved.

- **Quality control risk:** This is the risk that the auditor will fail to detect material error which is present in the financial statements because sufficient appropriate audit evidence is not collected and/or is not evaluated properly. This component of audit risk relates to 'human error' in areas such as:

  - understanding the client, its business, its industry and its key personnel;
  - assessing audit risk;
  - setting materiality levels;
  - planning the audit;
  - selecting, directing and supervising audit staff;
  - preparing and reviewing audit working papers.

As with internal control risk, some quality control risk will always be present, simply because audits are conducted by humans and they involve a considerable amount of judgment. Audit staff cannot be expected to make optimal judgments, and to per- form with perfection, on *every* occasion throughout an audit. Some human error is inevitable!

As noted above, the risk of the auditor failing to detect material misstatement which is present in the financial statements is under his or her direct control. Auditors should therefore take steps to reduce sampling risk and quality control risk (that is, detection risk) to the level it is economically feasible to do so. As explained in section 8.6 below, this level varies inversely with the level of inherent risk and internal control risk. (Reducing sampling risk and quality control risk are discussed in Chapters 11 and 6, respectively.)

8.5.3 Audit Risk Analysis

In today's climate of intense competition in the auditing arena, audit firms have focused their attention on conducting efficient, cost-effective audits. This has led them to adopt risk-based auditing, that is, assessing the risk of error occurring in the finan- cial statements and tailoring their audit procedures accordingly.

As for establishing materiality thresholds, the risk of error occurring in the (un- audited) financial statements (which may be referred to as pre-audit risk) needs to be considered at two levels, namely, the overall (financial statement) level and the indi- vidual account or audit segment level.

- *Pre-audit risk at the overall level* refers to assessing the risk of material misstate- ment being present in the financial statements as a whole and, based on this (together with planning materiality), determining the total amount of effort required for the audit as a whole. (The higher the likelihood of material misstatement being present, the greater the amount of audit work required.)

• *Pre-audit Risk at the Individual Account or Audit Segment Level* refers to identifying high audit-risk areas, that is, identifying specific accounts or audit segments where material misstatement is most likely to occur (or, alternatively stated, tolerable error is most likely to be exceeded). Once these have been identified, total audit effort may be allocated so as to ensure that audit work is concentrated primarily in the high-risk areas.

The objective of risk-based auditing is to achieve maximum efficiency and effectiveness. It is designed to ensure that neither the financial statements as a whole, nor any segment thereof, are under- or over-audited; that is, that neither too little, nor too much, audit evidence is gathered to achieve the auditor's desired level of assurance (or desired level of audit risk.) Too little audit evidence leaves the auditor with greater exposure to audit risk than (s)he wishes to accept; too much evidence means the auditor's exposure to risk is reduced to beyond the level (s)he is prepared to accept and, as a result, represents unnecessary expenditure of audit time and cost.

The auditor assesses the overall risk of material error being present in the financial statements, and identifies high audit-risk areas, primarily through:

• gaining a thorough understanding of the client, its business, its industry and its key personnel (this is discussed in Chapter 7);
• performing analytical procedures (this is discussed in section 8.7 below); and evaluating the client's system of internal control (this is discussed in Chapter 9).

Gaining an understanding of the client and performing analytical procedures are particularly important for assessing inherent risk; evaluating the client's system of internal control is the primary means of determining internal control risk.

8.6   RELEVANCE OF AUDIT RISK ASSESSMENTS AND MATERIALITY THRESHOLDS TO PLANNING AN AUDIT

8.6.1   Audit Risk Assessments and Audit Planning

It was noted in section 8.3 above that:

• auditors are required to be reasonably assured, not absolutely certain, that financial statements are free of material misstatement before issuing a 'clean' audit report;
• being reasonably assured that financial statements are free of material misstatement is the complement of accepting some risk that they are not free of such misstatement.

In section 8.5 it was further shown that audit risk derives from two primary sources:

- the risk that material misstatement is present in the (unaudited) financial statements. (This is a function of inherent risk and internal control risk) and
- the risk that the auditor will fail to detect material misstatement which is present; this is a function of sampling and quality control risk, collectively referred to as detection risk.

The relationship between audit risk and its components may be presented in the form of an equation as follows:

Audit risk =   risk of material error being present   +   risk of failing to
in the (unaudited) financial statements   detect material error

Audit risk =   inherent risk + internal control risk   +   detection risk

At this point it may be helpful to recall that audit procedures are basically of two kinds: compliance procedures; and substantive procedures.

- *Compliance Procedures*   These are designed to ascertain whether the entity's internal controls are operating effectively (that is, are being complied with). Therefore, in the context of the audit risk equation, they are relevant to the evaluation of internal control risk.

- *Substantive Procedures*   These are designed to substantiate, or to evaluate the substance (validity, completeness and accuracy) of, financial statement balances. They fall into two broad categories, namely:
- specific analytical procedures;
- tests of details. These tests are of two types: tests of transactions and direct tests of account balances.

Substantive procedures have a direct bearing on detection risk and thus on audit planning. In general terms, the lower the level of inherent risk and internal control risk (that is, the lower the risk of material error being present in the unaudited financial statements), the less the substantive procedures which are required to confirm that the financial statements are, in fact, free of material error. Expressed differently, where the auditor believes there is little likelihood of material misstatement occurring in the financial statements (inherent and internal control risks are low), the greater the risk (s)he is prepared to accept that a material error, if present, will not be detected (high detection risk). Therefore, the less the substantive procedures that will be performed.

When considering the relationship between the components of audit risk it should be remembered that:

- inherent risk is the risk of material error being present in the unaudited financial statements in the absence of internal controls; thus, conceptually, the auditor assesses the likelihood of error occurring in the unaudited financial statements in two stages:

(i) first, inherent risk is assessed; then

(ii) the extent to which the entity's internal controls reduce the likelihood of error occurring in the unaudited financial statements is evaluated;

- inherent risk and internal control risk are beyond the direct control of the auditor; as a consequence, the auditor must adjust detection risk, by increasing or reducing the extent of substantive procedures, in order to achieve his or her desired level of audit risk (or, alternatively stated, his or her desired level of assurance);

- inherent risk and internal control risk may both be assessed as high, or may both be assessed as low, or one may be assessed as high and the other as low; but, whatever their combined level of risk may be, this determines the extent of the substantive procedures the auditor must conduct in order to achieve his or her desired level of audit risk.

These relationships may be illustrated by reference to simple numerical examples.

Example 1:   Assume the following facts:

(i)   The auditor's desired level of audit risk is 5%. (His or her desired level of assurance is 95%).

(ii)   After assessing inherent risk the auditor believes there is a 60% risk of material misstatement being present in the unaudited financial statements.

(iii)   After also evaluating the entity's internal controls, the auditor has reduced his or her assessment of the risk of material misstatement occurring in the unaudited financial statements from 60% to 20% (a reduction of 40 percentage points).

Given the facts outlined above, it is evident that in order to achieve a desired level of audit risk of 5%, the auditor must reduce his or her assessment of audit risk by a further 15 percentage points through the performance of substantive procedures.

Desired level of audit risk	=	Inherent risk	–	Risk reduction through internal control assessment	–	Risk reduction through substantive audit procedures
5%	=	60%	–	40%	–	15%

Example 2:   Assume the following facts:

(i)   The auditor's desired level of audit risk is 5%. (His or her desired level of assurance is 95%.)

(ii)   After assessing inherent risk, the auditor believes there is an 85% risk of material misstatement being present in the unaudited financial statements.

(iii)   The risk of material misstatement occurring in the unaudited financial statements after the accounting data has passed through the entity's accounting system and internal controls is assessed as 75% (a reduction of 10 percentage points).

Given the above facts, it is evident that, in order to achieve a desired level of audit risk of 5%, the auditor must reduce audit risk by a further 70 percentage points through the performance of substantive procedures.

Desired level of audit risk	=	Inherent risk	–	Risk reduction through internal control assessment	–	Risk reduction through substantive audit procedures
5%	=	85%	–	10%	–	70%

In the first example the auditor plans to use substantive audit procedures to reduce overall audit risk by 15 percentage points, whereas in the second case such procedures need to reduce audit risk by 70 percentage points. It follows that in the second case the substantive procedures need to be far more extensive and powerful than in the first.

Some audit firms use a simple probability multiplication rule to indicate the detection risk which should be planned for. This states:

Desired level of audit risk	=	Risk of material error occurring in the unaudited financial statements	×	Risk of failing to detect material error [detection risk (D)]

In statistics the probability of two events (A and B) both happening is the multiple of the probability of $A[p(A)]$ and the probability of $B[p(B)]$. Thus the multiple of the risk (or probability) of a material error occurring in the unaudited financial statements, and the risk (or probability) of the substantive tests failing to detect it, gives the risk of the auditor failing to qualify materially misstated financial statements (that is, audit risk).

Applying this to the figures given in the examples set out above:

Example 1:

Desired level of audit risk	=	Risk of material error occurring (after inherent risk and internal control risk have been assessed)	×	Risk of failing to detect material error (detection risk)
$\frac{5}{100}$	=	$\frac{20}{100}$	×	$\frac{D}{100}$

Rearranging the equation to find detection risk:

$$D = \frac{5}{20} \times \frac{100}{1} = 25\%$$

Example 2:

Desired level of audit risk	=	Risk of material error occurring (after inherent risk and internal control risk have been assessed)	×	Risk of failing to detect material error (detection risk)
$\frac{5}{100}$	=	$\frac{75}{100}$	×	$\frac{D}{100}$

Rearranging the equation to find detection risk:

$$D = \frac{5}{75} \times \frac{100}{1} = 6.7\%$$

It may be seen that in Example 1 the auditor can accept a 25% risk of failing to detect material error, whereas in Example 2 such detection risk falls to 6.7%.

From Examples 1 and 2 it is evident that the greater the likelihood of material error occurring in the unaudited financial statements (the higher the combined level of inherent and internal control risk), the lower the risk the auditor can take of not detecting material error which is present. The lower the detection risk the auditor can accept, the more extensive the substantive audit procedures (s)he must conduct. It follows from this that the relationship between the components of audit risk has a significant impact on audit planning. Audits must be planned so as to ensure that inherent risk and internal control risk are properly evaluated and that adequate substantive procedures are performed so as to reduce overall audit risk to the desired level. In order to ensure that adequate substantive procedures are per-formed, the auditor must carefully plan the nature, timing and extent of these procedures.

The relationship between inherent risk, internal control risk and detection risk may be illustrated by reference to a town's water supply. For the purpose of illustration, assume that:

- the population of Jolleytown derives its water supply from Smillie Reservoir;
- three rivers flow into Smillie Reservoir;
- the water from the rivers passes through a purification filter before it passes into the reservoir.

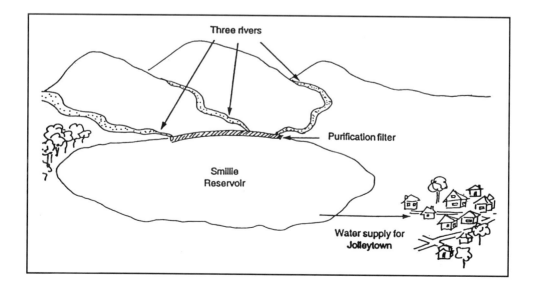

Jolleytown's water supply	Parallel in audit risk terms
Situation 1	
1. The rivers (mountain streams) flowing down towards the purification filter are crystal clear.	1. Management integrity appears to be high, there are no apparent pressures likely to motivate management to manipulate the financial statement information, and business risk is low. (Inherent risk is low.)
2. The purification filter is in excellent order and can be relied upon to filter out impurities in the river water.	2. Internal controls appear to be effective in preventing and detecting errors in the accounting data. (Internal control risk is low.)
3. In order for the authorities to be assured that the water in Smillie Reservoir is safe for the population of Jolleytown to drink, relatively little testing will be required.	3. The auditor, having assessed the inherent risk and internal control risk, will be fairly confident that the financial statements do not contain material misstatement. Thus (s)he will conduct relatively little testing to confirm that material error is not present.
Because the authorities believe the reservoir water is 'pure', they will not test it extensively. They thus run the risk of failing to detect impurities which may, in fact, have 'slipped through' the system.	By conducting relatively little substantive testing, the auditor runs the risk of not detecting material misstatement which may, in fact, have 'slipped through' the system. Thus detection risk is high.
Situation 2	
1. The three rivers flowing down from the hills towards the purification filter are muddy and carry lots of impediments such as rocks, stones and vegetation.	1. Management integrity appears to be fairly low and business risk is high. The risk of material error occurring in the unaudited financial statements in the absence of internal controls (i.e. inherent risk) is high.
2. The purification filter is not in a good state of repair. A number of holes have developed and the filter is in need of replacement.	2. Internal controls do not appear to be effective: they seem unlikely to prevent and detect errors which are present in the accounting data. (Internal control risk is high.)
3. Before the water in the reservoir can be accepted as safe for Jolleytown residents to drink, extensive testing will be required. (A large number of water samples will need to be taken from various parts of the reservoir.)	3. Before the financial statements can be adjudged 'true and fair', the financial statement account balances will need to be tested extensively.
As a result of the extensive testing, the failure to detect impurities in the water (if they are present) will be fairly low.	As a result of the extensive (substantive) testing, the chance of failing to detect material error is fairly low (i.e. low detection risk).

SAS 300: *Accounting and Internal Control Systems and Audit Risk Assessments* conveys these ideas as follows:

When planning their audit, auditors consider the likelihood of error [occurring in the financial statements] in the light of inherent risk and the system of internal control (control risk) in order to determine the extent of work (and hence the level of detection risk) required to satisfy themselves that the risk of error in the financial statements is sufficiently low. (para 12)

Auditors should consider the assessed levels of inherent and [internal] control risk in determining the nature, timing and extent of substantive procedures . . . to be performed to reduce detection risk, and therefore audit risk, to an acceptably low level. (paras 49 and 51)

8.6.2 Audit Risk at the Overall and Individual Account (or Audit Segment) Level

The discussion set out in section 8.6.1 above focuses on assessing inherent risk and internal control risk at the overall (financial statement) level and considers the extent of substantive procedures required to reduce detection risk, and thus audit risk, to the desired level for the audit as a whole.

However, as noted in section 8.5.3, audit risk is also considered at the individual account or audit segment level. The principles explained in relation to overall audit risk apply equally to audit risk at the account or audit segment level. Indeed, in practice, the audit risk equation and determination of the required substantive procedures probably have greater application at the individual account or audit segment level than at the overall (financial statement) level.

8.6.3 Audit Risk, Materiality and Audit Planning

From our discussion of audit risk, it is evident that the auditor's assessment of inherent risk and internal control risk has a major effect on the planning of audit procedures. In section 8.4.2 above, it was explained that materiality, both at the overall level (planning materiality) and individual account level (tolerable error), also has a significant impact on audit planning.

The relationship between the auditor's desired level of audit risk (or its complement, the auditor's desired level of assurance), materiality thresholds (or levels), detection risk, and substantive procedures is complex. In order to assist understanding of the relationship between these factors, the key ideas are presented diagrammatically in Figures 8.3(a) to 8.3(e).

• Figure 8.3(a) indicates that, other things remaining the same, as the auditor's desired level of audit risk is reduced (or, equivalently, the auditor's desired level of assurance is increased), the planned level of detection risk is reduced. (In other words, the greater the assurance sought by the auditor that the financial statements do not contain material error, the less risk (s)he is prepared to take of failing to detect error which is present.)

• Figure 8.3(b) indicates that, other factors remaining the same, as the materiality level (level of acceptable error) judged appropriate for users of the financial statements increases, the auditor can accept a higher level of detection risk. (This is the corollary of the point made in section 8.4.2(iii) above, namely, that the lower materiality thresholds are set, the greater the amount of evidence that needs to be gathered to determine whether or not these thresholds have been exceeded. The greater the amount of evidence collected, the lower the risk of failing to detect errors which are present – thus, the lower the level of detection risk.)

Figure 8.3   Interrelationship Between Desired Level of Audit Risk, Materiality, Detection Risk and Extent of Substantive Procedures

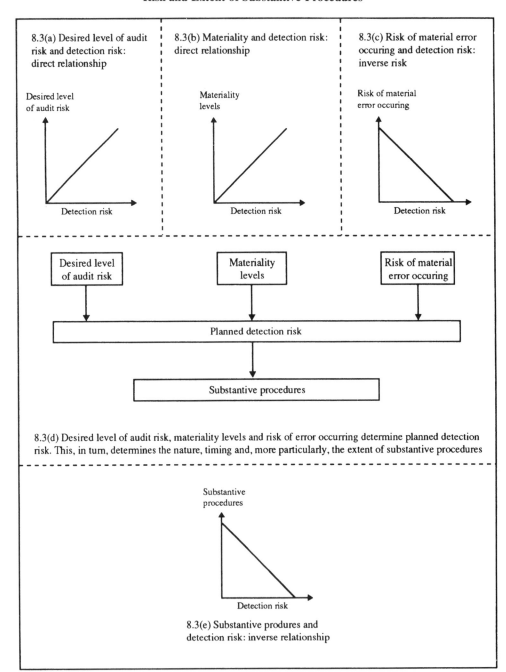

8.3(a) Desired level of audit risk and detection risk: direct relationship

Desired level of audit risk

Detection risk

8.3(b) Materiality and detection risk: direct relationship

Materiality levels

Detection risk

8.3(c) Risk of material error occuring and detection risk: inverse risk

Risk of material error occuring

Detection risk

Desired level of audit risk

Materiality levels

Risk of material error occuring

Planned detection risk

Substantive procedures

8.3(d) Desired level of audit risk, materiality levels and risk of error occurring determine planned detection risk. This, in turn, determines the nature, timing and, more particularly, the extent of substantive procedures

Substantive procedures

Detection risk

8.3(e) Substantive produres and detection risk: inverse relationship

• Figure 8.3(c) indicates that, other factors remaining the same, if the auditor considers there is a high risk of material error[12] occurring in the (unaudited) financial statements as a result of inherent risk and internal control risk, the lower the level of detection risk which is necessary. The inverse relationship between the risk of errors occurring in the unaudited financial statements and detection risk was explained in section 8.6.1.

• Figure 8.3(d) shows that, taken together (a) the desired level of audit risk (or desired level of assurance), (b) the materiality levels set by the auditor, and (c) the auditor's assessment of the risk of errors occurring in the unaudited financial statements, determine the level of detection risk the auditor plans to accept and this, in turn, determines the extent of the substantive procedures.

• Figure 8.3(e) indicates that the lower the planned level of detection risk, the more extensive and/or powerful are the necessary substantive procedures. The more assured the auditor wishes to be of not failing to detect material error in the unaudited financial statements, the more extensive the substantive procedures (s)he will plan to perform.

To illustrate the ideas conveyed in Figures 8.3(a) to 8.3(e), it may be stated that, if the auditor's desired level of audit risk is assumed to be low (the desired level of assurance is high), the materiality thresholds are low and the risk of material error occurring in the unaudited financial statements is high, then the planned detection risk will be low and the necessary substantive procedures are extensive.

8.7 ANALYTICAL PROCEDURES

8.7.1 Meaning of Analytical Procedures

Analytical procedures are the means by which meaningful relationships and trends in both financial and non-financial data may be analysed, actual data may be compared with budgeted or forecast data, and the data of an entity may be compared with that of similar entities and industry averages.

The procedures consist primarily of ratio, percentage, trend and comparative analyses, although they also include more sophisticated statistical techniques such as regression analysis.

SAS 410: *Analytical Procedures* explains:

Analytical procedures include the consideration of comparisons of the entity's financial information with, for example:

• comparable information for prior periods;
• anticipated results of the entity, from budgets or forecasts;
• predictive estimates prepared by the auditors, such as an estimation of the depreciation charge for the year; and
• similar industry information, such as a comparison of the entity's ratio of sales to trade debtors with industry averages, or with the ratios relating to other entities of comparable size in the same industry. (para 5)

Analytical procedures also include consideration of relationships:

---

[12] It should be recalled from section 8.4 that the lower materiality thresholds are set, the more readily errors – individually or in aggregate – cross the threshold and thus qualify as 'material errors'.

- between elements of financial information that are expected to conform to a predicted pattern based on the entity's experience, such as the relationship of gross profit to sales; and
- between financial information and relevant non-financial information, such as the relationship of payroll costs to number of employees. (para 6)

It should be noted that in financial accounting the term 'interpretation and analysis' is used to mean essentially the same thing as analytical procedures in auditing. Since the ratios, percentages, trends and comparisons used by financial statement users in the interpretation of financial statements are essentially the same as those used in analytical procedures, it follows that analytical procedures prompt consideration of the size of errors which would be material to financial statement users. For example, the auditor would seek an explanation for a gross profit percentage which moved from, say, 18% to 20% if such a change would cause the financial analyst to change his or her assessment of the entity's financial performance. In this case, it follows that any error in the sales or cost of sales which caused such a shift in the gross profit percentage would be material.

8.7.2 Importance of Analytical Procedures

Analytical procedures are generally regarded as highly efficient and effective audit tests; however, it must be borne in mind that their effectiveness is always dependent upon the quality of the underlying data. As indicated above, these procedures provide a useful means of establishing whether financial statement amounts display unexpected characteristics, that is, whether they deviate from the auditor's expectations, given his or her understanding of the client, its business, its industry, and detailed knowledge of events which have affected the client's financial position and/or performance over the reporting period.

As shown in Figure 8.4, analytical procedures are used at three different stages during an audit to achieve three different objectives:

1. *During the planning stage* they are used to help gain an understanding of the client's business, to help assess the likelihood of errors being present in the unaudited financial statements, to help determine appropriate levels of materiality, and to help determine the nature, timing and extent of audit procedures.
2. *During the substantive testing stage* they are used to obtain audit evidence in relation to individual account balances and classes of transactions.
3. *During the final review stage* they are used to help confirm (or challenge) conclusions reached by the auditor regarding the truth and fairness of the financial statements.

The use of analytical procedures as substantive tests and in the final review of the financial statements is discussed in Chapters 10 and 12, respectively.

8.7.3 Analytical Procedures in Planning the Audit

During the planning stage of an audit, analytical procedures are used, in particular, to assist the auditor:

Figure 8.4   The Use of Analytical Procedures in an Audit

Stage of the Audit	Objective	Nature of Procedures Used
Planning the audit	• To understand the client's business. • To assess the likelihood of errors being present in the unaudited financial statements. • To set materiality levels. • To identify high risk audit areas. • To plan the nature, timing and extent of audit procedures.	• Trend analysis. • Ratio analysis of entity data. • Comparative analysis of entity data with that of other similar entities and industry averages. (Focus is on the entity's overall financial position and performance).
Substantive procedures	To obtain evidence to confirm (or refute) individual account balances.	Ratio analysis based on direct relationships amongst individual accounts. (Focus is on the reasonableness of individual account balances).
Final review	To confirm conclusions reached with respect to the truth and fairness of: – profit and loss statement amounts; – balance sheet amounts; – cash flow statement amounts; – financial statement note disclosures.	• Trend and percentage analysis of individual accounts. • Ratio analysis of financial statement data. (Focus is on the truth and fairness of the financial statements as a whole in portraying the entity's financial position, performance and cash flows).

• gain an understanding of the client's financial affairs;
• assess the likelihood of the unaudited financial statements containing material errors;
• determine appropriate materiality levels;
• identify high-risk areas, that is, identify the accounts or audit segments where errors appear most likely to exist;
• plan the audit procedures to be performed during the rest of the audit.

On the basis of his or her general understanding of the client and its business, and knowledge of events which have affected the client's financial position and performance during the reporting period, the auditor will have certain expectations regarding the results of the analytical procedures performed during the planning stage of the audit. Where the results differ from the auditor's expectations, they raise questions about the accuracy of the financial and non-financial data used in the analysis (and, hence, about the accuracy of the financial statements) and/or about information previously obtained by the auditor on which his or her understanding of the entity and its financial affairs is based. Thus, analytical procedures performed in the planning phase of an audit are useful for confirming or challenging the auditor's understanding of the entity's business and its financial position and performance, as well as for ascertaining whether it is likely that material error is present in the financial statements and for identifying the accounts or audit areas in which material error is most likely to occur. Once the likelihood of errors being present in the financial statements has been established, the auditor can plan the nature, timing and extent of audit procedures to be performed during the rest of the audit and determine the areas in which audit effort is to be concentrated.

The analytical procedures performed during the planning phase of the audit concentrate on the overall financial position and performance of the entity. The analysis focuses in particular on the entity's liquidity, solvency (or capital adequacy) and profitability.

(i) *Liquidity*

When analysing the entity's liquidity, the auditor is primarily interested in the entity's ability to meet its short-term financial obligations when they fall due. Two ratios in particular are used by auditors to assess an entity's liquidity, namely:

- current (or working capital) ratio [current assets/current liabilities]; and
- quick assets ratio (or acid test), [(current assets minus stocks and prepayments)/ current liabilities].

In order to assess the results of these ratios, the auditor needs to consider:

- the quality of current assets – for example, whether debtors are stated at their net realisable value and how quickly they and stocks are likely to generate cash; and
- the nature of current liabilities – for example, how quickly they will have to be paid and whether unused bank overdraft (or other short-term funding) facilities are available.

To help evaluate these factors, the auditor usually calculates additional ratios, such as:

- the number of days debtors' balances are outstanding [(average debtors/sales) × 365];
- the number of days trade creditors' balances are outstanding [(average trade creditors/purchases) × 365];
- the rate of stock turn [cost of goods sold/average stocks].

(ii) *Solvency (or Capital Adequacy)*

When analysing the entity's solvency, the auditor is primarily interested in the entity's ability to continue in operation even if it encounters adverse trading conditions and experiences exceptional losses. The auditor wishes to assess, in particular, the ease with which the entity can meet its financing commitments, and the ease with which it is likely to be able to raise new capital should the need arise.

To assess an entity's solvency, auditors usually calculate ratios such as the following:

- asset structure [current assets/total assets; fixed assets/total assets];

- financial structure [current liabilities/total funds; long-term liabilities/total funds; shareholders' funds/total funds];
- times interest earned [earnings before interest and tax/interest];
- debt to equity ratio [total debt/total equity].

(iii) *Profitability*

Probably the most widely used measure of an entity's profitability is the return it earns on its assets (ROA), [net profit/average total assets].[13] This ratio is, in fact, built up from two other ratios, each of which provides a useful measure of profitability, namely:

- net profit margin [net profit/sales]; and
- asset turnover [sales/average total assets].

Other measures of profitability frequently used by auditors include:

- gross profit margin [gross profit/sales];
- sales to current assets [sales/average current assets];
- sales to fixed assets [sales/average fixed assets];
- return on shareholders' funds [net profit after tax/average shareholders' funds].

8.8 SUMMARY

In this chapter we have identified the two phases involved in planning an audit – developing the audit strategy and designing the audit programme – and we have discussed various aspects of developing the audit strategy. More specifically, we have examined the auditor's desired level of assurance (the desired level of audit risk), the concept of materiality, the distinction between planning materiality and tolerable error, and the setting of materiality thresholds. We have also discussed the concept of audit risk and shown that overall audit risk comprises two major components: the risk of material error being present in the financial statements and the risk of the auditor failing to detect material error which is present. We have also shown that each of these components of audit risk consists of two elements, namely, inherent risk and internal control risk, and sampling risk and quality control risk, respectively. Additionally, we have examined the relationship between the audit risk components and established that, while inherent risk and internal control risk are generally beyond the direct control of the auditor, detection risk is not. As a consequence, in order to achieve his or her desired level of audit risk, the auditor needs to assess inherent risk and internal control risk, and to plan the nature, timing and extent of audit procedures so as to ensure that detection risk, and hence audit risk, is reduced to the desired level.

In the final section of this chapter we have considered the meaning and importance of analytical procedures and discussed the use of these procedures in the planning phase of an audit.

---

[13] As a result of the equivalence of total assets and total funds invested, this ratio is also referred to as 'return on investment' (ROI), [net profit/average total funds invested].

A summary of the main ideas discussed in this chapter is presented in Figure 8.5.

Figure 8.5 Relationship Between Steps in the Audit Process, Planning the Audit, Establishing Materiality Thresholds, and Assessing Audit Risk

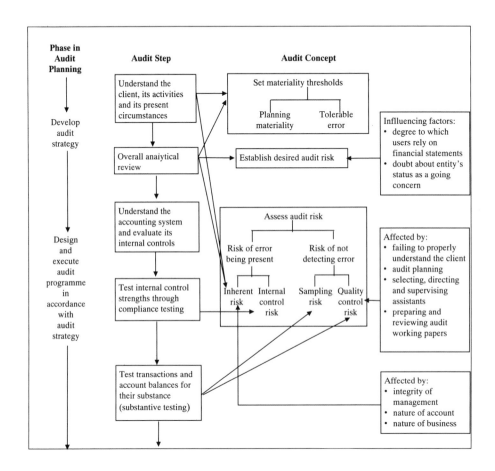

SELF-REVIEW QUESTIONS

8.1 State the two main phases in planning an audit and outline the main objective of each.

8.2 Define the auditor's 'desired level of assurance'. Explain how this relates to the auditor's desired level of audit risk.

8.3 Explain briefly the circumstances in which the auditor's desired level of assurance is likely to be particularly high.

8.4 Define 'materiality' and explain briefly the distinction between:
(i) planning materiality, and
(ii) tolerable error.

8.5 Define 'audit risk' and list the four components of audit risk.

8.6 Explain briefly why inherent risk and internal control risk are said to be 'uncontrollable risk', but sampling risk and quality control risk are referred to as 'controllable risk'.

8.7 Explain briefly how the auditor's assessment of inherent risk and internal control risk affects his or her planning of substantive procedures.

8.8 When planning an audit, the auditor must consider:
   • the extent of audit procedures,
   • the timing of audit procedures,
   • the nature of audit procedures.
   (a) Briefly explain the meaning of each of these terms.
   (b) Give one example for each term to illustrate its affect on planning an audit.

8.9 Define 'analytical procedures' and list three different ways in which these procedures are used in an audit.

8.10 List four ways in which analytical procedures can assist the auditor during the planning stage of an audit.

REFERENCES

Anderson, R.J. (1977). *The External Audit I: Concepts and Techniques*. Toronto: Cropp Clark Pitman.

Arens, A.A. & Loebbecke, J.K. (1980). *Auditing: An Integrated Approach* (2nd ed.). New Jersey: Prentice-Hall Inc.

Arens, A.A. & Loebbecke, J.K. (1991). *Auditing: An Integrated Approach* (8th ed.). New Jersey: Prentice-Hall Inc.

Pratt, M.J. (1990). *External Auditing: Theory and Practice in New Zealand*. New Zealand: Longman Paul Ltd.

Read, J.W., Mitchell, J.E. & Akresh, A.D. (1987). Planning materiality and SAS No. 47. *Journal of Accountancy*, **164**(12), 72–9.

ADDITIONAL READING

Adams, R. (1991). Audit risk. In Sherer, M. & Turley, S. *Current Issues in Auditing*, 2nd ed, Ch 10. London: Paul Chapman Publishing Ltd

Ameen, E.C. & Strawser, J.R. (1994). Investigating the use of analytical procedures: an update and extension. *Auditing: A Journal of Practice & Theory*, **13**(2), 69–76.

Charles, I. (1990). Audit risk, materiality and the examiner. *Accountancy*, **106**(1161), 98–100.

Chase, K.W. (1979). The limits of materiality. *CA Magazine*, **112**(6), 33–7.

Chinn, R. (1996). Crossing the threshold. *Accountancy*, **117**(1231), 123.

Colbert, J.L. (1987, September). Audit risk – tracing the evolution. *Accounting Horizons*, pp. 49–57.

Holder, W.W. & Colmer, S. (1990). Analytical review procedures: New relevance. *CPA Journal*, **50**(11), 29–35.

Lea, R.B., Adams, S.J. & Boykin, R.F. (1992). Modeling of the audit risk assessment process at the assertion level within an account balance. *Auditing: A Journal of Practice & Theory*, **11**(Supp), 152–79.

Lee, T.A. (1984). *Materiality*. Audit Brief. London: Auditing Practices Committee.

McKee, T. (1982). Developments in analytical review. *CPA Journal*, **52**(1), 36–42.

Pratt, M.J. & Dilton-Hill, K. (1982). The elements of audit risk. *The South African Chartered Accountant*, **18**(4), 137–41.

Warren, C.S. (1979). Audit Risk. *The Journal of Accountancy*, **148**(8), 66–74.

Westwick, C. (1981). *Do the Figures Make Sense? A Practical Guide to Analytical Review*. London: Institute of Chartered Accountants in England and Wales.

Chapter 9

Internal Controls and the Auditor

LEARNING OBJECTIVES

After studying the material in this chapter you should be able to:
- explain what is meant by 'an accounting system';
- explain why the accounting system is divided into sub-systems for audit purposes and the basis on which this is done;
- describe the techniques for reviewing and documenting the accounting system and its internal controls;
- explain what is meant by 'a walk through test' and why it is conducted;
- explain how an audit programme is developed;
- explain what is meant by 'an internal control system', 'the control environment' and 'control procedures';
- describe the elements of a good system of internal control;
- describe the objectives of internal accounting controls;
- discuss the inherent limitations of all systems of internal control;
- discuss the importance of the auditor identifying the strengths and weaknesses of the client's system of internal control;
- explain the meaning of the term 'compliance testing';
- describe the audit procedures used for compliance testing.

The following publication is particularly relevant to this chapter:

- Statement of Auditing Standards (SAS) 300: *Accounting and Internal Control Systems and Audit Risk Assessments* (APB, 1995).

9.1   INTRODUCTION

As the auditor has journeyed through the audit process to reach the present stage, (s)he has gained an understanding of the client and its activities, established a desired level of audit risk, defined materiality thresholds, assessed the likelihood of material error being present in the financial statements, and identified the accounts or audit segments where error is most likely to occur (see Appendix, Audit Steps 1–4).

The auditor will now wish to obtain a detailed knowledge of the client's accounting system and evaluate the effectiveness of the system's internal controls. Once the auditor has assessed the level of reliance (s)he can place on the internal controls to eliminate errors from the accounting data, (s)he is able to design the audit programme – that is, plan in detail the nature, timing and extent of audit procedures to be performed during the rest of the audit.

In this chapter we examine what is meant by an accounting system and how the system is segmented for audit purposes. We explore some conceptual aspects of internal control, and discuss how the auditor gains knowledge of the client's accounting system and evaluates its internal controls. We also investigate how the auditor develops an audit programme. Before concluding the chapter we consider the tests the auditor conducts to determine whether the internal controls on which (s)he plans to rely to prevent errors from occurring in the financial statements (and thus to reduce substantive tests) are operating as effectively as his or her preliminary evaluation suggests.

9.2   THE ACCOUNTING SYSTEM

Like all systems, the accounting system has an input, a processing and an output stage, as Figure 9.1 indicates:

- *the input stage* involves capturing a mass of accounting data from either:
  - source documents, which are completed when transactions take place; or
  - memoranda generated by the entity's accountant and which generally record non-transactions data – for example, writing off bad debts and closing adjustments;
- *the processing stage* involves converting the mass of raw data into useful information. This may be achieved using manual, mechanical or, as in most cases today, electronic data processing methods but in each case it is accomplished through recording, classifying and summarising the data;
- *the output stage* involves preparing the accounting information in a form useful to those who wish to use it – that is, appropriately classifying, grouping and heading the information in a meaningful manner.

In order to ensure that all, but only relevant, accounting data are captured as input to the system and to ensure that the data are properly and correctly processed during their conversion into output in the form of financial statements, special checking mechanisms or internal controls are built into the system. The elements and objectives of internal control systems are discussed in section 9.3 below.

The auditor has the task of forming an opinion on whether or not the entity's financial statements give a true and fair view of its financial position and performance.

Figure 9.1 The Accounting System

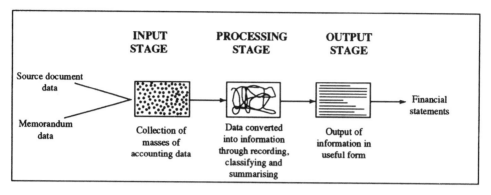

In order to reach this opinion, the auditor needs to understand the system which generates the financial statements – that is, the accounting system and its related internal controls. If the auditor tried to gain this understanding by approaching the entity's accounting system as a single unit, (s)he would find it extremely cumbersome and inefficient. In order to facilitate the audit or to put it on a more practical footing, the auditor (conceptually) dissects the accounting system into sub-systems or audit segments.

The audit segments recognised for any audit vary according to the nature, size and complexity of the audit-client and its activities; however, they are almost invariably based on either transaction categories (such as sales, purchases, administration expenses, long-term loans, etc.) or (more commonly) accounting cycles. When they are based on accounting cycles, groups of closely related accounts and associated transactions are audited as a single unit. As an example of audit segments based on accounting cycles, in an audit of a wholesale or retail business the following segments may be recognised:

- Sales-Debtors-Receipts cycle
- Purchases-Creditors-Payments cycle
- Stock-Warehousing cycle
- Payroll and Personnel cycle
- Financing and Investing cycle.

These audit segments are depicted in Figure 9.2. To illustrate related accounts which constitute audit segments, the accounts comprising the sales-debtors-receipts cycle are shown in Figure 9.3.

It should be noted that, until audit segments are identified during the review of the entity's accounting system, the audit is approached holistically. As is shown in Figure 9.2, the auditor gains an understanding of the client and its activities, establishes a desired level of audit risk, defines materiality thresholds, and assesses the likelihood of material error being present in the financial statements, based on the client as a whole. Once audit segments have been recognised, obtaining detailed knowledge of the accounting system, evaluating and testing its internal controls, and assessing the accuracy, validity and completeness of financial statement balances, revolve around particular audit segments. When the detailed segment-based work is complete, the auditor reviews as a whole the evidence gathered in the segments, and conducts the remaining audit procedures on an entity-wide basis. These final steps of the audit constitute the review and completion stage which is discussed in Chapter 12.

Figure 9.2   Steps in the Audit Process Conducted on an Entity-wide and Audit Segment Basis

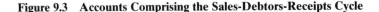

Figure 9.3   Accounts Comprising the Sales-Debtors-Receipts Cycle

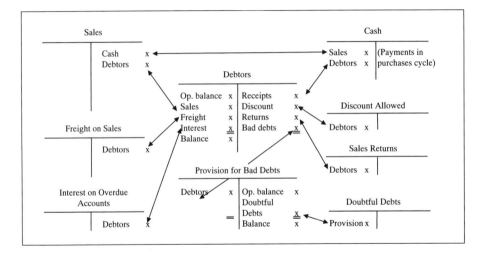

9.3 CONCEPTUAL ASPECTS OF INTERNAL CONTROL

9.3.1 Meaning of 'Internal Control' and 'Internal Control System'

When an entity is small, its owner or manager can personally perform, or directly oversee, all of the entity's functions. However, as the entity grows larger it becomes necessary to delegate functional responsibilities to employees. Once this occurs, mechanisms need to be introduced which enable the performance of the employees to be checked, to ensure they are fulfilling their responsibilities as intended. As Anderson (1977) explains:

> With the best of intentions, most people make mistakes. The mistakes may be errors in the end results of their work, needless inefficiencies in achieving those end results, or both. And sometimes, without the best of intentions, a few people deliberately falsify. Any organisation wishing to conduct its business in an orderly and efficient manner and to produce reliable financial accounting information, both for its own and for others' use, needs some controls to minimise the effects of these endemic human failings. When such controls are implemented within the organisation's systems they are described as internal controls . . . . (p.143)

It is significant that Anderson refers to internal controls as controls which are implemented within the *organisation's* systems rather than within its *accounting* system. This recognises the fact that internal controls are mechanisms designed to control *all* of an entity's functions, not just its accounting function. The wide application of the term is reflected in the definition of internal control proposed by the Committee of Sponsoring Organisations of the Treadway Commission (COSO, 1992):

> Internal control is broadly defined as a process, effected by an entity's board of directors, management and other personnel, designed to provide reasonable assurance regarding the achievement of objectives in the following categories:
>
> - Effectiveness and efficiency of operations.
> - Reliability of financial reporting.
> - Compliance with applicable laws and regulations.
>
> The first category addresses an entity's basic business objectives, including performance and profitability goals and safeguarding of resources. The second relates to the preparation of reliable published financial statements, including interim and condensed financial statements and selected financial data derived from such statements, such as earnings releases, reported publicly. The third deals with complying with those laws and regulations to which the entity is subject. (p.1)

To avoid confusion, it is useful to use different terms to distinguish between the broadly defined 'internal control process' (see COSO above) and the more focused internal control procedures. We have adopted the terms 'internal control system' and 'internal controls' (or 'internal control procedures'), respectively.

An 'internal control system' embraces both the control environment and internal control procedures. As Statement of Auditing Standards (SAS) 300: *Accounting and Internal Control Systems and Risk Assessments* explains:

> It includes all the policies and procedures (internal controls) adopted by the directors and management of an entity to assist in achieving their objective of ensuring, as far as practicable, the orderly and efficient conduct of its business, including adherence to internal policies, the safeguarding of assets, the prevention and detection of fraud and

error, the accuracy and completeness of the accounting records, and the timely preparation of reliable financial information. (para 8)

'Control environment' means the overall attitude, awareness and actions of directors and management regarding internal controls and their importance in the entity. The control environment . . . provides the background against which the various other controls are operated. . . . Factors reflected in the control environment include:
- the philosophy and operating style of the directors and management;
- the entity's organisational structure and methods of assigning authority and responsibility . . .; and
- the directors' methods of imposing control, including the internal audit function, the functions of the board of directors and personnel policies and procedures. (para 9)

'Control procedures' are those policies and procedures in addition to the control environment which are established to achieve the entity's specific objectives. They include in particular procedures designed to prevent or to detect and correct errors . . . Specific control procedures include:
- approval and control of documents;
- controls over computerised applications . . .;
- checking the arithmetical accuracy of the records;
- maintaining and reviewing control accounts and trial balances;
- reconciliations;
- comparing the results of cash, security and stock counts with accounting records;
- comparing internal data with external sources of information; and
- limiting direct physical access to assets and records. (para 10)

Where entities have internal auditors, these auditors are generally responsible for implementing, monitoring and maintaining all aspects of the internal control system. However, although external auditors need to be familiar with the internal control system and need to evaluate the quality of the control environment, they are primarily concerned with the internal controls which relate to the accounting function – in particular, those relating to safeguarding of assets and the provision of reliable financial statements.

9.3.2 Elements of a Good Internal Control System

If an entity's control environment possesses certain characteristics and certain control procedures are present, it is highly likely that the entity's assets will be adequately safeguarded and that its accounting data (and thus its financial statements) will be reliable. These control elements are as follows:

(i)   competent, reliable personnel who possess integrity;
(ii)   clearly defined areas of authority and responsibility;
(iii)   proper authorisation procedures;
(iv)   adequate documentation;
(v)   segregation of incompatible duties;
(vi)   independent checks on performance;
(vii) physical safeguarding of assets.

(i)   *Competent, reliable personnel who possess integrity*:   The most important factor in safeguarding an entity's assets and in securing reliable accounting data is the quality of the entity's personnel. If employees are competent, they are able to perform their duties efficiently and effectively; if they are also reliable and possess integrity, they will perform their duties carefully and honestly. Indeed, if this control element is satisfied, it is probable that the entity's assets will remain safe and its accounting data will be free of material errors, even if the other elements are missing or weak.

(ii) *Clearly defined areas of authority and responsibility*: Irrespective of how competent and reliable an entity's personnel may be, in order to ensure that all necessary tasks are performed – and performed in an efficient, timely manner – it is important that the authority and responsibility of each employee are clearly defined. This not only ensures that employees know what is expected of them, it also facilitates pinpointing responsibility in cases where tasks are not performed properly. Such identification of responsibility motivates employees to work carefully and also enables management to ascertain where corrective action is required.

(iii) *Proper authorisation procedures*: In order to safeguard its assets, an entity must have proper authorisation procedures. In other words, procedures must be established which ensure that all transactions are initiated or approved by a person who has the requisite authority. For example, an entity may establish procedures for approving credit sales whereby:

- all credit sales have to be authorised in writing by the credit manager before the goods are sold;
- the credit manager has discretion to extend credit to individual customers up to a maximum of, say, £5,000;
- if the £5,000 limit is to be exceeded, written authority for this to happen must be obtained from the managing director.

Similarly, a purchases manager may be granted authority to purchase stocks and/or supplies up to the value of a specified amount, or a departmental manager may be authorised to purchase capital equipment for his or her department up to a specified value. If the purchases or departmental manager wish to exceed their authorised limit, they must seek approval to do so from a higher authority, such as a divisional manager, managing director or the Board of Directors (depending on the procedures established in the entity).

It should be noted that delegating spending authority to the purchasing or departmental manager is not the same as delegating general authority to the relevant department *per se*. Members of a department can only enter transactions on behalf of the entity to the extent that they are authorised to do so by their departmental head.

(iv) *Adequate documentation*: If an entity is to secure reliable accounting data and to safeguard its assets, it is essential that it maintains adequate documents and records. This includes ensuring that:

- the entity's documents (such as order forms, receiving reports, sales invoices, receipts, and payments vouchers) are pre-numbered consecutively and are designed

so that they may be completed easily and fully at the time the transaction takes place;
- every transaction is supported by a source document;
- all accounting entries are supported by a source document (for transactions) or a memorandum generated by the entity's accountant (for non-transactions, such as closing adjustments and writing off bad debts);
- authorisations are supported by written evidence;
- an adequate chart of accounts is maintained to facilitate recording transactions in the correct accounts;
- adequate procedures manuals and job descriptions are maintained to ensure that employees:
  - know (or can find out) the procedures to follow when undertaking organisational activities; and
  - are aware of the requirements of their own position in the entity and how this relates to the duties attaching to associated positions.

(v) *Segregation of incompatible duties*: When defining areas of responsibility and assigning tasks to employees, it is essential that incompatible duties are vested in different people. In particular:

- no one person should have custody of assets and also maintain the records of those assets. For example, the cashier (who handles money) should not record cash received or paid. If the same person performs these duties (s)he is able to steal cash and cover his or her traces by making appropriate adjustments in the cash records;
- no one person should have custody of assets and also authorise transactions relating to those assets; for example, the stores manager should not be given the task of authorising purchases or sales of items under his or her control because if these tasks are vested in the same person it enables that person to obtain assets for his or her personal benefit by authorising fictitious transactions;
- no one person should have responsibility for all of the entries in the accounting records. Careful allocation of accounting duties enables the work of different employees to be arranged so that the work of one automatically cross-checks the work of another and this facilitates the detection of unintentional errors.

(vi) *Independent checks on performance*: Even if personnel are competent, reliable and trustworthy, and their responsibilities are clearly defined and carefully assigned so as to avoid one person performing incompatible duties, there remains the possibility that errors will occur. All employees are humans, not robots, and humans are prone to make mistakes. Unintentional errors may occur, for example, as a result of tiredness, boredom, or failure to concentrate fully on the task in hand. On occasions, employees may become careless in following defined procedures, or may deliberately fail to do so, either because they perceive an 'easier' way to accomplish the task or because they wish to defraud the entity. In any event, if accounting data are to be reliable and the entity's assets are to be safeguarded, it is important that independent checks on employees' performance take place.

One means of achieving these checks is to assign accounting duties so that the work of one employee automatically cross-checks the work of another. For example, one accounts clerk may maintain the Debtors Subsidiary Ledger and another the Debtors Control account in the General Ledger. Similarly, before preparing a cheque, the payments clerk may be required to match the supplier's invoice with a copy of the relevant order form (from the purchases department) and receiving note (from the receiving department), to check for authorised signatures on the order form and receiving note, and to verify and reconcile the items, quantities and monetary amounts shown on the documents. In other situations, two employees may be involved in a single task, so that each provides a check on the performance of the other; for example, two employees may be involved in opening the mail when it is expected to contain remittances from debtors. A further means of checking employees' performance is for supervisors to review the work of subordinates; for example, the financial controller may review journal and ledger entries and completed bank reconciliations.

(vii) *Physical safeguarding of assets*: As noted above, one of the key objectives of an internal control system is to safeguard the entity's assets. The most effective way to achieve this objective is to provide physical protection for assets, combined with restricted access. For example, stocks and supplies may be stored in a locked storeroom with access restricted to a limited number of authorised personnel; cash, cheques, marketable securities and similar items may be kept in a fireproof safe, with few personnel having access to the safe keys or being privy to the combination lock number; the entity's land and buildings may be protected by such things as fences, locked entry doors, closed circuit television, burglar and fire alarms, smoke detectors, water sprinklers and similar devices.

An entity's legal, accounting and other documents are important components of its assets and should be protected in the same way as its other assets, that is, facilities should be provided for their safekeeping and access should be strictly limited to authorised personnel. Additionally, back-up copies should be kept of entity information generated or stored in computers, and emergency use of computer facilities should be arranged in case the entity's system should fail. Internal controls in an IT environment are discussed in Chapter 14.

It was noted in section 9.3.1 above that internal controls become necessary only when an entity grows beyond the size at which the owner or manager can personally perform or oversee all of the entity's functions, and functional responsibilities have to be delegated to employees. It follows from this, that the extent of internal controls and their degree of formalisation are likely to vary according to the size of the entity. However, once functional responsibilities are delegated to employees, it is necessary to institute internal controls and, irrespective of the entity's size, if the seven elements of a good system of internal control (outlined above) are present, then it is likely that the entity's assets will be adequately safeguarded and its accounting data will be reliable.

9.3.3 Objectives of Internal Accounting Controls

As explained in section 9.2 above, an entity's accounting system is designed to capture accounting data and to convert and output this data as useful financial information. In order for financial information to be useful, it must be reliable. Thus, the underlying accounting data must be valid, complete and accurate. To secure data which meets these criteria, internal controls are built into the accounting system. These controls, which we refer to as 'internal accounting controls', are designed, in particular, to ensure that transactions which give rise to the accounting data are:

- properly recorded – that is, all relevant details of transactions are recorded at the time the transactions take place;
- properly authorised – that is, all transactions are authorised by a person with the requisite authority;
- valid – that is, transactions recorded in the accounting system represent genuine exchanges with *bona fide* parties;
- complete – that is, all genuine transactions are input to the accounting system; none are omitted;
- properly valued – that is, transactions are recorded at their correct exchange value;
- properly classified – that is, transactions are recorded in the correct accounts;
- recorded in the correct accounting period.

If these seven internal accounting control objectives are met, it is probable that the information presented in the financial statements will be reliable. If the seven elements of a good internal control system are present (as outlined in section 9.3.2 above), then it is likely that the internal accounting control objectives will be met.

9.3.4 Inherent Limitations of Internal Control Systems

Irrespective of how well designed an internal control system may be and how effectively it operates, it will always possess inherent limitations. These may be illustrated by the following examples:

1. The extent of an entity's internal control procedures depends on their cost-effectiveness. Beyond some point, the cost of instituting additional controls will exceed the benefits to be gained from more accurate accounting data or increased safeguarding of assets. There is, for example, little point in installing a £10,000 surveillance system to prevent the theft of, say, one 20p biro each week!
2. Internal controls are designed to prevent and detect errors and irregularities in the normal, frequently recurring transactions. However, errors are more likely to occur in relation to infrequent, unusual transactions – for the very reason that they are unusual.
3. The potential for error is always present because accounting personnel are human and therefore prone to make mistakes. Thus, internal controls may not always operate as intended.
4. There is the possibility that management will override the controls; alternatively, there may be collusion between two or more employees which results in the controls being circumvented.
5. Internal control procedures may become inadequate or inappropriate as a result of changes in the entity's internal and/or external environment and, as a consequence, compliance with the controls may deteriorate.

Because of the inherent limitations of all internal control systems, irrespective of how 'perfect' a system may appear to be, an auditor can never rely on the system to prevent and/or detect *all* material errors and irregularities in the accounting data. (S)he will always have to evaluate, at least to some extent, the accuracy, validity and completeness of the information presented in the financial statements; that is, some substantive audit procedures will always be necessary.

9.3.5 Significance of Internal Controls to the Auditor

External auditors are not responsible for establishing or maintaining an entity's internal control system: that is the responsibility of the entity's management. Nevertheless, the quality of the internal controls can, and usually does, have a significant impact on the audit.

If the internal control system is well designed (if it contains the seven elements of a good system of internal control, as outlined in section 9.3.2) and if it operates effectively to meet the seven internal accounting control objectives set out in section 9.3.3, then the auditor will gain a high level of assurance that any material errors or irregularities which might be present in the accounting data will be eliminated as the data passes through the accounting system. Thus, the auditor will feel fairly confident that the financial statements are free of material misstatement. Expressed in terms of audit risk, where an entity has a well designed and effective internal control system, the risk of material errors in the accounting data not being eliminated (that is, internal control risk) will be fairly low. However, as noted earlier, as a result of the inherent limitations of all internal control systems, this risk can never be reduced to zero. As demonstrated in Chapter 8, when inherent risk and internal control risk are low, there is little likelihood of material error being present in the (unaudited) financial statements and, as a result, substantive procedures need not be extensive.

However, if an entity's internal control system is poorly designed and is ineffective in meeting the internal accounting control objectives, the auditor will gain little assurance that the financial statements are free of material error (that is, internal control risk will be assessed as high.) As a consequence, before a 'clean' audit report can be issued, the auditor will need to conduct extensive substantive tests in order to gain sufficient assurance that the financial statements are, in fact, free of material misstatement (see Chapter 8, section 8.6).

9.4 REVIEWING THE ACCOUNTING SYSTEM AND EVALUATING ITS INTERNAL CONTROLS

9.4.1 Introduction to the Review and Evaluation of Accounting Systems

In section 9.2 above, it was pointed out that, in order to facilitate the audit, the auditor (conceptually) divides an entity's accounting system into sub-systems or audit segments. The auditor then conducts his or her detailed audit examination based on these audit segments.

As the starting point of the detailed examination, the auditor seeks to understand and to document the entity's accounting sub-systems, and to conduct a preliminary evaluation of the related internal controls.

9.4.2 Understanding the Accounting Sub-systems

The auditor gains an initial understanding of each of the accounting sub-systems and related internal controls primarily through the following audit procedures:

(i) *Enquiries of client personnel*: The auditor asks questions of relevant personnel from management, supervisory and staff levels of the audit-client about various aspects of the sub-system. For example, (s)he enquires how accounting data are captured and input to the accounting sub-system and how the data are recorded, classified and summarised within the sub-system. The auditor also makes enquiries as to which employees are responsible for what duties, how employees know what to do, how much guidance is provided by procedures manuals and similar documents, and what reviews of employees' work take place.

(ii) *Inspection of client documents*: The auditor gains significant insight into the structure and operation of the accounting sub-system by consulting the client's documents. S(he) examines, for example, the entity's organisation chart, the chart of accounts and guidance given on account classification of transactions, and the client's policies and procedures manuals insofar as they relate to the accounting sub-system. The auditor also inspects more detailed documents such as source documents, journals, ledgers and trial balances, and discusses the various documents with client personnel to ascertain how well they are used and understood.

(iii) *Observation of client personnel*: In addition to asking client personnel about their various duties and inspecting documents which specify the duties which should be performed, the auditor observes personnel at various levels of the organisation carrying out their normal accounting and review functions.

9.4.3 Documenting the Accounting Sub-systems

Once the auditor has gained a preliminary understanding of the accounting sub-system, (s)he documents that understanding. Two primary forms of documentation are used:

(i) narrative descriptions;
(ii) flowcharts.

(i) *Narrative Descriptions*

A narrative description is a detailed description of accounting routines which take place within an accounting sub-system. An example of part of a narrative description from the purchases–creditors–payments cycle is provided in Figure 9.4.

Figure 9.4   Narrative Description of Part of a Purchases-Creditors-Payments Cycle

> When the issue of a regular item of stock results in the re-order point for that stock item being reached, the Stores Department prepares a two-part requisition. The requisition is authorised by the manager or assistant manager of the department. Copy 1 of the approved requisition is sent to the Purchasing Department. Copy 2 is filed by requisition form number. The filed copy is subsequently matched with the purchases order (Copy 2) and receiving report (Copy 2). Discrepancies between goods requested, ordered and received are reported (by memorandum) to the Purchasing Department, Receiving Department and Creditors Ledger clerk. A copy of the memorandum is filed with the relevant documents.
>
> On receiving the approved requisition (Copy 1), the Purchasing Department prepares a five-part purchase order. Copy 1 is sent to the supplier, Copy 2 is sent to the Stores Department (see above), Copy 3 is filed by order form number, Copy 4 is sent to the Receiving Department, and Copy 5, together with approved requisition (Copy 1), is sent to the Creditors Ledger clerk.
>
> The Receiving Department files the purchase order (by number) pending the arrival of the goods. On arrival, the goods are inspected and counted and compared with the purchase order. A three-part receiving report is prepared. Copy 1 of the receiving report is sent to the Creditors Ledger clerk, Copy 2 is sent to the Stores Department (see above) and Copy 3 is filed, together with purchase order (Copy 4), by receiving report number . . .

A narrative description should include details of:

(a) all of the documents which are used in the accounting routine. For example, in a purchases routine the narrative description should refer to order forms, receiving reports, suppliers' invoices and credit notes, payments vouchers, etc.; the description should detail how each document is initiated, the steps through which it passes between initiation and filing, where and how it is filed (for example, alphabetically or by date), whether it is matched with related documents before filing, and who is responsible for preparing, reviewing, using and filing the document;

(b) all of the processes which take place within the routine: for example, what triggers goods to be ordered, how a supplier is selected, how quantities to be ordered are determined, how price is ascertained, how goods received are checked against goods ordered, how discrepancies between goods ordered and received are handled, and so on;

(c) internal control procedures: the narrative should refer to internal control procedures such as the segregation of incompatible duties, authorisation procedures, procedures which provide independent checks on performance, and asset and record safeguards (for example, use of locked storerooms and fireproof safes, and access being restricted to authorised personnel, etc.)

As a means of documenting the entity's accounting sub-systems, compared to flowcharts, narrative descriptions are generally less time-consuming and less technically demanding to prepare. However, they do not convey the sequence of processes or document flows as clearly as flowcharts, they are time-consuming to read, they may be difficult to comprehend, and the key points may not be readily apparent.

Narrative descriptions are appropriate for describing simple accounting routines or sub-systems, but their use requires a careful balance to be maintained between giving sufficient detail to provide an adequate description, and giving too much detail which mitigates clarity and ease of comprehension. Narrative descriptions are frequently used, and are useful, as supplements to flowcharts; to expand on elements of a flowchart where additional detail or explanation is considered necessary.

(ii) *Flowcharts*

A flowchart is a diagrammatic representation of the flow of documents or information through an accounting sub-system and the processes which take place in the system. An example of a flowchart of part of a purchases-creditors-payments cycle is presented in Figure 9.5.[1] (The flowcharting symbols used are shown in Figure 9.6.)

The prime advantages of a flowchart are the clear overview of the accounting system it provides and the ease with which internal control strengths and weaknesses can be identified. Compared with a narrative description, a flowchart is easier to read and understand and, when changes are made to the accounting system, it is easier to update. However, on the downside, a flowchart is time-consuming and technically demanding to prepare and its preparation is, therefore, costly.

9.4.4 Walk Through Test

Once the auditor has documented his or her understanding of the accounting sub-system, (s)he will test this understanding against the system itself. This is achieved by means of a 'walk through test' (also known as a 'cradle to the grave test'). One or two transactions of each major type (for example, credit sales, credit purchases, cash received, cash paid) are traced through the entire accounting system, from its initial recording at source to its final destination as a component of an account balance in the financial statements.

It should be remembered that a walk through test is not an audit procedure designed to test financial statement balances: instead, it is a procedure designed to confirm (or correct) the auditor's understanding of the flow of transactions data through the client's accounting system and the accuracy of the auditor's documents (narrative description and/or flowcharts) recording the system.

9.4.5 Evaluating Internal Controls

SAS 300: *Accounting and Internal Control Systems and Audit Risk Assessments* requires auditors to gain an understanding of the client's accounting system and control environment, and to evaluate and test, as appropriate, the operation of those internal

---

[1] The narrative description provided in Figure 9.4 describes part of the system depicted in Figure 9.5. This is for illustrative purposes only. In practical situations one or other method would be adopted to represent the system. However, this is not to say that one form may not be used to supplement the other. For example, a narrative description may be provided to clarify an element of a flowchart. Similarly, a flowchart component may be used to clarify a point in a narrative description.

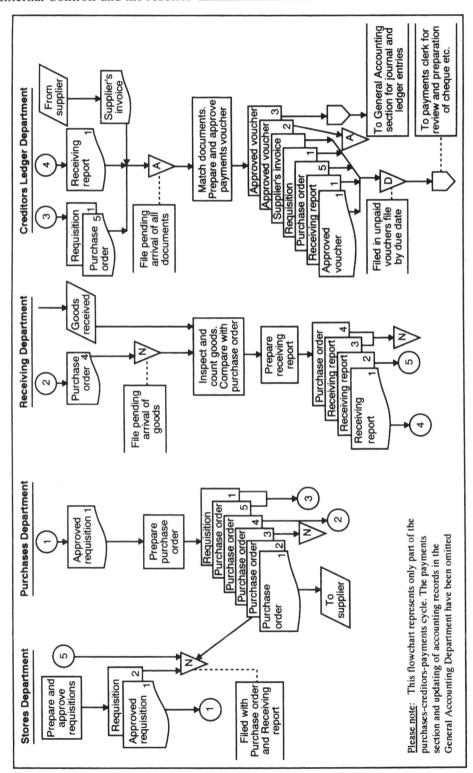

Please note:: This flowchart represents only part of the purchases-creditors-payments cycle. The payments section and updating of accounting records in the General Accounting Department have been omitted

Figure 9.6   Basic Flowcharting Symbols

GENERAL SYMBOLS

Document - paper documents and reports of all types or 'pro forma' documents prepared on a computer screen.

Process Symbol - any processing function. A defined operation which involves some action by a person or the computer.
Examples: Prepare purchase order; prepare cheque for payment.

Off-line Storage - files of paper documents and records, or records kept in computer.
N,D,A indicates order of filing: N = Numeric; D = Date; A = Alphabetic.
Examples: Purchase orders filed numerically; payments vouchers prepared for payment filed by due date.

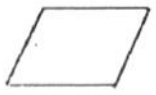

Input/Output Symbol - indicates information entering or leaving the system.
Examples: Purchase order sent to supplier; receipt of customer order.

On-page Connector - exit to/entry from another part of the flowchart.
Example: Document transferred from one department to another.

Directional Flowlines - direction of processing, or data (document) flow, or transmission of information through a computer network.

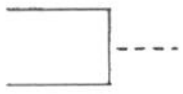

Annotation - descriptive comments or explanatory notes.
Example: 'File pending arrival of all documents'.

Off-page Connector - exit to/entry from another page of the flowchart.

control procedures upon which reliance is to be placed to reduce potentially costly substantive testing. It states:

> In planning the audit, auditors should obtain and document an understanding of the accounting system and control environment sufficient to determine their audit approach. (para 16)

> If auditors, after obtaining an understanding of the accounting system and control environment, expect to be able to rely on their assessment of [internal] control risk to reduce the extent of their substantive procedures, they should make a preliminary assessment of [internal] control risk for material financial statement assertions, and should plan and perform tests of control [compliance tests] to support that assessment. (para 27)

It is clear that auditors are not only required to gain an understanding of their clients' accounting sub-systems – the documents, processes and personnel involved, and the part played by each – they are also required to evaluate the internal accounting controls within the sub-systems. The purpose of this evaluation is to identify strengths and weaknesses in the internal accounting controls.

• *Strengths* are internal controls which operate effectively to prevent or detect errors and irregularities in the accounting data which pass through the control point. They are the controls on which the auditor may rely to prevent material misstatement from occurring in the financial statements and thus to reduce substantive tests.

• *Weaknesses* are points in the accounting system which are prone to errors or irregularities but effective controls to prevent or detect such occurrences are absent.
  Evaluation of the entity's internal control procedures involves two steps:

(i) gathering information about the procedures;
(ii) evaluating their effectiveness in preventing and detecting errors.

(i) Gathering Information

The primary means of gathering information about an entity's internal control procedures is an internal control questionnaire (ICQ). This consists of a series of questions relating to control procedures which are normally considered necessary to prevent or detect errors and irregularities occurring in each major type of transaction. The questions are usually phrased so that they require a 'yes' or 'no' response. As a result, ICQs are generally simple and quick to complete. A useful way to organise the questions, so as to ensure good coverage of each audit segment, is to link them to the internal accounting control objectives outlined in section 9.3.3 above. An example of part of an ICQ prepared on this basis, relating to purchase transactions, is presented in Figure 9.7.
  It should be noted that, although gathering information about the internal controls has been presented here as an audit step subsequent to the auditor gaining an understanding of, and documenting, the client's accounting system, ICQs are commonly completed during the 'understanding and documenting' stage.

(ii) Assessing the Adequacy of Internal Controls

Once information about the client's internal controls has been gathered, the auditor evaluates the adequacy of the controls. In conducting this evaluation the auditor considers, in particular:

• the errors and irregularities that could occur in each audit segment;
• whether effective control procedures are present to prevent or detect such occurrences;
• where effective control procedures appear to be absent, whether there are compensating controls which overcome the internal control weakness.

9.4.6 Internal Control Evaluation and Audit Planning

The purpose of evaluating the client's internal control procedures is to determine whether the auditor can rely on the procedures to prevent material misstatement from occurring in the financial statements. This, in turn, affects the nature, timing and extent of audit tests.

Figure 9.7   Part of an ICQ Relating to the Purchases-Creditors-Payments Cycle

Internal Control Questionnaire				Ref: C-4
Purchases				
Client: Jasper Limited		Prepared by: RB		Date: 12/12/x6
Period: Year to 31 March 19x7		Reviewed by: MC		Date: 15/12/x6

Control Procedure	Yes	No	N/A	Remarks
1. Are pre-numbered requisitions used to initiate purchase orders?	✓			
2. Are numbered requisitions accounted for?	✓			Copies are filed numerically. Cancelled requisitions also filed (crossed to indicate cancellation).
3. Are requisitions approved by a responsible official?	✓			Manager or Assistant Manager of Stores Department
4. Is access to blank requisitions limited to authorised personnel?		✓		All Stores Department employees have access
5. Can purchase orders be prepared without a requisition?		✓		
6. Are purchase orders pre-numbered?	✓			
7. Are all numbers accounted for?	✓			Copies are filed numerically (including cancelled order forms)
8. Are purchase orders prepared by a responsible official?	✓			Manager or Assistant Manager of Purchasing Department
9. Is access to blank purchase orders restricted to authorised personnel?	✓			
10. Do all purchase orders show: (a) Quantities ordered? (b) Prices of goods ordered? (c) Special terms of the order? (d) Initials of preparer? (e) Date of preparation?	✓ ✓ ✓ ✓ ✓			
11. Is there a limit to the value of goods that may be ordered?	✓			Maximum order size £5,000
12. Is a copy of the purchase order sent to: (a) Stores Department? (b) Receiving Department? (c) Creditors Ledger Clerk?	✓ ✓ ✓			

The more reliable the internal controls (that is, the lower the level of internal control risk) , the less likely it is that material misstatement will be present in the financial statements and, as a result, the less extensive the substantive audit tests need to be. However, before the auditor can rely on internal control procedures to eliminate material error from the financial statements, (s)he must test them to obtain evidence that they are working as effectively as his or her preliminary evaluation suggests, and that they have been so working throughout the reporting period. Therefore, the greater the reliance the auditor plans to place on internal controls, the more extensive the compliance tests which need to be performed.

Further, when the auditor considers that internal controls are reliable, a significant proportion of the audit procedures may be conducted during an interim audit, that is, about three months prior to year end. This enables the audit to be completed in a timely manner following the end of the financial year. It also facilitates efficient scheduling of audit work (and thus audit staff) over the calendar year and avoids 'bottlenecks' occurring when the balance sheet dates of a number of audit-clients coincide.

It can be seen that, when an auditor considers a client's internal controls can be relied upon, compliance procedures will be given greater emphasis, total audit testing will be less extensive, and more audit procedures will be conducted during an interim audit, than would otherwise be the case. Thus, the auditor's evaluation of the client's internal controls clearly has a direct impact on audit planning and, once the evaluation is complete, the auditor proceeds to develop the audit programme.

When considering the detailed audit procedures to be included in the audit programme, the following points need to be borne in mind:

1. Irrespective of how effective a client's internal controls may appear to be, the auditor may not rely upon them to reduce substantive procedures until they have been tested and found to be operating effectively and operating in this manner throughout the reporting period. This may appear to preclude the planning of substantive procedures until compliance testing is complete. However, such a delay would introduce inefficiencies into the audit process. As a consequence, the auditor may proceed to develop the audit programme on the assumption that the internal control procedures on which (s)he plans to rely operate generally as described and that they have functioned effectively throughout the reporting period. Nevertheless, the auditor must remain alert to the possibility that compliance tests may reveal that internal control procedures are not as effective as was first thought, and adjustments to the audit programme may be necessary.

2. Although particular internal controls may appear to be operating effectively, the auditor may decide not to rely on them to reduce substantive procedures because (s)he considers that the audit effort required to test compliance with the controls is likely to exceed the reduction in effort (in terms of reduced substantive testing) that would be achieved through reliance upon the controls. In this case, no testing of the relevant controls is undertaken and internal control risk is assumed to be high (see SAS 300, para 28).

9.5   DEVELOPING THE AUDIT PROGRAMME

The audit programme consists of a set of detailed audit procedures designed to meet the specific audit objectives of each audit segment. According to SAS 200: *Planning:*

> an audit programme . . . sets out the audit procedures the auditors intend to adopt and includes reference to other matters such as the audit objectives, timing, sample size and basis of selection for each area. It serves as a set of instructions to the audit team and as a means to control and record the proper execution of the work. (para 15)

The audit programme is usually prepared in two stages as follows:

(i)   planning format;
(ii) performance format.

(i)   *Planning Format*

In this stage, the audit objectives for each class of transactions and each financial statement balance within an audit segment are identified. For example, audit objectives for purchase transactions might be as follows:
Ascertaining whether:

• purchase transactions are recorded;
• purchase transactions are authorised;
• recorded purchase transactions are valid;
• recorded purchase transactions are complete;
• purchase transactions are properly classified;
• purchase transactions are stated at their correct amount;
• purchase transactions are recorded in their correct accounting period.

Based on the auditor's understanding of the client, the results of overall analytical review procedures, and his or her preliminary evaluation of the client's internal controls, the auditor determines how each identified audit objective is best met through compliance and/or substantive procedures, and identifies the specific procedure(s) to be performed. Certain procedures may be identified as appropriate for meeting more than one objective.
This process is repeated systematically for each audit segment.

(ii) *Performance Format*

Once the lists of audit procedures to be performed have been compiled, the procedures are arranged in a logical sequence and any overlapping procedures are eliminated. This results in a list of audit procedures which are set out in a manner suitable for their performance. This is the audit programme.

The final document specifies for each audit segment:
• the audit objectives to be met;
• the procedures (both compliance and substantive procedures) to be performed to meet the stated objectives;

- the timing of the procedures – that is, whether they are to be performed during the interim or final (year end) audit.

An example of part of an audit programme relating to purchase transactions is presented in Figure 9.8.

Review of Audit Programme

The audit programme is not a document which is prepared near the commencement of an audit and then followed slavishly. Rather, it is kept under continuous review. Its adequacy and appropriateness are re-evaluated as evidence is gathered, and it is revised as and when this is found to be necessary.

9.6 COMPLIANCE TESTING

9.6.1 Purpose of Compliance Procedures

During the preliminary evaluation of the client's internal controls, the auditor identifies internal control strengths – that is, internal control procedures which appear to be operating effectively to meet certain audit objectives. Two examples are set out below.

Audit objective	Internal control procedures meeting audit objective
1. Sales transactions are properly authorised.	The credit manager approves all credit sales before goods leave the premises and initials the sales document to indicate approval.
2. Sales transactions are properly valued.	All sales invoices are checked (prices are checked against price lists, and extensions and additions are checked) by an independent person, prior to the invoice being sent to the customer. The 'checker' initials the invoice to indicate that it has been checked.

Irrespective of how effective internal controls may appear to be, before the auditor can rely on them to eliminate errors and irregularities from the accounting data, their effectiveness must be confirmed through compliance procedures. When performing these procedures, particular attention needs to be given to the possibility that deviations from the internal controls may occur as a result of staff changes in key control functions – for example, a change of credit manager. Such staff changes may be permanent or temporary; they may occur, for example, during the holiday period. Care must be taken to ensure that compliance procedures cover these periods.

9.6.2 Types of Compliance Procedures

Compliance procedures fall into two main categories:

(i) those performed where the internal control procedures leave no audit trail;
(ii) those performed where an audit trail is left.

Figure 9.8   Part of an Audit Programme for Purchase Transactions

	Procedure	Completed by	Date	Workpaper Ref
1	*Test sequence of purchase orders.* Randomly select five purchase orders from total. Test number sequence – five forwards and five backwards.			
2	*Test purchase order approval.*			
3	*Test adherence to authority limits and compatibility with nature of client's business.* Randomly select 25 purchase orders: (i) Vouch for initials of purchasing officer. (ii) Compare value of order with authorised limit. (iii) Evaluate compatibility of goods ordered with nature of client's business.			
4	*Test sequence of receiving reports.* Randomly select five receiving reports from total. Test number sequence – five forwards and five backwards.			
5	*Test for matching of purchase orders with receiving reports.* Randomly select 25 receiving reports: (i) Check for matching with purchase orders. (ii) Vouch for independent check of items and quantities ordered and received.			
6	*Test sequence of purchase returns records.* Randomly select three purchases returns records. Test number sequence – five forwards and five backwards.			
7	*Test for matching of purchases returns records and suppliers' credit notes.* Randomly select 15 purchases returns records: (i) Check for matching with credit notes. (ii) Vouch for independent check of items and quantities returned and credited.			
8	*Test suppliers' invoices and payments vouchers.* Randomly select 25 payments vouchers: (i) Check for matching with – supplier's invoice – purchase order – receiving report – purchase returns report – supplier's credit note. (ii) Vouch supplier's invoice for evidence of independent check of: – items, quantities and prices of goods ordered and received – extensions and footings. (iii) Vouch payments vouchers for: – account classification shown – evidence of independent check of: • amount of payment • account codes. (iv) Test accuracy of amounts and account classifications: – recalculate extensions and footings on supplier's invoices and credit notes – recalculate VAT on invoices and credit notes – check propriety of account codes.			
9	*Review all outstanding purchase orders at year end.* Check for goods in transit at year end. • • •			

(i) *Procedures where the Internal Controls Leave No Audit Trail*

The primary compliance procedures performed where the internal controls leave no audit trail are enquiry and observation. For example, in order to ascertain whether the controls which are designed to secure the segregation of incompatible duties are being complied with, the auditor will enquire and observe which personnel perform what duties, and when and how these duties are performed. In order to determine whether controls designed to protect assets and records are being complied with, the auditor will observe if access to restricted areas is limited to authorised personnel.

(ii) *Procedures where the Internal Controls Leave an Audit Trail*

Where an audit trail is available (that is, where there is tangible evidence that a control procedure has or has not been performed) the primary audit tests are the vouching of source documents and inspection of other documents. For example, source documents are vouched for evidence of compliance with authorisation procedures and independent verification of prices, quantities, extensions and additions (such as the initials of the person performing the control procedure.) Similarly, other documents, such as reconciliations, journals and ledgers, are inspected for evidence indicating that independent review procedures have been performed.

9.6.3 Follow-up to Compliance Procedures

On the basis of the results of compliance procedures, the auditor will either:

- accept that the internal controls (or certain controls) are effective and reliable; or
- reject them as not operating effectively. In this situation the auditor should ascertain whether there is another relevant control on which reliance might be placed (after applying appropriate compliance procedures). Alternatively, the auditor should modify the nature, timing and/or extent of substantive audit procedures. Such modification will require the audit programme to be adjusted.

9.7 REPORTING INTERNAL CONTROL WEAKNESSES TO MANAGEMENT

Weaknesses identified in the internal control system (that is, points in the accounting system where errors and irregularities could arise and/or be present but not detected) are not tested by the auditor. The controls are absent or ineffective and therefore they cannot be relied upon to meet audit objectives. However, the auditor does not ignore them. Identified internal control weaknesses are reported to management or to the audit committee (if the entity has one) at the earliest opportunity,[2]

---

[2] Deficiencies in internal controls discovered during compliance testing are likewise reported to management or the audit committee.

preferably in writing, so that appropriate corrective action may be taken as soon as possible. Such action is usually suggested by the auditor at the same time as the weaknesses are reported.

At the conclusion of the audit these internal control weaknesses, together with other matters of concern arising during the audit, are documented in a formal management letter. This letter is discussed in Chapter 13.

9.8 SUMMARY

In this chapter we have considered what is meant by an accounting system and why and how a client's system is divided into sub-systems (or audit segments) for audit purposes. We have also examined the process by which an auditor gains a detailed understanding of each audit segment, and documents and tests this understanding.

Additionally, we have explored the issue of internal control. We have noted that the internal control system comprises the control environment and control procedures and that it embraces all of the controls which are instituted within an organisation's systems. However, the auditor is particularly interested in those controls which are designed to safeguard the entity's assets and ensure that its accounting data are free of material errors. (We have referred to the latter set of controls as 'internal accounting controls'.) We have discussed the seven elements of a good internal control system, identified the seven objectives of internal accounting controls, and observed that, irrespective of how effective a system of internal control may appear to be, it will always possess certain inherent limitations. We have also examined why and how the auditor conducts a preliminary evaluation of the internal controls in each audit segment.

Once the auditor has identified internal control strengths (controls which are effective in preventing or detecting errors in the accounting data) and weaknesses (controls which are required to prevent or detect errors but which are either absent or ineffective), the auditor is in a position to develop the audit programme. This is accomplished in two stages, a planning and a performance stage, and the final document comprises a list of audit procedures set out in a format which audit staff can follow.

We have emphasised throughout the chapter that, although certain internal controls may appear to be operating effectively, the auditor may not rely on them to prevent material error from occurring in the financial statements until their effectiveness and reliability have been tested. We have discussed compliance procedures (that is, procedures designed to test whether the internal controls on which the auditor plans to rely are operating as effectively as his or her preliminary evaluation suggests) and whether they have been so operating throughout the reporting period. If the compliance procedures confirm that internal controls are operating effectively, this will result in reduced substantive testing – the topic of the next chapter.

SELF-REVIEW QUESTIONS

9.1   Explain briefly what is meant by 'an accounting system'.

9.2 Explain briefly why a client's accounting system is divided into sub-systems (or audit segments) for audit purposes. State two bases on which this sub-division may be based.

9.3 Describe briefly two procedures which are used to document clients' accounting sub-systems.

9.4 Explain briefly the purpose of a 'walk through test' and how it is conducted.

9.5 Define the following terms:
   (i)   internal control
   (ii)   internal control system
   (iii) control environment
   (iv)   control procedures.

9.6 State the seven elements of a good internal control system.

9.7 Define in relation to internal controls:
   (i)   a strength
   (ii) a weakness.

9.8 List five examples of inherent weaknesses of internal control systems.

9.9 (a) Explain briefly the purpose of 'compliance procedures'.
     (b) Give two examples of compliance procedures and link each to the audit objective it is designed to test.

9.10 (a) Describe briefly what is meant by 'an audit programme'.
     (b) State the two stages in which an audit programme is developed.

REFERENCES

Anderson, R.J. (1977). *The External Audit I: Concepts and Techniques*. Toronto: Cropp Clark Pitman.

Committee of Sponsoring Organisations of the Treadway Commission (COSO). (1992). *Integrated Control – Integrated Framework*, Executive Summary. New Jersey: COSO.

ADDITIONAL READING

Georgen, W.D. (1975, April). Rating internal controls. *Financial Executive*, pp. 42–50.

Grant Thornton. (1990). *Audit Manual*. Chapter 14, Internal control as a source of audit reliance. London: Longman, 194–221.

Hatherly, D. (1980). *The Audit Evidence Process*, Chapter 4, Internal control. London: Anderson Keenan Publishing, 59–82.

Institute of Chartered Accountants in England and Wales (ICAEW). (1994). *Internal Control and Financial Reporting: Guidance for Directors of Listed Companies Registered in the U.K.* London: ICAEW.

Loebbecke, J.K. & Zuber, G.R. (1980). Evaluating internal control. *The Journal of Accountancy*, **149**(2), 49–56.

Chapter 10

Testing the Financial Statement Balances:[1] Substantive Testing

LEARNING OBJECTIVES

After studying the material in this chapter you should be able to:
- explain the significance of substantive testing in the audit process;
- state the audit objectives of substantive procedures;
- discuss the purpose and importance of analytical procedures as substantive tests (specific analytical procedures);
- explain what is meant by 'testing the details' of financial statement balances;
- distinguish between the two approaches to 'testing the details', namely:
  - testing transactions generating account balances
  - testing account balances directly;
- describe common audit procedures used to test the details of financial statement balances;
- discuss the importance of, and procedures used for, confirming the existence, ownership and value of stocks;
- discuss the importance and performance of confirmations as a substantive test of debtors;
- explain the factors the auditor should consider when assessing the adequacy of the client's allowance for bad debts.

The following publications are particularly relevant to this chapter:

- Statement of Auditing Standards (SAS) 300: *Accounting and Internal Control Systems and Audit Risk Assessments* (APB, 1995)
- Statement of Auditing Standards (SAS) 400: *Audit Evidence* (APB, 1995)
- Statement of Auditing Standards (SAS) 410: *Analytical Procedures* (APB, 1995)
- International Standards on Auditing (ISA) 501: *Audit Evidence – Additional Considerations for Specific Items* (IFAC, 1994)
- Auditing Guideline 3.2.405: *Attendance at Stocktaking* (ICAEW, 1983)

---

[1] As indicated in Section 10.1, 'Testing the financial statement balances' could be expressed more precisely as 'Testing the assertions embodied in financial statement balances'.

10.1   INTRODUCTION

The financial statements of a corporate entity comprise a set of statements by the entity's directors/management which, taken together, provide a picture of the entity's financial position, the results of its operations, and (in applicable cases) its cash flows. These statements are presented as account balances (appropriately grouped and classified), a statement of accounting policies and notes to the financial statements. The accounting policies and notes explain, amongst other things, the bases on which the financial statements have been prepared. In presenting the financial statement balances (and accompanying notes), the entity's directors/management are making implicit assertions about them. More specifically, they are implicitly asserting that the balances are valid, complete and accurate. (These assertions are explained in more detail in section 10.3.2 below.)

The auditor is required to express an opinion as to whether or not the financial statements give a true and fair view of the entity's state of affairs and profit or loss. To accomplish this, the auditor conducts substantive tests – tests which examine the substance of the financial statement balances. Expressed slightly differently, substantive testing is concerned with testing the assertions which are embodied in, or represented by, the financial statement balances.

In this chapter we examine the significance of substantive testing in the audit process and explore the different approaches which may be taken to test the financial statement balances. We also discuss the audit procedures commonly adopted for each approach. More particularly, we discuss specific analytical procedures and procedures used to test the details of the financial statement balances through testing the transactions which generate the balances or testing the balances directly.

After studying the principles of substantive testing, we examine in more detail the application of substantive procedures in auditing the balances of the stock and debtors accounts.

10.2   SIGNIFICANCE OF SUBSTANTIVE TESTING IN THE AUDIT PROCESS

When considering the significance of substantive testing in the audit process, it is important to appreciate the integrative character of an audit. The nature, timing and extent of substantive procedures are essentially determined by the preceding audit steps, more particularly:

- understanding the client and its activities;
- establishing the desired level of audit risk (or desired level of assurance) and setting materiality thresholds;
- assessing inherent risk, that is, assessing the likelihood of material error being present in the financial statements in the absence of internal controls;
- evaluating the quality of the client's internal control system and testing those control procedures on which the auditor plans to rely to prevent material misstatement from occurring in the financial statements.

These audit steps combine to give the auditor a certain level of confidence about the validity, completeness and accuracy of the information contained in the financial statements.

When the auditor is reasonably confident that the financial statements are free of material misstatement, (s)he will undertake less substantive testing than would otherwise be the case. However, substantive tests may not be omitted altogether. The auditor is required to form and express an opinion about the truth and fairness of the financial statements *per se* – not about inherent risk or the quality of the client's internal controls. Further, as noted in Chapter 9, no internal control system is perfect; they all possess some inherent limitations. Therefore, irrespective of how confident the auditor may be that the financial statements are not materially misstated, in order to form and express the required opinion, some substantive testing of the financial statement balances and related notes is always necessary.

These ideas are conveyed in Statement of Auditing Standards (SAS) 300: *Accounting and Internal Control Systems and Audit Risk Assessments*, which states:

> To form their audit opinion, auditors obtain sufficient appropriate audit evidence as to whether the financial statements are free of material misstatement. . . . The auditors' control risk assessment, together with the inherent risk assessment, influences the nature, timing and extent of substantive procedures to be performed to reduce detection risk, and therefore audit risk, to an acceptably low level. (para 51)

> Regardless of the assessed levels of inherent and control risks, auditors should perform some substantive procedures for financial statement assertions of material account balances and transactions classes. (para 53)

> The assessed levels of inherent and control risks cannot be sufficiently low to eliminate the need for auditors to perform any substantive procedures for material account balances and transaction classes. (para 54)

10.3 ALTERNATIVE APPROACHES TO SUBSTANTIVE TESTING

10.3.1 Specific Analytical Procedures and Tests of Details

All substantive testing has as its objective to determine the validity, completeness and accuracy of financial statement balances. However, two basic approaches may be adopted, namely:

(i) specific analytical procedures;
(ii) tests of details.

(i) *Specific analytical procedures*: Where this approach is adopted, meaningful relationships between account balances are examined to ascertain the reasonableness (or otherwise) of the relevant financial statement amounts.

(ii) *Tests of details*: This approach may take one of two forms:

(a) testing the transactions which give rise to the account balances;
(b) testing the closing account balances directly.

Where the transactions approach is adopted, attention is focused on the opening balance of the account in question and the transactions which affect the account during the reporting period. If the opening balance and the transactions are recorded correctly, the closing balance must, of necessity, be correct.[2]

Where closing account balances are tested directly, components of the balance are usually tested. For example, individual debtors' account balances are tested as a means of substantiating the debtors account balance in the balance sheet.

Although different approaches to substantive testing may be identified, it should be recognised that they are complementary and that they interlock in a mutually supportive manner. This may be illustrated by reference to the sales-debtors-receipts cycle, as shown in Figure 10.1.

Figure 10.1 Substantive Testing of Debtors and Related Accounts

Verified by	Debtors				Verified by
Previous year's audit ⟶	Opening bal	x	Receipts	x	⎫ Testing cash receipts
			Discount	x	⎭ transactions
Testing sales transactions ⟶	Sales	x			
			Returns	x	⎫ Analytical procedures or
Analytical procedures or testing transactions (depending on materiality) ⟶	⎰ Freight	x	Bad debts	x	⎭ testing transactions (depending on materiality)
	⎱ Interest	x			
		=		=	
Analytical procedures (for reasonableness) and direct tests of balance ⟶	Closing bal	x			

NB: Verification of complementary account balances (such as sales) simultaneously helps to confirm the debtors account balance.
Verification of the debtors account balance (through direct testing) simultaneously helps to confirm the balances of related accounts (such as sales).

Specific analytical procedures may be used to ascertain the reasonableness of the debtors closing balance. If it appears to be reasonable, the extent of further detailed testing may be reduced. Conversely, if analytical procedures indicate that the balance may be materially misstated, more extensive testing will be required to identify the nature and extent of the error(s). Specific analytical procedures may also be used to substantiate less material account balances such as 'interest on overdue accounts' and 'freight charged to credit customers'. Specific analytical procedures are discussed in section 10.4.2 below.

In order to determine the validity, completeness and accuracy of the sales account balance, individual sales transactions are tested. Similarly cash receipts, discount received and sales returns transactions may be tested to substantiate their respective account balances. It should be noted that testing these transactions serves two purposes: it confirms the relevant account balance in the balance sheet or profit and loss statement and it simultaneously provides support for an element of the debtors account. If the balance of the debtors account is also confirmed through direct testing

---

[2] In the case of balance sheet accounts, the opening balance is established from the audited closing balances of the previous period; for profit and loss statement accounts, the opening balance is, of course, zero.

this, by implication, provides support for the accuracy of the related (component) accounts. By obtaining mutually supportive evidence in this manner, the auditor can feel confident that all of the accounts constituting the sales-debtors-receipts cycle are fairly stated.

10.3.2 Objectives of Substantive Procedures

Whatever approach is taken towards substantive testing (that is, specific analytical procedures or tests of details), the overall objective is to confirm the validity, completeness and accuracy of the financial statement account balances. More specifically, the objective of substantive procedures is to confirm or refute the assertions underlying the financial statement balances; namely to confirm that:

- the account balances are valid, that is, they represent *bona fide* transactions: no fictitious amounts are included;
- the account balances are complete, that is, they include all relevant amounts: none has been omitted;
- the account balances represent items which are owned by the entity (or, as in the case of leased assets, the entity has rights to control the items which are similar to rights normally associated with ownership);
- the account balances are arithmetically accurate;
- items included in the account balances are properly valued;
- items included in the account balances are correctly classified;
- items included in, or excluded from, the account balances are allocated to the correct accounting period;
- the account balances, and any requisite notes, are properly disclosed.

Confirming each of these assertions constitutes a specific audit objective. If the specific audit objectives are met, the overall objective of confirming the validity, completeness and accuracy of the financial statement balances will also be met.

Statement of Auditing Standards (SAS) 400: *Audit Evidence* conveys similar ideas but expresses them differently. It states:

> In seeking to obtain audit evidence from substantive procedures, auditors should consider the extent to which that evidence . . . supports the relevant financial statement assertions. (para 10)

> Financial statement assertions are the representations of the directors that are embodied in the financial statements . . . . These representations or assertions may be described in general terms . . . as follows:
> a) existence: an asset or a liability exists at a given date;
> b) rights and obligations: an asset or a liability pertains to the entity at a given date;
> c) occurrence: a transaction or event took place which pertains to the entity during the relevant period;
> d) completeness: there are no unrecorded assets, liabilities, transactions or events, or undisclosed items;
> e) valuation: an asset or liability is recorded at an appropriate carrying value;
> f) measurement: a transaction or event is recorded at the proper amount and revenue or expense is allocated to the proper period; and

g) presentation and disclosure: an item is disclosed, classified and described in accordance with the applicable reporting framework (for example, relevant legislation and applicable accounting standards). (para 11)

It should be noted that substantive testing is concerned with the validity, completeness and accuracy of information presented in the financial statements. Its objective is very different from that of compliance testing. In compliance testing, the auditor is concerned to confirm that internal controls on which (s)he plans to rely to prevent material error from occurring in the financial statements are being complied with. Thus, compliance procedures conducted in relation to, for example, sales transactions, seek evidence which indicates, *inter alia*, that sales transactions have been authorised, and that extensions, additions, and account codings shown on sales invoices have been independently checked. In contrast to this, substantive procedures are concerned with examining the monetary amounts and correctness of recording of transactions.

Confusion between the two types of procedures frequently arises in relation to testing transactions. This is because the source documents recording transactions are used for both types of tests. For example, copies of sales invoices may be vouched to see if initials are present which indicate that extensions, additions and account classifications have been checked by an independent person. In this case, evidence of compliance with an internal control procedure is sought. The same document may be used for substantive testing; that is, for the auditor to check for him/herself that the extensions and additions are arithmetically correct, and that the transaction has been correctly classified. The same source document (and transaction) is used for two entirely different purposes.

10.4 SUBSTANTIVE AUDIT PROCEDURES

10.4.1 Overview of Substantive Audit Procedures

It was noted in section 10.3 above that there are two broad categories of substantive tests – namely, specific analytical procedures and tests of details. It was also noted that tests of details may be either tests of transactions or direct tests of account balances. The relationship between these types of substantive tests, and the procedures used for each, are depicted in Figure 10.2.

10.4.2 Specific Analytical Procedures

During the early stages of an audit, analytical procedures are used to help the auditor assess the likelihood of material error being present in the (unaudited) financial statements and to identify high-risk audit areas. At this stage, broad entity measures are important, such as the current ratio, debt to equity ratio, gross profit percentage, return on assets, and return on shareholders' funds. During the substantive testing stage, the focus of attention is individual account balances. To distinguish between the two uses of analytical procedures, the term 'overall analytical procedures' is frequently applied to the broad-risk assessment procedures, and 'specific analytical procedures' to the narrow account-focused substantive tests.

Figure 10.2   Overview of Substantive Audit Procedures

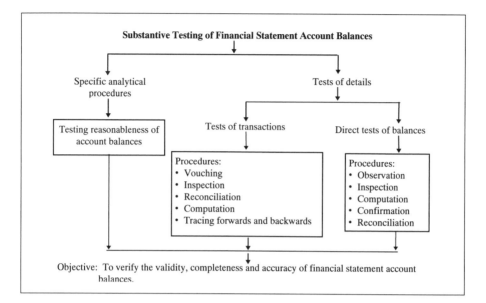

During the substantive testing phase of an audit, specific analytical procedures are usually used in two different ways as preliminary tests for account balances where extensive substantive procedures are required; and as complete tests where less extensive procedures are needed.

(i)   *Specific Analytical Procedures as Preliminary Tests*

For accounts where extensive substantive testing is required (such as debtors and stock), specific analytical procedures are generally used as preliminary tests – to test the reasonableness of the account balances as a basis for deciding the extent to which further substantive testing is required. When an account balance appears to be reasonable, material misstatement is generally unlikely. In these cases, less substantive testing is needed than in situations where material error seems likely. Use of specific analytical procedures as a preliminary test in auditing stocks is illustrated in section 10.6 below.

(ii)   *Specific Analytical Procedures as Complete Tests*

For accounts where less extensive substantive testing is required (such as often applies in the case of prepaid expenses and interest paid), specific analytical procedures are frequently used to test the reasonableness of their balances. If they appear to be reasonable, no further testing is undertaken. However, if error appears likely, then the relevant account is subjected to more detailed testing.

The following examples illustrate two ways in which specific analytical procedures may constitute complete substantive tests:

1. Historically, sales returns may possess a fairly stable relationship with sales. Thus, assuming that nothing has come to the auditor's attention which suggests that the relationship may not hold in the current year, if the sales returns account balance is calculated as a percentage of sales, the result should be similar to that for previous years. If it is, the account balance is assumed to be reasonable and is accepted as 'true and fair'.

2. The balance of the interest paid account may be estimated by using a known relationship between two variables. More specifically, the average debt and the average interest rate for the reporting period may be ascertained, and the average interest rate then applied to the average debt. This provides an estimate of the interest paid account balance. In the absence of exceptional circumstances known to the auditor, if the interest paid account balance is close to the estimated amount, it will be judged to be reasonable and accepted as 'true and fair'.

10.4.3 Tests of Details

As noted in section 10.3 above, substantive tests of details may involve testing the transactions which give rise to an account balance or directly testing the balance itself. The approach adopted is generally that which provides the most efficient means of determining the validity, completeness and accuracy of the account balance in question.

(i) *Testing Transactions*

Revenue and expense accounts commence the accounting period with a zero balance and the transactions comprising the account are generally of a similar type. For example, entries in sales and purchases accounts are usually confined to cash and credit sales and purchases, respectively. Such similarity of transactions facilitates their testing and results in the testing of the transactions generally being more efficient than directly testing the relevant account balances.

Similarly for some balance sheet accounts, where the number of transactions affecting the account during the reporting period is small relative to the size of the account balance, testing the transactions affecting the account may be more efficient than directly testing the closing balance. An example is afforded by the motor vehicle account in entities which have large fleets of vehicles (such as British Telecom). In the case of balance sheet accounts, the opening balance was verified during the previous year's audit and, as for the revenue and expense accounts, if the opening balance and the transactions affecting the account are recorded correctly, the closing balance must be correct.

As shown in Figure 10.2, the primary procedures used for testing the accuracy, validity and completeness of transactions are vouching, inspection, reconciliation, computation, and tracing. All of these procedures, other than tracing, are directed towards examining the accuracy of financial statement account balances – their accuracy as to amount, account and reporting period. These audit procedures may be illustrated as follows:

- *Vouching* of source documents may be used to determine whether transactions have been recorded in the correct account and period. The auditor checks the account code classifications of the transactions and, particularly for transactions near year-end, examines the dates and terms of the transactions to ascertain the period to which they belong.

- *Inspection* of documents such as price lists may be used to check that correct prices have been applied to goods and services bought and sold.
- *Reconciliation* may be used, for example, to ensure that related purchase orders, receiving reports, suppliers' invoices and payments vouchers all match – that the quantities and prices of goods ordered and received, invoiced and paid for, are in agreement. Similarly, source document totals are reconciled with journal entries, and journal entries are reconciled with ledger records.
- *Computation* of items such as extensions and additions on source documents may be performed in order to check that transactions have been recorded at their correct amounts.

Tracing backwards and forwards are substantive procedures designed to test the validity and completeness, respectively, of recorded transactions, rather than their accuracy.

- *Tracing backwards* involves tracing selected entries back through the accounting records, from the financial statements, through the ledgers and journals, to the source documents. This procedure is designed to check that the amounts recorded in the financial statements represent *bona fide* transactions and that financial statement account balances are not overstated. Because of the (usual) desirability of having more rather than less assets, there may be an incentive to inflate asset accounts. Tracing backwards has particular application in ensuring that asset account balances are valid and not overstated.
- *Tracing forwards* involves tracing selected transactions forwards through the accounting records, from source documents, through the journals and ledgers, to the financial statements. This procedure is designed to check that financial statement account balances include all relevant transactions and that they are not understated. Because of the desirability of having less rather than more liabilities, there may be an incentive to understate liability accounts. Tracing forwards has particular application for testing the completeness of liability account balances, and ensuring that they are not understated.

(ii) Direct Tests of Balances

For some accounts it is more efficient to audit the closing balance directly rather than examine the transactions which constitute the balance. This applies, for example, to many balance sheet accounts such as stock, debtors, investments and loans.

The primary audit procedures used to examine the validity, completeness and accuracy of account balances are observation, inspection, computation, confirmation and reconciliation. These may be illustrated as follows:

- *Observation* is used, for example, to establish the existence, quantity and quality of stocks and of fixed assets such as plant, equipment and motor vehicles. (In some cases, observation extends to observing identification numbers of fixed assets, for example, the engine and chassis numbers of motor vehicles.)

- *Inspection* of documents, such as marketable securities and loan, lease and hire purchase contracts, is used to confirm the existence of the items concerned and to ascertain their terms and conditions.
- *Computation* of accounts, such as depreciation and accumulated depreciation, doubtful debts and allowance for bad debts, is used to confirm the arithmetical accuracy of their balances.
- *Confirmation* is used to confirm certain information with parties outside the audit client – for example, the balance of debtors' and bank accounts, and items such as contingent liabilities and commitments. (Confirmation of debtors is discussed in detail in section 10.7 below.)
- *Reconciliation* is used, for example, to reconcile the bank account balance in the general ledger with the confirmation letter received from the bank, and to reconcile subsidiary ledger totals with the relevant control account in the general ledger.

10.5 INTRODUCTION TO SUBSTANTIVE TESTING OF STOCK AND DEBTORS

To illustrate the application of substantive procedures to direct tests of balances, some aspects of auditing stock and debtors are discussed in detail in sections 10.6 and 10.7 below. These accounts frequently constitute the greatest proportion of an entity's current assets and represent its chief source of short-term cash. They are also accounts which are prone to misstatement. In the case of stock this arises, in particular, from possible over-valuation of stock, resulting from stock obsolescence. For debtors, it results primarily from the subjectiveness involved in estimating the allowance for bad debts. As a consequence of these factors, the stock and debtors account balances almost always attract considerable audit attention. Particular interest in these accounts arose as a result of the infamous *McKesson & Robbins* case in the United States in the 1930s. Subsequent to this case, which involved many millions of dollars' worth of fictitious stock and debtors, auditors have been required to attend stocktakes and to confirm debtors in all audits where these items are material, which, as noted above, is usually the case.

10.6 SIGNIFICANT ASPECTS OF AUDITING STOCK

10.6.1 Overview of Auditing Stock

When auditing stock, the auditor is particularly concerned to confirm its existence, ownership and value. As shown in Figure 10.3, each of these audit objectives requires a different set of audit procedures.

Before testing the details of the stock account balance, in order to ascertain whether misstatement seems likely, specific analytical procedures may be performed. For example, the ratio of stock to cost of goods sold (COGS) may be calculated for each significant type of stock, at each significant location. The trend for the current and past

Figure 10.3   Procedures for Auditing Stock

Assertion/Audit Objective	Audit Procedures
Existence – Does stock exist?	Observation (attendance at stocktake)
Rights – Is stock owned?	Vouching of source documents and inspection of other documents for dates and terms of 'purchase' of stock
Valuation – is stock correctly valued?	• Observation (of quality of stock and degree of completion of work-in-progress) • Vouching of source documents and inspection of price lists for cost of stock • Computation of stock valuation

years may then be plotted and the resultant picture evaluated. Some possible scenarios are as follows:

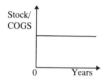

(1)   A steady relationship between stock and COGS is indicated, suggesting that significant misstatement is unlikely.

(2)   A steady increase in stock levels is indicated, suggesting the possibility of overstocking. This may indicate that stock obsolescence is a problem and that some write-down in value may be necessary.

(3)   A steady decrease in stock levels is indicated, suggesting the possibility of stockouts. This may indicate that future sales and profits are threatened. The reduction in stocks may signal liquidity problems.

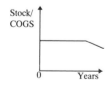

(4)   A marked decline in stock in the current year is indicated. This raises the possibility of theft, a material error in the accounts, or a reduction in stock in anticipation of a decline in sales.

(5)   A marked increase in stock in the current year is indicated. This raises the possibility of manipulation of the accounts by senior management, a material error in the accounts, or an increase in stock in anticipation of an increase in sales.

When assessing the results of specific analytical procedures (such as those set out above), it is essential that they are not viewed in isolation. The auditor must evaluate the results within the context of his or her understanding of the client, and must give due consideration to all of the relevant external and internal environmental factors. For example, the above graphs need to be assessed on the basis of the stock item(s) and/or location(s) to which they apply and how they compare with the graphs of other stock items and/or locations. Consideration must be given to pertinent policy decisions of management, such as planned changes in product mix, changes in target market(s), and/or changes in purchases and sales policies. Similarly, due allowance must be made for local and national economic, competitive and other factors which may have a bearing on stock levels.

It is important that specific analytical procedures be regarded, not as a source of answers, but as a means of identifying questions which need to be asked.

10.6.2 Ascertaining the Existence of Stock

The primary means by which an auditor ascertains that stock exists is attending the client's stocktake. Auditing Guideline 3.2.405: *Attendance at Stocktaking* recognises the importance of this audit procedure. It states:

> Where stocks are material in the enterprise's financial statements, and the auditor is placing reliance upon management's stocktake in order to provide evidence of existence, then the auditor should attend the stocktaking. This is because attendance at stocktaking is normally the best way of providing evidence of the proper functioning of management's stocktaking procedures, and hence of the existence of stocks and their condition. (para 5)

Audit procedures relating to a stocktake fall into three main groups:

(i)   those conducted prior to the commencement of the stocktake;
(ii) those conducted during the stocktake; and
(iii) those conducted when the stocktake is completed.

(i)   *Procedures Conducted Prior to the Stocktake*

Prior to the commencement of the stocktake the auditor should review the client's stocktaking procedures to ensure they are adequate. (S)he needs to establish, for example:

• when the stocktake is to take place and whether sufficient time has been allowed to enable the task to be completed satisfactorily;
• which personnel are to be involved in the count, their seniority and experience, and whether they are to work in pairs;
• how the count is to be performed; whether, for example, stocksheets or tags are to be used;
• whether the instructions given to the stocktaking teams are clear, easily understood and complete;
• whether management's control procedures are adequate; whether, for example, appropriate procedures have been established to facilitate accounting for used and

unused stocksheets or tags, for counting and recounting stock, and to prevent stock from being counted twice, or omitted from the count;
• whether management has established adequate procedures for identifying the stage of completion of work-in-progress, obsolete or damaged items, and/or stock owned by a third party (such as goods held on consignment).

If, having reviewed the client's stocktaking procedures, the auditor is of the opinion that they are not adequate, (s)he should discuss these concerns with management so that the deficiencies may be rectified before the stocktake begins.

(ii)   *Procedures Conducted During the Stocktake*

During the stocktake the auditor should observe whether the client's employees adhere to management's procedures and (s)he should also perform test counts. Auditing Guideline 3.2.405 notes that:

> When carrying out test-counts, the auditor should select items both from count records and from the physical stocks and should check one to the other to gain assurance as to the completeness and accuracy of the count records. In this context, he should give particular consideration to those stocks which he believes . . . have a high value either individually or as a category of stock. (para 15)

> The auditor should consider whether management has instituted adequate cut-off procedures, i.e. procedures intended to ensure that movements into, within and out of stocks are properly identified and reflected in the accounting records. . . . [T]he auditor should [also] test the arrangements made to segregate stocks owned by third parties and he should identify goods movement documents for reconciliation with financial records of purchases and sales. (para 17)

Most stocktakes involve the use of either stocksheets or tags. In a thorough system using stocksheets:

• all stocksheets are pre-numbered sequentially and a record is kept of the stocksheets which are issued to identified members of the stocktaking team;
• all items of stock at any location are identified and listed on the stocksheets;
• working in pairs, one team of stocktakers counts the stock and records the quantity on the stocksheets;
• a second team of stocktakers (also working in pairs) recounts the stock and records the quantity on duplicate stocksheets;
• the completed (and unused) stocksheets are returned to the stocktaking clerk who checks off the returned stocksheet numbers and compares the stock counts recorded by the two teams of stocktakers;
• any significant discrepancies in the counts recorded by the two teams are investigated and the affected stock items are recounted to establish the correct quantity.

In a thorough system using tags:

• pre-numbered tags (small cards, perforated across the centre, with the allocated number recorded on both the top and bottom half) are placed on all stock items and the relevant stock item number or description is entered on both halves of the tag;

- working in pairs, one team of stocktakers counts the stock and records the quantity on the bottom half of the tag; they initial both the top and bottom halves of the tag and remove (and retain) the bottom half;
- a second team of stocktakers (also working in pairs) recounts the stock and records the quantity on pre-numbered stocksheets; they initial the top half of the stock item tag;
- on completion of the counts, the completed bottom halves of the tags and the completed stocksheets are given to the stocktaking clerk who:
  - accounts for all issued tag and stocksheet numbers;
  - compares the quantities recorded on the tags and the stocksheets;
- any significant discrepancies in the counts recorded by the two stocktaking teams are investigated and the affected stock items are recounted to establish the correct quantity.

(iii) *Procedures Following Completion of the Stocktake*

When the stocktake is complete, under both the stocksheet and the tag system, a master stock listing is prepared. The auditor should test this listing to determine whether it accurately reflects the stock counts. (S)he should also compare the quantities listed on the master listing with the perpetual stock records. Discrepancies between the physical count and perpetual records should be noted and investigated. Additionally, the accounting records should be inspected to ascertain whether they have been adjusted appropriately.

10.6.3 Ascertaining Ownership of Stock

Stock recorded as a current asset in the financial statements should reflect the value of stock owned by the entity at balance sheet date. It should not include stock which is not owned by the entity, neither should it exclude stock which is owned. Therefore, as part of the audit of stock, the auditor vouches source documents and inspects other relevant documents in order to determine stock ownership. Two situations are of particular concern:

(i) *The ownership of goods bought and sold near year-end*: The auditor needs to determine, for example, whether legal title to goods purchased, but in transit on balance sheet date, had passed to the client by that date. [This usually depends on whether the terms of the contract are f.o.b. (free on board) at shipping point or destination.] The auditor must also ascertain whether the goods in question have been properly included in, or excluded from, the client's stock listing at balance sheet date.

Similarly, the auditor needs to ensure that where goods have been sold (and legal title has passed to the customer) but are still on the client's premises awaiting delivery at balance sheet date, these goods have not been recorded as part of the client's stock.

(ii) *Goods on consignment*: The auditor needs to ascertain whether any stock included in the client's stock listing is held on consignment, or under a franchise agreement, whereby title to the goods does not pass to the client until a specified condition is met – for example, the goods are sold to a third party. Such goods are not owned by the client and therefore do not form part of the client's stock.

By the same token, the auditor needs to ensure that stock owned by the client which is held on consignment, or under a franchise agreement, by a third party is included as part of the client's stock.

10.6.4   Ascertaining that Stock is Correctly Valued

In addition to establishing the quantity and ownership of stock, the auditor must verify that it is correctly valued. To accomplish this audit objective, the auditor performs the following procedures. (S)he:

- determines the valuation method adopted by the client and confirms that this method:
  - is in accordance with Statement of Standard Accounting Practice (SSAP) 9: *Stocks and Long-Term Contracts*
  - has been applied consistently across all stock items
  - is consistent with previous years;
- vouches suppliers' invoices and inspects price lists and other relevant documents to determine the cost of stock items;
- computes the value of stock based on its quantity (from the master listing), cost information, and the valuation method adopted;
- establishes that the degree of completion of work-in-progress has been determined appropriately, and that raw materials, work-in-progress and finished goods stock are properly classified;
- assesses the quality, condition and possible obsolescence of stock items, and determines whether the net realisable value of stock is lower than its cost;
- determines whether 'the lower of cost or market' rule has been applied correctly.

In relation to assessing the value of stock, it is important that the auditor evaluates his or her competence to estimate its value and, if necessary, seeks assistance from an appropriate expert. The most commonly cited example to illustrate this point is the auditor's inability, in general, to distinguish between diamonds and glass. The following case, reported in a BBC news broadcast in 1983, also provides a pertinent example. In this case the problem was an inability to distinguish between brass and gold.

> A North Wales jeweller committed suicide when it was discovered that his company's stock of gold was really brass. The Chester coroner was told that the jeweller had instructed his staff not to use the stock of what he said was gold wire, but when the bank sent investigators around, he admitted to a friend that the stock had been over-valued by £1 million. He then drove to a hotel where he drank a solution of cyanide poison.
> (BBC *'News about Britain'*, August 1983)

10.7   SIGNIFICANT ASPECTS OF AUDITING DEBTORS

10.7.1   Overview of Auditing Debtors

The debtors' account balance is audited as an element of the sales-debtors-receipts cycle. Auditing this cycle involves, *inter alia*:

- performing specific analytical procedures to test the reasonableness of relevant profit and loss statement and balance sheet accounts (for example, sales, sales returns, doubtful debts, allowance for bad debts, and debtors);
- confirming the validity, completeness and accuracy of sales and cash receipts transactions;
- directly testing the debtors' account balance.

In this section, our focus of attention is the debtors' account balance. When auditing this balance, the auditor is concerned, in particular, to confirm the existence, ownership and value of debtors. As for auditing stock, each of these audit objectives (or management assertions) requires a different set of audit procedures. These are shown in Figure 10.4.

Figure 10.4   Procedures for Auditing Debtors

Assertion/Audit Objective	Audit Procedures
Existence – Do debtors exist?	Confirmation
Rights – Are debtors owned?	Enquiry and inspection of documents for possible factoring of debtors
Valuation – Are debtors correctly valued?	• Confirmation • Computation of allowance for bad debts

10.7.2   Confirmation of Debtors

As noted in section 10.5 above, confirmation of debtors became a standard audit procedure as a result of the *McKesson & Robbins* case in the US in the 1930s. International Standards on Auditing (ISA) 501: *Audit Evidence – Additional Considerations for Specific Items,* reaffirms the value of confirmations in the audit of debtors. It states:

> Direct confirmation provides reliable audit evidence as to the existence of debtors and the accuracy of their recorded account balances. (para 20)

However, the Standard goes on to note that confirmations do not usually provide evidence as to the collectibility of balances or the existence of unrecorded debtors (para 20). It also draws attention to the fact that, in some circumstances, the auditor may consider it unlikely that debtors will respond to a confirmation request. In this situation, auditors are required to perform alternative procedures, such as examining post year-end cash receipts related to the year-end balance of the debtor(s) concerned (para 21).

Whilst acknowledging the caveats noted in ISA 501, it should be appreciated that confirmations provide the most widely used, and the most reliable, audit procedure available for verifying the existence and accuracy of debtors.

Seven steps may be identified in the confirmation process. These are as follows:

(i)   deciding on the type of confirmation to use;
(ii)   deciding on the timing of confirmations;

(iii) selecting the sample of debtors;
(iv) preparing and despatching the confirmations;
(v) following-up non-responses;
(vi) analysing discrepancies;
(vii) drawing conclusions with respect to the accuracy of the debtors' account balance.

(i) *Deciding on the Type of Confirmation to Use*

> The request for confirmation of balances may take a positive form, in which the debtor is asked to confirm agreement or to express disagreement with the recorded balance, or a negative form, in which a reply is requested only in the event of disagreement with the recorded balance. (ISA 501, para 24)

From the above passage, it is evident that confirmations may be of two types, positive and negative. Positive confirmations are generally considered to provide more reliable evidence as the debtor is requested to respond whether the amount stated in the confirmation request is correct or incorrect. This enables the auditor to perform follow-up procedures in cases where responses are not received. In the case of negative confirmations, the debtor is asked to respond only if the amount stated in the confirmation request is incorrect. Thus, all non-responses must be treated as if the amount stated in the confirmation request is correct even though the debtor may have merely ignored the request. However, negative confirmations are less expensive than positive confirmations (because there are no follow-up procedures) and, therefore, for a given total cost, more negative than positive confirmation requests may be sent.

Determining which type of confirmation to use in any given audit is a matter of judgment. Nevertheless, it is generally accepted that positive confirmations are appropriate when the following circumstances apply:

1. A small number of large accounts represent a significant proportion of the total debtors balance.
2. The auditor has reason to believe that there may be disputed or inaccurate accounts. For example, when internal controls are weak.
3. The auditor has good reason to expect that recipients of confirmation requests will not give them reasonable consideration. [For example, low response rates (for positive confirmations) have been experienced in previous years. In this circumstance negative confirmations are not appropriate.]

By way of contrast, it is generally accepted that negative confirmations are appropriate in the following circumstances:

1. The auditor considers that internal controls are reliable and that, as a result, material error in debtors' accounts is unlikely.
2. The auditor has reason to believe that the large majority of recipients will give serious consideration to the confirmation request.

It is pertinent to note that in some audits a combination of positive and negative confirmations is used. Where this occurs, positive confirmations are generally used for large balances and negative confirmations for small balances.

(ii) *Deciding on the Timing of Confirmations*

There is little doubt that the most reliable evidence from confirmations is obtained when requests are sent close to balance sheet date. When this occurs, the debtors' balances are tested directly, without any inferences having to be made about transactions which take place between confirmation date and balance sheet date. However, in order to complete the audit on a timely basis, and to facilitate scheduling of audit staff workloads, it is often convenient to confirm debtors at an interim date (generally, 2–3 months prior to year-end). This timing of confirmations is acceptable, providing the client's internal controls are evaluated as effective and the auditor can be reasonably assured that sales, sales returns and cash receipts transactions are properly recorded between the confirmation and balance sheet dates.

(iii) *Selecting the Sample of Debtors*

In order to select the sample of debtors to be confirmed, two separate decisions need to be made, namely:

(a) how large the sample is to be;
(b) how the sample is to be selected.[3]

(a) *The size of the sample* will depend on a number of factors, including the following:

* the materiality of the total debtors' account balance. (The more material the balance, the larger the sample size);
* the number of accounts which constitute the total debtors balance;
* the size distribution of individual debtor's account balances;
* the results of specific analytical procedures and internal control evaluation which indicate the likelihood (or otherwise) of material error being present in the debtors' accounts;
* the results of confirmations in previous years;
* the type of confirmation being used.

(b) *The sample selection* usually involves some stratification of the total population of debtors. In most audits where confirmations are to be sent, the population is stratified based on the size and age of outstanding balances. Emphasis is given to testing large and old accounts as these accounts are the most likely to contain a material error. However, it is important that the auditor's sample includes some items from every material stratum of the population.

In most cases, the auditor confirms all balances which exceed some designated monetary amount and all accounts beyond a specified age limit (for example, 90 days), and selects a random sample from the remainder.

---

[3] Determining sample size and selecting samples are discussed in detail in Chapter 11.

(iv) *Preparing and Despatching the Confirmations*

Once the auditor has decided on the type of confirmation to be used and selected the sample of debtors to be confirmed, the confirmation requests are prepared.

A confirmation request is essentially a letter, sent to a selection of the client's customers, which sets out the amount owed by the customer to the client as shown in the client's accounts on a specified date (confirmation date). As noted earlier, if a positive confirmation is used, the debtor is requested to confirm that the amount stated in the letter is correct or to indicate that it is not correct. If a negative confirmation is used, the debtor is asked to respond only if the amount stated is not correct. In either case, if the amount is incorrect, the debtor is asked to state what (s)he believes the correct amount to be. The letter is frequently prepared on the client's letterhead but, in any event, it should include an authorisation from the client to the debtor to disclose the requested information to the auditor.

Notwithstanding the use of the client's letterhead, it is essential that all aspects of the confirmation process remain completely under the control of the auditor. This includes preparing the confirmation requests, placing them in envelopes, stamping and posting the envelopes. A stamped addressed envelope should be enclosed with the confirmation request, with the envelope addressed to the audit firm. Additionally, the audit firm's address should be shown as the return address on the outside of the envelope addressed to the debtor. This is to ensure that any undelivered requests are returned to the audit firm.

When a confirmation request is returned as undelivered mail, the reason for the non-delivery needs to be carefully evaluated. In most cases it represents a customer who has moved away without settling his or her account but there is always the possibility that it represents a fictitious account. Further, even if the debtor is valid, a large number of undelivered confirmation requests could signal a serious collectibility problem which will need to be reflected in the allowance for bad debts.

(v) *Following-up Non-responses*

As noted above, when negative confirmations are used, it is assumed that amounts stated in confirmations which are not returned, are correct. Non-responses are not followed-up. However, when positive confirmations are used, no assumption is made as to the correctness or otherwise of amounts stated in confirmations which receive no response. Instead, second, and in some cases even third, confirmation requests are sent.

If a debtor still fails to respond, the auditor has to rely on alternative audit procedures to confirm the amounts in question. (S)he will, for example, examine the cash receipts records to ascertain whether the debtor paid an amount subsequent to the date of the confirmation. However, receipt of cash from the debtor does not necessarily establish that the amount being investigated was owed at confirmation date: it could relate to a subsequent sale. Therefore, in addition to examining the cash receipts records, the auditor needs to examine copies of:

• sales invoices – to confirm that the customer was billed for the relevant goods or services;

- despatch records – to confirm that the goods were despatched to the customer;
- sales returns records – to confirm that the goods were not returned by the customer.

In each case, careful attention must be paid to the dates and details of the records to ensure that they all relate to the same transaction(s).

Inspection of correspondence in a disputed accounts file may also provide evidence that a debtor who failed to respond to a confirmation request owed the amount in question at the confirmation date.

The extent and nature of follow-up procedures largely depend upon the materiality of the non-responses, the types of errors discovered in the confirmed responses, subsequent cash receipts from non-respondents, and the auditor's evaluation of the quality of the client's internal controls. However, in order for valid conclusions to be drawn about the population of debtors from the sample of accounts examined, all of the unconfirmed balances should be investigated using alternative procedures, even if the amounts involved are small.

(vi) *Analysing Discrepancies*

When confirmations are returned by customers to the auditor, any disagreements with amounts stated in the confirmation requests must be analysed carefully. In many cases these will result from timing differences between the customer's and the client's records (for example, a payment by a debtor may not have been recorded in the client's records by the confirmation date). However, in other cases, disagreements may signal errors in the client's accounts. These may arise, for example, from incorrect recording of amounts (that is, clerical errors), or from failure to record certain transactions, such as goods returned by the customer. Alternatively, they may reflect disputed amounts, where the customer claims, for instance, that the wrong price has been charged, incorrect quantities or items were received, or the goods arrived in a damaged condition.

All disagreements with amounts in confirmation requests should be investigated to determine whether the client's records are in error and, if this is the case, by how much. Generally, the auditor asks the client to perform the necessary reconciliation but, if necessary, will communicate with the customer to settle discrepancies which have come to light.

(vii) *Drawing Conclusions with Respect to the Debtors' Account Balance*

When all discrepancies found in the sample of debtors have been explained, including those discovered as a result of procedures performed as a follow-up to non-responses, the auditor needs to:

- re-evaluate the client's system of internal control and determine whether detected errors are consistent with the auditor's original assessment of the controls;
- generalise from the sample of debtors examined to the total population of debtors;
- draw conclusions as to whether sufficient appropriate evidence has been gathered on which to base an opinion and, if so, whether the debtors account balance, before allowing for doubtful debts, is 'true and fair'.

10.7.3 Adjusting Debtors for Doubtful Debts

Before concluding that the value of debtors is stated fairly in the financial statements, the auditor must assess the adequacy of the client's allowance for bad debts. To make this assessment, the auditor needs to consider whether, compared with previous years, there has been any change in factors such as the following:

- the client's credit policy;
- the client's credit approval procedures;
- the level of compliance by employees with the credit approval procedures;
- the number of days debtors' account balances are overdue (the longer debtors' balances are overdue the less probable it is that they will ever be paid);
- the volume of credit sales;
- general economic conditions which are likely to affect debtors' ability to meet their financial obligations.

Giving due weight to these and similar factors, the auditor will assess the propriety of the percentage applied by the client to gross debtors to establish the current year's allowance for bad debts. The auditor will also reperform the relevant calculation.

10.7.4 Ownership of Debtors

In most cases ownership of debtors does not give rise to problems: the amounts owed by debtors are owed to the client. However, the auditor must remain alert to the possibility that all or part of the client's debtors may have been factored, that is, sold to a financial institution at a discount. When this occurs, customers are frequently not aware of the change in the ownership of their debt because they continue to make payments to the client. As a consequence, factoring does not, in general, come to light through the confirmation process. The most common means of the auditor discovering that factoring has occurred is through discussions with management and inspection of documents such as minutes of directors' meetings and correspondence.

10.8 SUMMARY

In this chapter we have discussed substantive testing, that is, testing the substance of (or assertions embodied in) the financial statement account balances. It is these balances about which the auditor is required to form and express an opinion and, irrespective of how 'perfect' a client's internal control system may appear to be, some substantive testing is always necessary.

We have noted that substantive testing may take one of two basic forms: specific analytical procedures or tests of details, and that tests of details may involve testing either the transactions which give rise to a financial statement account balance or testing the balance directly. However, whichever form of substantive testing is used, the objective is always the same, namely, to test the validity, completeness and accuracy of the financial statement accounts.

In addition to discussing the general principles of substantive testing, we have discussed the application of commonly used substantive audit procedures (for example, observation, inspection, computation, tracing, confirmation and reconciliation) and examined in some detail, significant aspects of auditing stock and debtors.

SELF-REVIEW QUESTIONS

10.1 Explain briefly the significance of substantive testing in the audit process.

10.2 State the overall audit objective of substantive testing.

10.3 List eight specific audit objectives of substantive procedures.

10.4 Explain briefly what is meant by 'tests of details'.

10.5 Explain briefly the two ways in which specific analytical procedures are used as substantive tests.

10.6 (a) Describe briefly how the following audit procedures are performed:
     (i) tracing forwards
     (ii) tracing backwards.
     (b) Using a specific example to illustrate your answer, explain the purpose of each of the above audit procedures.

10.7 Describe briefly the 'tag system' which may be used for a client's stocktaking.

10.8 Explain briefly two special considerations the auditor must take into account when testing the audit objective: Is stock owned by the client?

10.9 In relation to auditing debtors, distinguish between a positive confirmation and a negative confirmation.

10.10 (a) List five aspects of the process of confirming debtors which must remain under the auditor's control.
      (b) Explain briefly why it is important that audit-client personnel are not permitted to assist the auditor in the process of confirming debtors.

ADDITIONAL READING

Bagshaw, K. (1994). Evidence: How much is enough? *Accountancy*, **113**(1209), 80–2.

Grant Thornton. (1990). *Audit Manual*. Chapter 16, Tests of Details, and Chapter 29, Sales cycle. London: Longman, 222–31, 383–400.

Hatherly, D. (1980). *The Audit Evidence Process*. Chapter 5, Substantive testing, and Chapter 6, Sales and debtors. London: Anderson Keenan Publishing, 83–128.

Hodgkinson, R. (1993). Taking stock. *Accountancy*, **112**(1203), 90.

Krogstad, J.K. & Romney, H.B. (1980). Accounts receivable confirmation – An alternative auditing approach. *The Journal of Accountancy*, **149**(2), 68–74.

Littrell, E.K. (1982). Creative accounting – Getting a bang out of inventory. *Management Accounting*, **63**(10), 56.

Chapter 11

Introduction to Audit Sampling

LEARNING OBJECTIVES

After studying the material in this chapter you should be able to:
- **explain what is meant by sampling;**
- **explain why sampling is important in auditing;**
- **distinguish between judgmental and statistical sampling and explain the advantages and disadvantages of each technique;**
- **describe the methods commonly used for selecting samples;**
- **explain the meaning of the basic terminology used in statistical sampling;**
- **distinguish between attributes sampling and variables sampling;**
- **explain the fundamental processes involved in attributes sampling;**
- **explain the basic principles of sampling with probability proportional to size (monetary unit sampling);**
- **discuss the follow-up to the results obtained by sampling.**

The following publication is particularly relevant to this chapter:

- Statement of Auditing Standards (SAS) 430: *Audit Sampling* (APB, 1995).

11.1 INTRODUCTION

The purpose of this chapter is to provide an introductory overview of the use of sampling techniques in auditing. First, the general principles of sampling are discussed. More specifically, the meaning and importance of sampling in auditing are explained, the differences between, and the advantages and disadvantages of, judgmental and statistical sampling are examined, and some commonly used methods of selecting samples are described.

In the second part of the chapter some aspects of statistical sampling are considered in more detail. The meaning of basic terminology relating to statistical sampling, and the difference between attributes and variables sampling, are explained; the process of attributes sampling and the principles of probability proportional to size (PPS) sampling are examined; and the ways in which the auditor follows-up the results obtained by sampling are discussed.

11.2 MEANING AND IMPORTANCE OF SAMPLING IN AUDITING

Statement of Auditing Standards (SAS) 430: *Audit Sampling* defines audit sampling as follows:

> 'Audit sampling' means the application of audit procedures to less than 100% of the items within an account balance or class of transactions to enable auditors to obtain and evaluate audit evidence about some characteristic of the items selected in order to form or assist in forming a conclusion concerning the population which makes up the account balance or class of transactions. (para 4)

Expressed in more general terms, sampling is the examination of a few items (or sampling units) drawn from a mass of data (or population), with a view to inferring characteristics about the mass of data as a whole. This may be illustrated by reference to a simple example.

Example: Assume that a client has 200,000 suppliers' invoices and that the auditor wishes to ascertain:

(i) whether, before payment, the invoices were:
  * matched with purchase orders and receiving reports;
  * checked for correct extensions and additions;
  * checked for correct account classifications; and
(ii) whether:
  * the extensions and additions are arithmetically correct;
  * the transactions have been coded to the correct account;
  * the correct amounts have been recorded in the accounting records.

Reviewing these audit objectives, it should be noted that the first group relates to the client's internal control procedures. In order to test the level of compliance with these procedures, the auditor will perform compliance tests. The second group of objectives relates to the accuracy of the recorded amounts and account classifications of the transactions and, in order to test these, the auditor will perform substantive tests.

Clearly, it is not feasible for the auditor to apply the six tests to all 200,000 invoices. Instead, (s)he will select a sample of, say, 40 invoices, and will perform the six tests on these. Based on the results of the tests, the auditor will draw conclusions about the population of suppliers' invoices with respect to each of the characteristics tested (That is, for each characteristic tested, the results obtained from testing 40 invoices will be inferred into the population as a whole.)

Sampling has been an accepted auditing technique since the early part of the 20th century and today is recognised as an essential feature of most audits. Three main reasons account for its importance, namely:

1. In the modern business environment, it is not economically feasible to examine the details of every transaction and account balance.
2. Testing a sample of transactions is faster and less costly than testing the whole population.
3. The auditor is required to form an opinion about the truth and fairness of the financial statements. The auditor is not required to reach a position of certainty, nor is (s)he concerned with the statements' absolute accuracy. The task can be accomplished by testing samples of evidence; there is no need to test the whole. This point is reflected in SAS 400: *Audit Evidence*, which states:

> Auditors seek to provide reasonable, not absolute, assurance that the financial statements are free from material misstatement. In forming their audit opinion, therefore, auditors do not normally examine all of the information available. Appropriate conclusions can be reached about a financial statement assertion using a variety of means of obtaining evidence, including sampling. (para 5)

Notwithstanding its undoubted advantages, reliance on sampling procedures introduces a matter of concern to the auditor. It exposes the auditor to sampling risk – that is, the risk that the auditor will draw incorrect conclusions about the population because the sample examined is not representative of the population. Although this risk cannot be avoided altogether if sampling procedures are used, it can be reduced by increasing sample size and by selecting sample units at random (see section 11.4.2 below). Additionally, sampling risk may be controlled and quantified through the use of statistical sampling techniques.

11.3 JUDGMENTAL AND STATISTICAL SAMPLING COMPARED

When discussing audit sampling, it is important to distinguish between judgmental and statistical sampling.

(i) *Judgmental Sampling*

Judgmental sampling refers to the use of sampling techniques in circumstances where the auditor relies on his or her judgment to decide:

- how large the sample should be;
- which items from the population should be selected;
- whether to accept or reject the population on the basis of the results obtained from the sample.

This sampling method has an advantage over statistical sampling in that it is generally faster, and therefore less costly, to apply. Additionally, it enables the auditor to incorporate in the sampling procedures allowance for factors known to him or her through gaining an understanding of the client and its business, and evaluating its internal controls. However, unlike statistical sampling, the method provides no measure of sampling risk and, should the auditor's judgment be challenged (particularly in a court of law), the decisions reached with respect to the sample may be difficult to defend. Further, when using judgmental sampling it is difficult not to introduce bias, whether it be in relation to sample size, the items selected, or the conclusions reached with respect to the population.

(ii)   *Statistical Sampling*

Statistical sampling refers to the use of sampling techniques which rely on probability theory to help determine:

- how large the sample should be;
- whether to accept or reject the population based on the results obtained from the sample.

It should be noted that when statistical sampling is used, sample units must be selected at random. (Random sample selection is discussed in section 11.4.2 below.)
   This sampling method has three important advantages over judgmental sampling:

1. It is unbiased.
2. Should aspects of the sampling be challenged, it is readily defensible.
3. It permits quantification of sampling risk. For example, if a sample is selected on the basis of a 95% confidence level, there is a 5% sampling risk—that is, there is a 5% risk that the sample is not representative of the population and, as a result, incorrect conclusions may be drawn about the population. (Sampling risk is discussed further in section 11.6 below.)

However, statistical sampling has the disadvantage that it is more complex and costly to apply than judgmental sampling. Further, in the main, only audits of large entities have populations which are sufficiently large and homogeneous for full application of statistical sampling methods. As a consequence, in many audits where these methods are applied, they tend to be applied in a modified form.
   In relation to statistical sampling it should be noted that, notwithstanding the distinction which is drawn between statistical and judgmental sampling, significant elements of judgment are involved in applying statistical sampling techniques. This is evident from the examination of attributes and PPS sampling procedures presented in section 11.6.

11.4 SELECTING SAMPLES

11.4.1 Introduction to Methods of Sample Selection

Once the auditor has decided to apply a certain audit procedure to a sample of items in a population, rather than to the population as a whole, two further decisions are necessary:

(i) how many items (or sampling units) to include in the sample. As noted above, this decision may be reached judgmentally or statistically;
(ii) how to select the items to include in the sample. This decision revolves around whether the sample is to be selected randomly or non-randomly.

11.4.2 Random Selection

The key feature of random sample selection is that each item in the population has an equal chance of selection. While maintaining this characteristic, a number of variations of random selection may be recognised. These include the following:

(i)   unrestricted random sampling;
(ii) stratified random sampling;
(iii) systematic sampling;
(iv) cluster sampling;
(v)   sampling with probability proportional to size [(PPS) or monetary unit sampling].

(i) *Unrestricted Random Sampling*

This method of sampling treats the total population as a homogenous mass of data and random number tables or computer-generated random numbers are used to select the required number of sampling units. A small portion of a random number table is reproduced in Figure 11.1.

Figure 11.1   Part of a Random Number Table

23874	36953	47611	53271
73595	29164	92997	75772
32003	66955	63762	96329
31000	68341	10444	00023
86017	59362	79230	37132
50273	93280	51093	05936
60119	06926	50848	18779
86145	12672	93824	60260
22551	34469	32143	77126
91478	75385	05441	09541

In order to select sampling units by means of unrestricted random sampling, the following procedures need to be followed:

1. *A numbering system* for the population under investigation needs to be established. Frequently this is provided by sequentially numbered documents, such as sales invoices, purchase order forms, payments vouchers, and page and item numbers in cash journals. However, where such numbers are missing, a numbering system must be established.
2. Where a random number table is to be used, a *correspondence* must be established between the items constituting the population and the numbers in the random number table. For example, if the numbers on sales invoices issued during the reporting period range from 2496 to 5121, a decision must be made as to whether to use the first four digits of each five-digit random number, or the last four digits.
3. *A route for selecting numbers* from the random number table must be established. For example, should the numbers be selected moving down columns, up columns, across rows from right to left, or left to right, diagonally, and so on. In order for the numbers to be selected at random, the route must be established in advance of the numbers being selected, and followed consistently.
4. In order to avoid any predictability of the numbers which are selected, *the starting point of the route* must be chosen at random. This can be accomplished in innumerable ways, for example, by blindly sticking a pin or pencil point in the random number table, or opening a telephone directory at random, selecting a number at random and using the last two digits to identify a column and the next two digits to identify a row in the random number table. The point at which the column and row intercept marks the start of the route for selecting numbers.
5. Beginning at the selected starting point and following the pre-established route, *the required number of random numbers* are selected. If a particular random number falls outside the range of the population numbers, it is ignored and the next number is selected. Similarly, if a particular unit within the population is identified more than once by the random numbers selected, the second selection is discarded and further numbers are chosen until sufficient numbers have been identified to facilitate selection of the required number of sample units.

Once the quantum of random numbers has been selected, the corresponding sample units can be identified in the population, and the relevant audit procedure(s) performed.

Example: In order to illustrate unstratified random sample selection, the following facts are assumed:

- A population of sales invoices has numbers ranging from 2496 to 5121.
- A sample of 125 units is to be selected.
- The auditor has decided:
  - to use the first four digits of each random number in the random number table,
  - to move up one column and down the next, working from right to left across the random number table.
- The starting point has been selected as the second column in from the right of the table and fourth row up from the bottom.

If Figure 11.1 depicts the relevant random number table, the starting point is number 50848. The relevant digits are 5084. Working up this column, the numbers

5084 and 5109 are selected; 7923, 1044, 6376 and 9299 all fall outside the relevant range of sales invoice numbers and are discarded. The number 4761 is within the range and is selected; moving to the next column to the left and working downwards, the numbers 3695 and 2916 are selected, 6695 is discarded . . . and so on, until 125 numbers have been identified.

Once the random numbers have been selected, 125 sales invoices with numbers corresponding to the random numbers are identified and the relevant audit procedure(s) are performed.

Instead of using a random number table, a computer program may be used to generate the required number of random numbers. In this case, the smallest and largest numbers in the population sequence, and the quantum of random numbers required, are input to the computer program. The program then generates the required number of random numbers from within the sequence of numbers provided.

Unrestricted random sampling possesses the advantages of being unbiased and readily defensible. However, particularly when random number tables are used, it can be time-consuming and, therefore, costly.

(ii)   *Stratified Random Sampling*

Stratified random sampling involves stratifying the population in some way before determining the size of the sample or selecting the sample units. For example, debtors account balances may be stratified according to size and/or age. Balances exceeding some specified monetary amount, and balances beyond some age limit (for example, 90 days), may be subjected to 100% sampling (that is, the total population of these account balances may be checked) and the remaining balances treated as a homogenous population from which an unrestricted random sample is selected.

The advantage of stratified random sampling is that it permits allowance to be made for variations in the risk attaching to identifiable components of the population. In the debtors example cited above, the risk of material error being present is higher for large and old account balances than it is for balances which are smaller and those which have been outstanding for a shorter period.

(iii)   *Systematic Sampling*

For systematic sampling, a selection interval is first determined by dividing the population by the sample size. For example, if the population of sales invoices has numbers ranging from 2496 to 5121 and the sample size is 125, the selection interval is:

$$\frac{(5121 - 2496)}{125} \;=\; 21$$

A number between 0 and 21 is selected at random and this gives the starting point. Every 21st item in the population is then selected, beginning with that point.

Systematic sampling is simple to use, and is generally quicker and therefore less costly, than unrestricted random sampling. However, it has the disadvantage that it can introduce bias into the sample if the characteristic of interest is not randomly distributed through the population. For example, the use of systematic sampling to select a sample of sales invoices to check for authorisations of credit sales will not generally cause any problem. However, if every 25th person on the payroll is fictitious, systematic selection using a sampling interval of 25 could result in a sample consisting entirely of fictitious employees. Alternatively, by selecting a different starting point and using a sampling interval of 25, the sample may fail to include any of the fictitious employees (a situation which is potentially more serious for the auditor).

(iv)   *Cluster Sampling*

Cluster sampling involves selecting clusters of items in the population (or groups of contiguous items or records) rather than individual items. For example, if a sample of 125 units is required, 25 clusters of five units may be selected. If the first unit in each cluster is selected using unrestricted random sampling, then the sample is regarded as a random sample.

This method of sampling provides a straightforward and relatively quick means of selecting a sample. However, in some circumstances it may be less efficient than samples comprising individually selected items as it may result in a larger sample size. For example, if a sample of sales invoices is to be checked for sales authorisations, a sample of 125 units selected individually may provide good coverage of invoices issued during the reporting period. However, 25 clusters of five units may not give adequate coverage, and the number of clusters may need to be increased. In other cases cluster sampling may be particularly appropriate, for example, in testing for completeness of records. If the auditor wishes to check that all sales invoices, purchase orders, stock-taking sheets, and similar documents are accounted for (that is, documents which are numbered sequentially), (s)he may check the number sequence of 125 documents in 25 clusters of five.

(v)   *Sampling with Probability Proportional to Size (PPS) (Monetary Unit Sampling)*

When PPS sampling is used, each individual monetary unit (that is, each individual £1) in a population is regarded as a separate population unit and each has an equal chance of selection.

This method may be explained by reference to the following example.

Example: Assume that the debtors' account balance in a client's balance sheet comprises 10 individual debtors' accounts and that the balances of these accounts at balance sheet date are as set out in Figure 11.2. Also assume that a sample of six units is required for testing.

The accounts are recorded in the order in which they appear in the subsidiary ledger and the cumulative pounds (£s) in the accounts are calculated (see Figure 11.2, column 3). These cumulative pounds constitute the population of 4690 individual pounds. Pounds 1 to 276 are contained in account 1, pounds 277 to 1470 in account 2, etc. Unrestricted random sampling or systematic sampling is used to select the required number of sample units—that is, individual identified pounds.

Figure 11.2   PPS Sampling: Population of Debtors

Account	Recorded balance	Cumulative total (pounds units)	Location of sample units
	£	£	
1	276	276	✓
2	1,194	1,470	✓
3	683	2,153	✓
4	25	2,178	
5	1,221	3,399	✓
6	94	3,493	
7	76	3,569	
8	684	4,253	✓✓
9	135	4,388	
10	302	4,690	

With reference to Figure 11.2, assume that unrestricted random sampling generated the following random numbers:[1] 2997, 3595, 3762, 2003, 0023, 0444. These
random numbers correspond to individual pounds in the cumulative total and result
in accounts 5, 8, 8, 3, 1 and 2 being selected for examination. Account 8 is a 'double
hit' but it is, of course, only examined once.

The advantage of PPS sampling is that larger account balances have a greater chance
of selection and it is these balances which, because of their size, are more likely to
contain a misstatement which is material. However, the method also has the disadvantage that small balances have a low probability of being included in the sample, yet a
small balance may be significantly understated and a series of errors in small balances
may together constitute a material misstatement. These concerns may be overcome by
treating balances which are smaller than a specified limit as a separate population and
selecting a sample from them using, for example, unrestricted random sampling.

Another problem of PPS sampling is the inability to include negative balances, for
example, debtors' accounts with credit balances. A possible approach to this difficulty
is to treat negative balances as if they were positive and to include them in the
cumulative total on that basis.

11.4.3   Non-random Selection

There are two main methods of non-random sample selection, namely:

(i)   haphazard selection;
(ii) judgmental selection.

(i)   *Haphazard Selection*

When using haphazard sampling, the auditor attempts to replicate random sample
selection but without following the formality of using a random number table or

---

[1] These numbers have been derived from the random number table of which Figure 11.1 is a part. The last four
digits of each random number have been used, moving across the table from right to left along consecutive
rows (downwards) starting with row 2 and ignoring numbers which fall outside the population range.

computer-generated random numbers. The auditor selects items from the population haphazardly, without regard to size, source, date, or any other distinguishing feature of the items.

The method is simple and quick, but it has the disadvantage that unintended bias may be introduced into the sample. Certain items in the population tend to have a greater chance of being selected than others; for example, items at the top, bottom or middle of a page; known (or unknown) persons; names which attract attention for some reason, and so on.

(ii) *Judgmental Sample Selection*

When using judgmental selection, the auditor deliberately tries to select a sample which is representative of the population and/or includes those items which (s)he considers require close attention.

When attempting to select a representative sample, the auditor will be particularly concerned to include, for example:

- a selection of items representing transactions occurring in each month (or even in each week) of the reporting period, and for each employee who has been involved in handling the transactions during the period;
- a selection of account balances or transactions which are representative of those in the population. Thus, the proportion of large and small account balances included in the sample will reflect the proportion of these balances in the population.

When the auditor wishes to select a sample which emphasises high-risk areas, care will be taken to include:

- a large proportion of large transactions or account balances, as an error in a large transaction or balance is more likely to be material;
- items representative of periods when internal controls may have been functioning less effectively than normal; for example, when the key control person (such as the credit manager, or supervisor responsible for reviewing bank reconciliations and journal entries) was on holiday or absent through illness.

The major advantage of judgmental sample selection is that it enables the auditor to tailor his or her sample to the unique circumstances of the client. However, it also has the significant disadvantage (which it shares with haphazard sampling) that, should the sample be challenged (for example, in a court of law), it may be more difficult to defend than random sample selection.

11.4.4 Documentation of Sample Selection

Before leaving the subject of sample selection, it should be noted that all aspects of selecting the sample must be clearly and fully documented in the audit working papers. The documentation should include details of:

- the size of the sample selected – and how this was determined;
- the method of sample selection.

When random sampling is used, the source of random numbers (for example, random number table, or computer program) should be noted. If a random number table is used, the digits selected from the random numbers, the starting point, and the route adopted should all be recorded.

When stratified random sampling is used, the basis and rationale of the stratification should be noted. Similarly, when judgmental sample selection is used, the factors the auditor took into account when exercising his or her judgment should be recorded.

11.5 JUDGMENTAL SAMPLING AND AUDIT PROCEDURES

As noted in section 11.2 above, sampling is used to facilitate the performance of a compliance or a substantive audit procedure. That is, instead of applying the audit procedure to all of the items constituting the population, the procedure is applied to a sample of the items. The results obtained by applying the procedure to the sample are then inferred into the population as a whole.

When judgmental sampling is adopted, the sampling process rests on the exercise of the auditor's judgment. The steps in the process are as follows:

(i)   the sample size is determined judgmentally;
(ii)   the sample is selected using either a random or a non-random sample selection method;
(iii) the sample is examined for the characteristic being tested; that is, compliance with a specific internal control procedure, or the validity, completeness and/or accuracy of the monetary amount of a class of transactions or account balance;
(iv)   the sample results are inferred into the population and, based on these results, the population is rejected or accepted as 'satisfactory'; that is, exercising judgment, the auditor concludes that the control being tested has (or has not) been adequately complied with, or that the class of transactions or account balance is (or is not) free of material misstatement.

As will be seen in the next section, when statistical sampling techniques are used, steps (i) and (iv) above are determined by applying probability theory, and step (ii) must be performed using random selection methods.

11.6 INTRODUCTION TO STATISTICAL SAMPLING

11.6.1 Terminology

In order to understand the fundamental principles of statistical sampling, it is necessary to have a good grasp of a few of the terms which are commonly used. These include the following:

1. *Population:* This refers to all of the items within an account balance or class of transactions which display a particular characteristic about which the auditor wishes to draw a conclusion.

2. *Frame:* This is the physical representation of the population. For example, if the auditor is interested in the initials of the credit manager on sales invoices as evidence of compliance with authorisation procedures, the sales invoices are the frame. If the auditor is interested in the accuracy of debtors' account balances, subsidiary ledger records may be the frame.
3. *Sample unit:* A sample unit is a unit selected from the population and included in the sample to be examined.
4. *Characteristic of interest:* This term refers to the characteristic the auditor wishes to test. There are two basic characteristics of interest, namely, an attribute and a variable:
   (a) An attribute is a characteristic of the population which is either present or absent. Attributes sampling measures how frequently the characteristic is present (or absent) – for example, the credit manager's initials on sales invoices signifying approval of credit sales.
   (b) A variable is a measurement which is possessed by every member of the population but which can take any one of a wide range of values. An example of a variable is the monetary amount of a transaction or account balance. In variables sampling the auditor is concerned with estimating a monetary value – for example, the estimated balance of the stock account, or the estimated amount by which this balance may be in error.
5. *Precision limits:* This term refers to how closely the results obtained from the sample match the results that would have been obtained had the total population been tested. For example, in attributes sampling, if the sample shows that a particular characteristic occurs in 2% of cases, how closely this reflects the rate of occurrence which would have been found if every item in the population had been checked. Alternatively, in variables sampling, if the auditor estimates, based on the sample, that the balance of the stock account is £750,000, how close this is to the amount that would have been arrived at if the value of every individual item of stock had been ascertained and added.
6. *Confidence levels:* This term refers to how confident the auditor wishes to be that his or her sample will have the desired precision. For example, if the auditor wishes to estimate the balance of the stock account and specifies a precision limit of £10,000 with a 95% level of confidence, this means that the auditor wishes his or her estimate of stock to be within £10,000 of the actual value of stock, at least 95 times out of every 100. By inference, it also means that the auditor is prepared to accept that, on five occasions out of 100, his or her estimate of stock (based on the sample examined) may differ from the actual value of stock by more than £10,000. (This 5% risk of the results derived from the sample falling outside the specified precision limits is referred to as sampling risk.)

11.6.2 Sampling Plans

Sampling plans are statistical sampling methods. The most common fall into two main categories – namely, attributes sampling plans and variables sampling plans. Banks (1979, p.113) provides a clear explanation of the difference between the two. He says:

> From a practical audit point of view, generally the extrapolation of the sample results to arrive at a population conclusion is limited to the following two techniques:

(a) sampling for Attributes (how many);
(b) sampling for Variables (how much).

In the case of attribute sampling the type of conclusion one would reach might read as follows:

'I am 95% confident, based upon the results of the bias-free [i.e. random] sample selected, that the population error rate will not exceed 5% in respect of those attributes being tested.'

With the variable sampling techniques the type of conclusion one might reach would read as follows:

'I am 95% confident, based upon the sample selected without bias, that the total monetary value of the entire population will be within the range of (say) $293,789 and $316,323.'

As may be seen from Figure 11.3, although the sampling plans used in auditing fall into two broad categories, different variations of attributes and variables sampling may be recognised.

Figure 11.3   Relationship between Sampling Methods[2]

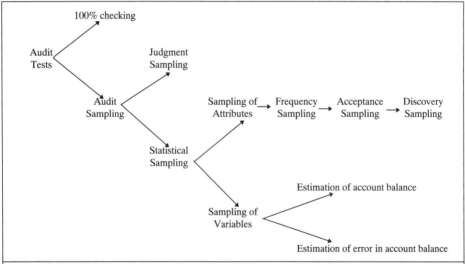

Note: PPS, or monetary unit, sampling is a hybrid of attributes and variables sampling. It is variables sampling in the sense that it measures monetary amounts, but attributes sampling techniques are employed to determine sample size and evaluate the sample results.

11.6.3   Attributes Sampling Plans

As noted above, attributes sampling is concerned with ascertaining whether a characteristic of interest is present or absent. Because evidence of compliance with internal control procedures (such as the credit manager's initials on sales invoices indicating authorisation of credit sales) is generally either present or absent, attributes sampling has particular application in compliance testing.

Three variations of attributes sampling are often used in auditing – namely, frequency estimation, acceptance sampling and discovery sampling.

---

[2] Adapted from McRae (1971, p.376).

1. *Frequency estimation:* This sampling plan involves examining a sample and, based on the occurrence (or, more usually, the absence) of a particular characteristic, estimating the rate of occurrence (or absence) of the characteristic in the population from which the sample is drawn. Frequency estimation might give rise to a statement such as: 'I am 95% confident that the rate of sales invoices in the population not carrying the credit manager's initials lies somewhere between 0.5% and 2.0%.'

   Although frequency estimation provides an estimate of the error rate in the population being investigated (in the above statement, the absence of the credit manager's initials on sales invoices), it does not directly address the question of whether or not the error rate is acceptable to the auditor. Expressed slightly differently, frequency estimation does not provide the auditor with an accept/reject decision rule: it does not give direct guidance as to whether the internal control being tested can be relied upon as planned.

2. *Acceptance sampling:* With acceptance sampling, before selecting and examining a sample from the population under investigation, the auditor needs to specify:
   (i) the tolerable error rate in the population (that is, the rate of error the auditor will accept in the population while still concluding that the control can be relied upon) and
   (ii) the expected error rate in the population (that is, the rate of error the auditor expects to exist in the population, given his or her assessment of inherent audit risk and preliminary evaluation of the client's internal controls). The expected error rate must clearly be less than the tolerable error rate.
   The difference between the tolerable error rate and the expected error rate determines sample size; the bigger the difference, the smaller the required sample.

   Unlike frequency estimation, acceptance sampling provides the auditor with a basis for deciding whether or not a population with a given error rate is acceptable (that is, whether compliance with a particular internal control procedure can be relied upon). Having specified the tolerable error rate in the population, the auditor can evaluate the sample results in this light. If the statistical evaluation of the sample results demonstrates that the tolerable error rate is unlikely to be exceeded, the population will be accepted and the relevant internal control relied upon. (A detailed example of acceptance sampling is provided below).

3. *Discovery sampling:* This is a subset of acceptance sampling where the expected error rate in the population is set at zero. This gives the smallest sample size possible under acceptance sampling. However, if a single error is found in the sample, then the tolerable error rate will be exceeded and the population cannot be accepted (or the relevant internal control relied upon) without further investigation.

   As the discovery of a single error in a sample results in the population not being acceptable to the auditor (at least, not without further investigation), discovery sampling reduces the number of populations which are accepted on the basis of the sample examined. However, discovery sampling is particularly useful to the auditor as it involves small samples and errors which are discovered in the sample provide guidance as to the nature and cause of errors in the population: discovery sampling is thus useful in directing the auditor's attention to areas which require more detailed investigation.

Detailed Illustration of Attributes Sampling

In order to provide an overview of attributes sampling, the procedure for acceptance sampling is set out below. For purposes of illustration, it is assumed that the audit client has 20,000 sales invoices and that the auditor wishes to establish whether or not credit sales are properly authorised.

The steps involved in acceptance sampling are as follows:

Steps involved in acceptance sampling	Illustration
1. Define the objective of the audit procedure.	To ascertain whether credit sales are properly authorised.
2. Define the attribute of interest.	Initials of credit manager on sales invoices signalling approval of credit sales.
3. Define the population (or, more correctly, the frame).	Sales invoices, with numbers ranging from 24,494 to 44,501.
4. Specify the tolerable error rate in the population (that is, the % error the auditor will tolerate in the population before concluding that the control cannot be relied upon).	4% tolerable error rate. The auditor will tolerate up to 4% of sales invoices not showing the credit manager's initials and still conclude that the control can be relied upon.
5. Specify the desired level of confidence, that is, the confidence the auditor wishes to have that the conclusion reached about the characteristic of interest in the population, based on the results of the sample, is valid. (The complement of the desired level of confidence is sampling risk—the risk that an incorrect conclusion about the characteristic of interest in the population will be reached, based on the sample results.)	A 95% confidence level is required. The auditor wishes to be 95% confident that if, based on the results of the sample, (s)he concludes that the error rate in the population does not exceed 4%, this conclusion is valid. [This is equivalent to the auditor accepting a 5% risk that the error rate in the population may, in fact, exceed 4% and thus (s)he may incorrectly conclude (based on the sample) that the control can be relied upon.]
6. Estimate the population deviation rate. (This is an estimation of the error rate based on the auditor's preliminary evaluation of the client's compliance with internal controls.)	It is estimated that 1% of sales invoices in the population do not contain the credit manager's initials.

Steps involved in acceptance sampling	Illustration
7. Use the relevant table to determine the required sample size.	See Figure 11.4 for the table entitled 'Sample size for attributes sampling'. (A different table exists for each desired level of confidence. The greater the desired level of confidence, other things being held constant, the larger the sample size.)
8. Using the table and the 'facts' established by judgment noted above, ascertain the sample size.	Tolerable error rate is 4% (see step 4 above). This identifies the relevant column in the table. The estimated population deviation rate is 1% (see step 6 above). This identifies the relevant row in the table. The required sample size is located at the intercept of the relevant column and row. It is seen to be 156
9. Randomly select a sample of the required size.	Using unrestricted random sampling select a sample of 156 sales invoices.
10. Perform the relevant audit procedure and record deviations	Vouch the 156 sales invoices and record all invoices which do not show the credit manager's initials. Assume one such invoice is found.
11. Generalise from the sample to the population using the relevant table for evaluating attributes sampling results.	See Figure 11.5 for the table entitled 'Evaluating attributes sampling results'. (A different table exists for each desired level of confidence.) The actual number of deviations found identifies the relevant column in the table. (In our example, one deviation is assumed: see step 10.) The sample size identifies the relevant row in the table. (In our example 150, being the closest to 156: see step 8.) From the table it is seen that (given our assumptions) the projected maximum error rate in the population (% of invoices without the sales manager's initials) is 3.1%. (This is not the most likely error rate but a 'worst case' possibility or upper boundary for the error rate.)

Steps involved in acceptance sampling	Illustration
12. Analyse detected deviations to ascertain whether they result from 'one-off' situations, or whether they are indicative of a more widespread problem – for example, the control failing to function properly when the key control person is absent.	Investigate the cause of the deviation detected. Assume this is found to be an isolated incident of control failure. (For example, two sales invoices were presented to the credit manager at one time for approval. (S)he reviewed both, but only initialed one invoice.)
13. Apply the decision rule for acceptance sampling. If the projected maximum population error rate shown in the table (based on the sample results) exceeds the tolerable error rate, conclude that the control may not be reliable. If the projected maximum population error rate is less than the tolerable error rate, subject to the analysis of detected deviations (see step 12), conclude that the control can be relied upon.	The projected maximum error rate in the population of 3.1% is less than the 4% tolerable error rate specified as acceptable by the auditor (see step 4). Additionally, the deviation detected has been found to be an isolated incident of control failure (see step 12). As a consequence of these findings, the auditor concludes that the control may be relied upon.

Figure 11.4 Sample Size for Attributes Sampling

95% Confidence Level (5% sampling risk)											
Expected Population Deviation Rate (in percentage)	Tolerable Deviation Rate (in percentage)										
	2	3	4	5	6	7	8	9	10	11	12
0.00	149	99	74	59	49	42	36	32	29	19	14
.25	236	157	117	93	78	66	58	51	46	30	22
.50	*	157	117	93	78	66	58	51	46	30	22
.75	*	208	117	93	78	66	58	51	46	30	22
1.00	*	*	(156)	93	78	66	58	51	46	30	22
1.25	*	*	156	124	78	66	58	51	46	30	22
1.50	*	*	192	124	103	66	58	51	46	30	22
1.75	*	*	227	153	103	88	77	51	46	30	22
2.00	*	*	*	181	127	88	77	68	46	30	22
2.25	*	*	*	208	127	88	77	68	61	30	22
2.50	*	*	*	*	150	109	77	68	61	30	22
2.75	*	*	*	*	173	109	95	68	61	30	22
3.00	*	*	*	*	195	129	95	84	61	30	22
3.25	*	*	*	*	*	148	112	84	61	30	22
3.50	*	*	*	*	*	167	112	84	76	40	22
3.75	*	*	*	*	*	185	129	100	76	40	22
4.00	*	*	*	*	*	*	146	100	89	40	22
5.00	*	*	*	*	*	*	*	158	116	40	30
6.00	*	*	*	*	*	*	*	*	179	50	30
7.00	*	*	*	*	*	*	*	*	*	68	37

Figure 11.5   Evaluating Attributes Sampling Results

Sample Size	\multicolumn{11}{c}{95% Confidence Level (5% sampling risk)}

	\multicolumn{11}{c}{Actual Number of Deviations Found}
Sample Size	0	1	2	3	4	5	6	7	8	9	10
25	11.3	17.6	*	*	*	*	*	*	*	*	*
30	9.5	14.9	19.5	*	*	*	*	*	*	*	*
35	8.2	12.9	16.9	*	*	*	*	*	*	*	*
40	7.2	11.3	14.9	18.3	*	*	*	*	*	*	*
45	6.4	10.1	13.3	16.3	19.2	*	*	*	*	*	*
50	5.8	9.1	12.1	14.8	17.4	19.9	*	*	*	*	*
55	5.3	8.3	11.0	13.5	15.9	18.1	*	*	*	*	*
60	4.9	7.7	10.1	12.4	14.6	16.7	18.8	*	*	*	*
65	4.5	7.1	9.4	11.5	13.5	15.5	17.4	19.3	*	*	*
70	4.2	6.6	8.7	10.7	12.6	14.4	16.2	18.0	19.7	*	*
75	3.9	6.2	8.2	10.0	11.8	13.5	15.2	16.9	18.4	20.0	*
80	3.7	5.8	7.7	9.4	11.1	12.7	14.3	15.8	17.3	18.8	*
90	3.3	5.2	6.8	8.4	9.9	11.3	12.7	14.1	15.5	16.8	18.1
100	3.0	4.6	6.2	7.6	8.9	10.2	11.5	12.7	14.0	15.2	16.4
125	2.4	3.7	4.9	6.1	7.2	8.2	9.3	10.3	11.3	12.2	13.2
150	2.0	(3.1)	4.1	5.1	6.0	6.9	7.7	8.6	9.4	10.2	11.0
200	1.5	2.3	3.1	3.8	4.5	5.2	5.8	6.5	7.1	7.7	8.3

It should be noted that the illustration generates a sample size of 156 invoices. This size of sample for a routine compliance test is probably impractical for all but the very largest audits. In practice, acceptance sampling is not used extensively and smaller judgmental samples are generally employed for compliance testing.

11.6.4   Variables Sampling

As noted earlier, variables sampling is concerned with estimating the monetary value of a financial statement balance, or estimating the amount by which it might be in error. Because of its focus on monetary amounts, variables sampling has particular application for substantive testing.

As may be seen from Figure 11.3, variables sampling includes estimation sampling which may take the form of estimating either an account balance or the maximum amount of error in an account balance.

1.   *Estimating an Account Balance*:

In this form of variables sampling, the auditor selects a sample of items (that is, a sample of transactions or components of an account balance, such as items of stock) and, based on this sample, estimates the range of values (between upper and lower bounds, or limits) within which the financial statement account balance should fall. This form of estimation sampling might give rise to a statement such as: 'From the items of stock examined, I am 95% confident that the value of the stock account balance lies between an upper bound of £765,000 and a lower bound of £683,000.'

2. *Estimating the Error in an Account Balance*:

In this case, rather than estimating the value of an account balance, the auditor estimates the amount of error (between upper and lower bounds) which may exist in the balance. It might give rise to a statement such as: 'From the items of stock examined, I am 95% confident that the amount of error in the stock account balance is between an upper bound of £50,000 and a lower bound of £8,000.'

Although variables sampling is a useful auditing technique, for many populations the application of variables sampling procedures results in a sample size which is impractically large. Additionally, variables sampling may not be appropriate for all population distributions and, as a result, use of this technique often requires specialist statistical expertise. For these reasons, variables sampling is not often used for audit purposes. A far more popular technique is PPS (or monetary unit) sampling.

11.6.5   Probability Proportional to Size (PPS) (or Monetary Unit) Sampling

As noted in Figure 11.3 above, PPS (or monetary unit) sampling is a hybrid of attributes and variables sampling. It is a technique which is based on monetary values in a population and therefore it possesses elements of variables sampling; however, attributes sampling techniques are employed in determining the sample size and evaluating the sample results.

In order to provide an overview of monetary unit sampling, the procedure followed is set out below. For purposes of illustration, it is assumed that the client's unaudited balance sheet shows total debtors at an amount of £3,198,426. The auditor wishes to confirm that this balance is not materially misstated.

The steps involved in monetary unit sampling are as follows:

Steps involved in PPS/monetary unit sampling	Illustration
1. Define the objective of the audit procedure.	To reach a conclusion as to whether the debtors' balance of £3,198,426 is materially misstated.
2. Define the population (or, more correctly, the frame).	3,198,426 individual one pound monetary units. (Each pound in the population is treated as equivalent to a physical unit in attributes sampling.)
3. Specify the tolerable error rate in the population (that is, the % error the auditor will tolerate in the population before concluding that the balance is materially misstated).	Assume a tolerable error rate of 4%, i.e. a materiality limit of £128,000 (4% of £3,198,426).
4. Specify the desired level of confidence. (The complement of the desired level of confidence is sampling risk.)	Assume a confidence level of 95% is required.

Steps involved in PPS/monetary unit sampling	Illustration
5. Estimate the expected error rate in the population. This is an estimate of the error rate in pounds (based on prior audit work). It is equivalent to the expected population deviation rate in attributes sampling.	Assume the expected error rate in the population is 1%; i.e. the auditor expects the population to contain a misstatement of £32,000 (1% of £3,198,426).
6. Use the relevant table to determine the required sample size.	See Figure 11.4 for the table entitled 'Sample size for attributes sampling'. (A different table exists for each desired level of confidence. The greater the desired level of confidence, other things being held constant, the larger the sample size.)
7. Using the table and the 'facts' established by judgment noted above, ascertain the sample size.	Tolerable error rate is 4% (see step 3 above). This identifies the relevant column in the table. The estimated population deviation rate is 1% (see step 5 above). This identifies the relevant row in the table. The required sample size is located at the intercept of the relevant column and row. It is seen to be 156.
8. Randomly select a sample of the required size.	Using PPS (monetary unit) sampling, select a sample of 156 pounds and identify the individual debtors' account balances in which they are contained (see section 11.4.2).
9. Perform the relevant audit procedure and record error (deviations).	Confirm the 156 debtors' balances containing the 156 sample pounds using confirmation techniques/alternative procedures in the normal way. Assume that one debtors' account balance recorded as £20,000 should be £10,000 and that no other errors are found.
10. Generalise from the sample to the population using the relevant table for evaluating attributes sampling results.	See Figure 11.5 for the table entitled 'Evaluating attributes sampling results'. (A different table exists for each desired level of confidence.) The actual number of errors (deviations) found identifies the relevant column in the table. (In our example, one deviation is assumed. Although the debtor's total balance of £20,000 is checked, only one of these 20,000 pounds was included in the sample. It is this one pound which is in error) (see step 9).

Steps involved in PPS/monetary unit sampling	Illustration
	The sample size identifies the relevant row in the table. (In our example 150, being the closest to 156: see step 7.) From the table it is seen that (given our assumptions) the projected maximum error rate in the population (% of pounds misstated) is 3.1%.
11. Analyse detected errors to ascertain whether they result from 'one-off' situations, or whether they are indicative of a more widespread problem – for example, a control failing to function properly when the key control person is absent.	Investigate the cause of the error detected. Assume this is found to be an isolated incident of control failure. (For example, two sales invoices of £10,000 were paid but only one was recorded as paid in the debtors' ledger.)
12. Apply the decision rule for acceptance sampling. If the projected maximum population error rate shown in the table (based on the sample results) exceeds the tolerable error rate, conclude that the account may be misstated. If the projected maximum population error rate is less than the tolerable error rate, subject to the analysis of the detected errors (see step 11), conclude that the account is not materially misstated.	The projected maximum error rate in the population of 3.1% is less than the 4% tolerable error rate specified as acceptable by the auditor (see step 3). Additionally, the error detected has been found to be an isolated incident of control failure (see step 11). As a consequence of these findings, the auditor concludes that the debtors' balance of £3,198,426 is not materially misstated.

It should be noted that, unlike the compliance testing example in section 11.6.3, where a sample size of 156 is probably impractically large, a debtors' confirmation exercise covering 156 debtors' account balances would not be an unreasonable sample size for a substantive test of an important account (debtors) in a fairly large audit.

Two further points need to be made in respect of this illustration. These are as follows:

1. It was noted in section 11.4.2 that PPS (monetary unit) sampling gives small balances a low probability of being included in the sample. It might be necessary, therefore, to supplement the sample of 156 account balances with a selection of small account balances to investigate the possibility of small balances containing significant understatements.
2. The error found in the illustration was a debtor's balance recorded at £20,000 which should be £10,000. This was treated as one deviation, being one debtor's pound included in the sample which was in error (step 10). Thus, in order to ascertain the projected maximum error rate, the relevant column in Figure 11.5 is that for one error (deviation) actually found. In reality the debtor's balance is not completely in error but 50% in error, since the £20,000 recorded should not be zero but £10,000. This is known as a 'partial' error. For such a 50% error (or 0.5 error) it is possible to 'interpolate' between the columns in Figure 11.5 for 0 errors and for one error,

giving a maximum projected error rate in the population of 2.55% [that is half way (50%) between the projected error rate for 0 errors (2.0%) and for one error (3.1%).] Such a refinement in respect of partial errors can reduce the projected maximum error rate (from 3.1% to 2.55% in our example) and, thus, can affect the acceptability of the population.

11.7 FOLLOWING-UP SAMPLE RESULTS

Irrespective of whether judgmental or statistical sampling techniques are used, the auditor does not slavishly follow the sampling method's accept/reject rule. For example, if the projected maximum population deviation rate in acceptance sampling is less than the specified tolerable deviation rate, this does not mean that the auditor will automatically accept the control as functioning effectively throughout the reporting period. Similarly, if the estimated value of an account balance falls within the auditor's specified tolerable error range, this does not automatically result in the conclusion that it is fairly stated. Instead, the auditor remains alert to the possibility that the control under investigation may not have functioned effectively throughout the reporting period, or the account balance being examined may be materially misstated. Thus, for example, as noted in sections 11.6.3 and 11.6.5 above, *all* deviations detected during the examination of sample units in acceptance and monetary unit sampling are analysed to ascertain their cause, irrespective of whether the auditor's tolerable error rate is, or is not, exceeded.

However, assuming that nothing has come to the auditor's attention to cause him or her to conclude otherwise, if a sample produces results which accord with the sampling method's 'accept' rule, the auditor will generally conclude that the internal control on which (s)he plans to rely to prevent material errors from occurring in the financial statements is functioning effectively, or that the account balance examined is not materially misstated. Nevertheless, the auditor remains aware of his or her exposure to sampling risk, and continues to watch for evidence which suggests that his or her conclusion about the internal control or account balance may be invalid.

Where sample results indicate that an internal control or account balance is not satisfactory, this finding must be followed up by alternative auditing techniques. In the case of a control which is found not to be operating effectively, other controls might be found and tested to see if reliance can be placed on them to detect or prevent the particular (potential) error, or substantive tests may be extended. If the sample indicates that an account balance might be materially misstated, alternative techniques must be employed to ascertain whether this is, or is not, the case.

11.8 SUMMARY

This chapter has provided an introduction to the use of sampling techniques in auditing. The meaning of sampling and terms associated with it have been explained, a distinction has been drawn between judgmental and statistical sampling, and the advantages and disadvantages of each of these sampling techniques have been discussed. In addition, some of the commonly used methods of selecting samples (randomly and non-randomly) have been described, and an overview has been provided of the application of attributes sampling to compliance testing and of PPS (monetary unit) sampling to substantive testing. The chapter has concluded with a discussion of the auditor's follow-up to sample results.

SELF-REVIEW QUESTIONS

11.1 Explain briefly what is meant by 'audit sampling'.

11.2 Distinguish between judgmental sampling and statistical sampling.

11.3 List two advantages and two disadvantages of each of the following:
    (i) judgmental sampling
    (ii) statistical sampling.

11.4 State the characteristic feature of a random sample.

11.5 List five methods (or variations) of random sample selection.

11.6 Distinguish briefly between:
    (i) haphazard sample selection; and
    (ii) judgmental sample selection.

11.7 Explain briefly the essential difference between attributes sampling and variables sampling.

11.8 In relation to statistical sampling, explain briefly what is meant by:
    (i) precision limits; and
    (ii) confidence levels.
    Give a specific example to illustrate your answer.

11.9 (a) Define a sampling plan;
    (b) List four types of sampling plans.

11.10 Explain briefly why PPS (monetary unit) sampling can be referred to as a hybrid of attributes and variables sampling.

REFERENCES

Banks, A. (1979). Current status of statistical sampling. *Accountants' Journal*, **58**(3), 113.
McRae, T.W. (1971). Applying statistical sampling in auditing: Some practical problems. *The Accountant's Magazine*, **LXXV**(781), 369–77

ADDITIONAL READING

Cosserat, G. (1983). Judgmental sampling rules O.K! *Accountancy*, **94**(1076), 91–2.
Grant Thornton. (1990). *Audit Manual*, Chapter 18, Statistical sampling. London: Longman, 255–62.

Grimlund, R.A. (1993). Tests of controls with interim-review populations: new results and recommendations for implementing professional pronouncements. *Accounting and Business Research*, **23**(91), 248–62.

Robertson, J.C. & Rouse, R. (1994). Substantive audit sampling—The challenge of achieving efficiency along with effectiveness. *Accounting Horizons*, **18**(1), 35–44.

Smith, T.M.F. (1976). *Statistical Sampling for Accountants*. London: Accountancy Age Books.

Vagge, R. (1980). Towards understanding statistical sampling. *CPA Journal*, **50**(5), 13–19.

Woolf, E. (1983). Audit sampling—without tears (or tables). *Accountancy*, **94**(1076), 84–7.

Chapter 12

Completion and Review

LEARNING OBJECTIVES

After studying the material in this chapter you should be able to:
- explain the place and the importance of completion and review procedures within the audit process;
- discuss the importance of, and procedures used for, the review for contingent liabilities and commitments;
- discuss the importance of, and procedures used for, the review for subsequent events:
- distinguish between subsequent events which necessitate adjustments to the financial statements and those which require only note disclosure;
- discuss the action auditors should take in relation to subsequent events which come to light after the audit report has been signed;
- explain the importance of re-assessing the validity of the going concern assumption during the completion stage of the audit;
- explain the nature and importance of management representation letters;
- discuss the nature and importance of the final review of audit working papers;
- explain the significance of dating the audit report.

The following publications and fundamental principle of external auditing are particularly relevant to this chapter:

Publications:
- Statement of Auditing Standards (SAS) 130: *The Going Concern Basis in Financial Statements* (APB, 1994)
- Statement of Auditing Standards (SAS) 150: *Subsequent Events* (APB, 1995)
- Statement of Auditing Standards (SAS) 160: *Other Information in Documents Containing Audited Financial Statements* (APB, 1995)
- Statement of Auditing Standards (SAS) 440: *Management Representations* (APB, 1995)
- Statement of Auditing Standards (SAS) 470: *Overall Review of Financial Statements* (APB, 1995)
- International Standards on Auditing (ISA) 501: *Audit Evidence – Additional Considerations for Specific Items* (IFAC, 1990)

Fundamental principle of external auditing: *association*
Auditors allow their reports to be included in documents containing other information only if they consider that the additional information is not in conflict with the matters covered by their report and they have no reason to believe it to be misleading.

12.1   INTRODUCTION

As explained in Chapter 9, in order to conduct the detailed work of evaluating and testing the effectiveness of the client's internal controls and confirming the validity, completeness and accuracy of transactions and account balances, the auditor divides (conceptually) the client's accounting system into sub-systems, or audit segments. Once the detailed audit work is complete, the auditor approaches the audit holistically (as is the case for the early part of the audit), and the completion and review stage is conducted on an entity-wide basis.

As shown in Figure 12.1, the completion and review phase of an audit comprises four main steps, namely:

(i)   the review for contingent liabilities and commitments;
(ii) the review for subsequent events and reassessment of the validity of the going concern assumption;
(iii) the review of the financial statements and audit working papers;
(iv) evaluation of the audit evidence and formulation of an opinion.

In this chapter we discuss each of these important audit steps.

Figure 12.1   Place of Completion and Review in the Audit Process

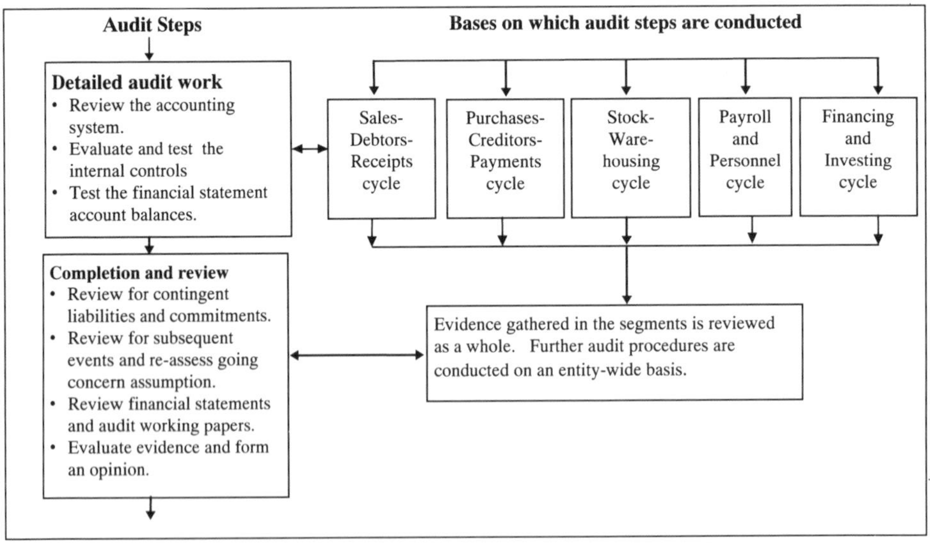

12.2   REVIEW FOR CONTINGENT LIABILITIES AND COMMITMENTS

Before considering the importance of the review for contingent liabilities and commitments, it is necessary to clarify the meaning of these terms.

• *Contingent liabilities*: are potential obligations which are expected to arise but which, at the balance sheet date, are uncertain as to amount. They are (potential) liabilities whose outcome is contingent upon the occurrence or non-occurrence of some uncertain future event. Examples include taxation in dispute and pending litigation for infringement of, for example, environmental, product safety, or product description regulations.

• *Commitments*: are contractual undertakings. Examples include bonus and profit-sharing schemes, and agreements to purchase raw materials or other stock at a fixed price at a particular date in the future, or to lease or buy fixed assets at a certain price, or to sell a certain quantity of goods, at an agreed price on a specified future date.

The auditor faces two major problems in relation to the review for contingent liabilities and commitments, namely:

(i) management may not feel disposed to disclose them in the financial statements;
(ii) as they do not involve transactions which are recorded in the accounting system, it is generally more difficult for the auditor to discover events and agreements which lie outside the accounting records.

Nevertheless, the existence of contingent liabilities and commitments may have a significant impact on the assessment of a reporting entity's financial position and performance by a user of its financial statements. Therefore, in order to provide a true and fair view of the entity's financial affairs, its financial statements must disclose any material contingent liabilities and commitments. As a consequence, when forming an opinion on the financial statements, the auditor has an obligation to determine the client's position with respect to these items.

The procedures most commonly adopted by auditors to ascertain the existence (or otherwise) of contingent liabilities and commitments include the following:

• enquiries of management;
• reviewing the minutes of directors' meetings;
• reviewing correspondence files [and, in particular, correspondence between the client and its solicitor(s)];
• reviewing the current and previous years' tax returns;
• reviewing the current year's audit working papers for any information that may indicate a potential contingent liability;
• obtaining confirmation from the client's solicitor(s) regarding any known existing, pending or expected contingent liabilities (especially arising from litigation) and commitments.

With respect to the last procedure noted above, International Standards on Auditing (ISA) 501: *Audit Evidence – Additional Considerations for Specific Items* states:

> When litigation or claims have been identified or when the auditor believes they may exist, the auditor should seek direct communication with the entity's lawyers. (para 33)
> The letter, which should be prepared by management and sent by the auditor, should request the lawyer to communicate directly with the auditor. When it is considered

unlikely that the lawyer will respond to a general inquiry, the letter would ordinarily specify:

- A list of litigation and claims.
- Management's assessment of the outcome of the litigation or claim and its estimate of the financial implications, including costs involved.
- A request that the lawyer confirm the reasonableness of management's assessments and provide the auditor with further information if the list is considered by the lawyer to be incomplete or incorrect. (para 34)

12.3   REVIEW FOR SUBSEQUENT EVENTS

12.3.1   Events between the Balance Sheet Date and Audit Report Date

The auditor has a responsibility to form and express an opinion on whether or not the audit client's financial statements give a true and fair view of its financial position and performance as at the balance sheet date. As a result, the auditor has an obligation to consider events which take place between the balance sheet date and the date on which the audit report is signed, which might affect a financial statement user's assessment of the entity's financial position and/or performance as at the balance sheet date.

The auditor's responsibility to review events which occur subsequent to the balance sheet date is normally limited to the period between that date and the date of the audit report. The review normally takes place during the final two to three weeks before the audit report is signed. The timing of the subsequent events review is depicted in Figure 12.2.

Figure 12.2   Timing of the Subsequent Events Review

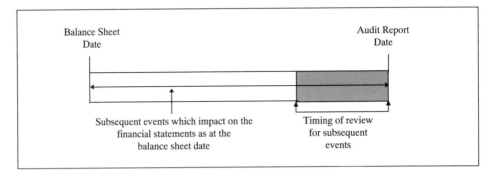

Subsequent events may be of two types, namely:

(i)   adjusting events
(ii)   non-adjusting events.

(i)   *Adjusting Events*

Adjusting events are events which clarify conditions which existed at the balance sheet date and/or which permit more accurate valuation of accounts in the financial statements at the balance sheet date. These events require the financial statements to be adjusted so that they reflect as accurately as possible the entity's financial position and performance as they existed at the balance sheet date.

Examples of adjusting events include the resolution of tax disputes and litigation which existed at the balance sheet date but the amount of which was then uncertain, and the unexpected collapse of a material debtor which was regarded as 'good' at the balance sheet date. This latter event is classified as an adjusting event if the conditions which caused the customer's collapse existed at the balance sheet date.[1] If the conditions arose subsequent to the balance sheet date, the event is classified as a non-adjusting event.

(ii) *Non-adjusting Events*

Non-adjusting events are events which relate to conditions which arose subsequent to the balance sheet date. These events represent changes in the situation as it existed at the balance sheet date and, as a result, they should not be incorporated in the financial statements as adjustments to account balances. However, if these events are considered to be material to financial statement users, in that they may affect users' evaluation of the financial position and/or future prospects of the entity, the events should be disclosed by way of a note to the financial statements.

Examples of non-adjusting events include a major fire or flood in the audit client entity subsequent to the balance sheet date where the resulting loss is not covered by insurance, and the entry of the entity into a significant transaction subsequent to the balance sheet date (such as the purchase of a subsidiary) which has a material impact on the entity's resources.

Statement of Auditing Standards (SAS) 150: *Subsequent Events* outlines procedures auditors should perform in order to identify subsequent events. These include the following:

- enquiring into, and considering the effectiveness of, the procedures management has established to ensure that subsequent events are identified;
- reading minutes of the meetings of members, the board of directors and audit and executive committees held after period end and enquiring about matters discussed at meetings for which minutes are not yet available;
- reviewing relevant accounting records and reading the entity's latest available financial information, such as interim financial statements, budgets, cash flow forecasts and other related management reports; and
- making enquiries of management as to whether any subsequent events have occurred which might affect the financial statements. (para 7)

Examples of specific enquiries which may be made of management are:

- the current status of items involving subjective judgment or which were accounted for on the basis of preliminary data, for example litigation in progress;
- whether new commitments, borrowings or guarantees have been entered into;
- whether sales of assets have occurred or are planned;

---

[1] It should be noted that, as the customer's collapse arose subsequent to the balance sheet date, the debt was not 'bad', and therefore the account should not be written off, at the balance sheet date. However, as the relevant conditions causing the collapse existed at the balance sheet date, the debt was under threat at that time and an adjustment should be made to the allowance for bad debts.

- whether the issue of new shares or debentures, or an agreement to merge or to liquidate, has been made or is planned;
- whether any assets have been destroyed, for example, by fire or flood;
- whether there have been any developments regarding risk areas and contingencies;
- whether any unusual accounting adjustments have been made or are contemplated; and
- whether any events have occurred or are likely to occur which might bring into question the appropriateness of accounting policies used in the financial statements as would be the case, for example, if such events might call into question the validity of the going concern basis. (para 8)

12.3.2   Events Subsequent to the Date of the Audit Report

(i)   *Prior to Issue of Financial Statements*

The auditor has an obligation to seek out events which occur between the balance sheet date and audit report date which might necessitate adjustment to, or disclosure in, the financial statements. However, (s)he does not have a responsibility to perform procedures to identify events after the audit report has been signed. Nevertheless, events may come to the auditor's attention after signing the audit report, but before the financial statements are issued, which (s)he considers should be reflected in the financial statements. In this circumstance, the auditor is required to discuss with management the possibility of amending the financial statements. If the financial statements are amended, the subsequent period is, in effect, extended to a later date. Appropriate subsequent events procedures should be performed relative to this extended period and the date of the audit report adjusted accordingly (SAS 150, paras 11 and 12).

If management refuses to amend the financial statements, the auditor's future action depends on whether the audit report has been released to the client. If the audit report has not been released, and the auditor considers the circumstances warrant it, a qualified or adverse audit opinion should be expressed. (These forms of opinion are discussed in Chapter 13.) If the audit report has been released to the client, the auditor should consider steps to take on a timely basis to prevent reliance on the report. SAS 150, para 19, notes that such steps may include making an appropriate statement at the annual general meeting. It may also include taking legal advice on the position.

(ii)   *Subsequent to Issue of Financial Statements*

Occasionally, a matter may come to the auditor's attention after the financial statements have been issued, which materially affects the truth and fairness of those financial statements. If this occurs, the auditor should discuss the situation with the client's directors and consider the implications for the audit report. The directors may decide to make an appropriate statement at the annual general meeting. Alternatively, or additionally, they may decide to issue a revised set of financial statements. If the latter course of action is followed, SAS 150, para 17, notes that the auditor should take the following steps:

- carry out the audit procedures necessary in the circumstances;
- for listed companies, consider whether Stock Exchange regulations require the revision to be publicised;

- for businesses authorised under the Financial Services Act 1986 or other regulated businesses, consider whether there is any requirement to communicate with the appropriate regulator;
- review the steps taken by the directors to ensure that anyone in receipt of the previously issued financial statements, together with the auditors' report thereon, is informed of the situation;
- issue a new report on the revised financial statements.

SAS 150 (para 18) states that when auditors issue a new report on the revised financial statements, they should:

- refer (in the audit report) to the note to the financial statements which explains the reason for the revision of the previously issued financial statements, or set out such reason in their report.
- refer to the earlier audit report issued on the financial statements;
- date the new audit report not earlier than the date the revised financial statements are approved;
- have regard to the guidance relating to reports on revised annual financial statements provided in the APB's Practice Note 8: *Reports by auditors under company legislation in the United Kingdom.*

If management does not take adequate steps to ensure that those in receipt of the (original) financial statements are notified that the information in those statements has been superseded (whether by issuing amended statements, or otherwise), the auditor should consider steps to take, on a timely basis, to prevent reliance on the original audit report. The auditor may also need to take legal advice (SAS 150, para 19).

An example of revised financial statements, accompanied by a revised audit report, is provided by the 1994 financial statements of Newarthill plc. As may be seen from Figure 12.3, Newarthill's original 1994 financial statements did not comply with Financial Reporting Standard No. 4 in respect of the redeemable convertible preference shares issued by an Australian subsidiary.

The directors have explained the reason for the revised financial statements, prepared a full set of revised financial statements, and provided an amendment to their Directors' Report. The auditors (Deloitte & Touche) have issued a revised audit report which complies with the requirements of SAS 150. (The format and content of standard audit reports are the subject of Chapter 13.)

12.4 REASSESSMENT OF THE GOING CONCERN ASSUMPTION

Financial statements are generally prepared on the assumption that the entity is a going concern. Statement of Standard Accounting Practice (SSAP) 2: *Disclosure of Accounting Policies* explains that 'going concern' means 'the enterprise will continue in operational existence for the foreseeable future.[2] This means in particular that

---

[2] The SSAP uses the term 'foreseeable future' without further elaboration.

Figure 12.3a   Directors' Note on Newarthill plc's 1994 Revised Financial Statements and Amendment to the Directors' Report

---

Newarthill p.l.c.

REVISION OF REPORT AND FINANCIAL STATEMENTS

Following discussion with the Financial Reporting Review Panel the Directors have concluded that the financial statements for the year ended 31st October 1994 did not apply Financial Reporting Standard No 4 in respect of the redeemable convertible preference shares issued by an Australian subsidiary. The financial cost of these shares had not been charged to minority interests within the profit and loss account and then released as a profit upon disposal of that subsidiary.

The Directors are therefore taking advantage of SI 1990 No. 2570 to revise the original financial statements.

The following statements and information replace that appearing in the original financial statements.

AMENDMENT TO THE REPORT OF THE DIRECTORS (Dated 13th April 1995)

Results and Dividends
The Group profit for the year after taxation and minority interests amounts to £15,262,000. Preference dividends totalling £322,000 have been paid, resulting in a transfer to reserves of £14,940,000.

The Directors do not recommend the payment of an ordinary dividend.

[there is no] intention or necessity to liquidate or curtail significantly the scale of operations' [para 14(a)].

When financial statements are prepared on the basis of the going concern assumption, assets and liabilities are recorded at the amounts which can reasonably be expected to be realised or discharged (as applicable) in the ordinary course of business. These amounts may differ quite significantly from those that would apply in the event of the entity's liquidation. Thus, when forming an opinion on the truth and fairness with which a reporting entity's financial statements portray the entity's state of affairs and financial performance, the auditor must consider whether adherence to the going concern assumption is justified.

Until SAS 130: *The Going Concern Basis in Financial Statements* came into effect in 1995, an auditor was merely required to remain alert to the possibility that the going concern assumption may not be valid. However, if questions regarding the continued existence of the entity arose, specific audit procedures to assess its going concern status were conducted. These generally included procedures such as:

- analysing cash flow, profit and other relevant forecasts and discussing these forecasts with management:
- reviewing the terms of debentures and loan agreements to determine whether these had been breached;
- reviewing the minutes of directors' meetings and of other relevant committees (such as an audit committee) for any reference to financial difficulties;
- confirming the existence, legality and enforceability of arrangements to provide financial support to, or receive financial support from, related and third parties, and assessing the financial position of these parties;

Figure 12.3b   Auditors' Report on Newarthill plc's 1994 Revised Financial Statements

AUDITORS' REPORT TO THE MEMBERS OF NEWARTHILL p.l.c.

We have audited the revised financial statements of Newarthill p.l.c. for the year ended 31st October 1994 drawn up so as to comply with FRS4. The revised financial statements replace the original financial statements approved by the directors on 13th April 1995 and consist of the attached supplementary note together with the original financial statements which were circulated to members on 28th April 1995.

Respective responsibilities of directors and auditors

As described in the supplementary note the directors are responsible for the preparation of financial statements. It is our responsibility to form an independent opinion, based on our audit, on these financial statements and to report our opinion to you. We are also required to report whether in our opinion the original financial statements failed to comply with the requirements of the Companies Act 1985 in the respects identified by the directors.

Basis of opinion

We conducted our audit in accordance with Auditing Standards issued by the Auditing Practices Board. An audit includes examination, on a test basis, of evidence relevant to the amounts and disclosures in the financial statements. It also includes an assessment of the significant estimates and judgements made by the directors in the preparation of the financial statements, and of whether the accounting policies are appropriate to the group's and company's circumstances, consistently applied and adequately disclosed. The audit of revised financial statements includes the performance of additional procedures to assess whether the revisions made by the directors are appropriate and have been properly made.

We planned and performed our audit so as to obtain all the information and explanations which we considered necessary in order to provide us with sufficient evidence to give reasonable assurance that the revised financial statements are free from material misstatement, whether caused by fraud or other irregularity or error. In forming our opinion we also evaluated the overall adequacy of the presentation of information in the revised financial statements.

Opinions

In our opinion the revised financial statements, drawn up so as to comply with FRS4, give a true and fair view, seen as at the date the original financial statements were approved, of the state of the group's and the company's affairs as at 31st October 1994 and of the group's profit for the year then ended and have been properly prepared in accordance with the provisions of the Company Act 1985 as they have effect under the Companies (Revision of Defective Accounts and Report) Regulations 1990.

As stated in our original opinion the original financial statements for the year ended 31st October 1994 failed to comply with the requirements of the Companies Act 1985 in the respects identified by the directors in the supplementary note.

Deloitte & Touche
Chartered Accountants and Registered Auditors
Hill House
1 Little New Street
London
EC4A 3TR
8th March 1996

- evaluating the entity's position with respect to unfilled customer orders;
- discussing with management their plans for dealing with the situation.

Evaluating the propriety of preparing the financial statements on a going concern basis was an audit step which was generally taken in the subsequent review period; however, the procedures outlined above could be performed at any time during the audit if something came to light which raised doubt in the auditor's mind regarding the ability of the entity to continue as a going concern. If, after investigating the circumstances and evaluating management's plans, the auditor still had doubts about the ability of the entity to continue as a going concern, (s)he was required to express those doubts in the audit report.

In the United Kingdom (UK), United States (US) and elsewhere, the auditor's duty in this regard has been clear for many years: if auditors had unresolved doubts about the ability of the auditee to remain in existence, they were required to express those doubts in the audit report and disclose the reasons therefor. However, the evidence suggests that, at least until recently, auditors did not, in general, fulfil this duty adequately. As Congressman Dingell (1985, p.22), the vocal critic of auditors in the US, observed, it is difficult to understand how a company can get a clean bill of health one day and collapse just one day later. Similarly, in the UK, auditors' failure to disclose doubts they had (or should have had) about entities' ability to continue in operation has been a major source of criticism of auditors in recent years (see, for example, Porter, 1993). The auditing profession in the UK and US (and elsewhere) has responded to this criticism by developing new auditing standards/guidelines which spell out auditors' duties with respect to the going concern assumption far more explicitly than has hitherto been the case.

Instead of merely requiring auditors to remain alert to the possibility that the going concern assumption may be subject to question, SAS 130 requires auditors to be proactive. They are now required to perform certain procedures on all audits to assess the auditee's going concern status. These are shown in Figure 12.4.

As may be seen from Figure 12.4, a preliminary assessment of the client's going concern status should be made during the planning phase of the audit. This is based on the auditor's understanding of the client's business, assessment of relevant risk factors and discussions with the client's directors (or their equivalent).

In relation to the procedures to be performed during the evidence gathering phase, SAS 130 states:

> The auditors should assess the adequacy of the means by which the directors have satisfied themselves that:
> (a) it is appropriate for them to adopt the going concern basis in preparing the financial statements; and
> (b) the financial statements include such disclosures, if any, relating to going concern as are necessary for them to give a true and fair view.
> For this purpose:
> (i) the auditors should make enquiries of the directors and examine appropriate available financial information; and
> (ii) having regard to the future period to which the directors have paid particular attention in assessing going concern, the auditors should plan and perform procedures specifically designed to identify any material matters which could indicate concern about the entity's ability to continue as a going concern. (para 21)

Figure 12.4 Assessment of the Auditee's Going Concern Status

Audit Steps	Audit Phase
Undertake preliminary assessment of the client's going concern status based on understanding the client's business, assessing risk factors, and discussions with the directors (or their equivalent).	Planning
Perform specific procedures regarding the client's going concern status. Perform other routine audit procedures. Decide on the need for a bankers' confirmation or meeting.	Evidence gathering
Consider and, if necessary, revise the preliminary going concern assessment. Determine and document the extent of concern (if any). Decide on the need for formal representations from the client's directors (or equivalent). Assess the need for, and adequacy of, disclosures relating to the client's going concern status.	Review
Express the appropriate opinion and, if necessary, make relevant disclosures regarding going concern uncertainties in the audit report.	Reporting

SAS 130 further notes (para 23) that the auditors may need to consider the following matters:

- whether the period to which the directors have paid particular attention in assessing going concern is reasonable in the entity's circumstances;
- the systems the entity has in place for identifying, in a timely manner, risks and uncertainties the entity might face;
- budget and forecast information, and cash flow information in particular;
- whether key assumptions underlying the budgets and/or forecasts appear appropriate in the circumstances;
- the sensitivity of budgets and forecasts to variable factors both within and outside the control of the directors;

- any obligations, undertakings or guarantees arranged with other entities for giving or receiving of support;
- the existence, adequacy and terms of borrowing facilities and supplier credit;
- the directors' plans for resolving any matters giving rise to doubts, if any, on the appropriateness of the going concern assumption.

With regard to confirmation of banking facilities, SAS 130 encourages meetings between auditors and directors or, if appropriate, auditors, directors and bankers, so that the auditors can form a view as to the likelihood of the continuation of loan facilities. Bankers are normally willing to provide (with caveats) written confirmation of their intentions. SAS 130, para 26, points out that auditors are more likely to seek confirmation of the existence and terms of bank facilities and the bank's intentions, when:

- financial resources available to the audit client are limited;
- the client entity is dependent on borrowing facilities shortly due for renewal;
- correspondence between the bankers and the entity shows that the last renewal of facilities was agreed with difficulty;
- a significant deterioration in cash flow is expected;
- the value of assets granted as security is declining; or
- the client entity has breached the terms of borrowing covenants or there are indications of potential breaches.

During the review phase of the audit the auditors should reconsider and, if necessary, revise their preliminary assessment of the entity's going concern status (made during the planning stage). They should also document the extent of their concern, if any, about the entity's ability to continue as a going concern and decide whether formal written representations from the client's directors are needed (SAS 130, paras 29 and 33). Whenever there are significant uncertainties regarding the auditee's ability to remain in existence, it is advisable for the auditors to obtain a written statement from the directors confirming the directors' considered view that the entity is a going concern, together with supporting assumptions or qualifications, as necessary. In a small audit, the auditor may help the directors form a view with respect to the company's going concern status and, in this situation, a minute of the meeting signed by the directors could suffice as the directors' representations.

In cases where the auditors believe there is uncertainty regarding the entity's ability to continue as a going concern, they are required to decide whether the matters giving rise to the uncertainty are adequately disclosed in the financial statements (SAS 130, para 36). Where the auditors consider that the uncertainty is adequately disclosed, an unqualified audit opinion is appropriate. However, if the level of uncertainty is significant, the auditors are required to include an explanatory paragraph (headed 'Fundamental Uncertainty'), drawing attention to the uncertainty, in the section of the audit report which sets out the basis of the auditors' opinion.[3] Should the auditors consider that the going concern uncertainties are not adequately disclosed in the financial

---

[3] Audit reports are discussed in Chapter 13.

statements, and that the deficiency is material to the truth and fairness of the financial statements, they are required to express an 'except for' opinion.[3] Such an opinion should also be expressed if the auditors consider that the directors have not taken adequate steps to satisfy themselves that adoption of the going concern basis for their entity's financial statements is appropriate (SAS 130, paras 42, 43 and 48).

In circumstances where the auditors conclude that disclosures in the financial statements relating to going concern uncertainties are so inadequate as to cause the financial statements to be seriously misleading, they are required to express an adverse opinion. They are similarly required to express an adverse opinion if the financial statements have been prepared on a going concern basis and the auditors consider that adoption of this basis is inappropriate (SAS 1430, para 49). However, it should be noted that the latter situation would arise only in extreme circumstances, such as impending liquidation.

From the above discussion it is evident that auditors are no longer required merely to remain alert to the possibility that adoption of the going concern assumption may not be appropriate. They are now required under SAS 130 to evaluate explicitly whether uncertainties exist regarding the ability of the entity to continue as a going concern and to assess the adequacy of disclosures in the financial statements where there are such uncertainties.

By helping to ensure that uncertainties regarding the going concern assumption are detected, adequately disclosed in the financial statements and, where appropriate, referred to in the audit report, application of SAS 130 should enable users of the financial statements to assess for themselves the impact of any major uncertainties and the consequent risk to the viability of the entity. It should also ensure that auditors meet, far more closely than previously, society's expectations of their 'flagging' doubts about the ability of an entity to continue in existence, and thus should reduce the criticism previously levelled against auditors for failing to perform this duty adequately.

12.5 MANAGEMENT REPRESENTATION LETTERS

When conducting an audit, the auditor frequently has cause to rely on information given to him or her by management. As part of the completion and review stage of the audit, the auditor usually seeks to have significant representations made by management recorded in writing. These are generally documented in what is known as a management representation letter.

These letters are technically written by the client's management to the auditor but, in practice, they are normally prepared by the auditor and signed by management. Their purpose is essentially twofold:

(i) to explicitly draw to the attention of the client's management,[4] and to place on record, that responsibility for the financial statements (and their truth and fairness) lies with them and not with the auditor;

---

[4] It should be remembered that, in the company context, 'management' includes the company's directors (see note in the Preface to this book).

(ii) to place on record management's responses to enquiries made by the auditor during the course of the audit. This ensures there is no misunderstanding between management and the auditor as to what was said – and gives management the opportunity to correct any response which the auditor has misinterpreted. It also ensures that management assumes responsibility for its representations to the auditor.

Although management representation letters are normally obtained by the auditor as a matter of routine, opinion differs as to their value as audit evidence. This is clearly illustrated by the following quotations:

- The letter of representation is, at the very least, a useful piece of corroborative audit evidence. It can be of vital importance if the auditor is in any doubt as to whether he has been given all the information and explanations he requires. (Davey, 1980, p.60)

- The audit utility of representation letters as primary evidence would appear to be limited. At best they may be corroborative, and then only to the extent that they support propositions on which the auditor should have formed his own judgment based on stronger forms of evidence. . . . While there may be circumstances unique to a particular audit that suggest the appropriateness of a representation letter, on balance there appears to be little audit justification for the representation letter to be formalised as a generally accepted auditing practice. (Pound and Besley, 1982, p.13)

Notwithstanding Pound and Besley's stance, SAS 440: *Management Representations*, makes it clear that auditors are expected to obtain written confirmation of management's oral representations (para 3). This applies, in particular, in those circumstances where management's representations concern matters which are material to the financial statements and other sufficient appropriate audit evidence cannot reasonably be expected to exist; for example, management's intention to hold a specific investment for long-term appreciation (paras 11 and 16).

With respect to management representation letters, SAS 440 notes that:

- when requesting a management representation letter, auditors request that it be addressed to them, that it contain specified information and that it be appropriately dated and approved by those with specific knowledge of the relevant matters (para 20);
- auditors should normally request that the letter be discussed and agreed by the board of directors (or similar body) and signed on their behalf by the chairman and secretary before they approve the financial statements. This ensures that the board as a whole is aware of the representations on which the auditors intend to rely in expressing their opinion on those financial statements (para 21);
- the management representation letter is normally dated on the date the financial statements are approved. If there is any significant delay between the date of the letter and the date of the auditors' report, the auditors may consider it necessary to obtain further written representations regarding the intervening period (paras 22 and 23).

An example of a management representation letter, appropriate for use in the audits of companies (derived from the appendix to SAS 440), is provided in Figure 12.5. A letter along similar lines is used in the audit of public sector entities (suitably modified to reflect relevant public sector legislation and conditions).

Before leaving the topic of management representation letters, it is pertinent to note that, should management refuse to confirm its representations in writing, this will normally constitute a limitation on the scope of the audit examination and, as such, give rise to a qualified audit report.[5] Further, in such circumstances, it may not be appropriate for the auditors to place reliance on other representations made by management during the course of the audit (SAS 440, paras 24 and 25).

Figure 12.5   Example of a Management Representation Letter

(Company letterhead)

(To the auditors)   (Date)

We confirm to the best of our knowledge and belief, and having made appropriate enquiries of other directors and officials of the company, the following representations given to you in connection with your audit of the financial statements for the period ended 31 December 19.

1) We acknowledge as directors our responsibilities under the Companies Act 1985 for preparing financial statements which give a true and fair view and for making accurate representations to you. All the accounting records have been made available to you for the purpose of your audit and all the transactions undertaken by the company have been properly reflected and recorded in the accounting records. All other records and related information, including minutes of all management and shareholders' meetings, have been made available to you.

2) The legal claim by ABC Limited has been settled out of court by a payment of £258,000. No further amounts are expected to be paid, and no similar claims have been received or are expected to be received.

3) In connection with deferred tax not provided, the following assumptions reflect the intentions and expectations of the company:
   a) capital investment of £450,000 is planned over the next three years;
   b) there are no plans to sell revalued properties; and
   c) we are not aware of any indications that the situation is likely to change so as to necessitate the inclusion of a provision for tax payable in the financial statements.

4) The company has not had, or entered into, at any time during the period any arrangement, transaction or agreement to provide credit facilities (including loans, quasi-loans or credit transactions) for directors or to guarantee or provide security for such matters.

5) There have been no events since the balance sheet date which necessitate revision of the figures included in the financial statements or inclusion of a note thereto.

As minuted by the board of directors at its meeting on . . . (date).

....
Chairman   Secretary

Source: SAS 440, *Management Representations*, APB (1995), Appendix

---

[5] Scope limitations resulting in qualified audit reports are discussed in Chapter 13.

12.6 FINAL REVIEW, CONCLUSION AND CONFERENCE

12.6.1 Final Review of Audit Working Papers and Conclusion

SAS 470: *Overall Review of Financial Statements* requires auditors to:

carry out such a review of the financial statements as is sufficient, in conjunction with the
conclusions drawn from the other audit evidence obtained, to give them a reasonable
basis for their opinion on the financial statements. (para 2)

In order to achieve this audit objective, once all the audit evidence has been
gathered and documented, the audit supervisor, manager and engagement partner will
each, in turn, review the audit working papers. In carrying out their review they will be
concerned to establish that:

- sufficient appropriate audit evidence has been collected in each audit segment, and
  for the audit as a whole, on which to base an audit opinion;
- all audit work has been properly performed, documented and reviewed;
- conclusions reached in relation to specific audit objectives are consistent with the
  results obtained from the audit procedures performed;
- all questions and difficulties arising during the course of the audit have been
  resolved;
- the information presented in the financial statements complies with statutory requirements, and the accounting policies adopted are in accordance with accounting
  standards, properly disclosed, consistently applied and appropriate to the entity;
- the financial statements as a whole, and the assertions contained therein, are consistent with the auditors' knowledge of the entity's business and with the results of
  other audit procedures, and the manner of disclosure is fair.

A checklist may be used to ensure that all aspects of the financial statements are
properly covered. When considering whether the accounting policies adopted by management are appropriate to the entity's circumstances, the auditors will have regard to:

- any policies commonly adopted in the particular industry to which the entity
  belongs;
- policies for which there is substantial authoritative support;
- whether any departures from applicable accounting standards are necessary in order
  for the financial statements to give a true and fair view;
- whether the financial statements reflect the substance of the underlying transactions
  and not merely their form (SAS 470, para 5).

Once the audit engagement partner has reviewed the evidence gathered and conclusions reached with respect to the financial statement account balances and disclosures,
(s)he forms an opinion as to whether the financial statements give a true and fair view
of the reporting entity's state of affairs and financial performance. In order to ensure
that this opinion is consistent with the audit evidence collected (as documented in the
working papers), that sufficient appropriate audit evidence has been gathered, and
that the working papers provide evidence that the audit was carried out in accordance
with auditing standards, a second audit partner (who has not been involved in the
audit) may review the audit file.

12.6.2 Review of Unaudited Information

Even if everything is found to be in order, before the auditor can prepare the appropriate audit report, one further audit procedure needs to be performed. (S)he is required by SAS 160: *Other Information in Documents Containing Audited Financial Statements*, to review unaudited information in the entity's annual report (or other documents containing the audited financial statements) to determine that it is not materially inconsistent with the financial statements. This is in accord with fundamental principle of external auditing – *Association:*

> Auditors allow their reports to be included in documents containing other information only if they consider that the additional information is not in conflict with the matters covered by their report and they have no cause to believe it to be misleading.

Explaining the importance of this audit procedure, SAS 160 states:

> An inconsistency exists when the other information contradicts, or appears to contradict, information contained in the financial statements. An inconsistency may raise doubt about the audit conclusions drawn from audit evidence previously obtained and, possibly, about the basis for the auditors' opinion on the financial statements. (para 9)

If the auditor discovers a material inconsistency, (s)he is required to determine whether it is the financial statements or the unaudited information which requires amendment and to advise the client accordingly. If the financial statements are in error and the client refuses to make the necessary adjustments, the auditor is required to consider the implications for his or her audit report (SAS 160, para 10). Such an error will almost certainly result in a qualified or adverse opinion. If, however, it is the unaudited information which is incorrect and the client refuses to correct it, then the appropriate action depends on the particular circumstances.

• If the auditee is a limited company and the directors' report is inconsistent with the financial statements, the auditors have a statutory responsibility to refer to the inconsistency in the audit report (SAS 160, para 11). Additionally, as SAS 160 (para 14) points out, auditors of limited companies have a right under the Companies Act 1985 (s.390) to be heard at any general meeting of the company's members on matters which concern them as auditors. Thus, they have an opportunity to explain the situation.
• If the auditee is not a limited company and/or the error the client refuses to correct is present in unaudited information other than the directors' report, then the auditors may wish to seek legal advice on appropriate action or even resign from the engagement (SAS 160, paras 13 and 15). As noted in Chapter 3, if auditors of a limited company resign, they are required (by the Companies Act 1985, s.394) to make a written statement of any circumstances they consider should be brought to the attention of the company's shareholders or creditors (or a statement that there are no such circumstances.) A copy of this statement is sent to the Registrar of Companies.

12.6.3 Final Conference

Once all audit matters have been resolved and the auditor has reached a conclusion with respect to the financial statements and prepared the audit report, a final conference is held between the client's directors (or their equivalent or, if it has one, its audit committee), the audit engagement partner and (usually) the audit manager.

The conduct and findings of the audit are discussed, the financial statements are signed by one or more directors[6] (or their equivalent, if this has not already been done at a previous directors' meeting) and, finally, the audit report is signed and dated by the audit engagement partner (who signs for and on behalf of the audit firm). It is important that the auditor does not sign the audit report prior to the directors (or their equivalent) signing the financial statements. By signing the financial statements, the directors signal their responsibility for, and acceptance of, the statements as presented. The auditor's report expresses an opinion on the financial statements prepared, presented and approved by the directors.

The date of the audit report is of the utmost importance because it signifies the end of the period considered by the auditor when expressing an opinion on the financial statements. It marks the end of the 'subsequent period' in which events may have occurred which impact on the truth and fairness of the financial statements, as they reflect the financial position and performance of the entity as at the balance sheet date.

12.7 SUMMARY

In this chapter we have discussed the steps which constitute the completion and review phase of the audit. More specifically, we have examined the importance of, and procedures used for, the review for contingent liabilities and commitments, and the review for events (adjusting and non-adjusting) occurring subsequent to the balance sheet date. We have also discussed the auditor's duty with respect to the going concern assumption and the meaning and significance of management representation letters. Additionally, we have reviewed the steps involved in the final review of evidence gathered during the audit and the forming of an opinion with respect to the truth and fairness of the financial statements and their compliance with relevant legislation. In the concluding sections of the chapter, we have drawn attention to the need for the auditor to review unaudited information in the client's annual report (or other documents containing the audited financial statements), and explained the importance of the auditor signing the audit report after the directors (or their equivalent) have signed the financial statements. The significance of the audit report date has also been noted.

SELF-REVIEW QUESTIONS

12.1 Define:
   (i)   contingent liabilities
   (ii) commitments

12.2 List five procedures auditors commonly use during their review for contingent liabilities and commitments.

---

[6] The statutory requirement for one or more directors to sign the auditee's balance sheet is referred to in Chapter 3, Section 3.2.6.

12.3 (a) Briefly distinguish between (i) adjusting and (ii) non-adjusting subsequent events.

 (b) Give one specific example to illustrate each of these types of subsequent events.

12.4 (a) State the period which is subject to the auditor's review for subsequent events.

 (b) List three procedures auditors commonly use during their review for subsequent events.

12.5 Explain briefly what is meant by the going concern assumption.

12.6 Explain briefly the auditor's duty when (s)he has unresolved doubts about the ability of the auditee to continue as a going concern.

12.7 Explain briefly what is meant by a 'management representation letter' and outline its two primary purposes.

12.8 List five items which are commonly referred to in a management representation letter.

12.9 List four objectives of the final review of audit working papers.

12.10 Explain briefly the significance of dating the audit report.

REFERENCES

Davey, J. (1980). Are letters of representation a waste of time? *Accountancy*, **91**(1038), 59–60.

Dingell, J. (1985). Accountants must clean up their act. *Management Accounting*, **66**(1), 21–3, 53–6.

Porter, B.A. (1993). An empirical study of the audit expectation-performance gap. *Accounting and Business Research*, **24**(93), 49–68.

Pound, G. & Besley, R. (1982). Are representation letters needed? *The Chartered Accountant in Australia*, **52**(8), 11–13.

ADDITIONAL READING

Constantine, J. (1992). The APB and going concern – the way ahead. *Accountancy*, **110**(1191), 89.

Cuthbert, S. (1982). How easy to hoodwink the auditor! *Accountancy*, **93**(1063), 136.

Grant Thornton. (1990). *Audit Manual*. Chapter 21, Completion procedures. London: Longman, 291–306.

Chapter 13

Auditors' Reports to Users of Financial Statements and to Management

LEARNING OBJECTIVES

After studying the material in this chapter you should be able to:
- state the auditor's statutory reporting obligation with respect to both private and public sector entities;
- explain what is required in order for financial statements to provide a true and fair view;
- explain what is meant by 'proper accounting records';
- describe the format of the standard audit report used for (i) companies and (ii) public sector entities;
- explain the various types of audit opinion expressed in the United Kingdom and Republic of Ireland and the circumstances in which each is appropriate;
- explain how inherent uncertainties are reflected in standard audit reports;
- describe significant differences between the standard 'expanded' audit report now in use and the former 'short form' report;
- discuss the purpose and content of management letters.

The following publications and fundamental principle of external auditing are particularly relevant to this chapter:

Publications:
- Statement of Auditing Standards (SAS) 600: *Auditors' Reports on Financial Statements* (APB, 1993)
- Statement of Auditing Standards (SAS) 610: *Reports to Directors or Management* (APB, 1995)
- Practice Note 10: *Audit of Central Government Financial Statements in the United Kingdom* (APB, 1996)

Fundamental principle of external auditing: *Clear Communication*
  Auditors' reports contain clear expressions of opinion and set out information necessary for a proper understanding of that opinion.

13.1 INTRODUCTION

The audit process culminates in the auditor's statutory report to shareholders and/or other users of the audited financial statements. This report is the end product of the audit examination and communicates to users of the financial statements the auditor's conclusions about, amongst other things, the truth and fairness with which the statements portray the entity's financial position and performance and compliance (or otherwise) of the financial statements with relevant legislation. The auditor also provides a report to the entity's management, known as a management letter. This usually covers various aspects of the audit and the entity's financial affairs but mentions, in particular, any material weaknesses in the entity's internal controls which were discovered during the audit, and recommends ways in which these might be overcome. The management letter is not a legal requirement but is a service provided by auditors to the client's management as a by-product of the audit. Its contents are generally not revealed to shareholders or other users of the entity's financial statements.

In this chapter we discuss the statutory reporting obligations of auditors of both private and public sector entities. We explore the issue of what is required for financial statements to be adjudged 'true and fair' and what is meant by 'proper accounting records'. We also examine the format of standard audit reports currently in use and consider the various types of audit opinion the auditor may express and the circumstances in which each is appropriate. We observe that the audit report is frequently the auditor's only opportunity to communicate with users of the audited financial statements and we discuss the differences between the 'expanded' audit report now in use and its predecessor 'short form' report. Before concluding the chapter we consider reports by auditors on corporate governance matters (issued in accordance with the Cadbury Committee's Code of Best Practice) and address the topic of management letters, focusing in particular on their content and purpose.

13.2 THE AUDITOR'S STATUTORY REPORTING OBLIGATIONS UNDER THE COMPANIES ACT 1985[1]

The Companies Act 1985 places a major duty on auditors. First, it specifies that the directors of every company must prepare financial statements comprising a balance sheet and profit or loss account. These financial statements are required to give a true and fair view of the company's state of affairs and its profit or loss for the accounting period and comply with the provisions of the Act as to form, content and notes.

The preparation of financial statements which meet the statutory requirements is a duty which belongs exclusively to the entity's directors (or their equivalent). However, except in the case of exempt companies,[2] the Act places on auditors the responsibility of examining the financial statements and forming and expressing an opinion as to whether they give the required true and fair view and have been properly prepared in accordance with the Companies Act 1985. Additionally, auditors are required to form an opinion as to whether:

---

[1] As amended by the Companies Act 1989.

[2] See Chapter 3 (section 3.2.2) for an explanation of 'exempt' companies.

- proper accounting records have been kept by the company;
- proper returns have been received from branches not visited by the auditors;
- the financial statements are in agreement with the underlying accounting records;
- they have received all the information and explanations they required for the purposes of their audit;
- the information given in the directors' report is consistent with the financial statements.

In cases where auditors are of the opinion that any of these requirements have not been met, they are required to report that fact in their audit report.

As noted in Chapter 3 (section 3.2.2), although most companies with a turnover of less than £350,000 and a balance sheet total of not more than £1.4 million are exempt from the audit requirement, those with a turnover of between £90,000 and £350,000 are required to have an 'exemption report' prepared by a reporting accountant. This report is required to state whether, in the reporting accountant's opinion:

- the company's financial statements are in agreement with the underlying accounting records;
- the financial statements have been drawn up in accordance with the Companies Act;
- the company has met the criteria enabling it to qualify for an exemption report in place of an audit report throughout the year (Companies Act 1985, s.249C).

Regarding the matters about which the auditors of non-exempt companies must form an opinion, two require some explanation, that is:

(i) proper accounting records;
(ii) a true and fair view.

(i) *Proper Accounting Records*

The Companies Act 1985 (s.221) requires all companies to maintain 'proper accounting records'. The Act explains that such records must be sufficient to show and explain the company's transactions and, amongst other things:

- enable the company's financial position to be disclosed, with reasonable accuracy, at any time;
- enable a balance sheet and profit and loss account which complies with the Companies Act to be prepared;
- record the day-to-day details of all receipts and payments of cash;
- provide details of the company's assets and liabilities;
- provide details of stock held by the company;
- provide details of trading goods bought and sold. The records must be in sufficient detail to enable the goods, the buyers and the sellers to be identified.

It can be seen from these requirements that the Act is both specific and strict as regards the criteria to be met in order for a company's accounting records to be considered 'proper accounting records'. It does not, however, lay down any detailed requirements for particular procedures or controls to be implemented.

It is important to appreciate that auditors must form an opinion in every audit as to whether or not proper accounting records have been kept. However, this opinion is only stated in the audit report if the auditor considers that proper accounting records have *not* been kept.

(ii)   *A True and Fair View*

As explained in Chapter 4, the concept of 'a true and fair view' has been subject to different interpretations and it has not been defined by statute or by a court of law. However, the Auditing Practices Board (APB) has provided guidance to auditors on the criteria financial statements should meet in order to be adjudged true and fair. In SAS 600: *Auditors' Reports on Financial Statements,* the Board explains that:

- compliance with accounting standards[3] is, in the absence of exceptional circumstances, necessary for financial statements to give a true and fair view (para 39);
- if an entity departs from an applicable accounting standard, the particulars, including the financial effects of the departure, should be disclosed in the entity's financial statements (para 40);
- although there is no legal requirement for companies to comply with accounting standards, the Companies Act 1985 (Schedule 4, clause 36A) requires large companies to state in their financial statements whether or not those statements have been prepared in accordance with such standards and to explain any departures therefrom.

Following on from the last point, the APB concludes:

> It is likely that a Court would infer from this requirement, taken together with other changes introduced into UK company law by the Companies Act 1989, that . . . in general, compliance with accounting standards is necessary to meet the requirement of company law that the directors prepare annual accounts which give a true and fair view of a company's (or group's) state of affairs and profit or loss. (para 43)

If (in exceptional circumstances) compliance with accounting standards would result in financial statements which do not provide a true and fair view of the entity's state of affairs and profit or loss, the directors of the reporting entity should depart from the relevant standard(s) and/or provide additional information and explanations so that a true and fair view is given. In forming an opinion as to whether or not a set of financial statements presents a true and fair view, the auditor must give due consideration to the information presented in the financial statements as a whole – including any 'additional information and explanations' which are provided.

With reference to the evaluation of financial statements by auditors, it should be remembered that the Companies Act 1989 requires all auditors of the financial statements of companies to be members of a recognised auditing body.[4] Further, every

---

[3] 'Accounting standards' means Financial Reporting Standards (FRSs) and Statements of Standard Accounting Practice (SSAPs) issued by the Accounting Standards Board (ASB).

[4] See Chapter 3, section 3.2.3.

member of a recognised auditing body who conducts an audit must conduct that audit in accordance with auditing standards issued by the APB. As a consequence of these requirements, all auditors of company financial statements judge whether or not a particular set of financial statements gives the required true and fair view based on the same criteria. This provides for some uniformity of opinion as between different auditors working in similar circumstances. Additionally, the auditors' reporting standard (SAS 600) ensures that auditors use a similar format to report their opinion.

Special features of auditors' reporting obligations in respect of the financial statements of public sector entities are discussed in section 13.7 below.

13.3   FORMAT OF AUDIT REPORTS

The format of standard audit reports is prescribed by SAS 600. The unqualified audit report given by Ernst & Young on the 1995 financial statements of British Airways Plc, presented in Figure 13.1, is an example of an audit report prepared in accordance with this auditing standard.

SAS 600 explains that its purpose is to:

> establish standards and provide guidance on the form and content of auditors' reports issued as a result of an audit of the financial statements of an entity. (para 1)

Figure 13.1   An Example of a Standard Unqualified Audit Report

---

Report of the auditors to the members of British Airways Plc

We have audited the accounts on Pages 16 to 47, which have been prepared under the historical cost convention as modified by the revaluation of certain fixed assets and on the basis of the accounting policies set out on Pages 20 to 22.

Respective responsibilities of Directors and auditors

As described above, the Company's Directors are responsible for the preparation of the accounts. It is our responsibility to form an independent opinion, based on our audit, on those accounts and to report our opinion to you.

Basis of opinion

We conducted our audit in accordance with Auditing Standards issued by the Auditing Practices Board. An audit includes examination, on a test basis, of evidence relevant to the amounts and disclosures in the accounts. It also includes an assessment of the significant estimates and judgements made by the Directors in the preparation of the accounts and of whether the accounting policies are appropriate to the Group's circumstances, consistently applied and adequately disclosed.

We planned and performed our audit so as to obtain all the information and explanations which we considered necessary in order to provide us with sufficient evidence to give reasonable assurance that the accounts are free from material misstatement, whether caused by fraud or other irregularity or error. In forming our opinion we also evaluated the overall adequacy of the presentation of information in the accounts.

Opinion

In our opinion the accounts give a true and fair view of the state of affairs of the Company and of the Group as at 31 March 1995 and of the profit of the Group for the year then ended and have been properly prepared in accordance with the Companies Act 1985.

Ernst & Young
Chartered Accountants
Registered Auditor
London
22 May 1995

It is pertinent to note that SAS 600 (para 1) refers to 'an audit of the financial statements of *an entity*' (emphasis added). It does not restrict its application to audit reports issued on the financial statements of companies. The Standard applies to audit reports issued in relation to *all* reporting entities, whether they be in the private or the public sector. Nevertheless, largely as a result of legislative differences, as will be seen from the examples presented in this chapter, audit reports issued on the financial statements of public sector entities differ in some respects from their private sector counterparts.

Referring to the content of audit reports, SAS 600 (para 14) specifies that audit reports should include:

- a title identifying the person or persons to whom the report is addressed;
- an introductory paragraph identifying the financial statements audited;
- separate sections, appropriately headed, dealing with:
  - the respective responsibilities of the directors[5] (or their equivalent) and auditors,
  - the basis of the auditors' opinion,
  - the auditors' opinion on the financial statements;
- a manuscript or printed signature of the auditors;
- the date of the auditors' report.

Regarding the respective responsibilities of the directors and auditors, SAS 600 (para 20) explains that the audit report should include:

- a statement that the financial statements are the responsibility of the reporting entity's directors;
- a reference to a description of those responsibilities if this is set out elsewhere in the financial statements or accompanying information; and
- a statement that the auditors' responsibility is to express an opinion on the financial statements.

In relation to the basis of the auditors' opinion, the Standard (para 24) states that auditors should include in their report:

- a statement as to their compliance or otherwise with Auditing Standards, together with the reasons for any departure therefrom;
- a statement that the audit process includes:
  - examining, on a test basis, evidence relevant to the amounts and disclosures in the financial statements,
  - assessing the significant estimates and judgments made by the reporting entity's directors in preparing the financial statements,
  - considering whether the accounting policies are appropriate to the reporting entity's circumstances, consistently applied and adequately disclosed;

---

[5] SAS 600 defines 'directors' as 'the directors of a company, proprietors or trustees of other forms of enterprise or equivalent persons responsible for the reporting entity's affairs, including the preparation of its financial statements' (para 10). Thus, the term is defined to embrace the governing body (or management) of public sector entities.

- a statement that they planned and performed the audit so as to obtain reasonable assurance that the financial statements are free from material misstatement, whether caused by fraud or other irregularity or error, and that they have evaluated the overall presentation of the financial statements.

As regards dating the audit report, it was noted in Chapter 12 that the audit report date is extremely important as it signifies the date to which the auditor has considered events, the occurrence of which might impact on the truth and fairness of the financial statements. SAS 600 further explains:

> Auditors should not express an opinion on financial statements until those statements and all other financial information contained in a report of which the audited financial statements form a part have been approved by the directors, and the auditors have considered all necessary available evidence. (para 76)

> The date of the auditors' report is, therefore, the date on which, following:
> a) receipt of the financial statements and accompanying documents in the form approved by the directors for release;
> b) review of all documents which they are required to consider in addition to the financial statements (for example the directors' report, chairman's statement or other review of an entity's affairs which will accompany the financial statements); and
> c) completion of all procedures necessary to form an opinion on the financial statements (and any other opinions required by law or regulation) including a review of post balance sheet events
> the auditors sign (in manuscript) their report expressing an opinion on the financial statements for distribution with those statements. (para 80)

> If the date on which the auditors sign their report is later than that on which the directors approved the financial statements, the auditors take such steps as are appropriate:
> a) to obtain assurance that the directors would have approved the financial statements on that later date . . .; and
> b) to ensure that their procedures for reviewing subsequent events cover the period up to that date. (para 83)

The APB has developed illustrative examples of audit reports incorporating the various requirements noted above, and these are presented in Appendix 2 to SAS 600. The APB clearly expects the examples to be followed closely, for the Standard states:

> [T]he use of common language in auditors' reports assists the reader's understanding. Accordingly, Appendix 2 [to the Standard] includes examples of auditors' reports on financial statements to illustrate wording which meets the Auditing Standards contained in this SAS. (para 16)

However, the Standard also notes that 'auditors draft each section of their report on financial statements to reflect the requirements which apply to the particular audit engagement' (para 16), therefore some differences may be expected.

Referring to Figure 13.1, it should be noted that, in accordance with SAS 600, the report identifies the persons to whom it is addressed (the members of British Airways Plc) and the financial statements on which the audit report is given. The report also contains separate, suitably headed, sections dealing with the directors' and auditor's responsibilities, the basis of the auditors' opinion and the auditors' opinion on the financial statements. The report also includes the auditors' signature (in printed form) and the report is dated (22 May 1995). The captions and the wording used follow the example of an unqualified audit report provided in SAS 600, Appendix 2 (Example 1).

13.4   TYPES OF AUDIT REPORT

13.4.1   Overview of Types of Audit Report

There are basically two types of audit report:

- an unqualified report (that is, a 'clean' report);
- a qualified report.

However, there are three types of qualified report, namely, those containing:

- an 'except for' opinion;
- an adverse opinion;
- a disclaimer of opinion.

As shown below, each type of report is appropriate for particular circumstances.

Irrespective of the type of audit report issued, the auditor should provide a clear expression of opinion on the financial statements and on any further matters required by statute or the particular engagement. The opinion should be based on an assessment of the conclusions drawn from evidence obtained during the audit (SAS 600, paras 2 and 30). As noted in fundamental principle of external auditing – *Clear Communication*, the audit report should also contain sufficient information for a reader to gain a proper understanding of the auditor's opinion. In the words of the principle:

> Auditors' reports contain clear expressions of opinion and set out information necessary for a proper understanding of that opinion.

13.4.2   Unqualified Audit Reports

SAS 600 explains:

> An unqualified opinion on financial statements is expressed when in the auditors' judgment they give a true and fair view (where relevant) and have been prepared in accordance with relevant accounting or other requirements. This judgment entails concluding whether *inter alia:*
> - the financial statements have been prepared using appropriate accounting policies, which have been consistently applied;
> - the financial statements have been prepared in accordance with relevant legislation, regulations or applicable accounting standards (and that any departures are justified and adequately explained in the financial statements); and
> - there is adequate disclosure of all information relevant to the proper understanding of the financial statements. (para 32)

The report on the 1995 financial statements of British Airways Plc is an example of an unqualified audit report (see Figure 13.1).

13.4.3   Qualified Audit Reports

According to SAS 600 (para 33), a qualified opinion is expressed when:

- there is a limitation on the scope of the auditor's examination (i.e. the auditor is unable to examine all of the evidence (s)he considers necessary to form an unqualified opinion); and/or
- the auditor disagrees with the treatment or disclosure of a matter in the financial statements.

Although SAS 600 recognises these factors as causes of qualified audit opinions, it also indicates that such opinions should be expressed only if, in the auditor's judgment, the effect of the matter giving rise to concern 'is or may be material to the financial statements' and, as a result, the 'statements may not or do not give a true and fair view of the matters on which the auditors are required to report or do not comply with relevant accounting or other requirements' (para 33).

In cases where the auditor considers the effect of the matter in question is material to the financial statements, the type of qualified opinion expressed depends on the circumstances.

- If the auditor considers the effect of a limitation on the scope of the audit, or the effect of a disagreement, is not so significant as to prevent the expression of an opinion, or to cause the financial statements to be seriously misleading, as the case may be, the auditor will express an *except for* opinion. (That is, the auditor states that, in his or her opinion, the financial statements give a true and fair view of the reporting entity's state of affairs and profit or loss except for the matters specified in the audit report) (paras 35 and 37).
- If the auditor considers the effect of a limitation on the scope of the audit is so material or pervasive that (s)he is unable to obtain sufficient evidence to support an audit opinion, a *disclaimer* of opinion is expressed. (That is, the auditor states that (s)he is unable to form an opinion on the financial statements) (para 36).
- If the auditor considers the effect of a disagreement is so material or pervasive that (s)he concludes that the financial report is seriously misleading, an *adverse* opinion is expressed. (That is, the auditor states that, in his or her opinion, the financial report does not give a true and fair view) (para 34).

13.5 CIRCUMSTANCES GIVING RISE TO AUDIT QUALIFICATIONS

13.5.1 Limitation of Audit Scope

Scope limitations arise when circumstances exist which prevent the auditor from obtaining all of the evidence considered necessary for the purpose of the audit. Examples of scope limitations include the following:

- the inability to carry out certain audit procedures as a result of:
  - circumstances related to the timing of audit work (for example, where the auditor is newly appointed and, as a consequence, was unable to attend the previous year's stocktake);

– circumstances beyond the control of the client and the auditor (for example, where accounting records are destroyed in a fire or flood);
– limitations imposed by the client (for example, where the client does not permit the auditor to send confirmation requests to certain debtors and the relevant balances cannot be verified by alternative procedures);

• significant weaknesses in the internal control system which cannot be compensated for by alternative auditing procedures.

When there has been a limitation on the scope of the auditor's work, the auditor must decide whether the limitation is sufficient to prevent him or her from forming an opinion on the entity's financial statements. In reaching this decision the auditor should assess:

a) the quantity and type of evidence which may reasonably be expected to be available to support the particular figure or disclosure in the financial statements; and
b) the possible effect on the financial statements of the matter for which insufficient evidence is available; when the possible effect is, in the opinion of the auditors, material to the financial statements, there will be insufficient evidence to support an unqualified opinion. (SAS 600, para 69)

The next step is to decide whether the possible effect of the limitation on the scope of the auditor's work is so material or pervasive that a disclaimer of opinion is appropriate. If the limitation on scope is material in its effect, but not so significant as to warrant a disclaimer, an 'except-for' opinion should be expressed. In this event, SAS 600 requires the opinion to be worded so as to indicate 'that it is qualified as to the possible adjustments to the financial statements that might have been determined to be necessary had the limitation not existed' [para 68(c)].

Whenever an 'except-for' or disclaimer of opinion is issued as a result of a scope limitation, the auditor's report should include, in the opinion section of the report, a description of the factors leading to the limitation [SAS 600, para 68(a)]. This enables the reader of the financial statements to understand the reasons for the limitation and to distinguish between those limitations which are beyond the control of the auditor and the auditee (such as a fire which destroys accounting records) and those which are imposed on the auditor by the client (for example, preventing certain debtors from being approached for confirmations of their account balances) (SAS 600, para 71).

Examples of qualified audit reports arising from scope limitations are presented in Figures 13.2 and 13.3:

• Figure 13.2 illustrates an 'except for' opinion expressed on Usborne plc's 1994 financial statements. This has resulted from insufficient evidence being available to the auditors (KPMG Peat Marwick) to enable them to form an opinion on the opening figures for stock and fixed assets at one of Usborne's subsidiaries (Daisy Hill Pigs Limited);
• Figure 13.3 illustrates a disclaimer of opinion expressed on a company's financial statements which has resulted from the loss of a company's accounting records. Disclaimers of opinion are rare forms of audit report and, as a result, 'actual' examples are difficult to locate. As a consequence, Figure 13.3 presents a fictitious example.

Figure 13.2   An 'Except for' Opinion Arising from a Scope Limitation

USBORNE plc

Accounts for the year ended 30 June 1994

Auditors' Report
to the members of Usborne plc

We have audited the accounts on pages 9 to 24.

Respective responsibilities of directors and auditors
As described on page 7 the Company's directors are responsible for the preparation of accounts. It is our responsibility to form an independent opinion. based on our audit. on those accounts and to report our opinion to you.

Basis of opinion
We conducted our audit in accordance with Auditing Standards issued by the Auditing Practices Board. except that the scope of our work was limited as explained below.

An audit includes examination. on a test basis. of evidence relevant to the amounts and disclosures in the accounts. It also includes an assessment of the significant estimates and judgements made by the directors in the preparation of the accounts, and of whether the accounting policies are appropriate to the Group's circumstances, consistently applied and adequately disclosed.

We were appointed as auditors on 4 July 1994 and planned our audit so as to obtain all the information and explanations which we considered necessary in order to provide us with sufficient evidence to give reasonable assurance that the accounts are free from material misstatement. whether caused by fraud or other irregularity or error. However. the evidence available to us to support stock and fixed assets at 30 June 1993 at one of the Company's subsidiaries. Daisy Hill Pigs Limited, was limited. We were unable to confirm that the basis of valuing the opening stock stated at £7.385,000 in the Group balance sheet at 30 June 1993 was in accordance with the Group's accounting policy. Neither were adequate information and explanations available to support the opening fixed assets stated at £4,001,000 in the Group balance sheet at 30 June 1993. As disclosed in note 2. there were substantial writedowns of livestock and fixed assets in the profit and loss account for the year ended 30 June 1994 and. because of the inadequate evidence available to us. we are unable to satisfy ourselves that the writedowns related solely to that year.

In forming our opinion we also evaluated the overall adequacy of the presentation of information in the accounts.

Qualified opinion arising from limitations in audit scope
In our opinion the accounts give a true and fair view of the state of affairs of the Company and the Group as at 30 June 1994.

Except for any adjustments that might have been found to be necessary had we been able to obtain sufficient evidence concerning opening stock and fixed assets at Daisy Hill Pigs Limited, in our opinion the accounts give a true and fair view of the Group's loss for the year ended 30 June 1994 and have been properly prepared in accordance with the Companies Act 1985.

In respect solely of the limitation on our work relating to stock and fixed assets at Daisy Hill Pigs Limited:

* · proper accounting records have not been maintained; and

* we have not obtained all the information and explanations that we considered necessary for the purpose of our audit.

Southampton, 3 November 1994

KPMG Peat Marwick
Chartered Accountants
Registered Auditors

Figure 13.3   A Disclaimer of Opinion Resulting from the Loss of Accounting Records

AUDITORS' REPORT TO THE SHAREHOLDERS OF PQR PLC

We have audited the financial statements on pages 34 to 55 which have been prepared under the historical cost convention as modified by the revaluation of certain fixed assets and the accounting policies set out on pages 39 and 40.

Respective responsibilities of directors and auditors
As described on page 56, the company's directors are responsible for the preparation of financial statements. It is our responsibility to form an independent opinion, based on our audit, on those statements and to report our opinion to you.

Basis of opinion
We conducted our audit in accordance with Auditing Standards issued by the Auditing Practices Board, except that the scope of our work was limited as explained below.

An audit includes examination, on a test basis, of evidence relevant to the amounts and disclosures in the financial statements. It also includes an assessment of the significant estimates and judgments made by the directors in the preparation of the financial statements, and of whether the accounting policies are appropriate to the company's circumstances, consistently applied and adequately disclosed.

We planned our audit so as to obtain all the information and explanations which we considered necessary in order to provide us with sufficient evidence to give reasonable assurance that the financial statements are free from material misstatement, whether caused by fraud or other irregularity or error. However, the evidence available to us was limited because, as stated in note 20 on page 41 of the financial statements, a fire at the company's head office destroyed many of the accounting records. The financial statements consequentially include a number of material amounts based on estimates.

In forming our opinion we also evaluated the overall adequacy of the presentation of information in the financial statements.

Opinion: disclaimer on view given by financial statements
Because of the possible effect of the limitation in evidence available to us, we are unable to form an opinion as to whether the financial statements give a true and fair view of the state of the company's affairs as at 31 March 1997, or of its profit for the year then ended. In all other respects, in our opinion, the financial statements have been properly prepared in accordance with the Companies Act 1985.

In respect alone of the limitation on our work resulting from the destruction of many of the company's accounting records:
  • we have not obtained all the information and explanations that we considered necessary for the purpose of our audit; and
  • we were unable to determine whether proper accounting records have been maintained.

....
Registered auditors   Newcastle
25 May 1997

Source: Adapted from SAS 600, Appendix 2, Example 9.

13.5.2 Disagreement

When the auditor disagrees with the accounting treatment of a particular item in the financial statements or disagrees with the way in which an item is disclosed, and the auditor considers that the effect of the matter with which (s)he disagrees is material to the financial statements, a qualified audit opinion is expressed. The type of qualification depends on the severity of the effect of the matter giving rise to the disagreement.

- If the effect of the matter in question is, in the auditor's opinion, so material or pervasive as to render the financial statements seriously misleading, an adverse opinion is expressed.
- If the effect of the matter is material to the financial statements, but not so material as to warrant an adverse report, an 'except for' opinion is expressed.

Whenever an 'except for' or adverse opinion is expressed as a result of a disagreement, the auditor is required by SAS 600, para 74(a), to include in the opinion section of the audit report:

- a description of all substantive factors giving rise to the disagreement;
- the implications of these factors for the financial statements; and
- whenever practicable, a quantification of the effect on the financial statements of the matter with which the auditor disagrees.

The auditor may also draw attention to relevant notes in the financial statements but, as SAS 600 emphasises:

> such reference is not a substitute for sufficient description of the circumstances in the auditors' report so that a reader can appreciate the principal points at issue and their implications for an understanding of the financial statements. (para 75)

Examples of qualified audit reports arising from disagreement are presented in Figures 13.4 and 13.5.

- Figure 13.4 illustrates an 'except for' opinion expressed on Newarthill plc's 1994 financial statements which has resulted from the auditors' (Touche Ross & Co) disagreement with the accounting treatment of convertible preference shares issued by a former Australian subsidiary of Newarthill plc.
- Figure 13.5 illustrates an adverse opinion expressed on the financial statements of a company which has arisen from the auditors' disagreement over the need to provide for an expected loss. Adverse opinions are rare forms of audit report and, as a result, 'actual' examples are difficult to locate. As a consequence, Figure 13.5 presents a fictitious example.

13.6   TREATMENT OF INHERENT UNCERTAINTIES

Inherent uncertainties are defined in SAS 600, para 12, to mean 'an uncertainty whose resolution is dependent upon uncertain future events outside the control of the

Figure 13.4   An 'Except for' Opinion Resulting from the Auditors' Disagreement with the Accounting Treatment of Convertible Preference Shares

REPORT OF THE AUDITORS TO THE MEMBERS OF NEWARTHILL p.l.c.

We have audited the financial statements on pages 8 to 29 which have been prepared under the accounting policies set out on pages 12 and 13.

Respective responsibilities of directors and auditors
As described above, the Company's directors are responsible for the preparation of financial statements. It is our responsibility to form an independent opinion, based on our audit, on those statements and to report our opinion to you.

Basis of opinion
We conducted our audit in accordance with Auditing Standards issued by the Auditing Practices Board. An audit includes examination, on a test basis, of evidence relevant to the amounts and disclosures in the financial statements. It also includes an assessment of the significant estimates and judgements made by the directors in the preparation of the financial statements, and of whether the accounting policies are appropriate to the circumstances of the Company and the Group, consistently applied and adequately disclosed. We planned and performed our audit so as to obtain all the information and explanations which we considered necessary in order to provide us with sufficient evidence to give reasonable assurance that the financial statements are free from material misstatement, whether caused by fraud or other irregularity or error. In forming our opinion we also evaluated the overall adequacy of the presentation of information in the financial statements.

Qualified opinion arising from disagreement about accounting treatment
The Group has not recognised the financial cost of redeemable convertible preference shares issued by a former Australian subsidiary in accordance with FRS4 for the period up to the date of disposal of its controlling interest on 3rd August 1994. At that date the Group's obligations to the holders of the redeemable convertible preference shares for these finance costs were extinguished. If the Group had accounted for the finance cost in accordance with FRS4 the profit attributable to shareholders for the year ended 31st October 1994 would be increased by £11.77m (1993 reduced by £6.228m) and shareholders' funds at 31st October 1993 would be decreased by £11.77m. Shareholder's funds at 31st October 1994 would, however, remain unchanged.

Except for the non compliance with FRS4 in the manner described above, in our opinion the financial statements give a true and fair view of the state of affairs of the Company and of the Group as at 31st October 1994 and of the profit of the Group for the year then ended and have been properly prepared in accordance with the Companies Act 1985.

Touche Ross & Co
Chartered Accountants and Registered Auditors
Hill House
1 Little New Street
London
EC4A 3TR
13th April 1995

Figure 13.5   An Adverse Opinion Resulting from the Auditors' Disagreement over the Need to Provide for an Expected Loss

---

AUDITORS' REPORT TO THE SHAREHOLDERS OF EDS PLC

We have audited the financial statements on pages 26 to 52 which have been prepared under the historical cost convention as modified by the revaluation of certain fixed assets and the accounting policies set out on pages 29 and 30.

Respective responsibilities of directors and auditors
As described above, the company's directors are responsible for the preparation of the financial statements. It is our responsibility to form an independent opinion, based on our audit, on those statements and to report our opinion to you.

Basis of opinion
We conducted our audit in accordance with Auditing Standards issued by the Auditing Practices Board. An audit includes examination, on a test basis, of evidence relevant to the amounts and disclosures in the financial statements. It also includes an assessment of the significant estimates and judgments made by the directors in the preparation of the financial statements, and of whether the accounting policies are appropriate to the company's circumstances, consistently applied and adequately disclosed.

We planned and performed our audit so as to obtain all the information and explanations which we considered necessary in order to provide us with sufficient evidence to give reasonable assurance as to whether the financial statements are free from material misstatement, whether caused by fraud or other irregularity or error. In forming our opinion we also evaluated the overall adequacy of the presentation of information in the financial statements.

Adverse opinion
As more fully explained in note 18, no provision has been made for losses expected to arise on certain long-term contracts currently in progress, as the directors consider that such losses should be off-set against amounts recoverable on other long-term contracts. In our opinion, provision should be made for foreseeable losses on individual contracts as required by Statement of Standard Accounting Practice 9. If losses had been so recognised the effect would have been to reduce the profit before and after tax for the year and the contract work in progress at 31 March 1997 by £2,874,000.

In view of the effect of the failure to provide for the losses referred to above, in our opinion the financial statements do not give a true and fair view of the state of the company's affairs as at 31 March 1997 and of its profit for the year then ended. In all other respects, in our opinion the financial statements have been properly prepared in accordance with the Companies Act 1985.

....
Registered auditors   Bristol
14 May 1997

Source: Adapted from SAS 600, Appendix 2, Example 10.

reporting entity's directors at the date the financial statements are approved'. Such an uncertainty is defined as a 'fundamental uncertainty' when:

> the magnitude of its potential impact is so great that, without clear disclosure of the nature and implications of the uncertainty, the view given by the financial statements would be seriously misleading.

> The magnitude of an inherent uncertainty's potential impact is judged by reference to:
> - the risk that the estimate included in financial statements may be subject to change
> - the range of possible outcomes, and
> - the consequences of those outcomes on the view shown in the financial statements. (para 13)

Inherent uncertainties frequently affect, to some degree, quite a wide range of items in the financial statements. They arise as a result of particular circumstances and, at the time the entity's directors approve the financial statements, it is not possible to remove the uncertainty. Examples include:

- uncertainty as to the outcome of litigation;
- doubts about the ability of the entity to continue as a going concern.

Although inherent uncertainties cannot be resolved at the time the financial statements are approved, the financial statements can reflect the directors' assumptions regarding their financial outcome and, where material, describe the circumstances giving rise to the uncertainties and their potential financial effect (SAS 600, para 55).

When forming an opinion on a set of financial statements, auditors are required to consider, in the light of evidence available at the date on which they express that opinion, the adequacy of the accounting treatment, estimates and disclosures of inherent uncertainties in the financial statements. In forming their opinion on the adequacy of the accounting treatment, they are required to consider:

- the appropriateness of the accounting policies dealing with the uncertain matters;
- the reasonableness of the estimates included in the financial statements in respect of the inherent uncertainties; and
- the adequacy of disclosures relating to the inherent uncertainties (SAS 600, paras 56 and 58).

When an auditor concludes that an inherent uncertainty has been properly accounted for and adequately disclosed in the financial statements, providing (s)he has no other concerns regarding the financial statements, an unqualified audit opinion is appropriate.

In some circumstances, the auditor may conclude that, although an inherent uncertainty has been properly accounted for and adequately disclosed in the financial statements, the degree of uncertainty about its outcome and potential impact on the view given by the financial statements is so significant (or fundamental) that attention should be drawn to it in the audit report. In such cases, SAS 600 [para 54(b)] requires auditors to include an explanatory paragraph referring to the fundamental uncertainty in the 'basis of opinion' section of the audit report. The Standard notes:

Figure 13.6   An Unqualified Opinion with an Explanatory Paragraph Referring to a Fundamental Uncertainty

---

Report of the Auditors

to the members of Queens Moat Houses P.L.C.

We have audited the accounts on pages 32 to 74.

Respective responsibilities of directors and auditors

As described on page 29 the company's directors are responsible for the preparation of accounts. It is our responsibility to form an independent opinion, based on our audit, on those accounts and to report our opinion to you.

Basis of opinion

We conducted our audit in accordance with Auditing Standards issued by the Auditing Practices Board. An audit includes examination, on a test basis, of evidence relevant to the amounts and disclosures in the accounts. It also includes an assessment of the significant estimates and judgements made by the directors in the preparation of the accounts, and of whether the accounting policies are appropriate to the company's circumstances, consistently applied and adequately disclosed.

We planned and performed our audit so as to obtain all the information and explanations which we considered necessary in order to provide us with sufficient evidence to give reasonable assurance that the accounts are free from material misstatement, whether caused by fraud or other irregularity or error. In forming our opinion we also evaluated the overall adequacy of the presentation of information in the accounts.

Going concern

In forming our opinion, we have considered the adequacy of the disclosures made in the accounts concerning the basis of preparation. The accounts have been prepared on a going concern basis and the validity of this depends on the successful completion of the financial restructuring, on the group's banks and other lenders continuing their support by providing adequate facilities pending the successful completion of the financial restructuring, and on the company's first mortgage debenture stockholders not seeking to enforce their security pending the successful completion of the financial restructuring. The accounts do not include any adjustments that would result should the group be unable to continue in operational existence. Details of the circumstances relating to this fundamental uncertainty are described in the accounting policies (note (a)). Our opinion is not qualified in this respect.

Opinion

In our opinion the accounts give a true and fair view of the state of affairs of the company and the group at 1 January 1995 and of the loss, total recognised losses and cash flows of the group for the year then ended and have been properly prepared in accordance with the Companies Act 1985.

Coopers & Lybrand

Chartered Accountants and Registered Auditors

London

29 March 1995

When adding an explanatory paragraph, auditors should use words which clearly indicate that their opinion on the financial statements is not qualified in respect of its contents. [para 54(c)]

An example of an unqualified audit report which includes an explanatory paragraph referring to a fundamental uncertainty (identified as 'Going concern') is presented in Figure 13.6. This report has been issued on the 1995 financial statements of Queen's Moat Houses plc.

If, after considering the adequacy of the accounting treatment and disclosure of an inherent uncertainty in the financial statements, the auditor concludes that an inappropriate accounting policy has been adopted and/or the estimate of the outcome of the uncertainty is materially misstated and/or the disclosures relating to the uncertainty are inadequate, the auditor is required to issue an 'except for' or adverse opinion, as appropriate, for disagreement (SAS 600, para 60).

13.7 SPECIAL FEATURES OF AUDIT REPORTS ISSUED ON THE FINANCIAL STATEMENTS OF PUBLIC SECTOR ENTITIES

As noted in Chapter 3 (section 3.3), the National Audit Act 1983 and the Local Government Finance Act 1982, amongst other public sector legislation, requires the management of public sector entities to prepare annually a set of financial statements relevant to that entity's activities. The legislation also requires that the financial statements be audited.

As examples of audit reports issued on the financial statements of public sector entities, Figures 13.7 to 13.9 present reports for:

- the appropriation account of the Serious Fraud Office: Administration, for the year ended 31 March 1995. (This affords an example of audit reports on issued Central Government Appropriation Accounts) (Figure 13.7);
- the financial statements of Edinburgh University for the year ended 31 December 1994. (This is an example of audit reports issued on the financial statements of the tertiary institutions) (Figure 13.8);
- the financial statements of Bedford Borough Council for the year ended 31 March 1995. (This provides an example of audit reports issued on the financial statements of Local Authorities) (Figure 13.10).

These reports serve to illustrate the variety of constitutional, accounting and auditing arrangements which apply to different types of public sector entities. It should be noted that these reports illustrate, in particular, differences with respect to:

(i)   the auditor appointed to perform the audit;
(ii) the locus of responsibility for the financial statements;
(iii) the addressee of the audit report;
(iv) the auditing standards applied in conducting the audit;

Figure 13.7 Audit Report on the Appropriation Account of the Serious Fraud Office: Administration

---

SERIOUS FRAUD OFFICE:
ADMINISTRATION   1994–95, Class IX, Vote 8

The Certificate of the Comptroller and Auditor General to the House of Commons

I have audited the financial statements on page 35 which have been prepared in accordance with the requirements of Government Accounting and other Treasury directions.

Respective responsibilities of the Accounting Officer and Auditors

As described on page 7 the Accounting Officer is responsible for the preparation of financial statements. It is my responsibility to form an independent opinion, based on my audit, on those statements and to report my opinion to you.

Basis of opinion

I certify that I have examined the financial statements referred to above in accordance with the Exchequer and Audit Departments Acts 1866 and 1921 and the National Audit Office auditing standards, which include relevant Auditing Standards issued by the Auditing Practices Board. An audit includes examination, on a test basis, of evidence relevant to the amounts and disclosures in the financial statements. It also includes an assessment of the judgements made by the Accounting Officer in the preparation of the financial statements.

I planned and performed my audit so as to obtain all the information and explanations which I considered necessary in order to provide me with sufficient evidence to give reasonable assurance that the financial statements are free from material misstatement, whether caused by fraud or other irregularity or error. In forming my opinion I also evaluated the overall adequacy of the presentation of information in the financial statements.

Opinion

In my opinion the sums expended have been applied for the purposes authorised by Parliament and the account properly presents the expenditure and receipts of Class IX, Vote 8 for the year ended 31 March 1995.

John Bourn   National Audit Office
Comptroller and Auditor General   157–197 Buckingham Palace Road
                                                                                     Victoria
16 November 1995   London SW1W 9SP

(v)   the wording of the auditor's opinion on the financial statements;
(vi) additional regulatory requirements addressed in the audit report.

(i)   *Auditor Appointed*

Reference to Figures 13.7 to 13.9 reveals that:

- the Serious Fraud Office's Appropriation Account is audited by the Comptroller and Auditor General (that is, the National Audit Office);
- the financial statements of Edinburgh University have been audited by one of the 'Big Six' international firms of Chartered Accountants (Ernst & Young);
- the financial statements of Bedford Borough Council have been audited by a District Auditor (of the District Audit Service). (As noted in Chapter 3, section 3.3.2, the auditors of local authorities in England and Wales are appointed by the Audit Commission. Both private sector firms of accountants and District Audit Offices are eligible for appointment.)

Figure 13.8   Audit Report on the Financial Statements of Edinburgh University

AUDITORS' REPORT TO THE COURT
OF THE UNIVERSITY OF EDINBURGH

We have audited the financial statements on pages 6 to 31 which have been prepared under the historical cost convention as modified by the revaluation of certain fixed assets and on the basis of the accounting policies set out on pages 6 to 8.

Respective Responsibilities of the Court and Auditors

As described on page 4, the University Court is responsible for ensuring that financial statements are prepared. It is our responsibility to form an independent opinion, based on our audit, on those statements and to report our opinion to you.

Basis of our Opinion

We conducted our audit in accordance with Auditing Standards issued by the Auditing Practices Board. An audit includes examination, on a test basis, of evidence relevant to the amounts and disclosures in the financial statements. It also includes an assessment of the significant estimates and judgements made by the Court in the preparation of the financial statements, and of whether the accounting policies are appropriate to the Group's circumstances, consistently applied and adequately disclosed.

We planned and performed our audit so as to obtain all the information and explanations which we considered necessary in order to provide us with sufficient evidence to give us reasonable assurance that the financial statements are free from material misstatement, whether caused by fraud or other irregularity or error. In forming our opinion we also evaluated the overall adequacy of the presentation of information in the financial statements.

Opinion

In our opinion:

- the financial statements give a true and fair view of the state of the affairs of the University and the Group at 31 July 1995 and of the Group's income and expenditure for the year then ended and have been properly prepared in accordance with the Statement of Recommended Practice: Accounting in Higher Education Institutions and in accordance with the Universities (Scotland) Acts 1858-1966;

- income from the Scottish Higher Education Funding Council grants and income for specific purposes and from other restricted funds administered by the University have been applied only for the purposes for which they were received;

- income has been applied in accordance with the Universities (Scotland) Acts 1858-1966 governing the University and, where appropriate, with the Financial Memorandum dated 12 July 1993 with the Scottish Higher Education Funding Council.

Ernst & Young
Chartered Accountants
Registered Auditors
11 December 1995
Edinburgh

Figure 13.9   Audit Report on the Financial Statements of Bedford Borough Council

DISTRICT AUDITORS REPORT

AUDITORS' REPORT TO BEDFORD BOROUGH COUNCIL   DISTRICT AUDIT

The audit of the financial statements on pages 19 to 44 has been carried out as described below and has been substantially completed. The audit cannot be formally concluded, because there is a police investigation into allegations of corruption relating to the Authority's European affairs. We are however satisfied that the amounts involved in the subject matter concerned are unlikely to have a material effect on the statement of accounts.

Respective Responsibilities of Chief Finance Officer and Auditors

As described on page 14 the Chief Finance Officer is responsible for the preparation of the statement of accounts. It is our responsibility to form an independent opinion, based on our audit, on the statement and to report our opinion thereon.

Basis of Opinion

We carried out our audit in accordance with Part III of the Local Government Finance Act 1982 and the Code of Audit Practice issued by the Audit Commission, which requires compliance with relevant auditing standards.

Our audit included examination, on a test basis, of evidence relevant to the amounts and disclosures in the statement of accounts. It also included an assessment of the significant estimates and judgements made by the Authority in the preparation of the statement of accounts and of whether the accounting policies are appropriate to the Authority's circumstances, consistently applied and adequately disclosed.

We planned and performed our audit so as to obtain all the information and explanations which we considered necessary in order to provide us with sufficient evidence to give reasonable assurance that the statement of accounts is free from material misstatement, whether caused by fraud or other irregularity or error. In forming our opinion we also evaluated the overall adequacy of the presentation of information in the statement of accounts.

Opinion

In our opinion the statement of accounts presents fairly the financial position of Bedford Borough Council at 31 March 1995 and its income and expenditure for the year then ended.

M S Robinson
District Auditor
22 December 1995
REF: 95/2465/0795

(ii) *Financial Statement Responsibility*

The public sector entity audit reports show that:

- the Accounting Officer of the Serious Fraud Office is responsible for the preparation of that Office's financial statements;
- the University Court of Edinburgh University is responsible for that University's financial statements;
- the Chief Financial Officer of Bedford Borough Council is responsible for the local authority's 'statement of accounts'.

(iii) *Addressee of the Audit Report*

Figures 13.7 to 13.9 show that:

- the report of the Comptroller and Auditor General on the Serious Fraud Office's Appropriation Account is addressed to The House of Commons. In practice, it is received and examined by the Public Accounts Committee (a Committee of the House of Commons);
- Ernst & Young have addressed their report to the Court of the University of Edinburgh. (This is curious since it is the University Court which is responsible for the preparation of the financial statements which Ernst & Young have audited and are reporting upon);
- the audit report on Bedford Borough Council's statement of accounts is addressed to Bedford Borough Council (that is, in effect, the Council members).

Conceptually, the question of to whom a public sector audit report should be addressed is difficult since many groups in society may have contributed finance (through taxes or rates, for example) or otherwise have a legitimate interest in the entity.

(iv) *Auditing Standards Applied*

Reference to Figures 13.7 to 13.9 reveals that:

- the audit of the Serious Fraud Office's Appropriation Account has been conducted in accordance with both relevant legislation and relevant APB auditing standards;
- Edinburgh University's financial statements have been audited in accordance with the APB's auditing standards;
- Bedford Borough Council's financial statements have been audited in accordance with both relevant legislation and the Code of Audit Practice issued by the Audit Commission; the latter requires the auditor to comply with relevant (APB) auditing standards.

(v) *Wording of the Auditor's Opinion*

From the examples of public sector entity audit reports provided in this chapter, it may be seen that:

- the auditor's opinion on the Serious Fraud Office's Appropriation Account states: 'the account properly presents the expenditure and receipts of Class IX, Vote 8 for the year ended 31 March 1995'. Unlike audit reports issued on company financial statements (in which the phrase 'in accordance with the Companies Act 1985' follows the words 'properly prepared'), the auditor's report on the Appropriation Account has no explanatory phrase following 'properly presents';
- the audit report on Edinburgh University's financial statements states that these financial statements:
  - give a true and fair view of the University's state of affairs and income and expenditure; and
  - have been properly prepared in accordance with relevant regulations and legislation;
- the audit report on Bedford Borough Council's financial statements refers to them 'presenting fairly' the Council's financial position and its income and expenditure.

The differences in the wording of the auditor's opinion may (or may not) imply different nuances in the nature of the opinion in each case. This issue remains largely unexplored in both the academic and professional literature.

(vi) *Additional Regulatory Requirements*

As Figures 13.7 to 13.9 show:

- in respect of the Serious Fraud Office's Appropriation Account, the Comptroller and Auditor General refers to 'the sums expended' being 'applied for the purposes authorised by Parliament';
- the auditors' opinion on the financial statements of Edinburgh University refers to the application of funds, grants and income being in accord with the purposes for which they were received, and with relevant legislation;
- no reference is made in the auditor's report on Bedford Borough Council's financial statements to additional regulatory matters. However, audit work is conducted on the propriety of receipts and payments but the auditor's report on this work is not attached to the financial statements.

Reviewing the illustrative audit reports provided in Figures 13.7 to 13.9, it may be seen that audit reports issued on the financial statements of public sector entities broadly follow the requirements of SAS 600. To this extent audit reporting practice is uniform across the public and private sectors.

13.8 THE AUDIT REPORT – THE AUDITOR'S CHANCE TO COMMUNICATE

When considering the standard form of audit report, it should be remembered that this report is the auditor's primary opportunity to communicate with users of the financial statements. If the auditor's opinion is to provide credibility to the financial statements [statements prepared by the entity's management, which essentially report on their own (that is, management's) performance], it is essential that financial statement users read and understand the audit report. Yet, as is shown below, evidence from many parts of the English-speaking world suggests that, particularly until the relatively recent adoption of the 'expanded' (or 'long form')[6] audit report, this was not the case. Indeed, it was primarily concern about the apparent ineffectiveness of the audit report as a means of communication which led to the former 'short form' standard audit report being replaced by the current 'expanded' report (as is required by SAS 600).

An example of the short form audit report, used in the United Kingdom prior to the adoption (in 1993) of the expanded report, is presented in Figure 13.10. It can be seen from this figure that the report was characterised by its brevity. It merely stated that the accounts had been audited in accordance with auditing standards, that they gave a true and fair view of the company's state of affairs and profit (or loss) and cash flows for the year, and that they complied with the Companies Act 1985.

Figure 13.10   Example of the Standard Unqualified (Short Form) Audit Report used until 1993

Report of the auditors

To the members of The Peninsular and Oriental Steam Navigation Company

We have audited the accounts on pages 27 to 49 in accordance with Auditing Standards.

In our opinion the accounts give a true and fair view of the state of affairs of the Company and the Group at 31 December 1991 and of the profit and cash flows of the Group for the year then ended and have been properly prepared in accordance with the Companies Act 1985.

London
24 March 1992

KPMG Peat Marwick
Chartered Accountants
Registered Auditor

From about the early 1970s, the apparent deficiencies of the short form audit report attracted considerable attention, particularly in the United States, Canada, United Kingdom and Australia. Studies by Lee and Tweedie (1975) in the United Kingdom and Wilton and Tabb (1978) in New Zealand, for example, found that little more than 50% of financial statement users read audit reports. Further, in the United States, the Commission on Auditors' Responsibilities (CAR, 1978; the Cohen Commission) found that the standard short form audit report (then in use) served to confuse rather than inform financial statement users. The Commission noted, for example, that 'users are unaware of the limitations of the audit function and are confused about the distinction between the responsibilities of management and that of the auditor' (p.71). Surveys conducted by researchers such as Lee (1970) in the United Kingdom, Beck (1973) in Australia, the Macdonald Commission (CICA, 1988) in Canada, and Porter (1993) in New Zealand, provide support for the Cohen Commission's conclusions.

---

6 The UK equivalent of what is known as the 'expanded' audit report is referred to as the 'long form' report in countries such as the United States, Australia and New Zealand.

These surveys found that a significant number of auditees (directors, senior executives, chief accountants and internal auditors of companies) and financial statement users believed that auditors are responsible for preparing auditees' financial statements, that auditors verify *every* transaction of the entity, and that a 'clean' audit report signifies that the auditor guarantees the financial statements are accurate and/or the reporting entity is financially secure.

Woolf (1979), looking at the issue from a different perspective, drew attention to the irony of the long and complex audit process culminating in such a brief report. He highlighted his point by citing a study conducted in the United States by Seidler:

> Seidler of New York University observed that the 1975 annual report of Arthur Andersen and Co. [one of the world's 'Big Six' audit firms] revealed that 6.6% of the firm's total revenue was received from five clients . . . whose annual fees averaged about $5.1 million each. . . . The audit fee element in each approximated $3.4 million[7] and further analysis showed that this fee represented approximately 95 man years, or 128,000 hours of work – a truly prodigious expenditure of skilled auditing labour. On the assumption that the five clients were among the firm's largest, Seidler identified . . . [them] and then proceeded to count the number of words in the audit reports to their shareholders. He found that such lavish audit scrutiny – the equivalent of work of 95 professionals labouring for an entire year – had resulted, on average, in an expression of findings occupying no more than 175 words! . . . A situation, one has to concede, which has no parallel in any other sphere of investigative reporting. (pp.223–4)

Concerned about the apparent shortcomings of the short form audit report, and stimulated by the Cohen Commission's (1978) observation that 'the auditor's standard audit report is almost the only formal means used both to educate and inform users of financial statements concerning the audit function', the professional accountancy bodies in most parts of the English-speaking world have adopted the expanded audit form report. More specifically, since 1988, new audit report auditing standards prescribing use of an expanded audit report have been published by the American Institute of Certified Public Accountants (AICPA), the Canadian Institute of Chartered Accountants (CICA), the Auditing Practices Board (APB) (UK), the Australian Accounting Research Foundation (AARF), the New Zealand Society of Accountants (NZSA), and the International Federation of Accountants (IFAC). In each case, unlike its predecessor short form report, the new expanded report includes, *inter alia*:

- a distinction between the responsibility of the entity's management[8] and auditor for the entity's financial statements;
- a statement that the audit was conducted in accordance with auditing standards;
- a statement that auditing standards require the auditor to plan and perform the audit so as to obtain reasonable assurance as to whether or not the financial statements are free of material misstatement;
- a brief description of the audit process.

The primary motive for the professional accountancy bodies adopting the expanded audit report was to educate financial statement users about the respective

---

[7] $3.4 million average audit fee was in 1975 – over 20 years ago!!

[8] Readers are reminded that, as stated in the Preface, except where indicated otherwise, the term 'management' is used in this book to include the directors of companies.

responsibilities of management and auditors for the financial statements, the level of assurance provided by the auditor's opinion, and the audit process. Studies by Kelly and Mohrweis (1989), Hatherly, Innes and Brown (1991), and Zachry (1991), among others, suggest that use of the expanded report has achieved some success in meeting its objectives. However, this has been at the cost of changing the audit report into a longer and more complex document. Further, questions have been raised, for example by Alfano (1979), about the ease with which a financial statement user can determine whether or not the auditor has reservations about the financial statements, and the value of explaining in the audit report the respective responsibilities of management and auditors for the financial statements. To Alfano, this merely enables financial statement users to allocate blame if something is wrong. Additionally, commentators such as Elliott and Jacobson (1987) have questioned the ability of a few sentences in the audit report to convey adequately the essence of the audit process. Further, Epstein (1976) found that financial statement users 'are not interested in the details of an audit' but 'are looking for a seal of approval' (as reported, CAR, 1978, p.164). As Alfano (1979) has expressed it: 'the reader wants to know whether the statements are right or wrong' (p.39). Certainly it seems pertinent to ask whether financial statement users require details of the auditor's and management's responsibilities, and a standard description of the audit process, in *every* audit report. Financial statement users need to be informed of these matters at least once but ways more appropriate than including it in every audit report could perhaps have been found. According to critics of the current expanded report (such as those named above), including the information in the audit report detracts from fulfilment of the report's primary function which is to convey the auditor's opinion on the accompanying financial statements.

Whether or not the standard audit report will undergo further revision in a few years' time, remains to be seen. One possibility is that, instead of each audit report containing a standard description of the audit process, each would contain a description of any particular features or difficulties encountered during that audit and how they were resolved. Such a move away from standardised wording is more likely to encourage each audit report to be read and the particular context of each audit opinion to be better understood.

13.9 AUDITORS' REPORTS ON CORPORATE GOVERNANCE MATTERS

In 1992, the Committee on the Financial Aspects of Corporate Governance (CFACG; the Cadbury Committee) published its 'Code of Best Practice'. This included the recommendation, among many others, that the directors of public companies report:

- on the effectiveness of their company's systems of internal control (clause 4.5);
- that the business is a going concern – with supporting assumptions and qualifications as necessary (clause 4.6).

The Committee also recommended that auditors be required to report on the directors' internal control and going concern statements (CFACG, 1992, paras 5.16 and 5.22).

Although compliance with the Cadbury Committee's Code of Best Practice is not a regulatory requirement, in 1993 the London Stock Exchange made it a listing requirement for companies to include in their annual reports a statement as to whether or not they comply with the Code. Since 1993, auditors of companies listed on the London Stock Exchange, in addition to reporting on the company's financial statements, have, as a general rule, reported on the company's 'corporate governance matters'. An example of such a report is presented as Figure 13.11.

Figure 13.11   Example of an Auditors' Report on Corporate Governance Matters

---

REPORT BY THE AUDITORS TO CANDOVER INVESTMENTS plc ON CORPORATE GOVERNANCE MATTERS

In addition to our audit of the financial statements, we have reviewed the directors' statement on page 29 on the Company's compliance with paragraphs of the Code of Best Practice specified for our review by the London Stock Exchange. The objective of our review is to draw attention to non-compliance with those paragraphs of the Code which are not disclosed.

We carried out our review in accordance with bulletin 1995/1 'Disclosures relating to corporate governance' issued by the Auditing Practices Board. That Bulletin does not require us to perform the additional work necessary to, and we do not, express any opinion on the effectiveness of either the Group's system of internal financial control or its corporate governance procedures nor on the ability of the Group to continue in operational existence.

Opinion

With respect to the directors' statement on internal control on pages 30 and 31, and going concern on page 30, in our opinion the directors have provided the disclosures required by paragraphs 4.5 and 4.6 of the Code (as supplemented by the related guidance for directors) and the statement is not inconsistent with the information of which we are aware from our audit work on the financial statements.

Based on enquiry of certain directors and officers of the Group, and examination of relevant documents, in our opinion the directors' statement on page 29 appropriately reflects the Company's compliance with the other paragraphs of the code specified for our review.

Grant Thornton   London
Registered Auditors   9th April, 1996
Chartered Accountants

As is indicated in Figure 13.11, the directors of Candover Investments plc have included in their 1995 annual report, statements on the company's:

• compliance with the Code of Best Practice;
• internal controls;
• status as a going concern.

Grant Thornton, Candover Investments' auditors, have reviewed the various statements and expressed the opinion that:

- the statement with respect to the company's compliance with the Cadbury Code 'appropriately reflects the Company's compliance' with the paragraphs of the Code the London Stock Exchange specifies they, as auditors, should review;
- the statements regarding the company's internal control and status as a going concern provide the disclosures required by the Code and are 'not inconsistent with the information of which we are aware from our audit work on the financial statements'.

It should be noted that Grant Thornton state in their report that they have performed their 'corporate governance matters' review in accordance with the APB's bulletin: *Disclosures relating to corporate governance.* Complying with this bulletin, the auditors have not performed additional work which would be necessary to, and they do not, 'express any opinion on the effectiveness of either [Candover Investment plc's] system of internal financial control or its corporate governance procedures nor on the ability of the Group to continue in operational existence.'

13.10   AUDITORS' REPORTS TO MANAGEMENT: MANAGEMENT LETTERS

In addition to issuing audit reports on the financial statements of companies and public sector entities and, in appropriate cases, issuing reports on corporate governance matters, it is standard practice for auditors to provide a written report to management on various aspects of the audit. SAS 610: *Reports to Directors and Management* provides guidance for auditors on these communications, which are generally referred to as 'Management Letters'. It states that:

> Auditors should consider the matters which have come to their attention during the audit and whether they should be included in a report to directors or management. (para 2)

It goes on to explain that the principal purpose of these letters is:

> for auditors to communicate points that have come to their attention during the audit:
> - on the design and operation of the accounting and internal control systems and to make suggestions for their improvement;
> - of other constructive advice, for example comments on potential economies or improvements in efficiency; and
> - on other matters, for example comments on adjusted and unadjusted errors in the financial statements or on particular accounting policies and practices. (para 5)

Notwithstanding the above guidance, the content of management letters varies quite widely in practice, depending on the auditor, the client and the circumstances. Nevertheless, certain items, such as weaknesses in the client's accounting and internal control systems which have come to light during the audit, are almost invariably present. In addition to noting the existence and effect of the weaknesses, recommendations are made as to ways in which they might be overcome.

A management letter is usually provided at the conclusion of both the interim and the final audit. The interim letter is usually confined to reporting accounting and internal control system weaknesses which have been discovered during the interim audit. It is sent to management as soon as possible after the audit attendance so that weaknesses can be rectified on a timely basis.[9] The final management letter is frequently broader in nature and usually includes comments on the conduct and findings of the audit as a whole. However, the main focus is generally on matters relating to the entity's accounting system and/or its financial affairs, where the auditor considers improvements could be made.

Management letters are private communications between the auditor and the management of the client entity. They can provide a valuable service to the client which, amongst other things, assists management improve the entity's accounting and internal control systems. With improvements in these regards, the auditor's confidence about the completeness, accuracy and validity of the accounting data may well increase, and thus the audit work required to form an opinion about the financial statements (and hence audit fees) may, in subsequent years, be reduced.

In well-managed entities, management letters are usually regarded as a useful by-product of the audit and steps are taken to ensure that the auditor's recommendations are acted upon. When companies and other reporting entities have audit committees, these committees usually discuss the contents of the management letter with the auditors and take steps to ensure that the auditor's recommendations are implemented.

13.11 SUMMARY

In this chapter we have discussed the reports which auditors provide for users of audited financial statements and the reports they provide for the reporting entity's management. We have examined the standard form of audit report used in the United Kingdom and Republic of Ireland for private and public sector entities and discussed the various types of audit opinion which may be expressed and the circumstances in which each is appropriate. We have also considered differences between the expanded form of audit report currently in use and its short form predecessor. We have noted that the expanded report was introduced to reduce misconceptions about the auditor's responsibility for the financial statements, the level of assurance provided by the audit report, and the audit function. But we have also seen that the result has been a longer and more complex document which some commentators maintain is less effective than the former short form report in communicating the auditor's key message about the accompanying financial statements.

In the final sections of the chapter we have given some attention to auditors' reports on corporate governance matters and to management letters. We have noted that the auditor's report to users of the financial statements is a statutory requirement whose content is largely defined by the Companies Act 1985 or relevant public sector legislation. The auditor's report on corporate governance matters is, in essence, circumscribed by the requirements of the London Stock Exchange. Each of these reports is a

---

[9] Indeed, SAS 610 requires auditors to report any material weaknesses in the client's accounting and internal control systems identified during the audit 'in writing to the directors, the audit committee or an appropriate level of management on a timely basis' (para 7).

public document. Management letters, however, are private communications between the auditor and the auditee's management. They are designed to help management improve its accounting and internal control systems and other aspects of the organisation's financial affairs but their content varies widely according to the client and the particular circumstances encountered during the audit.

SELF-REVIEW QUESTIONS

13.1 List the elements which the Companies Act 1985 requires auditors to refer to in their audit reports.

13.2 Explain briefly the requirements which, under SAS 600: *Auditors' Reports on Financial Statements*, financial statements must meet before they can be adjudged 'true and fair'.

13.3 Describe briefly the format of the standard audit report currently in use in the United Kingdom and Republic of Ireland.

13.4 State the criteria which SAS 600 requires to be met before an auditor may issue an unqualified audit report.

13.5 List three types of qualified audit report and briefly explain the circumstances in which each is appropriate.

13.6 Explain briefly the difference between a scope limitation and an inherent uncertainty.

13.7 Distinguish between a material inherent uncertainty and a fundamental inherent uncertainty and explain how each is reflected in the auditor's report.

13.8 Explain briefly the ways in which the expanded audit report currently in use differs from its short form predecessor.

13.9 Explain briefly an auditor's responsibility to communicate with management by means of a management letter.

13.10 Explain briefly the value of management letters to the audit-client.

REFERENCES

Alfano, J.B. (1979). Making auditor's reports pure and simple. *CPA Journal*, **46**(6), 37–41.
Beck, C.W. (1973). The role of the auditor in modern society: an empirical appraisal. *Accounting and Business Research*, **3**(10), 117–22.
Canadian Institute of Chartered Accountants (CICA). (1988). *Report of the Commission to Study the Public's Expectations of Audits* (Macdonald Commission). Toronto: CICA.
Commission on Auditors' Responsibilities (CAR). (1978). *Report, Conclusions and Recommendations* (The Cohen Commission). New York: AICPA.
Committee on the Financial Aspects of Corporate Governance (CFACG). (1992). Report of the Committee on the Financial Aspects of Corporate Governance (Cadbury Committee). London: Gee.

Elliott, R.K. & Jacobson, P.D. (1987). The auditor's standard report: the last word or in need of change? *Journal of Accountancy*, **164**(2), 72–78.

Epstein, M.J. (1976). The Corporate Shareholders' View of the Auditor's Report, in Commission on Auditors' Responsibilities. *Report, Conclusions and Recommendations.* New York: AICPA, p.164.

Hatherly, D., Innes, J. & Brown, T. (1991). The expanded audit report: an empirical investigation. *Accounting and Business Research*, **21**(84), 311–19.

Kelly, A.S. & Mohrweis, L.C. (1989). Bankers' and investors' perceptions of the auditor's role in financial statement reporting: The impact of SAS No.58. *Auditing: A Journal of Practice & Theory,* Fall.

Lee, T.A. (1970). The nature of auditing and its objectives. *Accountancy*, **81**(920), 292–6.

Lee, T.A. & Tweedie, D.P. (1975). Accounting information: an investigation of private shareholder usage. *Accounting and Business Research*, **5**(20), 280–91.

Porter, B.A. (1993). An empirical study of the audit expectation-performance gap. *Accounting and Business Research*, **24**(93), 49–68.

Wilton, R.L. & Tabb, J.B. (1978, May). An investigation into private shareholder usage of financial statements in New Zealand. *Accounting Education*, **18**, pp. 83–101.

Woolf, E. (1979). *Auditing Today.* London: Prentice Hall.

Zachry, B.R. (1991). Who understands audit reports? *The Woman CPA*, **53**(2), 9–11.

ADDITIONAL READING

Estes, R. (1982). *The Auditors' Report and Investor Behaviour.* Lexington, Mass: Heath.

Hatherly, D. (1992). Company auditing: a vision of the future? *Accountancy*, **110**(1187), 75.

Hatherly, D., Innes, J. & Brown, T. (1992). *The Expanded Audit Report*, London: Institute of Chartered Accountants in England and Wales.

Hodgkinson, R. (1993) Clear expressions of opinion. *Accountancy*, **112**(1201), 86–8.

Holt, G. & Moizer, P. (1990). The meaning of audit reports. *Accounting and Business Research*, **20**(78), 111–22.

Hopkins, L. (1996). A clear expression of opinion. *Accountancy*, **117**(1232), 145.

Seidler, L.J. (1976). Symbolism and communication in the auditor's report. In Stettler, H.F., (Ed). *Auditing Symposium III.* University of Kansas: ToucheRoss/University of Kansas Symposium on Auditing Problems.

Chapter 14

Auditing and the Computer

LEARNING OBJECTIVES

After studying the material in this chapter you should be able to:
- explain the impact of information technology (IT) on the accounting system and related internal controls;
- discuss the impact of computer processing of accounting data on the objectives and scope of an audit;
- explain the skills and competence required of auditors in today's computer (IT) environment;
- explain the impact of computer processing of accounting data on audit procedures, including the use of computer-assisted audit techniques (CAATs);
- discuss the use of computers as an audit tool.

The following publication is particularly relevant to this chapter:

- Auditing Guideline (AG) 3.2.407: *Auditing in a Computer Environment*, (ICAEW, 1984).

14.1 INTRODUCTION

Forty years ago computers were virtually unknown in the accounting environment. Today there are few organisations of any size whose accounting data are not processed by computers.

In this chapter we consider the effect of computer processing of accounting data on the audit process. More specifically, we discuss the impact of information technology (IT) on the objectives and scope of an audit, and on the skills and competence required of auditors. We examine the effect of IT on the auditor's evaluation of internal controls and also discuss the impact of computers on audit tests and, in particular, the use of computer-assisted audit techniques (CAATs).

The advent of computers has not only affected audit procedures; they have also become a valuable audit tool. In the final section of this chapter we examine some of the ways in which computers are used by auditors to assist them in the performance of their audits.

14.2 IMPACT OF INFORMATION TECHNOLOGY (IT) ON AUDIT OBJECTIVES AND PROCESS

The use of computers by organisations to process their accounting data has had a significant impact on organisations' accounting systems and related internal controls. These changes have generally resulted in changes to the procedures used by auditors to evaluate and test entities' internal control systems and to test the validity, completeness and accuracy of their financial statements.

However, although the adoption of computer processing of accounting data may have affected audit procedures, it has *not* affected the objectives and scope of the audit. Auditors are still required to express an opinion as to whether or not the financial statements of the reporting entity give a true and fair view of the entity's financial position and performance and are properly prepared in accordance with relevant legislation. It is particularly pertinent to note that the requirements of the Companies Act 1985 (s. 237) regarding the keeping of proper accounting records[1] are the same irrespective of whether the entity has a manual or a computer-based accounting system.

Further, the use of computers to process accounting data has not resulted in any change to the audit process. The audit still proceeds through the normal steps of:

- understanding the client, its business, and its industry;
- assessing audit risk through overall analytical review;
- setting materiality limits;
- reviewing and evaluating the entity's accounting and internal control systems;
- developing the audit programme based on knowledge of the client, overall analytical review, and preliminary evaluation of the internal control system;
- testing the internal control procedures on which reliance is to be placed to ensure the validity, completeness and accuracy of the accounting data (compliance testing);

---

[1] The requirements of section 237 are outlined in Chapter 13, section 13.2.

- substantive testing of transactions and account balances;
- completion and review procedures.

The adoption of computer-based accounting systems has, in many cases, influenced how these audit steps are performed, but it does not affect the steps *per se*.

14.3 SKILLS AND COMPETENCE REQUIRED FOR AUDITING IN AN IT ENVIRONMENT

As noted above, the use of computers to process accounting data has not affected the objectives and scope of an audit or the audit process, but it has had an impact on auditing procedures. Not surprisingly, it has also affected the skills and competence required of auditors.

Statement of Auditing Standards (SAS) 240: *Quality Control For Audit Work* specifies that audits are to be performed by persons who have adequate training, skills and competence in auditing (see Chapter 6, section 6.2.2). Auditing Guideline (AG) 3.2.407: *Auditing in a Computer Environment* adds to this by stating:

> When auditing in a computer environment, the auditor should obtain a basic understanding of the fundamentals of data processing and a level of technical computer knowledge and skills which, depending on the circumstances, may need to be extensive. This is because the auditor's knowledge and skills need to be appropriate to the environment in which he is auditing, and . . . he should not undertake . . . professional work which he is not himself competent to perform unless he obtains such advice and assistance as will enable him competently to carry out his task. (para 6)

The auditor may obtain such 'advice and assistance' from within his or her audit firm (especially from IT specialists) and/or from experts outside the firm. However, irrespective of how much, or from whom, assistance is sought, the auditor remains responsible for the audit and for expressing an opinion on the entity's financial statements. As a consequence, it is important that the auditor is sufficiently knowledgeable about IT to be able to direct, supervise and review the work of assistants from within the firm with special IT skills and/or to obtain reasonable assurance that the work performed by outside IT experts is adequate.

14.4 EFFECT OF IT ON ACCOUNTING SYSTEMS AND RELATED INTERNAL CONTROLS

14.4.1 Characteristic Features of an IT Environment

IT has advanced at a phenomenal pace in the last 20 years in particular and, as a result, the computer environment faced by the auditor is constantly developing. Moreover, at any point in time, an auditor will encounter different computer environments in different audit-clients, the variations depending upon the size of the business, the relevance of IT to that business, and the enthusiasm of the client's management for IT.

In the early years of using computers to process accounting data, computers were only found in major organisations which held a physically large 'mainframe' computer in a central computing or EDP[2] department. This department gathered the relevant data in manual form from other departments and coded it into a format and form accessible to the computer. The computing department would usually have its own programmers to write the necessary computer programs to process the data. Output from the computer would be in the form of hard copy or print-out which would be despatched from the computing department to the user departments. Today, in the more sophisticated environments, data is frequently input via a remote terminal, which may be many miles from the central computer processor and database, and it can be transmitted through a 'network' to the central processor, into storage, or to other remote terminals. It is not necessary for the input data to be printed out in hard copy. The remote terminal may be an 'intelligent' PC (personal computer) – intelligent in the sense that it may be capable of processing data locally before transmitting it to a central location. Alternatively, it may be capable of 'downloading' data from a central location to permit local processing of that data. There may be no need for processed data to be printed out and despatched to user departments. Instead, users can access the system, making 'enquiries' of the data, through their own remote terminals.

The most significant IT developments for accounting have been:

(i) the dramatic increase in the processing power and data storage abilities of the computer A typical modern PC has many times the power of the old 'mainframe' computers;
(ii) the ability to network computers, allowing them to 'talk' to each other and to input and output data through remote terminals or PCs.

Paralleling these developments, IT or computer departments have changed their character quite considerably. There is less emphasis on writing computer programs since most companies 'buy in' a package or suite of programs from a software house. There is greater emphasis on maintaining the network, managing databases, and controlling access to the system, although many of these activities can also be sub-contracted to a greater or lesser extent. In many cases, former EDP departments, with their focus on accounting functions, have developed into IT departments, responsible for all of the organisation's information technology and communications systems.

It is important for an auditor auditing in an IT environment to understand the characteristic features of that environment because different IT environments present the auditor with different challenges. However certain features, of which the auditor needs to be aware, are common to most IT environments. These include the following:

(i) *Concentration or Distribution of Data Storage and Processing*

In some IT environments accounting data and records are concentrated in the computing or IT department. This means, among other things, that:

• much of the data processing is carried out by people who have little, or no, accounting knowledge;

---

[2] EDP stands for Electronic Data Processing (i.e. computer processing).

- certain IT personnel may be the only people in the entity with detailed knowledge of the relationship between the source data, its processing and its distribution as output;
- the records of all types of transactions – for example, sales, purchases, wages, cash receipts and payments – are handled by the same people.

These factors clearly have implications for the auditor's evaluation of the entity's internal control system.

In other IT environments, computer networks have been introduced and these allow 'distributed' processing at local computers ('work stations') or PCs. In these environments, the problems related to processing and storage of accounting data can be quite different from those where there is only central processing. In the 'distributed' case, the potential difficulty is that local processing can take place without any standard controls being imposed from the centre.

(ii) *Difficulties in Accessing the Audit Trail*

In many computerised accounting systems much of the data is produced and stored on computer discs. Once hard copy (print-out) has been obtained, the related computerised data may be retained for only a short period. This imposes time constraints on the testing of such data. In other computer systems, especially those which are more advanced, a regular print-out of all processed data may be absent. Exception reports (that is, reporting data or information which requires some follow-up action) are often all that is produced, although these too can be kept on a computer file without hard copy print-out. Further, at a number (and an increasing number) of points within the accounting system, the computer itself is programmed to initiate transactions. These include, for example, the calculation and recording of interest accruing on accounts in savings banks, and payment of invoices (printing of cheques) when all of the necessary information has been received by the computer and matched (for example, when the purchase order, receiving report and supplier's invoice have all been input and matched). As a consequence of these factors, there may well be a general absence of input and output documentation for the auditor to scrutinise.

Where the computer-stored accounting data has a short lifespan or there is a general absence of documents, two major impacts on the audit may result. These are as follows:

(a) Planning the audit, as regards the timing of audit procedures and requesting that documents be printed and saved and/or computer files be copied or retained, can be far more demanding than was the case in the audit of an entity with a manual-based accounting system.
(b) Many features of an internal control system, which are generally regarded as fundamental in a manual accounting system, may be absent. If this is the case, other controls, more appropriate to the IT environment, must be present if the auditor is to gain assurance that the accounting data, and hence the financial statement account balances, are valid, complete and accurate.

(iii)   *Ease of Access to Data and Computer Programs and the Vulnerability of Storage Media*

As indicated above, accounting data (and computer programs) can frequently be accessed and altered through computer facilities at remote locations. As a consequence, in the absence of appropriate controls, there may be potential for unauthorised access to, and alteration of, data and programs from inside or outside the entity. Similarly, computer programs and/or accounting data may be exposed to computer viruses and hacking.

In addition, large volumes of data and programs will be stored on computer discs which may be highly portable. Unless these are carefully protected, such storage media are vulnerable to loss, theft and destruction.

(iv)   *Processing Features of the Computer*

The computer has special processing features, some of which have particular significance for the auditor. These include the following.

(a)   *Consistent performance*:   Computers have a repetitive and mathematical ability not possessed by humans: they perform repeatedly as programmed. As a consequence, providing they are programmed correctly, computerised accounting systems are generally more reliable and accurate than manual systems. This feature usually enables auditors to derive greater assurance about the reliability of accounting data from a smaller volume of audit tests than applies in the case of manual accounting systems. However, it must also be recognised that, if the computer is not correctly programmed, it will consistently process transactions and other data incorrectly. Thus, errors which occur are more likely to be material. The auditor should also be aware of the possibility of programming fraud whereby a computer may be programmed to recognise a specific condition which causes a transaction possessing that condition to be processed in a non-routine, fraudulent manner while all other transactions are processed correctly. Appropriate supervision of programmers and testing of programs are the relevant safeguards.

(b)   *Detailed records*:   Computers facilitate the maintenance of more detailed and up-to-date records; for example, detailed up-to-date listings of stock items and detailed fixed asset registers may be maintained. Further, the detailed records are generally readily retrievable. Such features are of considerable assistance to auditors in the performance of substantive procedures.

(c)   *Simultaneous update of multiple accounts and files*:   Computer capabilities may be used to update a number of accounts and/or files simultaneously. For example, when a single sales transaction is input to the computer, the sales and debtors' accounts and the perpetual stock records may all be updated automatically. The auditor must pay due regard to such simultaneous updating because, if a transaction is entered into the system incorrectly, it will cause errors in a number of different accounts. Further, if sales and cash receipts (and other relevant items) are recorded simultaneously in the relevant account in the debtors' subsidiary ledger and in the debtors' control account in the general ledger, the value of reconciling the subsidiary ledger total and the control account balance as a control procedure is reduced.

(d) *Programmed controls*:   The nature of computer processing enables internal control procedures to be embedded in computer programs. For example:

- access to the computer, or to data, programs or files, may be restricted through the use of passwords;
- regular and frequent reconciliations between, say, the debtors' control account in the general ledger and the debtors' subsidiary ledger may take place. In a manual system regular and frequent reconciliations may be precluded by time and cost factors;
- rejection and exception reports may be generated routinely. Rejection reports indicate why the computer program has rejected certain input. Exception reports indicate items which exceed pre-determined limits (for example, a debt which has been outstanding for 30 days or more, or a wage payment of £5,000 or more a week). These reports are of particular importance to auditors as they indicate the errors or conditions the computer is programmed to detect. The fact that incorrect input is rejected, and certain processing errors are detected and highlighted, helps to ensure that errors in the accounting data are minimised.

In relation to exception reports, it should be noted that these reports provide the basis for management by exception. For example, where the computer is programmed to generate a list of overdue debtors' balances, the credit manager does not have to review the entire debtors' ledger in order to obtain the required information. Indeed, the computer may be programmed not only to provide a list of overdue accounts; it may also generate suitable reminder letters and, at the appropriate time, print suitable threats!

14.4.2   Internal Controls in an IT Environment

As a result of the features of an IT environment noted above and, in particular:

- the concentration of processing and storage of accounting data in the computer or IT department or, at the other extreme, the distribution of processing and storage around the network,
- the difficulties of accessing the audit trail,
- the short lifespan of some computer-stored accounting data, and
- the ease of access to data and programs,

many of the 'traditional' internal control procedures employed in a manual system are not applicable in an IT environment and alternative, more appropriate, controls need to be designed and implemented.

Nevertheless, the overall objectives of internal controls, namely, to secure reliable accounting data and to safeguard the entity's assets, are not affected. Similarly, although the detailed application of the seven elements of a good internal control system may differ from the way in which they are applied in a manual accounting system, the importance of the elements remains unchanged. The elements (which are discussed in Chapter 9, section 9.3.2) are as follows:

- competent reliable personnel who possess integrity;
- clearly defined areas of authority and responsibility;
- proper authorisation procedures;
- adequate documentation;
- segregation of incompatible duties;
- independent checks on performance;
- physical safeguarding of assets.

In an IT environment, two broad categories of internal controls may be recognised, namely:

(i)   general (or environmental) controls, and
(ii) application controls.

(i)   General (or Environmental) Controls

General controls are designed to control both the IT environment and the development and maintenance of computer systems. They include:

- restricting access to the computer, data, programs, and files to authorised personnel;
- ensuring that duties are clearly assigned and that incompatible duties are segregated; for example, assigning systems analyst, programming, program testing, computer operating, and library (storage) duties to different employees;
- ensuring that there are adequate back-up facilities for both software and hardware, should they be needed;
- ensuring that the development or acquisition of new programs (or packages), and the testing and implementation of new programs and program changes, are properly authorised and adequately planned;
- ensuring that all computer applications, and modifications thereof, are properly and fully documented;
- ensuring that computer systems are used only for authorised purposes, and that only authorised programs and data are used.

(ii)   Application Controls

Application controls are controls over the input, processing and output of accounting applications. More particularly, they are controls which are designed to ensure that:

- all transactions input to the system are properly authorised;
- input data are complete;
- invalid and incorrect data are rejected;

- transactions are completely, properly and accurately processed (in particular, they are accurate as to their amount, account classification and reporting period);
- processing errors are identified and corrected on a timely basis;
- data files are properly maintained and protected;
- output is checked against input data;
- output is provided to appropriate, authorised personnel on a timely basis;
- exception reports are acted on promptly and appropriately;
- only the latest versions of programs and data are used for processing.

It should be noted that, although two broad groups of internal controls may be identified in an IT environment and both are essential to an effective internal control system, they are not of equal importance. If the general controls are weak or defective, then it is likely that the application controls will not be applied correctly and the internal control system as a whole will be ineffective. Weaknesses in the general or environmental controls cannot be adequately compensated for by 'foolproof' application controls. However, by the same token, the presence of 'perfect' general controls does not mean that application controls may be dispensed with. They remain an essential element of an effective internal control system.

14.5   AUDIT TESTS IN AN IT ENVIRONMENT

14.5.1   Auditing Around or Through the Computer

Until fairly recently, input and output documentation in a computerised accounting system was fairly extensive; also, computer systems were relatively unsophisticated. These factors left auditors (who, in the main had very limited computer knowledge or experience) with a choice between two approaches to auditing computer systems, namely:

(i)   auditing around the computer; and
(ii) auditing through the computer.

(i)   *Auditing Around the Computer (or the 'Black Box' Approach)*

Under this approach the input to, and output from, the computer is examined, but the detailed processing within the computer (the contents of the 'black box') is ignored. It is assumed that, providing the output matches the input, the processing function is satisfactory.

(ii) *Auditing Through the Computer*

Under this approach, not only is the input to, and output from, the computer examined, but also the processing which goes on inside, that is, the programs used to process the data are also examined. This is achieved through the use of computer-assisted audit techniques (CAATs) which are discussed in section 14.5.2 below.

In recent years, as input and output documentation has been reduced, and computer systems have become more commonplace and sophisticated, it has become increasingly necessary for auditors to audit through the computer. Indeed, it seems likely that, as most corporate entities today use computer systems to process all, or nearly all, of their accounting data, if auditors do not examine the computer processes, they could be adjudged negligent for failing to do so.

14.5.2 Computer-Assisted Audit Techniques (CAATs)

CAATs are audit procedures which use computer facilities to investigate the reliability (or otherwise) of the client's computerised accounting system. The two most well known CAATs are:

(i)   test data (or test decks or test packs).
(ii) audit software.

(i)   *Test Data*

The test data technique is primarily designed to test the reliability of internal controls which are incorporated in the client's computer programs. It is therefore essentially a compliance procedure.

The technique involves entering data (such as a sample of transactions) into, and having the data processed by, the client's system, and comparing the output with predetermined results. The data may be used to test the effectiveness of controls, such as on-line passwords, which are designed to restrict access to specified data and programs to authorised personnel.

Alternatively, the data may comprise a set of transactions representing all types of transactions normally processed by the client's programs, and including a variety of errors. These transactions (and errors) are designed to ascertain whether programmed procedures are operating effectively; for example, whether exception reports are generated in appropriate cases, and whether transaction dates and amounts lying outside specified parameters are rejected.

Use of the test data technique is generally straightforward and does not require the auditor to possess a sophisticated knowledge of computer processes. Further, the tests are usually fairly quick to perform and generally cause little or no disruption to the client's normal processing schedules. However, a major disadvantage of the technique is that the test data are usually processed separately from the client's normal processing runs. Although the auditor can establish whether the controls are, or are not, operating effectively at the time the audit procedure is performed, (s)he does not know whether the controls operate effectively at other times.

In order to overcome this disadvantage, the test data technique can be extended to an 'integrated test facility' (ITF). This involves establishing a 'dummy' department, employee, or other unit appropriate for audit testing. Transactions affecting the dummy unit are interspersed amongst, and processed with, the client's ordinary transactions. The resultant output, relating to the dummy unit, is compared with predetermined results.

When the ITF technique is used, the auditor must be alert to the danger of contaminating the client's files and care must be taken to reverse out all of the audit test transactions.

(ii) *Audit Software*

In contrast to the test data technique, which requires the auditor to input test data to be processed by the client's computer programs, the audit software technique involves the auditor using audit software (audit computer programs) to process the client's accounting data.

There are three main types of audit software.

(a) *Utility programs and existing programs used by the entity*:   In this case, general (non-audit specific) application programs, or enquiry facilities available within a software package, are used to perform common data processing functions such as sorting, retrieving and printing of computer files. These programs may assist the auditor perform a variety of audit procedures but they are not specifically designed for audit purposes and, in general, their audit application is limited. They are used primarily to extend or to speed up procedures which would otherwise be performed manually (for example, accessing and printing all or part of the debtors' account balances or items comprising the stock account balance).

(b) *General audit software*:   This software consists of generally available computer packages which have been specially designed to perform a variety of data processing functions for audit purposes. These include reading computer files, selecting and retrieving desired information and/or samples, performing various calculations, making comparisons and printing required reports.

(c) *Specialised Audit Software*:   This software comprises specially developed programs which are designed to perform audit tests in specific circumstances, usually the circumstances pertaining to a particular entity. These programs may be prepared by the auditor (or audit firm), the entity's computer (IT) personnel, or by an outside programmer engaged by the auditor.

Although the development of specialised audit software may be appropriate for certain clients (for example, clients in specialised industries such as banking or mining), and may be a desired ideal in other cases, developing such software is extremely expensive and is usually beyond the expertise of the auditor. Whenever specialised audit software is to be developed for use in certain audits, it is essential that the auditor is actively involved in designing and testing the programs. This is necessary to ensure that the auditor fully understands the operation (and limitations) of the software and also to ensure that it adequately meets the requirements of the audit.

During recent years, the availability of general audit software has increased significantly and these packages are now used extensively to assist auditors perform a wide range of audit procedures. They are used, for example, for performing analytical procedures, for selecting and testing a sample of transactions or account balances, and for performing statistical sampling techniques such as monetary unit sampling (see Chapter 11).

In entities which rely heavily on computers to process accounting data, audit software may be invaluable to the auditor. However, its use may be resisted by an entity's management or IT personnel because the running of additional programs for audit purposes may interrupt and cause delays to the entity's normal processing runs. Be that as it may, where an entity's accounting system involves extensive use of computer processing, manual audit procedures may be rendered inappropriate and application of audit software may be the only means by which a satisfactory audit can be conducted. In such circumstances, if the client's management restricts the use of audit software, this could amount to a limitation on the scope of the audit and give rise to a qualified audit report.

14.5.3   Use and Control of CAATs

CAATs may be used to assist the auditor with a variety of audit procedures. They may, for example, assist the auditor perform:

- compliance tests of general (IT) controls – for example, to analyse processing or access logs, or to review the effectiveness of library (or other storage facility) access procedures;
- compliance tests of application controls – for example, using test data to test the effectiveness of programmed controls, such as the rejection of data outside specified parameters;
- analytical procedures – for example, using audit software to identify unusual fluctuations or items;
- detailed tests of transactions and balances – for example, using audit software to test all (or a sample) of transactions in a computer file.

CAATs are generally user-friendly so auditors do not require high-level computer knowledge in order to apply them. Although this is clearly an advantage to many auditors, it also carries the danger that auditors may be lulled into a false sense of security. This danger is particularly high when auditors require the co-operation of client computer (IT) personnel (who have an extensive and detailed knowledge of the client's system) in order to use CAATs, or where they use the client's own enquiry facilities. Such an enquiry facility could, for example, be programmed by client staff not to reveal certain records when accessed by means of the auditor's password.

Before using CAATs, the auditor must ensure that (s)he understands the process by which the audit procedures are to be performed by the computer and the limitations of, or pitfalls related to, the process. As noted in section 14.3 above, where the auditor has limited computer knowledge, (s)he should obtain assistance from, or have ready access to, assistants within the audit firm who have computer expertise, or suitable experts from outside the firm. The auditor must guard against the temptation to rely upon the client's IT personnel for explanations in circumstances which render it inappropriate to do so. The auditor must ensure that the performance of CAATs remains under his or her control and that client personnel are not able to influence improperly the results obtained therefrom.

When planning an audit in which CAATs are to be used, the auditor must be cognisant of the fact that certain computer files, such as transaction files, may be retained by the client for only a short period of time. In such cases, the auditor may need to make special arrangements for certain data to be retained, or to alter the timing of audit work in order to facilitate the testing of data while they are still available.

An interesting sideline to the advent of CAATs is that they are once again making possible, for some audit tests, an examination of *all* accounting data, instead of just samples thereof.[3] As in the 19th and early 20th centuries when detailed checking of all transactions was the norm, this may increase the likelihood of detecting certain types of corporate fraud (although not necessarily computer fraud). Further, this is occurring at a time when the courts, politicians, the public, and a significant number of individual auditors are pressing the profession to assume greater responsibility for detecting fraud. However, it is also happening at a time when the increasing sophistication of computer networks is opening up new possibilities for computer fraud. This seems likely to present new challenges – and difficulties – for auditors.

It is suggested that it is likely that the development of CAATs and the increasing sophistication of IT systems, combined with the demand for auditors to accept greater responsibility to detect corporate fraud, will add impetus to the move (noted in Chapter 3) towards re-establishing fraud detection as an important audit objective. It was noted in Chapter 2 that history shows that changes in the audit environment, changes in audit techniques and changes in audit objectives, go hand in hand. It appears that this is being demonstrated at the present time in relation to corporate fraud.

14.6   THE COMPUTER AS AN AUDIT TOOL

It is clear from the material presented in this chapter that the advent of computers has had a significant impact on the conduct of an audit. However, even if an audit client does not rely on computers to process its accounting data and/or if CAATs are not used during the audit, computers are a useful audit tool. Indeed, few audits are performed today without some assistance from computers. In particular, many audit working papers are compiled using computers and stored on disc. Indeed, major audit firms are speaking of 'paperless' audits and predicting that, by the turn of the century, (hard-copy) audit working papers will be replaced entirely by computer storage. To-day, audit juniors typically arrive at clients' premises armed with briefcase, audit files and laptop computer. It seems likely that the briefcase and audit files will soon be superfluous and the laptop computer will be all that is needed. The laptop can contain the audit manual as well as facilities to help the auditor perform a wide range of audit procedures. These include, for example:

• performing analytical procedures and risk assessments;
• developing the audit programme;

---

[3] This can happen whenever the audit procedure does not require reference to evidence held outside the computer system. For example, a CAAT can check calculations on the value of all stock items but it cannot check on the condition of the stock.

- generating random numbers for sample selection;
- producing debtors' confirmation requests.

Significant though these developments are, the major audit firms are predicting more than paperless audits. They are also suggesting that, within the next decade or so, auditors will have direct on-line access to their audit-clients' accounting data and, thus, they will be able to audit the data whenever they wish to do so throughout the reporting period. Such a development is likely to have a major impact on the nature, timing and extent of audit procedures, and the skills and competence required of audit staff.

14.7 SUMMARY

In this chapter we have considered the impact of computer processing of accounting data on the audit process. We have noted that the change from manual to computerised accounting systems has not affected the objectives or scope of an audit or the audit process *per se*. However, we have also observed that computer systems differ from manual systems in respect of, for example, the processing and storage of accounting data and the nature of the audit trail, and that these differences have affected audit procedures. In particular, they have impacted on the conduct of the auditor's evaluation of internal controls and the performance of compliance and substantive audit procedures.

Additionally, we have noted that, although until fairly recently auditors could audit around the computer, the present widespread use and sophistication of IT systems mean that, in general, such an approach is no longer acceptable. Today, auditors are expected to examine not only the input to, and output from, a computerised accounting system, they are also expected to investigate the programs used to process the data. This is achieved through the use of computer-assisted audit techniques.

Although computers have placed new demands on auditors in terms of the skills and competence they are required to possess and they have necessitated the development of new audit procedures, they have also provided auditors with a valuable audit tool. In the final section of this chapter we have noted a variety of ways in which computers may be used to assist auditors.

SELF-REVIEW QUESTIONS

14.1 Explain briefly the skills and competence required of auditors as a consequence of audits being conducted in a computer (IT) environment.

14.2 Outline the main changes which have taken place during the last 20 years in the IT environment which have significance for the auditor.

14.3 Describe four distinctive processing features of computers and explain their particular significance to auditors.

14.4 List seven elements of a good internal control system in an IT environment.

14.5 Explain briefly the purpose of each of the two broad categories of internal controls which may be recognised in an IT environment:
(i) general controls
(ii) application controls.

14.6 List five general controls which should be present in an IT environment and five application controls.

14.7 Explain briefly what is meant by:
(i) auditing around the computer
(ii) auditing through the computer.

14.8 With reference to CAATs, explain briefly the test data technique.

14.9 List three types of audit software.

14.10 List four ways in which the computer can be used to assist auditors.

ADDITIONAL READING

Allen, B. (1977). The biggest computer frauds: Lessons for CPAs. *The Journal of Accountancy*, **147**(5), 40–50.
Croft, M. (1992). Let the computer take the strain. *Accountancy*, **110**(1187), 60–1.
Fisher, R. (1993). Auditors and electronic data interchange. *Accountants' Journal*, **73**(7), 49–51.
Grant, J. (1991). Planning for an effective and efficient audit in a computerized environment. In Sherer, M. & Turley, S., *Current Issues in Auditing*. 2nd ed. Chapter 11. London: Paul Chapman Publishing.

Chapter 15

Legal Liability of Auditors

LEARNING OBJECTIVES

After studying the material in this chapter you should be able to:
- distinguish between auditors' statutory and common law duties;
- discuss auditors' contractual liability to their client entities;
- discuss auditors' liability to third parties for negligence;
- explain how auditors' duty of care to third parties was extended by a series of cases starting in 1931 with *Ultramares* v *Touche* through to the 1980s with the cases of *Jeb Fasteners* and *Twomax Ltd*;
- explain the significance of the House of Lords' decision in the *Caparo* case;
- discuss the effect of out-of-court settlements.

15.1   INTRODUCTION

When an auditor[1] accepts an audit engagement it is assumed that this denotes an undertaking to perform the audit in accordance with certain statutory and common law obligations. If these obligations are not met, the auditor is liable to parties who suffer loss as a result. These parties may include the client entity with whom the auditor has a contractual relationship, and also third parties who do not have a contractual relationship with the auditor but who, nevertheless, rely on the proper performance of the auditor's duties (that is, on the opinion expressed in the auditor's report).

In this chapter we address the issue of auditors' legal liability. More specifically, we examine auditors' contractual liability to audit clients and trace the development (in an international setting) of their liability to third parties. We also consider the House of Lords' decision in the *Caparo* case (1990). This is currently the most influential case in the UK with respect to auditors' liability and is particularly notable for reversing the trend towards extending auditors' liability to third parties and returning the law to where it stood some 30 years ago. Before closing the chapter, we discuss some cases decided subsequent to *Caparo,* and explore the effect of out-of-court settlements on the development of the law relating to auditors' liability and indemnity insurance.

15.2   OVERVIEW OF AUDITORS' LEGAL LIABILITY

15.2.1   Auditors' Exposure to Legal Liability

As noted above, when an auditor accepts an audit engagement it is understood that (s)he agrees to perform the audit in accordance with certain statutory and common law obligations. If either of these sets of obligations are not met, the auditor is exposed to liability. Auditors' exposure to liability is depicted in Figure 15.1.

15.2.2   Breach of Statutory Duties

Some of the auditor's duties are specified by statute for example, in the Companies Act 1985 and the Theft Act 1968. If the auditor fails to perform these duties, the breach may constitute either:

* a civil wrong, whereby the client entity or some individual suffers loss as a result of the auditor failing to meet his or her statutory obligations; or
* a criminal act; this arises, for example, when an auditor deliberately signs a report knowing it to be false.

In either case, the maximum penalty the auditor will face (which will be in the form of a fine or imprisonment) is specified in the statute the auditor has breached. For

---

[1] Under the Companies Act 1989, s.25(2), an audit firm may be appointed as 'the auditor'. Thus, 'the auditor' should be taken to mean either an individual or an audit firm. The principles of legal liability apply equally in either case. If the audit firm is a partnership (which is usually the case), the partners are jointly and severally liable. This means they are liable jointly with the other partners of the firm for any damages awarded by a court against any one of the firm's partners; they are also liable individually to meet damages awarded against any of the firm's partners, should the other partners of the firm not be able to pay.

Figure 15.1   Auditors' Exposure to Legal Liability

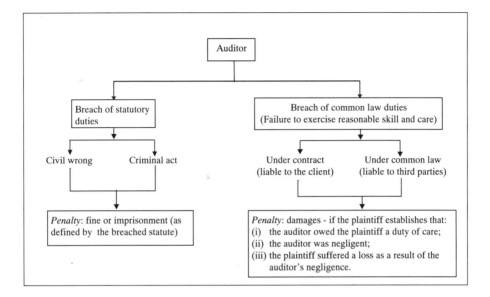

example, under the Companies Act 1989 (s.28), if the auditor of a company becomes ineligible, during his or her term of office, to hold the position of auditor (s)he is required to vacate the position and inform the company in writing. Failure to give such written notice, renders the auditor liable:

(a) on conviction on indictment, to a fine, and
(b) on summary conviction, to a fine not exceeding the statutory maximum (currently, £5,000) (Companies Act 1989, s.28).

15.2.3   Breach of Common Law Duties

In addition to statutory obligations which arise when an auditor agrees to perform an audit, a common law duty also arises, namely, a duty to perform the audit with reasonable skill and care appropriate to the circumstances. If the auditor fails to exercise reasonable skill and care, (s)he will be liable to make good any resultant loss suffered by those to whom a duty of care is owed. Such a duty of care may result from a contractual relationship or may arise under common law to parties outside a contractual arrangement. The circumstances in which the courts have held that auditors owe a duty of care to third parties are discussed in section 15.4.1 below.

The penalty for proven negligence (that is, failure to take due care) is the award of damages. However, before damages will be awarded against an auditor, the plaintiff must prove three facts, namely:

• that the auditor owed him or her a duty of care;
• that the auditor was negligent (that is, the auditor did not exercise a reasonable standard of skill and care in the particular circumstances); and

- the plaintiff suffered a loss as a result of the auditor's negligence.

Although these three requirements have been clearly established in law, two of them create difficulties for auditors as they are not static. These are as follows:

(i) *What Qualifies as Negligence? (What amounts to a reasonable standard of skill and care in the particular circumstances?)*

As Moffit J made clear in the Australian case of *Pacific Acceptance Corporation Limited* v *Forsyth and Others* (1970) 92 WN (NSW) 29, compliance with generally accepted auditing standards may not be enough to protect the auditor from being judged negligent. Moffit J observed that professional standards and practice must change over time to reflect changes in the economic and business environment. Although the courts are guided by professional standards and current best auditing practice, they will not be bound by them and, if the courts see fit, they will go beyond them. It is for the courts, not the auditing profession, to determine, in the light of society's norms of the time, what is reasonable skill and care in the particular circumstances of the case.

This leaves auditors in a difficult and unenviable position. Not only do they lack a clear standard to which they are expected to work (the standard of skill and care required of them varies over time and as between different sets of circumstances) but additionally, when the courts evaluate whether or not they have exercised the required standard of skill and care, it is with the wisdom of hindsight.

(ii) *The Parties to Whom Auditors Owe a Duty of Care*

As indicated in Figure 15.1, a duty of care may arise under either:

(a) *contract*, that is, as part of the contractual arrangement between the auditor and the client. This duty is generally clear-cut and does not give rise to uncertainty; or
(b) *common law*. This duty of care to third parties (that is, parties outside a contractual relationship) is imposed on auditors when the courts consider it reasonable and equitable to do so. As will be shown in section 15.4.1 below, between the early 1960s and the end of the 1980s, the parties to whom auditors were held to owe a duty of care were extended progressively. Then, as a result of the *Caparo* case, they were reduced significantly once more. The various changes leave auditors unsure as to their contractual liability should they fail to exercise a reasonable standard of skill and care in the particular circumstances of the audit.

15.3 AUDITORS' CONTRACTUAL LIABILITY TO THEIR CLIENTS

15.3.1 Auditors' Contractual Duties

When an auditor accepts an audit engagement, (s)he contracts with the client to perform certain duties. Some of these are specified in legislation (such as the

Companies Act 1985); others have been determined over the years by the courts as a result of various cases being brought against auditors. (Some of these cases are discussed in Chapter 3, section 3.4). If the auditor does not perform his or her duties with a reasonable standard of skill and care and, as a consequence, the client[2] suffers a loss, then the auditor is liable to make good the loss suffered.

An example of an auditor being held liable for breach of contractual duties is provided by the Australian case of *AWA Limited* v *Daniels, trading as Deloitte Haskins & Sells & Ors* (1992) 10 ACLC 933. In this case, AWA's manager of foreign exchange operations, whilst appearing to trade profitability in foreign exchange dealings, in fact caused AWA to incur a loss of $A50 million. The manager concealed the losses by various means, including undertaking unauthorised borrowing from a number of banks, allegedly on behalf of AWA. AWA sued the auditors for damages in breach of contract, claiming that the loss suffered was caused by Deloittes' failure to draw attention to serious deficiencies in the company's internal controls and accounting records, and for failing to qualify their audit reports.

Rogers, C J found that Deloittes failed to perform their contractual duties in three ways:

(i)   It was clear that the books and records relevant to AWA's foreign exchange transactions were 'inaccurate and inadequate' and 'the auditors should have formed the opinion that proper accounting records had not been kept' (Rogers, C J at 959). They failed to fulfil this duty.

(ii) The auditors had doubts about the extent of the foreign exchange manager's authority to enter into foreign exchange transactions on behalf of AWA. In such circumstances, the auditors had a duty to make enquiries from an appropriate level of management. This, Deloittes failed to do.

(iii) Notwithstanding that the auditors had discussed the inadequate system of recording foreign exchange transactions with the general manager of AWA, they did nothing to ensure that the matter was dealt with urgently and effectively, nor did they ensure that it was referred to AWA's board of directors. Rogers, C J held that simply identifying shortcomings and bringing them to the attention of management below board level is insufficient discharge of an auditor's duty in cases where the auditor is aware that management fails to respond adequately. Management's failure to take action to rectify the position imposes on the auditor an obligation to inform the board. Further, this duty to report to the board is not discharged by relying on the possibility that the chief executive officer will already have done so.

It was decided in the AWA case that the auditors had been negligent in the performance of their duties and that their negligence had contributed to the loss suffered by AWA. However, AWA's senior management was also found to have contributed to the company's loss by virtue of deficiencies in its system of internal controls and record keeping.

---

[2] It should be noted that 'the client' is the client entity, not the entity's shareholders or any other interested party.

Deloittes appealed the trial judge's ruling but the Court of Appeal upheld Rogers, C J's findings.[3] However, the Appeal Court gave greater weight than did the trial judge to the part played by AWA's management in the loss suffered by the company. Indeed, Shanahan (1995) reports:

> The court [of Appeal] was satisfied that the omissions of the board [of directors] were a cause of the ultimate loss suffered by AWA in the sense that grossly negligent management was permitted to persevere with [foreign exchange] operations in an entirely unsatisfactory manner. (p.214)

In the Court of Appeal's view, the crux of Deloittes' negligence lay in their failure to give appropriate advice to the board of directors regarding the absence of controls over the foreign exchange operations and the failure of senior management to respond to their (the auditors') warnings regarding the absence of controls (Shanahan, 1995, p.214). Taking due cognisance of the contributory negligence by AWA's management, the Court of Appeal reduced the damages awarded against Deloittes from $A17 million to $A6 million. [It should be noted that this is an Australian case and that, in the United Kingdom, the concept of contributory negligence (proportionate liability), although currently being looked at by the British Government, is not yet accepted as an applicable legal principle.]

With respect to auditors' contractual liability to their clients, the AWA case is particularly interesting as it illustrates both:

(i) a breach of auditors' statutory duties – that is, their failure to qualify their audit report for the company's failure to maintain proper accounting records, as required by section 331E(2) of the Australian Corporations Law; and

(ii) a breach of their common law duties – that is, their failure to make the necessary enquiries of AWA's senior management about matters of which they were uncertain (for example, the extent of the foreign exchange manager's authority), and their failure to report to the appropriate level of the entity's management (namely, the board of directors) serious deficiencies they had discovered in the entity's internal controls and record keeping.

It should be noted that, in order for contractual liability to be invoked, the aggrieved party must be a party to the contract. In the case of auditors appointed to perform a statutory audit under the Companies Act 1985, the contract is between the auditor and the company *per se*, *not* individual shareholders (or their equivalent). As the *AWA* case illustrates, if an auditor fails to perform his or her statutory duties or fails to take due care in performing the audit, the client entity (in this case, AWA Limited) may sue for breach of contract. Should a shareholder wish to take action against the auditor(s), (s)he can do so only by exercising his or her rights as a third party under the common law (see section 15.4.1 below). However, as a result of the House of Lords' decision in the *Caparo* case (1990), even this avenue of relief for shareholders as individuals has been brought into question (see section 15.4.2 below).

---

[3] *Daniels (formerly practising as Deloitte Haskins & Sells)* v *AWA Ltd*; 15 May 1995, (NSW) CA.

15.3.2 The Importance of Engagement Letters

Statement of Auditing Standards (SAS) 140: *Engagement Letters* recommends that, when an auditor is engaged to perform an audit, an engagement letter be prepared to clarify the terms of the contract.[4] The engagement letter does not (indeed, cannot) excuse the auditor from performing his or her statutory or common law duties, or from performing those duties with a reasonable standard of skill and care appropriate to the circumstances of the audit. However, the letter can reduce to a minimum any mis-understanding between the client and the auditor with respect to the duties to be performed and the terms of the engagement.

Although engagement letters are important to clarify the terms of an audit engage-ment, as the United States case of *1136 Tenants' Corporation* v *Max Rothenberg & Co* (1971) 319 NYS2d 1007 demonstrates, they are even more important when the engagement does not include an audit. In the *1136 Tenants' Corporation* case, a firm of certified public accountants was engaged to write up the books of a co-operative block of flats. It was successfully sued for negligence for not uncovering an embezzlement by the managing agent. Damages were awarded against the accountants despite the fact that each set of accounts they submitted to the corporation was accompanied by a letter which began:

> Pursuant to our engagement, we have reviewed and summarised the statements of your managing agent, and other data submitted to us by the managing agent.

The letter concluded:

> The following statements were prepared from the books and records of the Corporation. No independent verifications were undertaken thereon . . .

The financial statements themselves were marked

> Subject to comments in letter of transmittal . . .

The accountants argued that the statement in the transmittal letter that 'no indepen-dent verifications were undertaken' was sufficient warning to all users of the financial statements that they were unaudited. The court nevertheless found them to be guilty of negligence (Woolf, 1979, p.263).

15.4 LIABILITY TO THIRD PARTIES UNDER COMMON LAW

15.4.1 Duty of Care to Third Parties

As noted above, if auditors breach their statutory duties or fail to perform their duties with reasonable skill and care, they may be held liable to make good any consequen-tial loss suffered by their client. This liability arises as a result of the contractual relationship between the auditor and the client.

Over the past 30 or so years, the courts in the UK (and elsewhere) have held that auditors also owe a duty of care to certain third parties who suffer loss as a

---

[4] Engagement letters are discussed in Chapter 7, section 7.3.

consequence of auditors failing to perform their duties with due care. Through a series of cases, beginning in 1931 in the US when it was held that auditors' liability should be restricted to contractual relationships and not extended to third parties, the parties to whom auditors have been held to owe a duty of care were widened progressively. This trend was reversed with the *Caparo* decision in 1990. The relevant cases are summarised in Figure 15.2.

In 1931, in the US case of *Ultramares Corporation* v *Touche* (1931) 255 NY 170, it was held that auditors' liability can arise only under a contractual relationship. Cardozo, J decided that it would be too much to impose on accountants a liability to third parties for financial loss as this may expose them to liability out of all proportion to the gravity of their actions. As Cardozo, J expressed it (at 179):

> [it] may expose accountants to liability in an indeterminate amount for an indeterminate time to an indeterminate class.

In 1932, the English case of *Donoghue* v *Stevenson* (1932) AC 562 started the process of recognising a liability to parties outside a contractual relationship. This case involved a young man who purchased a bottle of ginger beer, complete with decomposed snail, and gave it to his girlfriend to drink. Not surprisingly, the girlfriend became ill. The court held that a duty of care is owed to third parties in circumstances where it can be reasonably foreseen that failure to take care may result in physical injury. Thus, this case established that liability may arise outside a contractual relationship in circumstances involving possible physical injury.

Nearly 20 years later, in the case of *Candler* v *Crane Christmas & Co.* [1951] 2 KB 164, the court confirmed that no duty of care is owed to third parties in the case of financial loss. In this case, the defendant firm of chartered accountants negligently prepared a set of financial statements for their clients, knowing that they would be shown to the third party plaintiff for the purpose of making an investment decision. The investment failed and the plaintiff sued the accountants.

The majority of the court, re-iterating the fears expressed by Cardozo, J in the *Ultramares* case, held that a duty of care is not owed to third parties in the case of financial loss. However, the dissenting judgment of Lord Denning signalled the way the law would develop in the future. He said:

> [Accountants] owe a duty, of course, to their employer and client and also, I think, to any third party to whom they themselves show the accounts or to whom they know their employer is going to show the accounts so as to induce him to invest money or to take some other action on them. But I do not think the duty can be extended still further so as to include strangers of whom they have heard nothing . . .

Twelve years later, in *Hedley Byrne & Co Ltd* v *Heller and Partners* [1963] 2 All ER 575, [1964] AC 465, the court accepted as correct the reasoning of Lord Denning in the *Crane Christmas* case. The *Hedley Byrne* case involved a telephone enquiry by a bank to a merchant bank (Heller & Partners Ltd) regarding the creditworthiness of a company for which Heller was banker. The bank communicated Heller's reply, that the company was 'considered good for its normal business engagements' and in particular for a proposed advertising contract, to one of its customers (Hedley Byrne & Co Ltd). The court held that a duty of care is owed to third parties where it can be shown that a 'special relationship' exists. Such a relationship will exist when the person giving the information knows, or ought to know, that another particular person is

Figure 15.2   Summary of Significant Cases Relating to Auditors' Liability to Third Parties

Case	Significance
1. *Ultramares Corporation* v *Touche* (1931) 255 NY 170 [US case]	Accountants' liability should not be extended to third parties. It can only arise under a contractual relationship.
2. *Donoghue* v *Stevenson* (1932) AC 562 [UK case]	A duty of care is owed to third parties in circumstances where it can reasonably be foreseen that failure to take care may result in physical injury.
3. *Candler* v *Crane Christmas & Co.*[1951] 2 KB 164 [UK case]	No duty of care is owed to third parties in the case of financial loss. Lord Denning's dissenting judgment indicated things to come. He considered that accountants owe a duty of care to any third party to whom they know the accounts are to be shown in order to induce him or her to invest money or to take some other action on them. He did not think that the duty could be extended to include strangers: i.e. persons of whom the auditor knows nothing at the time of the audit.
4. *Hedley Byrne & Co. Ltd* v *Heller and Partners* [1963] 2 All ER 575 [1964] AC 465 [UK case]	A duty of care is owed to third parties for financial loss where it can be shown that a 'special relationship' exists: i.e. where the auditor knows, or ought to know, that someone is going to rely on the accounts for some specific purpose. The duty of care does not extend to strangers.
5. *Diamond Manufacturing Company* v *Hamilton* [1969] NZLR 609 [NZ case]	A 'special relationship' was said to exist because one of the auditors had been involved in negotiations with the investor; a duty of care therefore existed.
6. *MLC* v *Evatt* [1971] AC 793 [Australian case]	A 'special relationship' can arise only where the person giving the advice holds him/herself out to be an expert. (The *Hedley Byrne* principle was effectively narrowed.)
7. *Haig* v *Bamford* [1976] 3WW R331 (SC Can) [Canadian case]	No duty of care is owed to a stranger. Auditors do not owe a duty of care to those whom, at the time of the audit, they are not aware will rely on the audited financial statements for a particular purpose.
8. *Anns* v *Merton London Borough Council* [1977] 2 All ER 492, [1978] AC 728 [UK case]	The requirement for a 'special relationship' was replaced by a 'relationship of proximity or neighbourhood', and the test of 'knowledge' that someone would rely on the advice given, and may suffer loss as a result of a failure to take care, was replaced by one of 'reasonable foreseeability'. This case extended quite considerably the third parties to whom a duty of care is owed.
9. *Scott Group Ltd* v *McFarlane* [1978] 1 NZLR 553 [NZ case]	This case established that a duty of care is owed by auditors who could or should reasonably foresee that a particular person or group of persons will rely on the audited financial statements for a particular type of investment decision. The *Hedley Byrne* principle of knowledge of reliance on the audited financial statements was replaced by a test of reasonable foreseeability. Attention was drawn to the fact that audited financial statements of public companies become a matter of public record through filing with the Companies Office.
10. *Jeb Fasteners Ltd* v *Marks, Bloom & Co.* [1981] 3 All ER 289 [UK case]	The court confirmed that the auditor owes a duty of care to any person or class of persons whom they do not know, but should reasonably foresee might rely on the audited financial statements when making decisions about the company. The case extended the *Scott Group* case from circumstances in which a takeover is reasonably foreseeable, to circumstances in which any form of financial support seems likely to be needed – and reliance on audited financial statements could/should be expected.
11. *Twomax Ltd* v *Dickson McFarlane and Robinson* [1982] SC 113, [1983] SLT 98 [UK – Scottish case]	The duty of care owed by auditors to third parties established in the *Scott Group* case was extended to virtually anyone who can prove they relied on negligently audited financial statements when making an investment decision and suffered loss as a consequence.
12. *Caparo Industries plc* v *Dickman and Others* [1990] 1 All ER 568; [1990] 2 AC 605; [1990] 2 WLR 358, HL, reversing [1989] 1 All ER 798; [1989] QB 653; [1989] 2 WLR 316, CA [UK case]	The court held that, in the absence of special circumstances, auditors owe a duty of care only to (i) the company and (ii) the company's shareholders as a body. A duty of care is owed to third parties only when the tests of foreseeability, proximity and fairness are satisfied.

Case	Significance
13. *Al-Saudi Banque & Others* v *Clark Pixley* [1990] Ch 313 [UK case]	The court followed *Caparo* and held that, in order for auditors to owe a duty of care to a third party they must have given the third party a copy of their audit report, or know that their audit report will be supplied to the third party.
14. *James McNaughton Papers Group Ltd.* v *Hicks Anderson* [1991] 1 All ER 134; [1990] BCC 891; (1991) 9 ACLC 3,091 [UK case]	The court applied *Caparo* but specified that when deciding whether a 'special relationship' exists, such as to give rise to the auditor owing a duty of care to a third party, the following matters are to be considered: the purpose for which an audit report is prepared, the purpose for which it is communicated to the third party, the relationship between the auditor and third party, the size of the class to which the third party belongs, the knowledge of the third party, and the extent of the third party's reliance on the auditor's report.
15. *Berg Sons & Co. Ltd.* v *Mervyn Hampton Adams* [1993] BCLC 1045 [UK case]	The court held that, in order for a company to succeed in an action against its auditors, it must show that the company or its shareholders were misled. Further, in order to establish that auditors owe a duty of care to a third party, it must be shown that: 1. a specific relationship exists between the audit function and the transaction in relation to which reliance was placed on the audit report; 2. there was a specific transaction to which the performance of the audit was directed; and 3. the case was brought within the period in which reasonable foreseeability of reliance on the financial statements applies.
16. *Galoo Ltd* v *Bright Grahame Murray* [1994] 1 WLR 1360; [1995] 1 All ER 16 [UK case]	The court followed *Caparo* but established that, in a takeover situation, if an auditor is made aware that a particular bidder will rely on the audited financial statements, and intends that the bidder should rely on them, a duty of care to the bidder will arise. However, this duty of care may be negated if the bidder has the right to undertake a due diligence examination.
17. *ADT Ltd* v *BDO Binder Hamlyn* (Dec 1995, unreported). [UK case]	This case was distinguished from *Caparo* on the grounds that it concerned the purpose for which a statement was made at a meeting, not the purpose of the audit. It was held that because Binder Hamlyn's partner knew the purpose for which ADT required the information and knew they would place reliance on it without independent enquiry, Binder Hamlyn assumed a responsibility to ADT and thus owed it a duty of care.
18. *R Lowe Lippmann Figdor & Frank* v *AGC (Advances) Ltd* (1992) 10 ACLC 1168 [Australian case]	The court followed *Caparo* and held that, although the auditors knew that AGC would rely on the audited financial statements for a lending decision, no duty of care was owed to AGC.
19. *Columbia Coffee & Tea Pty Ltd* v *Churchill* (1992) 10 ACLC 1659 [Australian case]	The court distinguished this case from *Caparo* and held that the auditors owed a duty of care to an unknown future purchaser of shares who relied on the audited financial statements of the company. The duty of care arose primarily as a result of the auditors' audit manual acknowledging an assumed responsibility to 'interested parties who read and rely upon our [audit] reports'.
20. *Esanda Finance Corporation* v *Peat Marwick Hungerfords* (1994) 12 ACLC 199 [Australian case]	The court followed *Caparo* and held that, in cases where the plaintiff is not a member of the company to whom the auditor owes a duty of care, in the absence of: • an assumption of responsibility to the plaintiff to exercise care in preparing the audit report; and • an intention that the plaintiff act in reliance upon the audit report, the auditor does not owe the plaintiff a duty of care. This decision of the South Australian Full Supreme Court indicates that in Australia the *Caparo* decision will be adopted.
21. *South Pacific Manufacturing Co. Ltd* v *New Zealand Security Consultants & Investigations Ltd* [1992] 2 NZLR 282 [NZ case]	This case, which was decided by a full bench of the Court of Appeal, indicates that it is unlikely that *Caparo* will be followed in New Zealand. Instead, NZ courts are likely to continue applying the two step *Anns* rule: (i) imposing a duty of care when it is reasonably foreseeable that harm will result from a failure to take care; (ii) limiting liability when this is dictated by policy considerations.

going to rely on the information for a specific purpose. However, the court emphasised that a duty of care does not extend to strangers – that is, persons of whom the person giving the information knows nothing at the time.

Hedley Byrne is a landmark decision in that it recognised third party liability in a case involving financial loss. Until then, liability to third parties had been limited to situations involving physical injury.

The next two cases in the series helped to clarify the meaning of a 'special relationship'. In the New Zealand case of *Diamond Manufacturing Company* v *Hamilton* [1969] NZLR 609, a member of an audit firm showed the financial statements the firm had audited to another party, knowing that the statements would be used in an investment decision. The court held that the auditors were liable to the third party as a special relationship existed, and therefore a duty of care was owed. The special relationship arose because one of the auditors was involved in the negotiations with the investor. However, the court confirmed that a duty of care did not extend to strangers.

In 1971, in the Australian case of *Mutual Life & Citizens' Assurance Co. Ltd* v *Evatt* [1971] AC 793, the circumstances in which a special relationship could arise were narrowed somewhat. This case involved an insurance agent who was negligent in giving financial advice. It was held that, in order for a special relationship to exist, the person giving the financial advice must not only know that someone is going to rely on the advice proffered but, further, he (or she) must be giving the advice in a professional capacity. The special relationship can only arise in circumstances where the person giving the advice holds him- or herself out to be an expert.

Five years later (and 12 years after the *Hedley Byrne* principle was established) a Canadian court, in *Haig* v *Bamford* [1976] 3WW R331 (SC Can), confirmed that in cases involving financial loss, no duty of care is owed to a stranger: liability to third parties cannot arise in the absence of knowledge that a particular person will rely on the financial advice given (or the audited financial statements) for a specific purpose. This principle was to be tested in the UK just one year later.

The case of *Anns* v *Merton London Borough Council* [1977] 2 All ER 492, [1978] AC 728, involved the failure of a local authority to inspect a faulty building. The court held that the authority owed a duty of care to the occupiers of the building. Although not involving auditors or accountants, this case is of singular importance to the extension of auditors' liability to third parties. It introduced a relationship of proximity or neighbourhood in place of a special relationship, and replaced the test of knowledge that someone would rely on the advice given and may suffer damage or loss as a result of failure to take care, with one of reasonable foreseeability. The court provided a two-step approach as a guideline for determining whether or not a duty of care exists in particular circumstances. In the words of Lord Wilberforce:

> In order to establish whether a duty of care arises in a particular situation, two questions must be asked:
>
> 1. As between the alleged wrongdoer and the injured party there must be a relationship of proximity or neighbourhood, such that in the reasonable contemplation of the former, carelessness on his part may be likely to cause damage to the latter, in which case a *prima facie* duty of care arises.
> 2. If the question is answered affirmatively, it is necessary to consider whether there are any considerations which ought to negative, or to reduce or limit the scope of, the duty or class of person to whom it is owed.

The principles enunciated in this case extended quite considerably the third parties to whom a duty of care is owed in circumstances involving non-physical injury. However, it is pertinent to note that it also brought the law in these cases into line with that obtaining in situations involving physical injury: the reasonable foreseeability test was established in circumstances involving physical injury in *Donoghue* v *Stevenson* in 1932 (supra).

The courts did not have long to wait before *Anns* was applied in a case involving auditors. In the New Zealand case of *Scott Group Ltd* v *McFarlane* [1978] 1 NZLR 553, auditors failed to detect a basic double counting error which resulted in assets being significantly overvalued.

At the time of the audit, the defendant auditor had no knowledge that the plaintiff had any intention of making a takeover offer. However, the court held that the company's rich assets and low profits situation made it a prime target for takeover or merger and, therefore, the auditor should have foreseen that some person or group of persons was likely to rely on the audited financial statements to make such an offer.

Thus, this case extended the *Hedley Byrne* test of *knowledge* to one of *reasonable foreseeability* in situations involving audited financial statements. It established that a duty of care is owed by auditors who can, or should, reasonably foresee that a particular person or group of persons will rely on the audited financial statements when deciding whether to make a takeover offer. Applying the two-part *Anns* test for a duty of care to be recognised, Woodhouse, J identified four factors which give rise to a *prima facie* duty of care in the case of auditors. These are as follows:

1. Auditors are professionals in the business of providing expert advice for reward. If they did not intend their audited accounts to be relied upon, their work would be pointless.
2. Confidence in the ability of a company to handle its commercial arrangements would disappear if the audit report authenticating the company's accounts could not be relied upon.
3. In ordinary circumstances there is no opportunity for a person to make any intermediate examination of the company's accounts, nor is it practicable for many persons to do so.
4. Auditors are aware that the audited accounts will be filed with the Companies Office and therefore they become a matter of public record; they are available to the public, and anyone interested in the company has direct access to them.

Considering whether there are any factors which might negate or limit the scope of auditors' duty of care or the persons to whom it is owed, Woodhouse, J found the only argument in favour of negating liability was that raised by Cardozo, J in *Ultramares* v *Touche* (supra) over 45 years earlier – namely, the fear that auditors may be exposed to liability of indeterminate amount for an indeterminate time to an indeterminate class. However, his Honour considered that this need not be a matter of concern because of the difficulty of bringing a successful action for negligence. To succeed in such an action, the plaintiff must prove that:

• it is reasonable to expect the auditors to have anticipated that the plaintiff would act on the audited financial information;

- the plaintiff actually relied on the audited financial information; and
- the auditors' failure to take care when auditing the financial information was the cause of the plaintiff's loss.

Woodhouse, J concluded:

> [The auditors] must be taken to have accepted . . . a duty to those persons whom they can reasonably foresee will need to use and rely on [the audited financial statements] when dealing with the Company in significant matters affecting the Company's assets and business.

The *Scott Group* decision was applied and extended in the case of *Jeb Fasteners Ltd v Marks Bloom & Co.* [1981] 3 All ER 289. In this case, the defendants conducted an audit for a company which they were aware was undergoing a liquidity crisis and needed to raise finance. The company's financial statements contained assets which were seriously overvalued, a fact the auditors failed to detect. The plaintiffs had reservations about the assets figure but nevertheless proceeded with the takeover. The court re-affirmed that the auditor owes a duty of care to any person or class of persons whom they do not know but should be able to reasonably foresee might rely on the audited financial statements when making an investment decision relating to the company. Woolf, J, citing *Scott Group* with approval, stated:

> When he audited the accounts, Mr Marks would not know precisely who would provide the financial support, or what form the financial support would take, and he certainly had no reason to know that it would be by way of takeover by the plaintiffs. However, this was certainly one foreseeable method, and it does not seem to me that it would be right to exclude the duty of care merely because it was not possible to say with precision what machinery would be used to achieve the necessary financial support. Clearly, any form of loan would have been foreseeable, including the raising of money by debenture and, while some methods of raising money were more obvious than others, and a takeover was not the most obvious method, it was certainly one method which was within the contemplation of Mr Marks.

Woolf, J concluded that the auditors should have foreseen that a person might rely on the audited financial statements for the purpose of making an investment decision and that the person could, therefore, suffer loss if the accounts were inaccurate.

Analysing Mr Justice Woolf's judgment (above) it appears that, although the case involved a takeover, he extended the *Scott Group* decision from circumstances in which a takeover is reasonably foreseeable, to circumstances in which any form of financial support seems likely to be needed, and reliance on audited financial statements can (or should) be expected.

In the Scottish case of *Twomax Ltd* v *Dickson, McFarlane & Robinson* [1982] SC 113, [1983] SLT 98, the facts are similar to those of the *Jeb Fasteners* case, and Lord Stewart had little hesitation in applying Woolf, J's judgment. He held that although the auditors did not know the plaintiffs would rely on the audited financial statements to make an investment decision, they were aware that the auditee company (Kintyre Knitwear Ltd) needed capital. Given these circumstances, the auditors should have reasonably foreseen that some person (or group of persons) would rely on the audited financial statements and would suffer loss if they were inaccurate. This case is significant because it confirmed the *Scott Group*'s and *Jeb Fasteners*' extension of auditors' duty of care to third parties whom they do not know but should reasonably foresee might rely on the audited financial statements when making a decision relating to the reporting entity. But, further, unlike the plaintiffs in the *Scott Group* and *Jeb Fasteners* cases, the plaintiffs in the *Twomax* case were able to prove to the satisfaction of the court that they not only relied on the financial statements when making their investment decision, they also suffered loss as a result of relying on those statements which had been audited negligently. As a consequence, damages were awarded against the defendant auditors.

Reviewing the cases outlined above, it is evident that between 1931 and 1983 the auditor's duty of care to third parties evolved from nothing to a very wide duty. Prior to 1963, influenced by the *Ultramares* case, auditors' liability was restricted to that arising under a contractual relationship. By the mid-1980s, auditors' duty of care extended to virtually anyone who the auditors could, or should, reasonably foresee might rely on the audited financial statements when making a decision in respect of the reporting entity. When it is remembered that the audited financial statements of public companies are filed with the Registrar of Companies and are readily available for public scrutiny, auditors' duty of care and their exposure to potential liability had become very wide indeed.

In this regard it is interesting to note the remarks of Savage (1981), made after the *Jeb Fasteners* but before the *Twomax* decision:

> [I]t is not beyond the bounds of possibility that a British Court might hold that an auditor owes a duty of care to anyone who consults audited accounts at the Companies Registry and sustains a loss as a result of a negligent audit. To that extent the Jeb decision only brings the law into line with the public's expectations. If the auditor carries out his work with reasonable care and competence . . . he has nothing to fear.[5] If he fails to do so then, rightly, justice and equity demand that the law give remedy to those who have suffered as a direct result of his negligence. (p.341)

Nevertheless, as is shown below, Savage's views were not shared by the Law Lords in the case of *Caparo Industries plc* v *Dickman & Others* [1990] 1 All ER 568; [1990] 2 AC 605; [1990] 2 WLR 358, HL, reversing [1989] 1 All ER 798; [1989] QB 653; [1989] 2 WLR 316, CA. They apparently felt that the law had gone too far.

15.4.2 The *Caparo* Decision

The facts of this case are briefly as follows. In June 1984 Caparo Industries plc (Caparo) purchased shares in Fidelity plc, a public company listed on the London Stock Exchange. Prior to the purchase (in May 1984), Fidelity's directors announced that the company's profits for the year were £1.3 million – well short of the forecast profit of £2.2 million. Nevertheless, relying on the audited financial statements, Caparo purchased more shares in Fidelity and, later in the year, made a successful takeover bid for the company.

---

[5] This has been clearly demonstrated in the case of *Lloyd Cheyham & Co. Ltd* v *Littlejohn & Co.* (1987) BCLC 303. This case established that:
  1. Auditors are not required to do any more than a person can or should do for himself. A person is not entitled to place unwarranted reliance on the financial statements.
  2. Auditors who have performed good quality audits' and who have good defensible working papers which show that their conclusions were justified on the basis of the evidence gathered, are able to defend themselves.

Subsequent to the takeover, Caparo brought an action against the auditors (Touche Ross) alleging that, notwithstanding the unqualified audit report, Fidelity's accounts were inaccurate and the reported pre-tax profit of £1.3 million should, in fact, have been a reported loss of £0.46 million. In bringing its action, Caparo claimed that Touche Ross, as auditors of Fidelity, owed a duty of care to investors and potential investors and, in particular, to Caparo in respect of the audit of Fidelity's accounts. More particularly, Caparo asserted that:

* Touche Ross knew or ought to have known:
  (a) that in early March 1984 a press release had been issued stating that profits for the financial year would fall significantly short of £2.2 million;
  (b) that Fidelity's price fell from 143 pence per share on 1 March 1984 to 75 pence per share on 2 April 1984; and
  (c) that Fidelity required financial assistance.
* Touche Ross therefore ought to have foreseen that Fidelity was vulnerable to a take-over bid and that persons such as Caparo might well rely on the accounts for the purpose of deciding whether to take over Fidelity and might well suffer loss if the accounts were inaccurate.

The Law Lords were unanimous in their decision that, in general, auditors do not owe a duty of care to individual shareholders or to potential investors. Rather, a duty of care is owed to the company's shareholders as a body. In reaching this decision, the Law Lords held that *Scott Group Ltd* v *McFarlane & Others* (supra), and the subsequent English and Scottish decisions which had relied on *Scott Group*, namely, *Jeb Fasteners Ltd* v *Marks Bloom & Co.* (supra) and *Twomax Ltd* v *Dickson, McFarlane & Robinson* (supra), had been decided wrongly.

Analysis of the House of Lords' decision in the *Caparo* case reveals that the Law Lords focused their attention on two main themes, namely:

(i) the circumstances which give rise to a duty of care; and
(ii) the purpose for which the legislation requires financial statements to be produced.

However, underlying the arguments relating to both of these themes is a concern by the Law Lords to ensure that the scope of liability arising in professional negligence cases is not extended beyond reasonable limits. They referred with considerable respect to Cardozo, J's statement in the *Ultramares* case (supra) namely, that auditors' liability should not be extended to the point where it may exist 'in an indeterminate amount for an indeterminate time to an indeterminate class.'

(i) *Duty of Care*

The Lords considered that, in order to establish a duty of care, a three-part test needs to be satisfied, namely:

* *foreseeability*: When a person (A) makes a statement for another (B) to rely upon, A should be able to reasonably foresee that B might suffer loss if the statement is incorrect;

- *proximity*: With respect to the statement made, there must be a relationship of proximity between A and B. Such a relationship will exist if, when making the statement, A knew:
  - that the statement would be communicated to B;
  - that the statement would be communicated in relation to a specific transaction or kind of transaction; and
  - B would be very likely to rely on the statement when making a decision with respect to the transaction(s) in question;
- *fairness*: The court must consider it fair, just and reasonable to impose a duty of care on A for the benefit of B.

These ideas are reflected in Lord Bridge's judgment. His major concern was that, in assessing the liability of an auditor (or other professional person), the court should not only consider the question of foreseeability of damage, but should give due weight to the other necessary ingredients which give rise to a duty of care. In the words of Lord Bridge:

> [T]here should exist between the party owing the duty and the party to whom it is owed a relationship characterised by the law as one of proximity or neighbourhood and the situation should be one in which the court considers it fair, just and reasonable that the law should impose a duty of a given scope upon the one party for the benefit of the other.

Referring to the principle enunciated in *Hedley Byrne*, Lord Bridge went on to note:

> The salient feature of [cases decided on the Hedley Byrne principle] is that the defendant giving advice or information was fully aware of the nature of the transaction which the plaintiff had in contemplation, knew that the advice or information would be communicated to him directly or indirectly and knew that it was very likely that the plaintiff would rely on that advice or information in deciding whether or not to engage in the transaction in contemplation. In these circumstances the defendant could clearly be expected . . . specifically to anticipate that the plaintiff would rely on the advice or information given by the defendant for the very purpose for which he did rely on it.

The Lords' concern to keep auditors' exposure to liability within reasonable bounds (and hence their imposition of a test of proximity in addition to one of foreseeability of damage) is reflected in Lord Oliver's statement:

> To apply as a test of liability only the foreseeability of possible damage without some further control would be to create a liability wholly indefinite in area, duration and amount and would open up a limitless vista of uninsurable risk for the professional man.

(ii) Purpose of Financial Statements

Whilst recognising that audited financial statements might be used for a variety of purposes, including the making of investment decisions, the Lords were of the view that the legislature considered their primary purpose is to protect the interests of the company *per se*, and to enable shareholders and debenture holders to evaluate the quality of the stewardship exercised by the company's directors and to exercise their rights as a group. Their purpose is not to protect the interests of individuals who choose to use the financial statements for a particular purpose. As Lord Oliver explained:

The original, central and primary purpose of [the legislative provisions requiring companies to provide annual financial statements] . . . is the informed exercise by those interested in the property of the company, whether as proprietors of shares in the company or as the holders of rights secured by a debenture trust deed, of such powers as are vested in them by virtue of their respective proprietary interests . . . I find it difficult to believe . . . that the legislature, in enacting provisions clearly aimed primarily at the protection of the company and its informed control by the body of its proprietors, can have been inspired also by consideration for the public at large and investors in the market in particular.

The auditor's function was seen by the Law Lords in the context of this interpretation of the purpose of financial statements. For example, Lord Oliver stated:

It is the auditor's function to ensure, so far as possible, that the financial information as to the company's affairs prepared by the directors accurately reflects the company's position in order, first, to protect the company itself from the consequences of undetected errors . . . and, secondly, to provide shareholders with reliable intelligence for the purpose of enabling them to scrutinise the conduct of the company's affairs and to exercise their collective powers to reward or control or remove those to whom that conduct has been confided.

The Lords' understanding of the position of a shareholder, such as Caparo plc, seeking redress for harm suffered as a consequence of auditors performing their duties negligently, flows from their interpretation of the purpose of financial statements and auditors' function in relation thereto. This is reflected in the following statement by Lord Bridge:

The shareholders of a company have a collective interest in the company's proper management and insofar as a negligent failure of the auditor to report accurately on the state of the company's finances deprives the shareholders of the opportunity to exercise their powers in general meeting to call the directors to book and to ensure that errors in management are corrected, the shareholders ought to be entitled to remedy. But in practice no problem arises in this regard since the interest of the shareholders in the proper management of the company's affairs is indistinguishable from the interest of the company itself and any loss suffered by the shareholders – for example, by the negligent failure of the auditor to discover and expose a misappropriation of funds by a director of the company – will be recouped against the auditors in the name of the company, not by individual shareholders.

The House of Lords' decision in the *Caparo* case has established that, in the absence of special circumstances, auditors do not owe a duty of care to anyone relying on their report, other than (i) the company and (ii) the company's shareholders as a body. More particularly, in general, no duty of care is owed to individual shareholders or potential investors, irrespective of any reliance they may place on the audited financial statements for their investment decision(s). In order for a duty of care to arise, other than to the company or the shareholders as a body, the three-part test of foreseeability, proximity and fairness must be satisfied.

This returns the law roughly to where it stood some 30 years ago at the time of *Hedley Byrne* v *Heller and Partners* (supra). However, many commentators regard the reversal of the law as unfortunate. Baxt (1990a), for example, notes that as a result of the *Caparo* decision both professional investors, such as Caparo, and individual or average investors are denied a possible avenue for relief when they suffer loss as a result of negligence on the part of auditors. He states:

Clearly, we do not wish to see the prophecy come true of Chief Justice Cardozo, nor do we wish to identify any particular group of professionals as being more subject to liabilities than others. But some protection is needed for the investor in circumstances such as [Caparo], assuming (and this is important and tends to be overlooked in cases of this kind) that liability can be established. (Baxt, 1990b, p.18)

Picking up on the last point made by Baxt in the above quotation, he (Baxt, 1990a), Gwilliam (1988), and others (including Woodhouse, J in the *Scott Group* case), have emphasised the difficulty of an investor bringing a successful action against auditors. As noted in section 15.2 above, in order to do so, the investor must satisfy the court that:

- the auditor in question owed him or her a duty of care;
- the auditor was negligent in the performance of his or her duties;
- the investor suffered a loss as a result of relying on the negligently audited financial statements.

It seems that in the *Caparo* case, the Law Lords, in seeking to ensure that auditors are not exposed to unbounded liability,[6] focused on the first requirement (above). They appear to have given little attention to the third factor. Yet, as cases such as *Scott Group* and *Jeb Fasteners* have demonstrated, this is the most difficult factor to prove. Most investors would find it very difficult to prove to the satisfaction of the court that audited financial statements provided the sole or main basis for an investment decision. As Baxt (1990a) observes:

> There must be a number of factors that will influence a shareholder to buy more shares in a company for investment purposes – a comparative analysis of other companies' performances, the market reaction to the information about those companies, the individual shareholder's financial position, his/her interests and needs, and a myriad of other individual factors. Each case will see different shareholders having to prove different things in order to show that the particular investment decision taken was based on the auditor's report, and that any loss is linked to the report, assuming further, that the report was negligent. (p.9)

In the case of a large investor such as Caparo, it must surely be extremely difficult to prove reliance on negligently prepared audited financial statements. A large investor would almost certainly be expected to seek additional information from the company and elsewhere before committing significant resources to the investment, such as occurs when a takeover offer is made.

15.4.3 Some Relevant Cases Decided Subsequent to *Caparo*

Since *Caparo* a number of cases relevant to auditors' duty of care have been decided in the UK and various British Commonwealth countries and, as the following examples serve to demonstrate, the law in this area is continuing to evolve.

In the UK, cases such as *Al-Saudi Banque and Others* v *Clark Pixley* [1990] Ch 313, *James McNaughton Papers Group Ltd* v *Hicks Anderson & Co* [1991] 1 All ER 134; [1990] BCC 891; (1991) 9 ACLC 3,091; *Berg Sons & Co. Ltd* v *Mervyn Hampton*

---

[6] See, for example, Lord Oliver's statement, quoted under (i) *Duty of care*, above.

Adams [1993] BCLC 1045; *Galoo Ltd* v *Bright Grahame Murray* [1994] 1 WLR 1360; [1995] 1 All ER 16, and *ADT Ltd* v *BDO Binder Hamlyn* (December 1995, unreported), have helped to clarify how the *Caparo* decision will be applied. In the *Al-Saudi Banque* case, for example, the court helped to clarify what is required for a 'special relationship' to exist such as to give rise to auditors owing a duty of care to third parties.

The case involved a company whose business consisted of providing finance to overseas customers in return for bills of exchange. The company then used the bills of exchange (which constituted virtually all of the company's assets) to negotiate advances from the ten plaintiff banks. In 1983 the company was compulsorily wound up and the bills of exchange were found to be worthless. The banks sued the auditors for negligence, alleging that they ought reasonably to have foreseen that the banks would rely on the auditors' reports when deciding whether to continue, renew or increase loans to the company, that they did so rely on the reports and were misled thereby. At the time of the relevant audit reports (1981 and 1982), seven of the plaintiff banks were existing creditors of the company but three were not.

Millet, J held that the auditors did not owe the banks a duty of care:

- In respect of the three banks which were not existing creditors at the dates of the audit reports, the judge noted that the auditors had not reported directly to the banks and had not intended or known that the reports would be communicated to them. He held that, even though it was foreseeable that a bank might ask a company for copies of its audited financial statements when making loan decisions with respect to the company, the element of proximity necessary to find a duty of care was lacking.
- Regarding the other seven banks, Millet, J observed that, although their identities and amounts of exposure were known to the auditors when they signed their audit reports, their position was not comparable to that of the company's shareholders to whom the auditors owed a statutory duty to report. As the auditors had not sent copies of their reports directly to the banks, or sent copies to the company with the intention or knowledge that they would be supplied to the banks, the auditors owed no duty of care to the plaintiffs.

From this case it is evident that, in order for auditors to owe a duty of care to third parties (or, more particularly, the audit client's bankers) they must either give the third party a copy of their audit report or intend or know that their report will be supplied to the third party. The case of *James McNaughton Papers Group Ltd* v *Hicks Anderson & Co* (supra) clarified the position further. In this case, James McNaughton Ltd was involved in the takeover of another company (MK). Draft accounts for use in the negotiations were prepared by Hicks Anderson and, at a meeting of the negotiators, a representative of the firm stated that MK was breaking even. After the takeover was completed, discrepancies were found in the accounts and MK was found to be insolvent. McNaughtons sued the accountants for negligent preparation of the accounts and stated that, in proceeding with the takeover, they had relied on the accounts and the statement made at the negotiating meeting by the accountants' representative.

The court of first instance found that the accountants owed McNaughton Ltd a duty of care. However, this was reversed on appeal. The Court of Appeal, applying the

Caparo judgment, held that when a statement or advice is acted on by a person (C) other than the person intended by the giver of the statement or advice (A) to act on it, the factors to be considered in determining whether A owes C a duty of care include:

- the purpose for which the statement is made;
- the purpose for which the statement is communicated;
- the relationship between A, C and any relevant third party;
- the size of any class to which C belongs;
- the state of knowledge of A;
- the reliance by C on A's statement or advice.

Considering these factors, the court found that the accountants owed no duty of care to McNaughton Ltd in respect of the draft accounts because:

- the accounts were produced for MK and not McNaughtons;
- the accounts were merely draft accounts and the accountants could not have reasonably foreseen that McNaughtons would treat them as final accounts;
- the accountants did not take part in the negotiations;
- McNaughtons were aware that MK was in a poor financial state and, thus, could have been expected to consult their own accountants;
- the statement made at the negotiating meeting was very general and did not affect the figures in the accounts. The accountants could not reasonably have foreseen that McNaughtons would rely on the statement without further inquiry or advice.

It can be seen that the *McNaughton* case added to the *Al-Saudi* decision in that it provided guidance as to the matters [other than knowledge (or intention) of reliance on the audit report] the court would consider when deciding whether or not auditors owe a duty of care to a plaintiff. These include the purpose for which an audit report is prepared and the purpose for which it is communicated to a third party.

The case of *Berg Sons & Co. Ltd* v *Mervyn Hampton Adams* (supra), focused primarily on auditors' duty of care to the auditee but also explored further auditors' duty of care to third parties. This case involved a small company in which all of the shares were held by the sole executive director, his wife and his son. In 1985 the company was put into liquidation and the company's liquidator, together with a discount house which had provided Berg Sons & Co. with finance, sued the auditors for negligence. It was alleged that, as a consequence of the auditor's unqualified audit report on the company's 1982 financial statements:

- the company was able to continue in business and borrow money which it had no prospect of repaying;
- the discount house discounted bills receivable which should have been shown in the financial statements as irrecoverable.

Hobhouse, J found that the auditors were not negligent even though they had received unsatisfactory assurances from the acceptor of certain bills and also from Berg which should have prompted an audit report qualified on grounds of uncertainty. His Honour stated:

> [T]he purpose of the statutory audit is to provide a mechanism to enable those having a proprietary interest in the company . . . to have access to accurate financial information about the company. Provided that those persons have that information, the statutory purpose is exhausted . . . In the present case the . . . plaintiffs have based their case not upon any lack of information on the part of the company's executive director but rather upon the opportunity that the possession of the auditor's certificate is said to have given for the company to continue to carry on business and borrow money from third parties. Such matters do not fall within the scope of the duty of the statutory auditor.

With respect to the company, the court held that, in order for a company to bring a successful action against its auditors, it must show 'that the company or its members were in some way misled or left in ignorance of some material fact' (per Hobhouse, J). A 'one man' company such as Berg Sons & Co. could never prove that it had been misled because its controlling director and shareholder would always know better than anyone else the true position of the company and its business.

The court also held that the auditors owed no duty of care to the discount house. Hobhouse, J reaffirmed but went beyond the *Caparo* decision. He stated that before a duty of care to third parties will arise, two tests need to be met:

1. There must a specific relationship between the function the defendant has been requested to perform and the transaction in relation to which the plaintiff relied upon the proper performance of that function (in this case, between the statutory audit and the discounting of bills receivable).
2. The case must be brought within a limited period of the alleged negligence. There is only a limited period of time within which it would be reasonably foreseeable that a bank or discount house would rely upon a given set of financial statements.

Davies (1992) has pointed out that:

> The effect of these additional limitations is to place such stringent restrictions on the circumstances in which the creditors of a company can sue its auditors that it is now difficult to imagine any circumstances when such a claim could succeed arising out of the statutory audit function. (p.4)

Davies concludes that, as a result of the *Berg Sons & Co.* judgment, it is most unlikely that a successful case can now be brought in the UK against auditors by their small company audit clients or by such clients' creditors. The case of *Galoo Ltd* v *Bright Grahame Murray* (supra) serves to confirm the difficulty a company's creditors will experience in trying to establish that the company's auditors owed them a duty of care. It also helps to clarify what the UK courts will accept (in the wake of the *Caparo* decision) as a 'special relationship' which may give rise to auditors owing a duty of care to a third party.

In the *Galoo* case, fraud was alleged in relation to stocks held by Galoo Ltd which were progressively over-valued in Galoo's financial statements between 1985 and 1990. The auditors were sued for negligence by Galoo Ltd and Hillsdown Holdings. The latter company purchased 51% of Galoo's holding company in 1987 and another 44% in 1991. It also made loans to Galoo and its holding company.

The Court of Appeal was asked to rule whether a sustainable cause of action existed against the auditors. It found in favour only in respect of Hillsdown's initial 51% investment. In response to Galoo's claim, the court held that the company was only entitled to nominal damages for breach of the auditors' responsibilities. Regarding the advances made by Hillsdown to Galoo and its holding company, the court considered that such loans were subject to normal business risks. Notwithstanding that Hillsdown alleged it would not have made the loans had the auditors detected the fraud and reported the stock over-valuation in their audit report, the court held that it was difficult to attribute the losses sustained by Hillsdown to the auditors.

With respect to its equity investment in Galoo's holding company, Hillsdown argued that it would not have purchased the shares had the correct position been disclosed in the company's financial statements. The initial purchase of 51% of the holding company was purchased in 1987, pursuant to an 'acquisition agreement' which provided a purchase price calculated on the company's net profits as shown in its 1986 financial statements, to be audited by Bright Grahame Murray.

The court stated that mere foreseeability that a potential bidder may rely on the audited financial statements does not impose a duty of care on the auditor to the bidder but, if the auditor is made aware that a particular identified bidder will rely on the audited financial statements, and intends that the bidder should rely on them, the auditor will be under a duty of care to the bidder and may be liable for any breach of this duty. In the present case, the auditors were aware that the 1986 audited financial statements were to be used to fix the price payable by Hillsdown for its purchase of 51% of Galoo's holding company. The court held that, in this regard, there was sufficient for a case to go to trial. However, Hillsdown was supported in its investment decision by an international accounting firm which had access to Galoo's books and records for the purpose of undertaking a due diligence exercise. Evans, L J expressed the view that the success of Hillsdown's claim against the auditors could depend on the bidder's right to undertake due diligence. 'This right of examination could negate any duty of care otherwise owed by Galoo's auditors to an identified bidder such as Hillsdown' (as reported, Ross, 1994, p.59).

Hillsdown's further claim against the auditors in respect of its 1991 purchase of an additional 44% of Galoo's holding company was dismissed. This purchase was not made pursuant to the original acquisition agreement and the auditors of Galoo owed no duty of care to Hillsdown in relation to its decision to make a further equity investment.

From the post-*Caparo* cases reviewed above it is clear that, in the UK, it is extremely difficult for small companies to sue their auditors successfully for breach of their contractual duties. It is equally difficult for third parties to establish that auditors owe them a duty of care. To do so, they must show that the auditors knew they would rely on the audited financial statements for a specific transaction, that there is a nexus between the audit and the transaction, and that they brought their case against the auditors within a limited period of the auditors' alleged negligence. It seems almost certain that such circumstances will occur very rarely. Nevertheless, the case of *ADT Ltd* v *BDO Binder Hamlyn* (December, 1995; as yet, unreported),[7] shows that, in appropriate cases, the courts will impose a duty of care on auditors to third parties. In the *ADT* case, Binder Hamlyn issued an unqualified report on the 1989 financial statements of Britannia Securities Group (BSG) – a company ADT Ltd was contemplating purchasing. In January 1990, a partner of Binder Hamlyn attended a meeting with a director of ADT

---

[7] Information about this case is derived from Wade (1996).

and confirmed that he 'stood by' BSG's 1989 audited financial statements. On the strength of Binder Hamlyn's advice, ADT purchased BSG for £105 million. It was subsequently found that BSG's true value was £40 million.

The question in this case is not whether the auditors owed ADT a duty of care in the performance of the audit. Following *Caparo*, it is clear they did not. Instead, the point at issue is whether Binder Hamlyn assumed responsibility to ADT, and thus owed it a duty of care, as a result of the assurance given to the ADT director by Binder Hamlyn's partner in respect of BSG's audited financial statements.

May, J held that Binder Hamlyn's partner gave the information or advice directly to ADT knowing the purpose for which it was required and knowing they would place reliance on it without further enquiry. Wade (1996) explains:

> Accordingly, the judge found that Binder Hamlyn assumed a responsibility for the statement that the audited accounts showed a true and fair view of BSG. Furthermore, he held that ADT relied, to its subsequent detriment, on the information provided by [Binder Hamlyn's partner]. Having found that the underlying audit work had been carried out negligently, Binder Hamlyn was held liable for the difference in the amount paid by ADT and the true value of BSG. (p.135)

The judge awarded damages of £65 million for the difference in the amount paid for BSG (£105 million) and its true value (£40 million) plus £40 million as interest (Accountancy, 1996, p 11). The case is subject to Appeal.

Although the courts in the UK appear to have created a fairly certain and protected environment for auditors in terms of their exposure to liability, the situation in Australia is far less clear. Some courts have applied the *Caparo* ruling, others have not. In *R Lowe Lippmann Figdor & Frank* v *AGC (Advances) Ltd* (1992) 10 ACLC 1168, the Supreme Court of Victoria followed *Caparo*. In this case, AGC relied on the 1981 audited financial statements of Lyvetta Weaving Mills Pty Ltd when it decided to increase its loan to Lyvetta. As a result of false stock sheets, Lyvetta's 1981 financial statements showed a profit of some $A30,000, instead of a loss of about $A205,000. Although they knew of the existence of correct stock sheets, and had been informed that the financial statements would be required by AGC for the purpose of reviewing its financial arrangement with Lyvetta, the auditors signed an unqualified audit report. Subsequently, AGC sued the auditors for negligent misstatement, arguing that they owed AGC a duty of care in respect of the 1981 financial statements.

The Supreme Court of Victoria, following *Caparo*, held that as the auditors had not supplied their report directly to AGC (and had not been under any obligation to do so) they owed no duty of care to AGC. Further, although AGC had informed the auditors that they would be requiring the audited financial statements to review the loan to Lyvetta, this was not sufficient to give rise to a duty of care by the auditors to AGC. Indeed Brooking, J noted that reliance on audited financial statements in such circumstances was to be expected. He stated that it would have been extraordinary if a lender in AGC's position had not been 'concerned to possess itself . . . a copy of the audited accounts so as to be better placed to form a view of the financial position of the borrower . . . ' (at 1172).

The crux of the court's judgment was that, in order for the auditors to be under a duty of care, the plaintiff had to prove that the auditors made a statement with the intention of inducing the plaintiff, or a class of persons including the plaintiff, to act in reliance upon it. Because the auditors' report was issued, not to induce the plaintiff to rely upon it when making a lending decision, but to meet a statutory obligation, no duty of care was owed to the plaintiff.

Many commentators considered this case (like *Caparo*) left the law in Australia in an unsatisfactory position. Baxt (1993) for example, observed:

> The message from this case is that auditors' reports in general may not be worth the paper that they are written on. Auditors would be quite disappointed . . . to learn that as a result of these decisions [in Al-Saudi Banque, Caparo and R Lowe Lippmann] it can be said to the investing public and to those who look to audited statements as giving a reasonable representation of what the company's financial position is, that auditors' statements cannot be relied on at all. If they are relied on and you suffer loss you can make no recovery. (p.22)

The Supreme Court of New South Wales may also have felt that the law had reached an unsatisfactory position because, in its decision in the case of *Columbia Coffee & Tea Pty Ltd* v *Churchill* (1992) 10 ACLC 1659, it adopted a markedly different approach. This case involved the purchase of Columbia Coffee shares by Donyoke Pty Ltd. After purchasing the shares, Donyoke discovered errors in Columbia's 1987 audited financial statements on which it relied when making the purchase. Donyoke sued Columbia's auditors (Nelson Parkhill BDO) for negligence.

The court distinguished *Columbia Coffee* from *Caparo* primarily on the grounds that the auditors, in their audit manual, assumed responsibility to a wide range of interested parties. More specifically, the court noted that the audit manual stated:

> It is the policy of the firm that any audit which we undertake will be conducted in such a way as will fulfil our responsibilities properly. . . . The use of the word 'responsibilities' . . . rather than the word 'contracts' is deliberate. It acknowledges that there will be interested parties who read and rely on our reports, and this extends beyond the persons who employ us in the first instance or those to whom the report is addressed initially. . . . Many readers of a company's accounts rely upon them as a basis for assessing the company's prospects. (sections 2.2 and 2.28)

Rolfe, J relied on these statements to conclude:

> Whatever may otherwise have been the restriction on . . . those to whom the duty was owed, the auditors accepted that it was owed to a class of persons wider than the company for which the audit was being conducted, and its shareholders. It was an acceptance . . . of responsibility to anyone who may reasonably and relevantly rely upon the audited accounts for the purpose of ordering their business affairs.

The court found that, although the auditors were not aware that the plaintiff would rely on the audited financial statements for their purchase of Columbia's shares, this did not matter as the plaintiff fell within the class of persons who might rely upon the 1987 audit report in arranging their business affairs.

As Livanes (1993) has pointed out, the statements contained in Nelson Parkhill's audit manual are implied in many professional publications. For example, the objectives of the Auditing Practices Board (APB, 1993, para 4) make it clear that the APB intends meeting the developing needs of users of financial information. In order to help achieve this objective, the Board regularly consults with a wide range of users and includes some user groups on the Board. It seems that, like Nelson Parkhill BDO, the auditing profession in the UK, as well as elsewhere, acknowledges a responsibility to a range of interested parties which extends well beyond audit-clients and those to whom audit reports are specifically addressed. Given this situation, the court's decision in the *Columbia Coffee* case, if widely adopted, has the potential to widen substantially the auditor's duty of care. However, as shown above, such a widening of the auditor's duty in the UK seems improbable. Further, as a consequence of the case of *Esanda Finance Corporation* v *Peat Marwick Hungerfords* (1994) 12 ACLC 199, a broadly applying duty of care for auditors seems unlikely to become established in Australia.

The *Esanda* case revolved around a loan made by Esanda Finance Corporation to Excel Pty Ltd. When Excel was placed in receivership, Esanda sued Peat Marwick Hungerfords for negligence, alleging that it had relied on the audited financial statements when it extended finance to Excel. It is significant that Esanda did not plead that the auditors had intended it should rely on the audited financial statements – merely that it had done so.

The South Australian Full Supreme Court discussed a number of relevant cases (including *Lowe Lippmann* and *Columbia Coffee*), then endorsed the approach adopted in the *Caparo* case. The Court held that, in cases where the plaintiff is not a member of the company to whom the auditor owes a statutory duty of care, in the absence of an assumption of responsibility to the plaintiff to exercise care in relation to the preparation of the audit report, and in the absence of an intention on the part of the auditor that the plaintiff act in reliance upon the report, the auditor is not under a duty of care to the plaintiff. Following this decision of the Supreme Court of South Australia it appears that, in general, the liability of auditors in Australia will be limited to their client companies unless there are special circumstances suggesting that wider liability might be said to arise (Baxt, 1994).

In New Zealand a contrary stance is evident. In the case of *South Pacific Manufacturing Co Ltd* v *New Zealand Security Consultants & Investigations Ltd* [1992] 2 NZLR 282, the Court of Appeal indicated that it would not be following the *Caparo* decision. The case involved insurance assessors who reported suspected arson in two separate incidents of suspicious fires preceding insurance claims. The insured sued the assessors for preparing their reports negligently. The Court of Appeal was asked to decide whether a duty of care was owed by insurance assessors to an insured.

The Appeal judges essentially took the view that a duty of care (and thus liability for negligence) should be imposed whenever this is just and reasonable in the particular circumstances. They noted, amongst other things, that proper standards of care should be imposed on people who undertake tasks which require skill and judgment and on whom others are dependent. They also noted that, when deciding whether a duty of care exists in a particular case, the following factors should be considered:

- the foreseeability of harm;
- the kind of harm (physical or purely economic);
- the immediacy, degree and magnitude of risk;
- the degree of reliance of one party on the other and the extent to which the defendant is aware of such reliance;
- the availability of other remedies;
- the extent of the burden the imposition of a duty of care would place on the defendant; in this regard the judges observed that the plaintiff's claim to compensation for avoidable harm must be balanced against the defendant's claim to be protected from an undue burden of legal responsibility.

The judges went on to note that considerations such as those set out above must be balanced by the policy considerations of one case opening the 'floodgates' to new claims of liability, general economic issues, and the need to preserve a fair and proper balance between the differing interests of people going about their business or daily lives. Casey, J observed that in assessing these policy considerations, the courts are likely to be influenced by their perceptions of prevailing community attitudes and goals. He noted that in cases involving economic loss arising through negligence, the New Zealand Court of Appeal had sought to adopt a stance which matched its understanding of community expectations (as reported, Ross, 1992). This seems to lend support to the view expressed by Savage (1981) after the *Jeb Fasteners'* decision[8], namely, that extending auditors' liability to all those who rely on audited financial statements and who suffer loss as a result of a negligent audit, is in line with public expectations.

From the above discussion of post-*Caparo* cases in the United Kingdom, Australia and New Zealand, it can be seen that different conclusions have been reached by different courts in different countries. It is particularly interesting to note the diametrically opposed approaches adopted in New Zealand and the United Kingdom.[9] In New Zealand, the courts have followed the two-part rule laid down in *Anns* v *Merton London Borough Council* (1978) that is, in appropriate cases, *prima facie* recognising a duty of care for auditors to third parties then restricting this if it is just and equitable in the circumstances so to do. However, in the UK, the courts have criticised *Anns* and adopted the opposite approach – that is, *prima facie* recognising no duty of care for auditors to third parties but then relaxing this if the circumstances of the case render it appropriate to do so. Despite these differing approaches, from an analysis of the post-*Caparo* cases in the United Kingdom and New Zealand, a common theme may be discerned. This is reflected in Sir Robin Cooke's observation in the *South Pacific Manufacturing* case (supra), namely, irrespective of whether judges follow the *Anns* rule or adopt a more conservative approach, they essentially seek to decide whether it is just and reasonable that a duty of care should be imposed in the particular circumstances of the case before them.

15.5 THE EFFECT OF OUT-OF-COURT SETTLEMENTS

Woolf (1983) has observed that one of the difficulties associated with the development of the law relating to auditors' liability and, more particularly, auditors' common law liability to third parties, is the predisposition of the auditing profession to settle out of court.

Given the costs involved in lengthy court hearings (not the least of which are the lost earnings of partners who spend days, if not weeks or months, in court, and the costs associated with damaged reputations as news of alleged negligence reaches the media headlines), it is not surprising that auditors are inclined towards settling out of court – even in circumstances where they believe they may be able to defend successfully an action brought against them. Added to this, they are frequently pressured by their

---

[8] Quoted in section 15.4 above.
[9] It should be remembered that the New Zealand legal system is based on that in the UK and the final Court of Appeal for New Zealand is the Privy Council of the House of Lords.

indemnity insurers to settle out of court, as the insurers consider this to be the least-cost option. Nonetheless, auditors' tendency towards out-of-court settlements is stifling the development (or clarification) of the law with respect to auditors' liability and is also causing indemnity insurance premiums to rise to unnecessarily high levels. Woolf (1983) explains the situation as follows:

> Why not, after all, let our indemnity insurers cough up? Surely that's why we pay them such fancy premiums. This view juxtaposes cause and effect. Treating insurance as an escape leads to an increase (not a decrease) in the risks against which further insurance cover is then needed – and so on, until the premiums exceed, by a very substantial margin, the damages which would be awarded against us if the issues in question were tested in the courts. Every out-of-court settlement leaves the underlying legal issues unresolved, and the only persons who suffer from such irresolution are ourselves; for you may be sure that our insurers, the plaintiffs and all the legal advisers involved, are only too delighted to leave matters where they are (or aren't – such is the present confusion!). (p.65)

As noted in section 15.2 above, one of the major difficulties facing auditors with respect to their liability for breach of their common law duties is that neither the parties to whom they owe a duty of care nor the requirements for a reasonable standard of skill and care are static. This leaves auditors uncertain as to their legal obligations and tends to encourage them to go on the defensive, to 'play safe' and agree readily with their insurers to an out-of-court settlement. Yet, as Woolf has observed, auditors' propensity to settle out of court does not allow the underlying legal issues to be resolved. Further, when news of an out-of-court settlement reaches the media (which it inevitably does), it seems to signify to interested parties, and to the public, that the auditors accept that they are in the wrong and that the action cannot be defended successfully. It is arguable that this is, in general, far more damaging to the reputation of the auditors concerned, and to the auditing profession as a whole, than having the facts of the case exposed in court – and the chance of the case being decided in favour of the auditors.

That the courts will not impose an intolerable burden on auditors has been clearly demonstrated. *Caparo,* and subsequent cases (including those discussed above), show that the courts have been concerned to limit the parties to whom auditors owe a duty of care, so as not to leave them exposed to liability which is indeterminate in amount for an indeterminate time to an indeterminate class. Similarly, examples such as the *Littlejohn* case (see footnote 5), may be cited to show that the courts have also been concerned to keep the standard of skill and care required of auditors within reasonable bounds. Further, as Gwilliam (1988) has shown:

> While the courts reserve for themselves the ultimate right to determine what reasonable skill and care entails, they have always been very reluctant to impose on professions standards higher than those regarded as appropriate by the profession itself. (p.22)

15.6 SUMMARY

In this chapter we have addressed the issue of auditors' legal liability. We have distinguished between a breach of auditors' statutory duties and a breach of their common law duties, and between auditors' contractual and third party liability. We have also traced the development of auditors' duty of care to third parties and noted the effect of the decision in the *Caparo* case. We have further noted that, since the *Caparo* decision, the law relating to auditors' liability to third parties has continued to evolve but the courts have been concerned to ensure that auditors are not exposed to an unreasonable liability burden.

In the final section of the chapter we have considered the effect of out-of-court settlements on the development of the law relating to auditors' liability and on auditors' indemnity insurance. In the next chapter we discuss measures individual audit firms, and the auditing profession as a whole, have taken (and are taking) to try to reduce auditors' exposure to liability through the performance of consistently high quality audits.

SELF-REVIEW QUESTIONS

15.1 Distinguish briefly between a breach of auditors' statutory duties and a breach of their common law duties.

15.2 Distinguish briefly between auditors' contractual liability and their liability to third parties.

15.3 List the three facts a plaintiff must prove before a court will award damages against auditors for negligence.

15.4 Explain the position adopted in the case of *Ultramares* v *Touche* (1931) with respect to auditors' liability to third parties. What reason did the judge give for his decision in this case?

15.5 Explain briefly the significance of the decision in *Hedley Byrne & Co. Ltd* v *Heller and Partners* (1963) to the development of auditors' liability to third parties.

15.6 Explain the position adopted in the cases of *Jeb Fasteners* (1981) and *Twomax Ltd* (1983) with respect to auditors' liability to third parties.

15.7 Explain briefly the principles enunciated in the *Caparo* decision (1990) with respect to the parties to whom auditors are liable.

15.8 Explain the approach adopted to applying the two-step rule enunciated in *Anns* v *Merton London Borough Council* (1977) by the courts in (i) the United Kingdom and (ii) New Zealand.

15.9 Since the *Caparo* case was decided, different courts in different parts of the British Commonwealth have adopted differing positions with respect to the parties to whom auditors owe a duty of care. Reviewing the cases discussed in section 15.4.3, what common theme can be discerned in the various courts' decisions?

15.10 Explain briefly the impact of out-of-court settlements on:
(i) the development of the law as it relates to auditors' liability; and
(ii) auditors' professional indemnity insurance.

REFERENCES

Auditing Practices Board (APB). (1993). The Scope and Authority of APB Pronouncements. *Accountancy*, **114**(1198), 117–118.

Baxt, R. (1990a). Shutting the gate on shareholders in actions for negligence – the Caparo decision in the House of Lords. *Companies and Securities Forum*, pp.2–12. CCH Australia Ltd.

Baxt, R. (1990b). A swing of the pendulum. *Charter*, **61**(5), 16–18.

Baxt, R. (1993). A swing of the pendulum. *Charter*, **61**(1), 20–2.

Baxt, R. (1994). Comfort from the courts. *Charter*, **65**(6), 20–2.

Davies, J. (1992). *Auditors' Liabilities: Who can sue now?* Unpublished paper written for Reynolds Porter Chamberlain, UK.

Gwilliam, D. (1988). Making mountains out of molehills. *Accountancy*, **101**(1135), 22–3.

Livanes, G. (1993). A U-turn by the courts? *Charter*, **64**(1), 46–8.

Ross, M. (1992). Casebook: Negligence: Auditors' liability. *Accountants' Journal*, **71**(8), 79.

Ross, M. (1994). Casebook: Auditors' Negligence. *Chartered Accountants' Journal*, **73**(7), 59.

Savage, N. (1981). The auditor's legal responsibility to strangers? *The Accountant's Magazine*, **85**(904), 338–41.

Shanahan, J. (1995). The AWA case: an auditor's view, reported in *Butterworths Corporation Law Bulletin*, (Australian Corporation Law), No. 10, (19 May 1995), 213–15.

Wade, R. (1996). What price 'audit' advice? *Accountancy*, **117**(1233), 134–5.

Woolf, E. (1979). *Auditing Today*. London: Prentice Hall.

Woolf, E. (1983). Auditing and staying out of court. *Accountancy*, **94**(1074), 65–6.

ADDITIONAL READING

Arnheim, M. (1991). Auditors' fate in the crucible? *Accountancy*, **107**(1193), 94–5.

Gwilliam, D. (1991). The auditor's liability to third parties. In Sherer, M. & Turley, S. *Current Issues in Auditing*. 2nd ed. Chapter 5. London: Paul Chapman Publishing, 22–33.

Livanes, G. (1992). When the numbers fall. *Charter*, **63**(9), 34–5.

Mills, C. (1991). The Caparo Case: A Victoria view. *Accountancy*, **108**(1177), 25.

Mitchell, A. (1993). The liability charade – the consumers' view. *Accountancy*, **112**(1204), 75.

O'Sullivan, N. (1993). Auditors' liability: its role in the corporate governance debate. *Accounting and Business Research*, **23**(91A), 412–20.

Passmore, C. (1995). Directors beware? Auditors rejoice? *Accountancy*, **116**(1228), 152–3.

Pearse, C. (1992). Liability: Case law accumulates. *Accountancy*, **110**(1188), 114

Ross, M. (1994a). Casebook: Audit Liability. *Accountants' Journal*, **73**(2), 76.

Ross, M. (1994b). Casebook: Audit Liability. *Chartered Accountants' Journal*, **73**(8), 70.

Swinson, C. (1986). The Littlejohn case. *The Accountants' Magazine*, **90**(956), 49–50.

Swinson, C. (1992). Duty and definition. *Accountancy*, **110**(1188), 112–13.

Woolf, E. (1993). A return to rational concepts. *Accountancy*, **111**(1196), 119–20.

Chapter 16

Avoiding and Limiting Auditors' Liability

LEARNING OBJECTIVES

After studying the material in this chapter you should be able to:
- describe and evaluate measures taken by audit firms and by the auditing profession to ensure that high quality audits are performed;
- discuss suggestions which have been advanced as means of limiting auditors' liability.

The following publication is particularly relevant to this chapter:

- *Towards Better Auditing* (The Auditing Committee, ICAEW, 1993)

16.1 INTRODUCTION

In Chapter 15 we reviewed a number of cases in which auditors were sued by their audit clients and/or third parties for allegedly performing their duties negligently (that is, without due skill and care). Despite the effect of the *Caparo* decision in reversing the trend evident in the courts in the United Kingdom and elsewhere, towards extending auditors' liability to third parties, auditors have continued to face staggering claims for damages. Price Waterhouse and Ernst & Young, for example, faced a combined claim of $US11 billion (approximately £5 billion) as a consequence of their (allegedly) negligent auditing of the failed Bank of Credit and Commerce International (BCCI) (Economist, 1994). Further, in a few cases, the damages awarded against auditors in recent years have been enormous. For instance, the Economist (1994) reports settlements, between January and July 1994, which include $US312 million (about £160 million) by Deloitte & Touche in a case involving United States Federal regulators, and $US12 million (£5 million) by Horwarth & Horwarth in relation to their audit of the Australian National Safety Council. Similarly, in the United Kingdom, in December 1995, damages of £105 million were awarded against the former BDO Binder Hamlyn partnership for their negligent audit of Britannia Security Group's 1989 financial statements. Binder Hamlyn's partners faced a shortfall in the insurance cover of the damages of some £34 million[1] (Accountancy, 1996a, p.11). Such damages, claims and settlements have prompted auditing firms to call for, and suggest, ways in which auditors' liability may be limited. The firms are particularly concerned that damages settlements bear no relationship to the size of the audit fee or the extent of the auditors' negligence.

Notwithstanding the successful actions which have been brought against auditors, as we noted in Chapter 15 (section 15.5), the courts have, in general, shown themselves reluctant to impose on auditors a standard of skill and care higher than that generally regarded as appropriate by the auditing profession. It seems to follow from this that the most effective way for auditors to address the problem of liability for negligence is to avoid it by performing high quality audits.

In this chapter we explore ways of avoiding and limiting auditors' liability. More specifically, we discuss measures introduced by individual audit firms, and by the profession as a whole, which are designed to ensure that auditors consistently perform high quality audits. We also examine three proposals which have been advanced as means of limiting auditors' liability – namely, incorporation of audit firms, imposing a statutory cap on auditors' liability, and gaining acceptance of the legal principle of proportionate (or contributory) liability.

16.2 MAINTAINING HIGH QUALITY AUDITS

16.2.1 Reasons for Establishing Quality Controls

It was noted above that auditors have been encouraged to seek ways to ensure that high quality audits are performed in order to avoid exposure to legal liability. Flint (1988), however, looks at the issue from a different perspective. He states:

---

[1] As noted in Chapter 15, the High Court's decision in this case is subject to appeal proceedings.

Auditors have both a legal duty and a professional obligation to work to the highest standards which can reasonably be expected. . . . In a profession whose authority is dependent among other things on public confidence . . . a demonstrable concern individually and collectively, to control and maintain the highest quality of audit work, is a matter of basic principle. (pp.159, 161)

To Flint (1980), the key issue is minimising the prospect of audit failure. He explains, 'this is what society in general, and those who rely on audit in particular, expect'. He adds, 'this is what the professional accountancy bodies as the regulatory authority have an obligation to pursue in the public interest' (p.64).

Whether it be prompted by concern for the public interest, concern for the interests of the beneficiaries of audit services, concern about potential damage to the profession's reputation if poor quality audits are performed, or concern about possible exposure to legal liability (or a mixture of these factors), both individual firms and the auditing profession as a whole have established procedures designed to ensure that all audits are performed to the highest standards.

16.2.2   Quality Control within Audit Firms

As noted in Chapter 6 (section 6.4), SAS 240: *Quality Control for Audit Work* requires audit firms to establish appropriate quality control policies and procedures at both the audit firm and individual audit level (para 2). It was also noted that if certain simple and common-sense procedures are established within audit firms and adhered to, then the risk of performing poor quality audits can be reduced to a minimum. Such procedures include ensuring that:

- high quality audit staff are employed, that is, personnel with the necessary qualities of integrity, honesty, objectivity and intelligence, who also possess the required academic knowledge and an ability and willingness to learn;
- audit staff are given adequate 'on the job' training in a wide range of circumstances, regular performance appraisals, and encouragement to attend professional development/continuing education courses;
- when work is delegated to assistants, care is taken to ensure that it is within their competence to perform and that they are given adequate direction and supervision;
- all audit work is fully and properly documented and the work of each member of the audit team is reviewed by his or her immediate superior;
- the audit engagement partner reviews the audit working papers to ensure that:
  - sufficient appropriate audit evidence has been gathered in relation to each audit segment and for the audit as a whole;
  - conclusions drawn in relation to each audit segment and the audit as a whole are consistent with the results of audit procedures performed;
  - the opinion formed on the financial statements is adequately supported by the audit evidence obtained and documented, and is consistent with the conclusions drawn therefrom;
  - there are no issues which have arisen during the audit which remain unresolved;
- a second partner, who has not been involved in the audit, reviews the audit working papers to ensure that they reflect the fact that the audit has been conducted in

accordance with Auditing Standards and that the opinion formed on the financial statements is supported by the audit evidence.

In order for high quality audits to be performed, all of the quality controls outlined above should be adhered to within each office of each audit firm. Where audit firms have a number of offices nationally and/or internationally (for example, the 'Big Six' international firms of chartered accountants), intra-firm quality control reviews may be conducted. These involve teams of about five audit partners, drawn from different offices of the firm in the United Kingdom (for national reviews) or from different countries (for international reviews), who visit various offices of the firm to review the adequacy of, and level of compliance with, the firm's quality control procedures. Such reviews are internal matters of the firms concerned and are designed to ensure that the risk of members of the firm performing poor quality audits (and thus, the exposure of the firm's partners to liability) is kept to a minimum. At the same time, ensuring that all offices of the firm (nationally and internationally) maintain adequate quality control procedures, helps to enhance the reputation of the firm for the professional quality of its audit work.

16.2.3 Quality Control within the Profession: Introduction

During the 1970s and 1980s, largely as a result of some well-publicised cases involving negligent auditing, auditors, particularly in the United States and the United Kingdom,[2] faced widespread and scathing public and political criticism. Largely as a response to such criticism, the professional accountancy bodies in these countries and elsewhere (for example, Canada, New Zealand and Australia) established mechanisms to monitor the performance of their members. These monitoring mechanisms have different titles in different countries. In the United States they are referred to as peer review or quality review,[3] in the United Kingdom as monitoring, and in Canada, New Zealand and Australia as practice review.

Notwithstanding their different titles, each of the schemes is designed to serve three key purposes, namely:

1. to ensure auditors meet their obligation to society to provide professional work of the highest quality. Monitoring provides a means of ensuring that all members of the profession adhere to the profession's technical and professional standards. As Flint (1988, p.167) has noted, it also assists auditors protect themselves against the adverse consequences of sub-standard work;
2. to sustain public confidence in the profession by demonstrating a concern for maintaining high standards of professional work;

---

[2] Public and political criticism of auditors was particularly rife in the US in the mid to late 1970s and in the UK in the mid to late 1980s.

[3] Peer review applies to CPA firms which join the AICPA's Division of CPA firms. To qualify for membership of this Division, all principals of the firm who are eligible for AICPA membership must be members, and a majority of the firm's principals must be AICPA members. Firms which do not meet these requirements but have at least one AICPA member must join the Quality Review Program. The peer review program operates on a national basis; the quality review program is run by the AICPA's State Societies.

3. to demonstrate to the public, and more particularly the government, that the professional body is discharging satisfactorily its self-regulatory responsibilities. In the United States, for example, Cook and Robinson (1979) observed that the 'AICPA[4] leadership hoped that a strong self-regulatory program [that is, peer review] . . . would satisfy the profession's critics in Congress who were calling for direct government regulation' (p.12).

Although the monitoring mechanisms established in the United States and United Kingdom were introduced for essentially the same reasons, as is shown in Figure 16.1 and described below, they differ in a number of important respects.

Figure 16.1 Significant Differences in the Monitoring Mechanisms in the United States and United Kingdom

Element of monitoring scheme	United States		United Kingdom
	Peer Review	**Quality Review**	**Monitoring**
Reviewee	Firm with majority of AICPA members	Firm with at least one AICPA member	Audit firm
Reviewer	Peer CPA firm or review team appointed by peer review committee	Peer CPA firm or review team appointed by quality review committee	JMU[1] and ACCA[2] monitoring unit
Frequency of visits (excluding follow-up visits)	Once every three years	Once every three years	ACCA & AAPA[3] firms and firms with listed clients, once every 5 years, other firms, once every 60+ years[5]
Scope of peer review	Membership requirements; audit and other reporting engagement quality controls	Membership requirements; audit and other reporting engagement quality controls	Registration requirements; audit quality controls
Confidentiality of report	Placed in public files	Kept confidential	Kept confidential
Public representation	Public Oversight Board	None	Lay members on Institutes' Registration Committees

1 Joint Monitoring Unit
2 The Chartered Association of Certified Accountants
3 Association of Authorised Public Accountants

---

[4] American Institute of Certified Public Accountants.
[5] The time interval is explained on page 468.

16.2.4 Monitoring Auditors' Performance in the United States

In the United States, as noted above, auditors' performance is monitored under either the peer review or the quality review scheme. The peer review program has its origins in a scheme established by the AICPA in 1971 whereby local CPA firms conducted reviews of other firms. The intent was to provide a counterpart for small firms of the intra-office reviews conducted by large national firms (Cook and Robinson, 1979, p.11). However, the peer review program as it exists today dates from 1977 when it was introduced as a response to searing attacks on the profession by the Congressional Moss Committee and Senate Metcalfe Committee which raised the spectre of government regulation of the profession. In 1977, the AICPA established a Division for CPA firms (previously only individuals could be members) with two sections: a Securities and Exchange Commission (SEC) Practice Section (SECPS) and a Private Companies Practice Section (PCPS). As a condition of membership of either section, the firms must agree, amongst other things, to:

• subject their audit practices to peer review once every three years;
• ensure their personnel meet minimum standards of continuing professional education;
• adhere to standards established by the Quality Control Standards Committee; and
• maintain minimum amounts of liability insurance (Wood and Sommer, 1985).

In addition to establishing the Division for CPA firms, the AICPA established a Public Oversight Board to oversee the activities of the SECPS. This Board, consisting of five experienced competent people drawn primarily from areas other than accounting, is independent of the AICPA. It oversees every peer review performed within the Section and reports to the SEC and the public on its evaluation of the effectiveness of the Section's self-regulatory efforts (Cook and Robinson, 1979, p.12).

Until 1989, joining the AICPA's Division of CPA firms and being subject to peer review was voluntary. In that year it became obligatory for all firms with AICPA members who engage in audits or other reporting assignments to join one of the sections of the Division of CPA firms or the newly established Quality Review Program.[6] In either case, the firm's membership requirements and system of quality controls are subject to peer or quality review at least once every three years. The key difference between the peer and quality review programs is that, while peer review is intended to be 'preventive' in nature (Wood and Sommer, 1985, p.130), the thrust of quality review is 'educational, rehabilitative and correctional' (Accountancy, 1987, p.8). Thus, peer review is more exacting than quality review.

All firms with AICPA members are required to have a quality control system for their accounting and auditing practices which complies with the AICPA's Statement of Quality Control Standards, no.1: *System of Quality Control for a CPA firm*. This Standard embodies nine elements, namely, independence, consultation (ensuring assistance is sought when necessary), assignment of personnel to engagements, supervision, hiring, professional development, advancement (ensuring all levels of responsibility are filled by competent staff members), acceptance and continuance

---

[6] See footnote 3.

with clients, and inspection (conducting periodic internal reviews of the firm's quality controls). Peer and quality reviews focus on the adequacy of the CPA firm's quality control policies and procedures for each of the nine elements, and the level of compliance therewith.

The reviews are conducted, at the reviewee's option, by either a review team appointed by the SECPS or PCPS peer review committee or the quality review committee (as applicable), or by another CPA firm (see Figure 16.1). Where the reviewee elects to be reviewed by another firm, the firms must be independent of each other and reciprocal reviews are prohibited. Further, where the reviewee is a member of the SECPS, a quality control review panel (of one to three members) is appointed by the SECPS review committee to oversee the review. All SECPS peer reviews and most PCPS peer reviews and quality reviews of firms with audit clients are conducted on-site. Some small CPA firms belonging to either the PCPS or the quality review program have their reviews conducted off-site. These firms submit documentation relating to selected engagements to the review team for review.

The focus of peer and quality review is the adequacy of the CPA firm's quality control procedures and the degree to which they are complied with. The review process is analogous to the auditor's review of an audit client's internal controls and testing compliance therewith. For on-site reviews, the review team:

- assesses whether the firm's quality control policies and procedures are appropriate to the size of the firm and the nature of its practice;
- evaluates whether the policies and procedures are adequately documented and communicated to professional staff within the firm; and
- tests compliance with the documented policies and procedures. This is primarily achieved by interviewing relevant personnel within the firm, reviewing personnel and administration files, and reviewing accounting and auditing engagement working papers and reports.

At the conclusion of the review, the review team holds a conference with appropriate people in the firm and discusses its findings. In particular, it highlights:

- deficiencies noted in the quality control policies and procedures adopted by the firm; and
- instances of non-compliance with the documented policies and procedures.

The review team then prepares a written report which is similar to an audit report. The report may be unqualified or, if significant quality control deficiencies or instances of non-compliance with controls have been found, the report may be modified. In some cases, quality control deficiencies or instances of non-compliance may be detected but they are not sufficiently serious to give rise to a modified report. In either event, when deficiencies in, and/or non-compliance with, controls are found, the review team issues a letter of comments which refers to matters that require action by the firm.

The review report and letter of comments are sent to the firm's managing partner, and the SECPS or PCPS peer review committee or the quality review committee (as applicable) is informed that the review is complete. The firm is responsible for sending a copy of the report, the letter of comments and any response it wishes to make to the relevant review committee. For all peer reviews, the report, letter of comments and any response made by the firm are filed in the AICPA's public files. Reports and comments arising from a quality review are submitted on a confidential basis to the relevant State society's quality review committee.

If a firm subject to peer review receives a modified report, the relevant peer review committee reviews the report, the letter of comments and any response made by the firm and decides on appropriate action. This may include sanctions such as a requirement to correct detected deficiencies, the performance of a follow-up peer review, a requirement for staff members to undertake additional continuing professional education, a fine, censure, or suspension from the relevant practice section. If a modified report is issued in relation to a quality review, the action taken by the State society's quality review committee depends on the firm's plan for corrective action. Realistic plans are taken at face value. However, some form of monitoring may be imposed to give the committee assurance that the plans are being implemented. There may also be some requirement for staff members to take certain types of continuing professional education (Localzo, 1979; CPA Journal, 1989).

Judging from surveys of peer review reports and letters of comments (for example, Evers and Pearson, 1990; Wallace and Wallace, 1990), peer review has reaped benefits in that deficiencies in CPA firms' quality control procedures have been detected and, in most cases, corrected. Overall, the quality controls in most firms have been found to be satisfactory. Evers and Pearson (1990), for example, report that 91% of the 295 SECPS firms reviewed during 1986 and 1987 received 'clean' reports; however, only 8% did not receive a letter of comments. The most commonly encountered deficiencies in the 1986 and 1987 reviews related to supervision (found in 83% of reviewed firms). A significant proportion of these (and other) deficiencies related to inadequate documentation. For example, in relation to supervision, 11% of firms were found to have documented inadequately the performance of key audit procedures or conclusions reached in key auditing areas. Wallace and Wallace (1990, p.52) similarly note that over one third of the 232 files they examined covering peer reviews conducted between 1980 and 1986 contained comments relating to inadequate documentation. The single most common deficiency they found was the absence of audit planning guidelines or documentation being inconsistent with such guidelines (reported in 22% of the filings).

16.2.5 Monitoring in the United Kingdom

In the United Kingdom, monitoring of auditors' professional conduct was an element of the regime for regulating auditors introduced by the Companies Act 1989. As noted in Chapter 3 (section 3.2.3), under this regime only 'registered auditors' are eligible for appointment as company auditors. Such auditors may be either individuals, or firms with a majority of individuals, who have qualified with a Recognised Qualifying Body (RQB) and registered with a Recognised Supervisory Body (RSB). In order to become a RSB, a professional body must have, *inter alia,* rules relating to auditors being fit and proper persons, technical standards applying to audit work, and procedures for maintaining competence, monitoring and enforcing the rules, investigating complaints and meeting claims arising out of audit work. Thus, monitoring auditors' compliance with auditing standards and other rules is a condition of a professional body gaining RSB status.

At present, the monitoring function of the five RSBs[7] is discharged by two units: the Joint Monitoring Unit (JMU), which operates on behalf of the three Institutes, and the ACCA monitoring unit which monitors auditors registered with the two Associations. Unlike peer and quality reviews in the United States, which are performed by practising auditors, monitoring of audit firms in the United Kingdom is performed by full-time staff of the two monitoring units.

The focus of monitoring is the audit firm. In September 1993, there were nearly 14,000 registered audit firms in the United Kingdom but the number and profile of firms registered with the three Institutes and two Associations differed markedly. Some 10,900 firms were registered with the Institutes: about 68% were sole practitioners, 31% had between 2 and 50 principals, and 1% (18 firms) had more than 50 principals. Of the Institutes' registered audit firms, 167 (2%) had listed company clients, with the largest 18 firms auditing approximately 88% of such companies. By comparison, nearly 3,400 firms were registered with the Associations; approximately 84% were sole practitioners and the remaining 16% had between 2 and 50 principals. Few of the Associations' audit firms had listed clients (ICAEW *et al,* 1993; Moizer, 1994). It is possibly as a result of differences in the number, size and nature of audit firms registered with the Institutes and Associations, respectively, that the JMU and ACCA monitoring unit have approached the task of sampling firms for monitoring rather differently. The JMU has differentiated between firms with, and those without, public interest clients and has developed a policy of visiting annually approximately 30 (20%) firms with listed clients and a random sample of about 150 (1.5%) of the other firms. On this basis, firms with listed clients are visited once every five years; the other firms can expect a visit once every 65 years.[8] The ACCA monitoring unit seeks to review each year 20% of the audit firms for which it is responsible, thus, each firm is visited once every five years. According to Moizer (1994), the difference in the sampling approaches of the two monitoring units reflects a difference in their intent:

> The purpose of the [JMU] visits has been to gather evidence on what is wrong [in the few firms visited] and then to educate all the audit firms registered with the three Chartered Institutes to correct the identified weaknesses. . . . The purpose of the visit [is] not primarily to improve the practices of the firm visited, but to improve the practices of the general population. In contrast, the ACCA and AAPA have taken the view that the monitoring process is concerned primarily with improving the quality of each firm visited. (p.1)

The remit of the monitoring units is to ascertain whether registered auditors are complying with the audit regulations. Thus, their monitoring activities embrace audit

---

[7] Institutes of Chartered Accountants in England and Wales (ICAEW), of Scotland (ICAS) and in Ireland (ICAI), the Chartered Association of Certified Accountants (ACCA), and the Association of Authorised Public Accountants (AAPA).

[8] In addition to visiting firms, the JMU requires all audit firms registered with the three Institutes to file annually a detailed return. This provides information on such things as the number of principals and employees, ownership and control of the firm, number and nature of audit-clients, fee income, the fit and proper status of principals and employees, maintenance of the competence of principals and employees, and audit compliance reviews conducted by the firm (JMU, 1994).

firms' compliance with all aspects of the regulations including, for example, technical auditing standards, ethical guidelines, independence, professional competence and professional indemnity insurance. Before visiting an audit firm, the JMU inspectors send a detailed pre-visit questionnaire (PVQ) to enable them to plan the visit. The visit begins with a meeting between the inspectors and relevant principals to follow up on matters covered in the PVQ and to plan the file reviews to be carried out. During the review, the inspectors focus on eight key areas, namely, proper registration, integrity, independence, proper procedures for audit work, individual competence, quality assurance procedures, proper performance of individual assignments, and other ethical matters (ICAEW *et al*, 1993, p.12).

At the conclusion of the visit, the JMU inspectors meet with the firm's principals to discuss their findings and, where applicable, the firm's proposed corrective action. The JMU prepares a report on its visit which is sent, together with the notes made by the firm, to the relevant Institute's Audit Registration Committee (ARC). Where no matters requiring corrective action have been found, the JMU prepares a short form report; in other cases a long form report is prepared. The latter includes factual information about the visit and also suggests regulatory action the ARC may wish to take.[9] A copy of the report is also sent to the firm which is invited to submit comments direct to the ARC, on the visit and the JMU's report.

The ARC reviews the report and the firm's comments and decides on appropriate regulatory action. It may accept the firm's proposals for corrective action and/or ask for, or impose, additional requirements. If the ARC considers that a firm's non-compliance with the audit regulations, although serious, does not warrant withdrawal of registration, it will require a follow-up visit by the JMU to confirm that the required remedial action has been taken. Alternatively, a firm may be required to have a follow-up visit conducted by another registered auditor. The ARC may also impose conditions on the firm's registration; for example, it may prohibit the firm from accepting any new audit clients. (This sanction was imposed on 20 firms registered with the three Institutes in the year to 31 March 1993.) As a final measure, the ARC may withdraw a firm's registration. This action was applied to nine Institute-registered firms in the year to 30 September 1993 and a further 11 voluntarily surrendered their registration following the JMU visit (ICAEW *et al*, 1993).

The most common instances of non-compliance with the audit regulations encountered by the JMU relate to the 'proper performance of individual assignments'. This caused concern in some 73% of the 312 firms visited in the year to 31 March 1993. The main problems identified were lack of evidence of audit planning, lack of assessment of the adequacy of clients' accounting systems, audit reports not complying with the auditing standard, and failure to ensure that required financial disclosures had been made (ICAEW *et al*, 1993, Moizer 1994).

The ACCA monitoring unit follows essentially the same process as the JMU. However, the ACCA unit compliance officers spend less time on each visit[10] and are less concerned with procedural matters than their JMU counterparts (Moizer, 1994).

---

[9] In the year to 30 September 1993, the JMU submitted 263 reports to the ARCs: 66 (25%) were short form reports and 197 (75%) were long form.

[10] Moizer (1994) found that, on average, visits to firms by the ACCA monitoring unit took one day compared to 4.1 days for visits conducted by the JMU.

Further, instead of recording comments under what might loosely be termed 'operational heads', as is done by the JMU, the ACCA unit seeks to grade audit firms in one of four categories as follows:

- *Grade A:* The conditions for eligibility as a registered auditor, and the continuing obligations on the practice, have been satisfied. Audit quality controls are well developed and the audit work examined appears appropriate in scope and extent and forms a reasonable basis for the audit opinions issued. (Outcome of visit: satisfactory.)
- *Grade B:* The conditions for eligibility as a registered auditor have been satisfied. However, there have been minor breaches of the continuing obligations on the practice, and/or there are shortcomings in audit quality controls, and/or deficiencies were found in the audit work examined but these did not appear to undermine the audit opinions issued. (Outcome of visit: less than satisfactory; but an early revisit is a low priority.)
- *Grade C:* The conditions for eligibility as a registered auditor have been satisfied. However, there have been serious breaches of the continuing obligations on the practice, and/or audit quality controls are poorly developed, and/or instances were found of audit opinions not adequately supported by the work performed and recorded. (Outcome of visit: less than satisfactory; an early revisit is required.)
- *Grade D:* The conditions for eligibility as a registered auditor have been breached and/or breaches of the Rules of Professional Conduct or deficiencies in audit work were found which are sufficiently serious to require immediate action by the Association. (Outcome of visit: referral to Authorisation Committee.) (ACCA, 1992, pp.22–3; 1993, pp.12–13).

During the year to 30 September 1993, 409 ACCA-registered audit firms and 138 AAPA-registered firms (a total of 547 firms) were visited by the ACCA monitoring unit. Of these, 196 firms (36%) were classed as Grade A, 150 firms (27%) as Grade B, 140 firms (26%) as Grade C, and 61 firms (11%) as Grade D (ACCA, 1993, p.12; Moizer, 1994, p.34). The main problems encountered by the ACCA monitoring unit were similar to those found by the JMU. They derive primarily from departures from auditing standards and, more particularly, from failing to record (or record adequately) audit work done (ACCA, 1993, p.20).

At the conclusion of a monitoring visit, the ACCA compliance officer, like the JMU inspectors, meet with the firm's partners to discuss the visit's findings and agree, where applicable, the remedial action to be taken. After the visit, the compliance officer drafts a report covering the matters discussed at the meeting. Instead of the report being referred to a committee, as happens with the JMU, the draft report, together with the completed programme, file inspection checklists and any supplementary working papers, is reviewed by another member of the monitoring staff. It is then sent to the reviewee. In the case of visits which result in a Grade D, a further review of the visit report and documents is conducted by the Head of the Monitoring Unit. These cases are also referred to the relevant Association's Authorisation Committee as questions arise as to the eligibility of the firm concerned to continue as a registered auditor. In any case where deficiencies are found, the firm may be required to confirm in writing action taken to correct the identified weaknesses or to provide written details of proposed corrective action. In appropriate cases, a follow-up visit is also arranged (ACCA, 1992, p.22).

Unlike peer review reports in the United States, reports produced by the JMU and ACCA monitoring unit are not accessible to the public; neither is there provision currently for public scrutiny of the monitoring process by a body similar to the POB.[11] However, the JMU reports are reviewed by the Institutes' ARCs and these include non-accountant members. The Institutes view the inclusion of such members as important 'in order to demonstrate [their] determination to act in the public interest even where that may conflict with members' interests in the short term'. The terms of reference of the non-accountants include providing assurance to the public that regulatory decisions take full account of public interest issues (if necessary, overriding the interest of the firm concerned or the profession), that they are taken fairly and properly, and that firms' interests are taken into account (ICAEW *et al*, 1993, p.25). The Associations' monitoring process does not make any provision for public representation. The monitoring visit reports are reviewed by the Associations' Authorisation Committees only if the firm is classed as Grade D, and these committees do not include non-accountants. Public representation is introduced only at the Authorisation Appeal Committee level.

16.2.6 Effectiveness of Monitoring Auditors' Performance in the United States and United Kingdom

From Figure 16.1 and the above descriptions, it is evident that the monitoring schemes operating in the United States and United Kingdom differ significantly. As shown in summary form in Figure 16.1, the schemes differ in respect of the reviewee, reviewer, frequency of review visits, scope of the review, confidentiality of the review report, and the public's representation in the review process. These differences exist, notwithstanding that the rationale and key objective of the schemes are, to all intents and purposes, the same. In essence, the rationale is to demonstrate to the public, and more particularly the government, that the profession can regulate its own affairs and ensure that its members provide high quality professional work. Based on this rationale, the key objective is to monitor the performance of members of the profession to ensure they are complying with the profession's standards.

Despite the differences in each scheme's mode of operation, the professional literature reveals that the outcomes are remarkably similar. Surveys conducted in both the United States and United Kingdom suggest that, in general, monitoring has resulted in an overall improvement in the quality (or, probably more precisely, the recording) of audit work. This improvement has been achieved primarily through improved quality control systems and documentation procedures (see, for example, Evers and Pearson, 1990; Wallace and Wallace, 1990, Fearnley and Page, 1992, 1993; Moizer, 1994). The deficiencies most frequently identified by the reviews – those of inadequate audit planning and, more particularly, documentation – are also common to both countries.

The monitoring schemes in both the United States and United Kingdom have apparently uncovered numerous instances of non-compliance with professional

---

[11] In January 1996 it was reported that the introduction of an independent public review body, similar to the POB in the US, has tentatively been agreed by the UK accountancy bodies (Accountancy, 1996b, p.10).

standards- and generated innumerable suggestions for improvements in auditing procedures. It also seems likely that the 'threat' of monitoring visits has motivated practitioners to effect improvements in their auditing procedures and quality control systems prior to the visit. Additionally, the professional bodies, when reporting on the effectiveness of their monitoring schemes, have drawn attention to the large number of reviewees who received qualified or adverse reports from their initial reviews but who 'cleaned up their act' before the follow-up visit. The professional bodies have also noted that members of the profession who persist with their defective performance are disciplined and, if necessary, excluded from the profession.

Given the improvements which peer review and monitoring have apparently brought, it may be asked why instances of auditor negligence still occur. In answer, commentators such as Wood and Sommer (1985) note that it is not known how many audit failures have been avoided as a result of auditors being required to conform to prescribed standards in the performance of their audit work. They also point out that the monitoring process focuses on quality control systems and that no system can prevent *all* undesirable events from occurring. Woodley (1991) echoed this theme when he stated, on the eve of monitoring being introduced in the United Kingdom:

> It would be foolish to believe that there will be no audit failures in the future. No amount of monitoring can eliminate the possibility of errors of judgement or failures to follow laid down procedures. But . . . the extra emphasis on quality control procedures, the possibility of a [monitoring] visit, and the dire consequences of failing to comply with the regulations [should] result in fewer audit failures in the future. (p.61)

It should also be recognised that monitoring is largely concerned with quality control procedures and compliance therewith, rather than with the substance of audit judgments. Thus, although audit firms may effect improvements in their control procedures, faulty audit judgments may persist.

Wood and Sommer (1985), among others, note that, although monitoring cannot prevent all audit errors from occurring, society has other checks in place to ensure that those responsible for causing harm to others as a result of sub-standard professional work do not go unpunished. For example, when questions of audit failure arise, authorities such as the SEC in the United States and Department of Trade and Industry (DTI) in the United Kingdom investigate and, if justified, appropriate sanctions are imposed on the culprits. Further, as evidenced by cases such as those discussed in Chapter 15, those harmed as a result of auditors' sub-standard work may seek redress through the courts.

16.3 SUGGESTIONS FOR LIMITING AUDITORS' LIABILITY

When investors and others suffer loss as a consequence of a company collapsing unexpectedly, they seek to recover their loss from any hopeful avenue. Although a company's failure is frequently the result of mismanagement by (or, sometimes, dishonesty of) its directors and/or senior executives, when the company fails, the fortunes of its directors often go with it. As a consequence, suing the directors is usually perceived as an option which is unlikely to bear fruit. However, auditors are known to carry indemnity insurance and, if any fault can be found with the way in which they performed their duties, they are often regarded as a potential source from which losses may be recouped. It is generally accepted that this 'deep pocket' syndrome has been a prime motivator in the large and increasing number of suits brought against auditors over the last couple of decades in English-speaking countries, particularly in the United States and United Kingdom.

In some cases, as is noted in the Introduction to this chapter, auditors have faced enormous claims for damages, amounting to many millions of pounds. Further, the damages awarded against auditors frequently bear no relation to the size of the audit fee or the extent of the auditors' negligence. The extent of such potential liability has caused some commentators, such as Hardcastle (1988), to conclude that there is a very real risk that it will result in a shortage of suitable people prepared to enter the auditing profession. Hardcastle states, for example:

> There is no doubt that, if current trends in litigation continue without check, the flow of people prepared to enter the professions will slow up and professional standards will fall, as the most able people come to regard a professional career as too risky. (p.15)

The potential burden auditors face has given rise to calls by auditing firms for auditors' liability to be limited in some way. The three main proposals which have been suggested are:

(i)   permitting auditors to form limited liability companies;
(ii)   placing a statutory cap on auditors' liability;
(iii)   introducing proportionate (or contributory) liability.

(i)   *Limited Liability Companies*

Prior to the Companies Act 1989, a body corporate was precluded from being appointed as auditor. Audit firms had to exist as sole practitioners or partnerships. As noted in Chapter 15, under partnership law, all partners within a firm have joint and several liability. If a court awards damages against a partner in an audit firm, to the extent that the damages exceed the firm's indemnity insurance cover, the personal assets of the errant partner are used. If there is still a shortfall, the assets of the other partners in the firm are called upon to make good the deficiency. Thus, a particular partner may lose his or her personal assets as a consequence of negligence on the part of another partner in the firm – a partner who (s)he may not even know!

The Companies Act 1989 changed the law to permit audit firms to form limited liability companies. In cases where firms take advantage of this option, to the extent that any damages awarded against the company exceed the company's insurance cover, the assets of the company are called upon to meet the damages claim. Additionally, the personal assets of the individual 'partner' (or, more correctly, shareholder/director) responsible for the negligence giving rise to the damages, may be pursued through the corporate front and used to meet any deficiency. However, the assets of 'partners' not associated with the defective audit cannot be called upon.

It is thus seen that incorporation benefits audit 'partners' (shareholder/directors) who are not themselves guilty of negligence in that their personal assets are safe from seizure to meet damages awarded to a successful plaintiff. However, it does not alter the fact that, if the damages awarded against the audit company exceed the company's indemnity insurance cover, the damages might still result in the company losing all its assets (thus forcing the auditors out of business) and the successful plaintiffs not recovering all their losses.[12]

Another argument raised against auditors forming limited liability companies is that auditors are members of a profession and, as such, they are accorded certain rights and privileges in society. As a consequence, they should not expect to be permitted to hide behind a corporate front while retaining their professional status. One of the hallmarks of a professional is a preparedness to stand by the quality of his or her work and reputation as an individual. Although this argument has merit, as indicated above, incorporation does not result in the identity of the professional responsible for the audit being lost. The individual can still be traced through the corporate front in the event of failing to perform an audit without due skill and care.

Notwithstanding the apparent benefits in terms of reduced exposure to potential liability, audit firms have demonstrated some reluctance to take advantage of the ability to form limited liability companies. By mid-1996, only about 200 audit firms had taken the incorporation route – including just one of the 'Big Six' firms, namely, KPMG Peat Marwick (see Accountancy, 1995, p.3, re KPMG Audit plc). The reasons for audit firms' reluctance to incorporate seem to be associated with company (as compared with individual) tax rules and the requirement to produce an annual report – complete with audited financial statements which show a true and fair view of the audit company's financial position and profit or loss for the year. It is also possible that some firms have reservations about whether an incorporated entity provides the appropriate environment within which professional services should be performed. In the United States, the major audit firms have formed limited liability partnerships (LLPs), registered in the State of Delaware. These have the advantage of providing limited liability whilst retaining the ethos of a partnership. In the United Kingdom, a similar opportunity may be available under the laws of Jersey in the Channel Islands (Accountancy, 1996c, p.3).

(ii) *Statutory Cap*

As an alternative to the formation of limited liability companies, it has been suggested that legislation be enacted to 'cap' the liability to which auditors may be exposed. A widely canvassed proposal is that the cap or limit on auditors' liability be fixed as a factor of the audit fee (for example, ten times the fee). Such arrangements are already in place in Germany and some other European countries.

This suggestion possesses the advantages of simplicity, linking the size of the sanction associated with a negligently performed audit to the size of the reward resulting from the audit, and preventing (or reducing) the likelihood of auditors being forced out of business by a single act of negligence. However, as with limited liability companies, the proposal to limit auditors' liability by means of a statutory cap has some disadvantages. These include the following:

---

[12] It should be recalled that, in order to be successful, the plaintiffs must have proved to the satisfaction of the court that they have suffered loss as a result of the auditor's negligence (i.e. they made an economic decision based on financial statements which the auditor had audited without exercising due skill and care).

(a) The possibility that auditors would be encouraged to reduce the size of their audit fee to a bare minimum so as to limit their exposure to liability. It seems likely that this would result in a reduction in the quality of audits, as cost-cutting measures were put in place. This, in turn, may lead to an increase in the number of actions brought against auditors for poorly performed audits. Further, as the general quality of audits was reduced and litigation against auditors increased, public confidence in the audit function and audited financial statements would be undermined. It seems likely that this would have serious and far-reaching undesirable consequences in the financial markets.

(b) It would result in auditors being treated differently from other professional groups and may well result in the government imposing some compensating restrictions on the profession. For example, the government may assume responsibility for regulating/controlling the profession.

(c) The introduction of a statutory cap on auditors' liability could result in an innocent client or third party, who suffered loss as a consequence of auditors failing to perform their duties with reasonable skill and care, being prevented from recovering the full amount of his or her loss. When it is remembered that the evidence suggests that plaintiffs do not succeed easily in actions brought against auditors (see Chapter 15, section 15.4), it seems inequitable to prevent those who are successful from recovering in full the amount lost as a result of auditors' negligence.

Pratt (1990, p.78) points out that rather than an innocent party, who relied on an auditor's skill and professional judgment in good faith, bearing the cost of the auditor's negligence (as a consequence of auditors' liability being limited in some way), it is preferable for the audit firm to shoulder the burden. Indeed, to Pratt, a particularly strong argument against any form of limitation of auditors' liability is that an audit firm can spread the risk of potential damages for negligence through professional indemnity insurance.

Referring to claims, such as those made by Hardcastle (1988) (see above), that auditors' liability may be reaching the point where it is prejudicial to the survival of the auditing profession, Pratt observes:

> [T]he accountancy profession will only continue to offer services if it can achieve a satisfactory return. Given that the market for statutory audit services is not a free one (public companies are required by law to have an audit and the qualifications of auditors are likewise prescribed), these oligopolistic characteristics would suggest, according to fundamental economic theory, that higher [indemnity insurance] costs will simply be passed on to audit clients in the form of increased fees. (p.79)

A federal judge, in the American case of *Rusch Factors* v *Levin* [1968] 284 F Supp.85, appears to agree with Pratt's view. He asked:

> Why should an innocent reliant party be forced to carry the weighty burden of an accountant's professional malpractice? Isn't the risk of loss more easily distributed and fairly spread by imposing it on the accounting profession, which can pass the cost on to the entire consuming public? (as reported by Pratt, 1990, p.79)

Against these views, audit firms would point to the decline in the capacity of the insurance market and their inability to secure the level of professional indemnity insurance they desire and need.

(iii) *Proportionate (or Contributory) Liability*

An alternative suggestion for limiting auditors' liability, other than through incorporation or imposing a statutory cap, is that of proportionate (or contributory) liability. Under this proposal, damages are awarded against those responsible for a plaintiff's loss in proportion to their responsibility for that loss. For example, if a court held that a plaintiff's loss was caused equally by negligence on the part of the company's directors and its auditors, then the directors and auditors would each be responsible for meeting half of the damages awarded.

Such an arrangement has recently been introduced in the United States and, as the AWA case discussed in Chapter 15 (section 15.3) shows, it is also in place in Australia. It is currently being pursued as a favoured option by the auditing profession in the United Kingdom, but so far the proposal has not found favour with the British Government.

Proportionate liability offers significant advantages for auditors and plaintiffs alike. For example, auditors will in most cases be called upon to meet only a proportion, rather than the full amount, of damages awarded to a successful plaintiff. As a result, there is less likelihood of audit firms being forced out of business by meeting damages settlements. Similarly, because damages awarded to a successful plaintiff are derived from more than one source, there is greater likelihood of him or her receiving the full amount. Although these benefits are clearly important, probably the single most important advantage of proportionate liability is the equity it introduces; it attempts to apportion damages against errant parties in accordance with their proportion of (or contribution towards) the cause of the loss suffered by the plaintiff.

It remains to be seen if, and when, the British Government will recognise the merits of this means of reducing auditors' exposure to liability.

16.4 SUMMARY

In this chapter we have considered how auditors' exposure to legal liability may be avoided or limited. More particularly, we have discussed measures which individual audit firms may implement in order to ensure that audits conducted by the firm are of a consistently high standard. We have also examined the peer and quality review programs in the United States, and the monitoring scheme in the United Kingdom, each of which is designed to monitor the performance of auditors to ensure they are complying with the profession's auditing and other relevant standards.

In addition, we have discussed three proposals which have been advanced as means of limiting auditors' exposure to liability – namely, the incorporation of audit firms, the introduction of a statutory cap on liability, and the introduction of proportionate (or contributory) liability. We have observed that, although the law has been changed to enable audit firms to incorporate, so far, relatively few firms have taken advantage of this opportunity and KPMG Peat Marwick is alone amongst the 'Big Six' firms in so doing. We have further noted that proportionate liability is an option the auditing profession in the United Kingdom is pursuing as a means of restricting auditors' liability. However, to date, it is not a proposal which has found favour with the British Government.

SELF-REVIEW QUESTIONS

16.1. List five quality control procedures which audit firms can adopt as means of ensuring that high quality audits are performed by the firm.

16.2. Explain briefly the rationale underlying the auditing profession's introduction of mechanisms designed to monitor auditors' performance.

16.3. Describe briefly the key features of peer review in the United States.

16.4. Describe briefly the key features of the monitoring system in the United Kingdom.

16.5. List three significant differences between peer reviews in the United States and monitoring in the United Kingdom.

16.6. Evaluate the relative merits of the monitoring schemes as practised by the Joint Monitoring Unit and ACCA monitoring unit.

16.7. Given that quality control systems have been established in audit firms and that mechanisms to monitor auditors' performance have been introduced by the professional bodies, audit failures should be a thing of the past.

Explain briefly:
(i) why audit failures still occur, and
(ii) the checks which society has in place to ensure those responsible for causing harm to others as a result of sub-standard work do not go unpunished.

16.8. List two advantages and two disadvantages of audit firms forming limited liability companies.

16.9. List two advantages and two disadvantages of the introduction of a statutory cap on auditors' liability.

16.10 Discuss briefly the merits of proportionate (or contributory) liability as a means of limiting auditors' liability.

REFERENCES

Accountancy. (1987). New peer review plans invented. *Accountancy*, **110**(1130), 8.
Accountancy. (1995). The Audit Co. Ltd. *Accountancy*, **116**(1227), 3, (Editorial).
Accountancy. (1996a). More court actions soon. *Accountancy*, **117**(1229), 9.
Accountancy. (1996b). CCAB finds common ground. *Accountancy*, **117**(1229) 6.
Accountancy. (1996c). The offshore auditors. *Accountancy*, **117**(1230), 3, (Editorial).
Chartered Association of Certified Accountants (ACCA). (1992). *Audit Regulation: First Annual Report of The Chartered Association of Certified Accountants to the President of the Board of Trade*. London: ACCA.
Chartered Association of Certified Accountants (ACCA). (1993). *Audit Regulation: Second Annual Report of The Chartered Association of Certified Accountants to the President of the Board of Trade*. London: ACCA.
Cook, J.M. & Robinson, H.G. (1979). Peer review – The accounting profession's program. *CPA Journal*, **49**(3), 11–16.

CPA Journal (1989). News and Views: Quality review or peer review – What's the difference? *CPA Journal*, **59**(11), 6.8.

Economist (1994, 9 July). Partners in pain. *The Economist*, p.61–2.

Evers, C.J. & Pearson, D.B. (1990). Lessons learned from peer review. *Singapore Accountant*, (June), 19–23.

Fearnley, S. & Page, M. (1992). Counting the cost of audit regulation. *Accountancy*, **109**(1181), 21–2.

Fearnley, S. & Page, M. (1993). Audit regulation – one year on. *Accountancy*, **111**(1193), 59–60.

Flint, D. (1980). Quality control policies and procedures – the prospect for peer review. *The Accountant's Magazine*, **84**(884), 63–6.

Flint, D. (1988). *Philosophy and Principles of Auditing*, London: MacMillan.

Hardcastle, A. (1988). Going to the Government, cap in hand. *Accountancy*, **101**(1133), 15–16.

Institute of Chartered Accountants in England and Wales (ICAEW), Institute of Chartered Accountants of Scotland (ICAS), Institute of Chartered Accountants in Ireland (ICAI) (1993). *Audit Regulation: Report to the DTI for the Year Ended 30 September 1992*. London: ICAEW, ICAS, ICAI.

Joint Monitoring Unit (JMU). (1994). *Chartered Accountants' Audit Annual Return*. London: JMU.

Localzo, M.A. (1979). What is peer review all about? *The Journal of Accountancy*, **148**(10), 78–82.

Moizer, P. (1994). *Review of Recognised Supervisory Bodies: A Report to the Department of Trade & Industry on the Audit Monitoring Process*.

Pratt, M.J. (1990). *External Auditing: Theory and Practice in New Zealand*. New Zealand: Longman Paul.

Wallace, W.A. & Wallace, J.J. (1990). Learning from peer review. *CPA Journal*, **60**(5), 48–53.

Wood, A.M. & Sommer, Jr, A.A. (1985). Statements in quotes. *Journal of Accountancy*, **156**(5), 122–31.

Woodley, K. (1991). Introducing audit regulation. *Accountancy*, **107**(1169), 60–1.

ADDITIONAL READING

Acher, G. (1996). Jointly, severally and unfairly liable. *Accountancy*, **117**(1232), 80.

Brown, P. (1995). Partial incorporation: will it work? *Accountancy*, **116**(1227), 81.

Douglas, P. (1994). Liability capping is the wrong solution. *Accountancy*, **113**(1209), 70.

Fearnley, S. & Page, M. (1994). Audit regulation – where are we now? *Accountancy*, **113**(1207), 81–2.

Fogarty, T.J. (1996). The imagery and reality of peer review in the U.S.: Insights from institutional theory. *Accounting, Organizations and Society*, **21**(2/3), 243–68.

Garvey, H. & Dickson, A. (1996). What the JMU found; and found again. *Accountancy*, **117**(1234), 126–7.

Institute of Chartered Accountants in England and Wales (ICAEW). (1996). *Finding a Fair Solution. A Discussion Paper on Professional Liability*. London: ICAEW.

McCabe, R.K., Luzi, A.D. & Brennan, T. (1993). Managing partners' perceptions of peer review. *Auditing: A Journal of Practice & Theory*, **12**(2), 108–15.

Pratt, M.J. (1991a). Limitation of liability. Statutory cap not the answer. *Accountants' Journal* **70**(2) 39, 42.

Pratt, M.J. (1991b). Legal liability, contributory negligence and corporatisation. *Accountants' Journal*, **70**(6), 18–20.

Pratt, M.J. (1991c). Auditors' liability and the public interest. *Accountants' Journal*, **70**(9), 41–4.

Singleton-Green, B. (1996). 'Convincing arguments' against liability reform. *Accountancy*, **117**(1233), 81.

Swinson, C. (1994). Professional standards – is monitoring a big mistake? *Accountancy*, **114**(1214), 77.

Ward, G. (1996). Time to be fair to auditors. *Accountancy*, **117**(1234), 84.

Appendix

Summary of Steps in the Audit Process

STEPS IN THE AUDIT PROCESS

The steps in the audit process are depicted in the diagram on page 364.

Step 1   Appointment (see Chapter 3)

In the case of private sector entities, the auditor is formally appointed (or re-appointed) by the shareholders at their annual general meeting. For public sector entities, the auditor is appointed under relevant public sector legislation.

Step 2   Engagement Letter (see Chapter 7)

At the commencement of the audit, an engagement letter is prepared by the auditor and sent to the client. This is to ensure there is no misunderstanding between the auditor and the client, and it sets out things such as:

- the scope (extent) of the audit, including any work the auditor is to do in addition to that required for the statutory audit;
- confirmation of any verbal agreements, including the basis on which fees are to be charged;
- confirmation of any work to be performed by the client – for example, the preparation of schedules such as stock on hand (prior to stocktaking) and an aged analysis of debtors;
- a statement emphasising that, under the Companies Act 1985 and other relevant legislation, the financial statements are the responsibility of the auditee's management[1] and that the statements are required to give a true and fair view[2] of the entity's financial position and performance and comply with relevant legislation;

---

[1] Readers are reminded that, in the company context, the term 'management' includes directors. (See Preface to this text, p.viii).
[2] For some public sector entities, the words 'present fairly' are used in place of 'true and fair view'.

Summary of Steps in the Audit Process

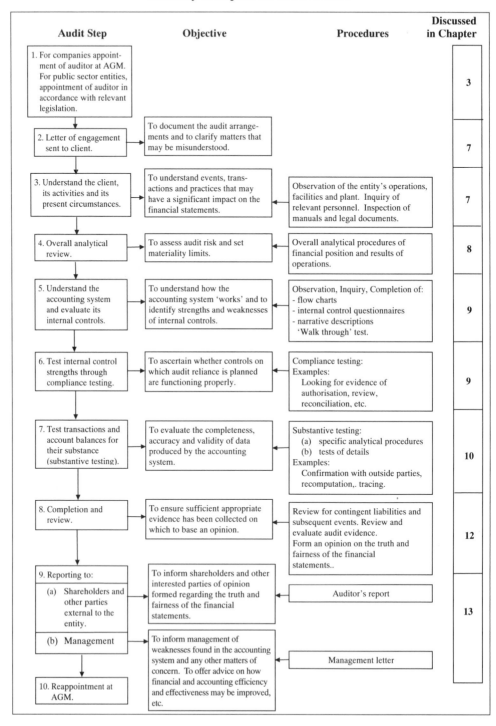

Audit Step	Objective	Procedures	Discussed in Chapter
1. For companies appointment of auditor at AGM. For public sector entities, appointment of auditor in accordance with relevant legislation.			3
2. Letter of engagement sent to client.	To document the audit arrangements and to clarify matters that may be misunderstood.		7
3. Understand the client, its activities and its present circumstances.	To understand events, transactions and practices that may have a significant impact on the financial statements.	Observation of the entity's operations, facilities and plant. Inquiry of relevant personnel. Inspection of manuals and legal documents.	7
4. Overall analytical review.	To assess audit risk and set materiality limits.	Overall analytical procedures of financial position and results of operations.	8
5. Understand the accounting system and evaluate its internal controls.	To understand how the accounting system 'works' and to identify strengths and weaknesses of internal controls.	Observation, Inquiry, Completion of: - flow charts - internal control questionnaires - narrative descriptions 'Walk through' test.	9
6. Test internal control strengths through compliance testing.	To ascertain whether controls on which audit reliance is planned are functioning properly.	Compliance testing: Examples: Looking for evidence of authorisation, review, reconciliation, etc.	9
7. Test transactions and account balances for their substance (substantive testing).	To evaluate the completeness, accuracy and validity of data produced by the accounting system.	Substantive testing: (a) specific analytical procedures (b) tests of details Examples: Confirmation with outside parties, recomputation,. tracing.	10
8. Completion and review.	To ensure sufficient appropriate evidence has been collected on which to base an opinion.	Review for contingent liabilities and subsequent events. Review and evaluate audit evidence. Form an opinion on the truth and fairness of the financial statements..	12
9. Reporting to: (a) Shareholders and other parties external to the entity.	To inform shareholders and other interested parties of opinion formed regarding the truth and fairness of the financial statements.	Auditor's report	13
(b) Management	To inform management of weaknesses found in the accounting system and any other matters of concern. To offer advice on how financial and accounting efficiency and effectiveness may be improved, etc.	Management letter	
10. Reappointment at AGM.			

- an indication of how the auditors will approach their work and guidance as to the approximate timing of the work to be done;
- a statement noting that the objective of the audit is to form an opinion on the truth and fairness of the financial information, not to detect fraud. However, it is also pointed out that audit procedures are designed to give reasonable assurance that any material frauds will be detected.

The auditor prepares two copies of the engagement letter. They are both sent to the client for signing; one is retained by the client, the other is returned to the auditor for inclusion in the audit file.

It should be noted that the engagement letter does not absolve the auditor from any statutory, common law or professional duties in relation to the audit. Its principal purpose is to clarify the role and scope of the audit and to confirm that the client entity's management is aware of the nature of the audit engagement. It also outlines some administrative matters.

Step 3   Understanding the Client (see Chapter 7)

It is essential that the auditor gains a thorough understanding of the client entity, its operations, its industry and its key personnel. This understanding:

- makes the auditor aware of any particular events, transactions or accounting practices which may have a significant impact on the financial statements;
- enables the auditor to assess whether there are circumstances which increase the likelihood of errors being present in the (unaudited) financial statements;
- provides a background against which evidence gathered during the course of the audit can be evaluated to see it if 'makes sense' and 'looks right'.

This understanding of the client is acquired primarily through the following procedures:

- visiting the client entity, touring the premises and meeting key personnel (for example, the managing director, the financial director, and the marketing, production and personnel department managers);
- discussing with key personnel, in relation to the past year, the trading and financial position of the entity, problems and successes experienced, and any significant changes in activities, accounting or personnel policies and procedures;
- reviewing the entity's legal documents (including, for example, its Memorandum and any debenture trust deeds), policy and procedures manuals, and any significant commercial agreements (e.g. franchise and leasing agreements).

Step 4   Overall Analytical Review (see Chapter 8)

In this step of the audit process, meaningful relationships in the entity's accounting data are examined. Primarily by means of trend and ratio analysis, the auditor gains a better understanding of the entity's financial position, the results of its operations and its cash flows, as presented in the financial statements. The results of this analysis are evaluated against what the auditor expected, based on his or her understanding of the client's circumstances. Key indicators such as net profit to sales, return on shareholders' funds, debt to equity ratio, and working capital ratio, are compared with averages for these indicators in the client's industry (or business sector). Based on the auditor's knowledge of the client, its 'normal' position in its industry and any known exceptional circumstances, the auditor can assess whether things 'look right', or whether it appears that there are errors in the accounting data.

Based on this overall analytical review the auditor can assess:

- audit risk: the likelihood that material error is present in the (unaudited) financial statements;
- materiality limits: the amount of error the auditor is prepared to accept in individual financial statement account balances, and in the financial statements as a whole, before concluding that they are materially misstated. (A material misstatement is one which is likely to affect the decisions or actions of a reasonable user of the financial statements.)

Step 5 Understanding the Accounting System and Evaluating its Internal Controls (see Chapter 9)

Before the auditor can assess the truth and fairness with which the financial statements portray the entity's financial position and performance, (s)he must understand the accounting system and the controls which are built into the system to prevent and detect errors and irregularities in the accounting data (i.e. the internal accounting controls). The auditor must understand how the transactions data are captured, how they are processed through the accounting records, and how they are 'converted' into financial information in the form of financial statements. (S)he also needs to know which personnel are responsible for doing what tasks.

The auditor gains this understanding of the accounting system primarily through:

- observation: observing various aspects of the client's accounting system;
- enquiry: asking questions of client personnel;
- completing a flow chart of the system;
- completing an Internal Control Questionnaire (ICQ). This usually consists of a list of questions which require 'yes', 'no' or 'not applicable' answers. The auditor completes this on the basis of observation and enquiry.

The flow chart and/or ICQ, together with any narrative descriptions of parts of the accounting system, are important audit documents and are kept in the audit file.

In order to test his or her understanding of the accounting system, the auditor conducts a 'walk through' test. For this test, one or two transactions are followed through the accounting system, from their recording on a source document (e.g. sales invoice) at the time the transaction takes place, through the journals, ledger, trial balances, etc., to their presentation in the financial statements (that is, as an element of account balances presented in the financial statements; e.g. as an element of 'Sales' and 'Debtors').

In addition to gaining knowledge of how the accounting system 'works', the auditor makes a preliminary evaluation of the system's internal controls. Specifically, the auditor identifies internal control 'strengths' and 'weaknesses':

- *Strengths* are controls within the accounting system which, if operating properly, will prevent or detect errors and irregularities.
- *Weaknesses* are aspects of the system which are susceptible to error or irregularities, but which lack a control to prevent or detect such occurrences.

Based on the results of the overall analytical review and preliminary evaluation of the internal controls, the auditor can make decisions concerning the nature, timing and extent of audit procedures.

- *The nature of audit procedures* refers, for example, to whether the auditor will rely primarily on:

- compliance tests: audit procedures which test whether the internal controls on which the auditor plans to rely to protect the integrity of the accounting data, are functioning as intended (i.e. are being complied with); or
- substantive tests: audit procedures which test the validity, completeness and accuracy of transactions and/or account balances.

Both types of test are used in virtually every audit, but the emphasis on one or the other largely depends on the auditor's preliminary evaluation of the internal controls. Where internal controls are regarded as effective, greater reliance is placed on compliance testing than on substantive testing. Where internal controls are regarded as weak, the emphasis is on substantive tests. Because the auditor is required to express an opinion on the truth and fairness of the information presented in the financial statements (not on the quality of the internal controls), some substantive testing *must* be undertaken in *every* audit.

The 'nature of audit procedures' also refers to choices the auditor makes between alternative procedures (s)he may use to accomplish a particular audit objective: for example, whether the auditor uses analytical procedures or tests of transactions to evaluate the accuracy, validity and completeness of the interest paid account balance.

- *The timing of audit tests* refers to whether (and the extent to which) the auditor conducts audit tests during an interim audit (some months before the balance sheet date) rather than during the final audit (around and shortly after the balance sheet date). Some testing must always be done in a final audit but, where internal controls are strong, some tests may be conducted earlier in the year. This enables the auditor to spread audit work more evenly throughout the financial year and to complete the final audit in a shorter period.

- *The extent of audit procedures* refers to the amount of evidence the auditor needs to gather before (s)he can be confident that the financial statements do or do not contain material error and/or inadequate disclosure. In general, the more effective the internal controls are in preventing and detecting errors, the more likely it is that the financial statements will be free from error and, therefore, the less the evidence the auditor needs to gather in order to form an opinion that this is, in fact, the case.

Step 6   Testing Internal Control Strengths through Compliance Testing (see Chapter 9)

Before the auditor can rely on 'strengths' in the accounting system (i.e. effective internal controls) to prevent or detect errors in the accounting data, compliance tests must be conducted to make sure that:

• these controls are, in fact, working effectively; and
• they have been so working throughout the financial year.

To illustrate a compliance test: One objective of internal controls is to ensure that all transactions are properly authorised. A control might be that, before any credit sale is made to a customer, it must be authorised by the credit manager. The credit manager is required to initial the sales invoice to indicate that the sale has been approved. An audit procedure to test whether this control has been complied with is to examine copies of sales invoices for the credit manager's initials.

Step 7   Testing the Validity, Completeness and Accuracy of Transactions and Account Balances (Substantive Testing) (see Chapter 10)

Because the auditor is required to express an opinion as to whether or not the reporting entity's financial statements give a true and fair view of the entity's financial position and performance and comply with relevant legislation, (s)he must always conduct some substantive tests. There are two main types of substantive tests:

(i)   analytical procedures;
(ii) tests of details.

(i)   *Analytical procedures*: In these tests the relationships in accounting data are examined to determine the 'reasonableness' of individual account balances. For example, in order to verify the interest paid balance, the auditor may ascertain the entity's average debt and average interest rate for the year. By applying the interest rate to the debt, an indication of the interest which should have been paid (or payable) during the year can be determined. By comparing the recorded amount of interest paid with the calculated amount, the auditor can decide whether or not the recorded amount is 'reasonable'. If it is, in many cases, no further testing of this account will be performed. However, if it is not, then the disparity between the recorded and calculated amounts will need to be investigated.

(ii)   *Tests of details*: In these tests, the validity, completeness and accuracy (as to amount, account classification, and reporting period) of transactions and account balances are examined. For example, the auditor, may:

- compute such items as depreciation, totals of sales or purchases transactions, bank reconciliations, etc. This checks for arithmetical errors;
- trace transactions forwards from source documents to financial statements. This checks for completeness: to make sure all relevant transactions have been included in the financial statement account balances and that none has been 'lost' on its way through the system;
- trace transactions backwards from financial statements to source documents. This checks for validity: to make sure that account balances shown in the financial statements reflect the totals of genuine transactions;
- request confirmations from outside parties. For example, a sample of customers may be asked to confirm that they owed the client entity the amount stated in the entity's ledger accounts, and banks are asked to confirm the client's bank balances as at the balance sheet date;
- observe such items as stock. This usually includes attendance at the entity's stock-take when stock is counted. However, it also includes observing the type and quality of stock on hand in order to assess whether, and how much of it, is obsolete or substandard;
- inspection of documents such as marketable securities (for example, share certificates) and loan, lease or hire purchase contracts.

Step 8   Completion and review (see Chapter 12)

This step, which completes the evidence gathering and evaluation phase of the audit, comprises four separate sub-steps:

(i)   review for contingent liabilities and commitments;
(ii)   review for subsequent events;
(iii) reassessment of the validity of the going concern assumption;
(iv)   final review of evidence gathered during the audit and formation of opinion.

(i)   *Review for contingent liabilities and commitments*: Before concluding the audit, the auditor must ascertain whether the entity has any contingent liabilities or commitments which should be disclosed in the financial statements.

- *A contingent liability* is a potential obligation which is expected to arise but which, at the balance sheet date, is uncertain as to amount. An example is litigation for infringement of, say, environmental or product safety regulations. The outcome of the litigation will not be known until the case is heard in court.

- *A commitment* is a contractual undertaking; for example, an undertaking to purchase a certain amount of raw materials at a fixed price at a particular time in the future, or an agreement to lease or buy fixed assets at an agreed price on a specified future date.

The auditor faces two major problems when reviewing for contingent liabilities and commitments:

(a) management may not want to disclose these items in the financial statements;
(b) it is more difficult to discover unrecorded transactions and events than it is to evaluate recorded information.

However, financial statements are required to show a true and fair view of the reporting entity's state of affairs and this necessitates disclosure of any material contingent liabilities and commitments. Therefore, the auditor must attempt to ascertain whether they exist. This is accomplished primarily through:

- making enquiries of management;
- reviewing the minutes of directors' (or equivalent) meetings;
- reviewing correspondence files;
- reviewing audit working papers prepared during the course of the audit for information that may indicate a potential contingent liability;
- obtaining confirmation from the client's solicitor(s) regarding known, pending or expected liabilities or commitments.

(ii) *Review for subsequent events*: The auditor is required to review transactions and events which occur during the period between the balance sheet date and the date of the audit report to see if anything has happened which might affect the truth and fairness of the financial statements as at the balance sheet date. Two types of subsequent events may have occurred:

(a) *Adjusting events*: These are events which clarify conditions existing at the balance sheet date and/or which permit more accurate valuation of account balances as at that date. For example, the commencement of bankruptcy proceedings against a major customer during the subsequent events period may indicate that his or her financial position was not sound at the balance sheet date. In this case, some adjustment to the Allowance for Bad Debts might be called for.

(b) *Non-adjusting events*: These are events which indicate conditions which have arisen subsequent to the balance sheet date. As these conditions do not affect the financial position or performance of the entity as they existed at the balance sheet date, they should not be incorporated in the financial statements. However, where a non-adjusting post-balance sheet event is material, it should be disclosed by way of a note to the financial statements, so that users of the financial statements can gain a proper understanding of the entity's financial position and performance. An example of this type of event is a major expansion (or contraction) of the organisation, such as the purchase (or sale) of a subsidiary subsequent to the balance sheet date.

If the post-balance sheet event is such that it brings into question the validity of the going concern concept – for example, as a result of a fire or flood occurring after the balance sheet date which results in a significant loss not covered by insurance – then it should be considered in the reassessment of the going concern assumption.

(iii)   *Re-assessment of the validity of the going concern assumption*: In normal circumstances, financial statements are prepared on the basis of an assumption that the entity will continue as a going concern for the foreseeable future. As part of their audits, auditors are required to consider whether adoption of this assumption is justified. Under SAS 130 they are required to:

* plan and perform procedures specifically designed to identify material matters which might indicate that adoption of the going concern assumption might not be valid;
* determine and document the extent of their concern (if any) about the entity's ability to continue as a going concern.

If auditors believe that the entity's ability to continue as a going concern is in question, they are required to consider whether the relevant information is adequately disclosed in the financial statements. Where auditors believe the relevant matters relating to the entity's (uncertain) future are adequately disclosed, (assuming the auditors are satisfied in all other respects) they are required to express an unqualified opinion. However, they may also be required to include an explanatory paragraph referring to the uncertainty regarding the entity's status as a going concern in the 'basis of opinion' section of the audit report. If auditors consider the relevant information is not adequately disclosed, they are required to express an 'except for' or 'adverse' opinion, as appropriate.

(iv)   *Review of evidence gathered during the audit and formation of an opinion*: At the conclusion of the audit, the auditor must carefully review the audit working papers. (S)he must consider:

* the objectives, nature, timing and extent of audit procedures performed, the results obtained, and the conclusions reached;
* problems encountered during the audit and how these have been resolved;
* whether sufficient appropriate audit evidence has been gathered, in each audit segment and for the audit as a whole, on which to form an opinion.

The auditor must then form an opinion (based on the evidence collected and documented in the working papers) as to whether or not the financial statements present a true and fair view of the entity's financial position and performance, and comply with relevant legislation.

Step 9   Reporting (see Chapter 13)

The concluding step in the audit process is the preparation of reports addressed to:

(i)   the company's shareholders or their equivalent in public sector entities. This report may also be read by other stakeholders external to the entity;
(ii)   the entity's management.

(i) *Report to shareholders (or their equivalent)*: Auditors are required by the Companies Act 1985 and equivalent public sector legislation to report to shareholders (or their equivalent) on the reporting entity's financial statements. The report may be unqualified or qualified.

- *An unqualified audit report*: This indicates that, in the auditor's judgment, the financial statements give a true and fair view of (or presents fairly) the entity's financial position and performance and comply with relevant legislation and regulations.

- *A qualified audit report*: This indicates that:
  - there has been a limitation on the scope of the auditor's examination; or
  - the auditor disagrees with the treatment or disclosure of a matter in the financial statements,

  and, in the auditor's opinion, the effect of the scope limitation or the matter with which (s)he disagrees is material to the financial statements. The qualified audit report may be of three types: 'except for', adverse or disclaimer.

  A qualified audit report will also be issued if the auditor considers:
  - the entity has not kept proper accounting records; and/or
  - all the required information and explanations have not been received.

  Additionally, in the case of companies, a qualified report will be issued:
  - if the financial statements are not in agreement with the underlying accounting records;
  - proper returns have not been received from branches not visited by the auditor;
  - the information given in the directors' report is not consistent with the financial statements.

In addition to the audit report required by statute (outlined above), for companies listed on the London Stock Exchange it has become customary for auditors to express an opinion on the directors' corporate governance statements – more particularly on the directors' statements with respect to:
- their compliance with the Cadbury Committee's Code of Best Practice;
- the company's internal controls;
- the company's status as a going concern.

(ii) *Report to management*: In addition to the auditor's report(s) to parties external to the entity on the entity's financial statements and, in relevant cases, corporate governance statements, it is normal professional practice for the auditor to provide a written report to the entity's management on various aspects of the audit. This communication is known as a 'management letter'.

The content of management letters varies quite widely in practice – depending on the auditor, the client and the circumstances. However, certain items, such as internal control weaknesses which have come to light during the audit, are almost invariably included. In relation to internal controls, the letter not only specifies weaknesses which have been detected, it also explains the effect of these weaknesses and recommends steps which could be taken to rectify them.

Index

Note: Page references in *italics* refer to Figures

Compiled by Annette Musker